NEW TOOLS FOR SOCIAL SCIENTISTS

NEW TOOLS FOR SOCIAL SCIENTISTS

Advances and Applications in Research Methods

Edited by
William D. Berry
Michael S. Lewis-Beck

SAGE PUBLICATIONS
The Publishers of Professional Social Science
Beverly Hills London New Delhi

For information address:

SAGE Publications, Inc.
275 South Beverly Drive
Beverly Hills, California 90212

SAGE Publications India Pvt. Ltd.
M-32 Market
Greater Kailash I
New Delhi 110 048 India

SAGE Publications Ltd
28 Banner Street
London EC1Y 8QE
England

Printed in the United States of America

Library of Congress Cataloging-in-Publication Data

Main entry under title:

New directions in social science research.

1. Social sciences—Research—Methodology. I. Berry, William D. II. Lewis-Beck, Michael S. III. Title.
H62.N3894 1986 300′.72 85-19653

ISBN 0-8039-2625-1
ISBN 0-8039-2256-6 (pbk.)

FIRST PRINTING

contents

preface

The seed for this edited volume is a seminar series on social science research methods sponsored by the Department of Political Science and other social science departments at the University of Kentucky. During the 1982-1983 academic year, students and faculty at the University of Kentucky were privileged to hear six lectures on research approaches and techniques by scholars widely known for both their methodological expertise and their substantive contributions to the social science literature. The methods and approaches presented were quite varied, but they were united by the fact that each has seen only limited use in social science research, yet each could be applied to study a wide variety of topics. Furthermore, the lectures neatly wove method and substance. After presenting the general nature of a technique or approach, speakers grappled with the problems involved in its application to a substantive social science question. The positive response to the series convinced us that the lectures would form the core of an excellent collection on new tools for social science research methods.

The attention to both method and application that we believe responsible for the warm reception given the lectures has been preserved in the contributions to this volume; it is perhaps the key distinguishing feature of the book. Many textbooks that introduce quantitative methods fail to present substantive illustrations; those that do typically offer only very cursory presentations. So, to find substantive applications, graduate students generally must turn to the articles that appear in social science journals. Unfortunately, the editors of journals—reacting to the intense competition for limited space—often require authors to trim the discussion of their methodology to the bare bones. Rarely do authors of journal articles have the luxury to present fully the assumptions of their techniques and describe and defend carefully the specific choices that had to be made in applying the techniques. This segregation of method and substance in the literature can lead an unsophisticated reader into the misperception that the methodological choices one must make in research are cut and dried.

We believe this volume is an exception to the rule of "segregation." Each chapter introduces a technique or approach for social science research. Both the assumptions underlying the method and the properties of the coefficients generated are reviewed carefully. (Where space limitations prevent detailed discussions, citations to other books and articles are offered.) Yet each chapter also includes an extensive treatment of just one or two substantive applications. The limitation to a small number of applications allows authors to discuss the methodological choices involved in research at a depth rarely found in the literature. As an added bonus, the chapters present provocative substantive research findings not previously published.

The chapters are designed to be as accessible as possible to readers with limited knowledge of quantitative methods—even those exposed only to the basic regression model. But it is unavoidable that the level of sophistication required of readers varies somewhat from chapter to chapter. For instance, a full understanding of Chapters 2 (Edward Carmines on analysis of covariance structures) and 7 (Herbert Kritzer on contingency table analysis) requires knowledge of matrix algebra. Despite this, we encourage readers without such knowledge to tackle these chapters. Kritzer relegates matrix algebra equations to an appendix. And while some readers may not be able to grasp all the detailed discussion in Chapter 2, Carmines is careful to outline the general nature of the analysis of covariance structures without matrices before venturing into a more technical discussion; we believe this makes his chapter the best "entry-level" treatment of the method around.

The volume is divided into three parts, each dealing with a major methodological problem confronting social science research. The first is the problem of *measurement*: How do we get good measures of the concepts fundamental to social science theories? The second is how to deal with the *noninterval*-level data that permeate the social sciences: How can we conduct multivariate analysis when interval-level data are not available? The third is how to make reasonable inferences about the determinants of a *dynamic* process. Each part begins with a brief chapter written by the editors. Our introductory remarks are intended to serve as an overview of the issues discussed in the chapters in that section, and to provide readers with background necessary for understanding the chapters that follow.

Clearly, the most commonly used multivariate technique in the social sciences is regression. In a typical application, the unit of analysis is the individual, the household, the organization, or the nation. Cross-sectional data are collected for a sample of cases, and analyzed to obtain coefficient estimates. If the assumptions of the regression model are met, the estimates obtained have several desirable properties; indeed, they are BLUE—the best (i.e., having minimum variance) linear unbiased estimates. Yet, more often than not, these assumptions are not met in a real-world substantive research setting. And if the assumptions of regression are not met, the regression technique must be modified or abandoned entirely. (Indeed, five of the techniques examined in this volume can be viewed as modifications or extensions of the regression model: the analysis of covariance structures [Chapter 2], probit and logit [Chapter 6], contingency table analysis [Chapter 7], interrupted time-series analysis [Chapter 9], and transfer function analysis [Chapter 10].)

For instance, the regression model assumes that all variables are measured perfectly. If—as is more likely—there is measurement error, regression coefficient estimates are no longer assured to be BLUE. And while the effects of measurement error on other techniques are not as thoroughly studied, it is clear that measurement error impedes our ability to make valid inferences with all types of empirical analysis. For this reason, we have included a set of chapters in Part I that examine alternative approaches for measuring social science concepts and strategies for appropriately incorporating the indicators of such concepts into research designed to test social science theories.

The regression model also makes an assumption about the level of measurement of variables included in the analysis; each variable is assumed to be measured at the interval level. But in the real world we are often restricted to (1) indicators of concepts measured at the ordinal level (such as degree of agreement with a statement: strongly agree, agree, disagree, strongly disagree), or (2) concepts that can be measured only nominally (such as an individual's race). Under such conditions, the data do not conform to the assumptions of classical regression. Yet alternative techniques for analyzing noninterval data have only limited exposure in the social sciences. Part II presents two chapters that together offer techniques appropriate when the dependent variable—and/or one or more independent variables—is measured at either the nominal or the ordinal level.

While regression analysis can accommodate time-series data, in the social sciences most applications of regression use cross-sectional data. Perhaps many scholars—aware of the problems that autocorrelation poses for regression, but unaware of how to deal with the problems—shy away from time-series analysis. Nevertheless, most social science theories attempt to explain *dynamic* processes. Furthermore, most of our hypotheses propose statements of causality, and a critical feature of demonstrating causality is showing the proper "*time* ordering" of independent and dependent variables. Thus the development and use of appropriate techniques for dynamic analysis is a critical step in the advancement of social science research methodology. The chapters in Part III are contributed with this in mind.

I

MEASUREMENT STRATEGIES

1

Introduction

WILLIAM D. BERRY
MICHAEL S. LEWIS-BECK

The typical social scientist's knowledge of measurement techniques and measurement problems has increased dramatically in recent years. Measurement techniques such as Likert and Guttman scales are now part of the tools learned by nearly all social science graduate students. More important, the effects of measurement error on the results of empirical research are becoming more widely known. Each year it seems that one hears less often among students and colleagues the misconception that "so long as measurement error is *random* in nature, it will not bias my statistical results."[1] For example, the result from classical measurement theory that random measurement error in variables attenuates correlations is becoming common knowledge: If X' is an indicator of the theoretical concept X, and Y' is an indicator of the theoretical concept Y, where both X' and Y' are measured with *random* measurement error, then the correlation between X and Y can be expressed by

$$r_{XY} = \frac{r_{X'Y'}}{r_{XX} \; r_{YY}} \qquad [1.1]$$

where r_{XX} and r_{YY} represent the *reliabilities* of X' and Y', respectively, as indicators of their concepts (Carmines and Zeller, 1979: 30–32). Thus, to overcome the effect of measurement error on correlations, one can try to estimate the reliabilities of variables using one of several approaches (Carmines and Zeller, 1979: chap. 3; Nunnally, 1978: chaps. 6–7), and plug these estimates (along with an observed correlation, $r_{X'Y'}$) into equation 1.1 to calculate an estimate of the correlation uncontaminated by measurement error (that is, an estimate of r_{XY}).

This approach for overcoming the effects of measurement error is consistent with a view that "measurement" and "theory/hypothesis testing" are distinct and separable stages of the research process, with the measurement stage logically prior to the "testing" stage.[2] In this view, theoretical hypotheses containing abstract concepts are formulated. Then indicators for the concepts included in hypotheses are developed and measured for a sample of cases (and sometimes reliabilities are estimated as well). Finally, when measurement is completed, hypothesis testing begins: The indicators typically are used with some multivariate technique such as regression analysis to see if empirical analysis confirms or disconfirms the hypotheses.

Although the three chapters in this section are on diverse topics, they are similar in that they all address issues of measurement, and they all reflect an assumption that measurement and theory/hypothesis testing are best "intertwined" rather than viewed as separate stages of the research enterprise. Indeed, we believe that such an assumption is essential for improving the quality of research in the social sciences. Social scientists live in two worlds: the unobservable world of theory and concepts, and the world of observation. It is vital to recognize that any *observed* relationship is likely a product of relationships both among unmeasured theoretical concepts and between the unmeasured concepts and the variables serving as empirical indicators.

For example, educational researchers often have examined the empirical relationship between college achievement test scores and scores on one or another of the common IQ tests. An accurate understanding of this observed relationship likely necessitates a statement about the relationship between the theoretical concepts "intelligence" and "achievement"—a statement such as, *ceteris paribus*, the greater a college student's intelligence, the greater will be his or her academic achievement. But this would not be enough to account for the empirical relationship between scores on the IQ test and scores on the achievement test, as the test scores do not reflect the theoretical concepts perfectly; some measurement error is bound to be present. This means that the theoretical analysis must go one step further, and extend to a statement about the relationships between the unmeasured concepts and their empirical indicators. For instance, we must include a proposition about the relationship between IQ test scores and intelligence. Here such issues as the extent of racial and cultural bias in the IQ test come into play directly. Blalock (1968) has termed a specification of the relationship between abstract concepts and their empirical indicators an *auxiliary theory*, perhaps to emphasize that such a theory is every bit as important in accounting for empirical relationships as the theory introduced to describe relationships among theoretical concepts.

Thus to study empirically the relationship between intelligence and academic achievement, it is best to merge the tasks of measurement and theory development so that the model chosen for empirical analysis reflects assumptions about relationships both among unmeasured concepts

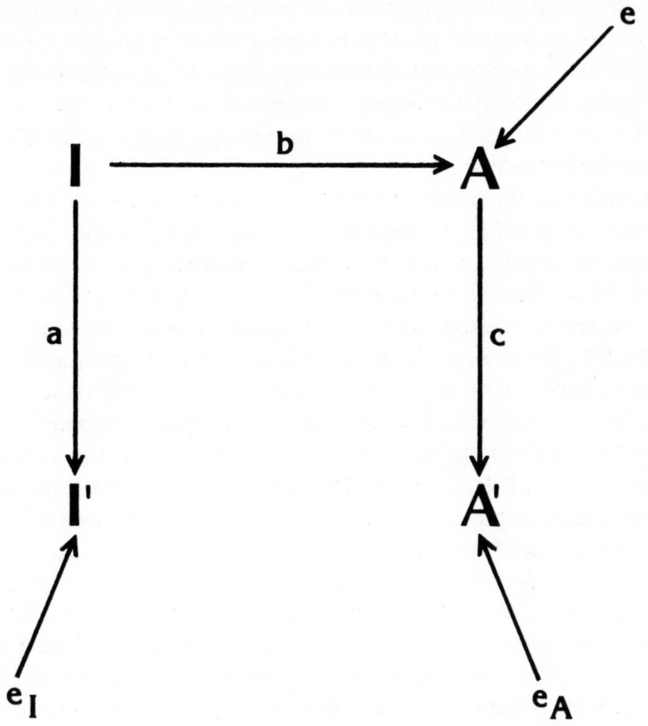

Figure 1.1: Path-Analytic Model

and between the concepts and observable indicators. One way to accomplish this goal is to develop a causal model containing both measured and unmeasured variables.[3] A simple example would be the path-analytic model expressed informally by the diagram in Figure 1.1 and more formally by the following equations:

$$I' = aI + e_I \qquad [1.2]$$

$$A' = cA + e_A \qquad [1.3]$$

$$A = bI + c \qquad [1.4]$$

where I denotes the unmeasured theoretical concept intelligence, A denotes the unmeasured concept academic achievement, I' and A' denote scores on tests of intelligence and achievement, respectively, and e_I, e_A, and e are error terms—the first two representing all those factors not included in the model but that affect test scores (in addition to I and A), and the last representing all variables apart from intelligence (I) that affect academic achievement (A). In the model, a, b, and c are path coefficients representing the effects of one variable on another. Thus this model suggests that intelligence is a variable influencing both academic achievement and the IQ test score, and that academic achievement has a direct effect on the achievement test score.

The great advantage of the model in Figure 1.1 is that it contains both a substantive proposition about the relationship between the two theoretical concepts of interest (I and A) and an auxiliary theory linking the unmeasured and measured variables. Making these propositions explicit also focuses attention on the measurement problems affecting the analysis. For example, the presence of the error term, e_I, affecting I' calls our attention to the other factors that affect IQ test performance apart from intelligence. A more sophisticated model might explicitly include some of these factors—such as race and ethnic background—in the model. This could be done by adding the variable R (denoting race) to equation 1.2 to yield the following:[4]

$$I' = aI + dR + e_I \qquad [1.5]$$

Edward Carmines formalizes this approach in Chapter 2, entitled "The Analysis of Covariance Structure Models." He shows how causal (or structural equation) models can be developed that contain both measured and unmeasured variables, and how the coefficients of such models can be estimated using a technique called LISREL. He illustrates the technique by examining a model designed to explain adolescent political participation.

A complete presentation of LISREL necessarily requires matrix algebra, and Carmines's presentation is no exception; thus a knowledge of matrix algebra is required for full understanding of the material in Chapter 2. However, Carmines's discussion is exceptional in that all types of models presented in matrix notation are illustrated as well with simple models involving only scalar (that is, nonmatrix) equations. Thus those familiar with basic regression analysis yet unfamiliar with matrix algebra should be able to understand the fundamental nature of the approach presented.

The general model for the analysis of covariance structures that Carmines presents can be viewed—as the author himself notes—as a model combining two more simple (and more familiar) types of models: (1) factor analysis models, and (2) structural equation (i.e., causal) models involving only *measured* variables. Indeed, both types of models can be totally subsumed under the more general model. Many of those familiar with factor analysis may never have thought about factor analysis as a type of structural equation model containing both *measured* variables and *unmeasured* variables (or factors). But this is precisely what a factor analysis model is. Indeed, there is an important advantage in considering factor analysis under the more general framework of causal modeling. Treating factor analysis as a type of causal modeling forces the analyst to make assumptions that are inherent in the factor model explicit. For example, the logic underlying factor rotation (which can be quite confusing to the novice) can be fairly easily understood by recognizing that factor rotations can be interpreted as assumptions about relationships among unmeasured variables. A user of factor analysis requesting an orthogonal rotation is merely making a nontestable assumption that all unmeasured variables (or factors) are completely uncorrelated with one another. In another example, the common factor model in Figure 2.2 of Carmines's chapter assumes that there are *no* direct causal effects of one measured variable on another, or of a *measured* variable on an *unmeasured* variable.

The factor analysis models that Carmines discusses—and that are most frequently used in the social sciences—are sometimes called *R factor analyses*. To define this term, some notation must be specified. The raw data for factor analyses (indeed for any covariance structure model) are the scores of each of a set of *persons* on each of a set of *variables*.[5] Assume, for specificity, that we have a set of n persons (denoted 1, 2, . . . , n), a set of k variables (X_1, X_2, . . . , X_k), and a score for each person on each variable—where X_{ji} denotes the score of person i on the variable X_j.

In R factor analysis, the n persons are the cases for analysis. The factors—or unmeasured variables—are "linear combinations of the *variables*," and the factors can be used to determine factor scores for each *person*. More specifically, each factor F can be expressed as

$$F_i = w_1X_{1i} + w_2X_{2i} + \ldots + w_kX_{ki} \qquad [1.6]$$

where F_i represents the score of person i on factor F, and where w_1, w_2, . . . , w_k are the weights for the k variables in the linear combination. Furthermore, R factor analysis is based on correlations (or sometimes covariances) among *variables*. The information required to determine factors is the bivariate correlation—across the n persons—for all pairs of variables in the analysis.[6]

Steven Brown's report in Chapter 3—"Q Technique and Method: Principles and Procedures"—presents (among other topics) a type of factor analysis that has been termed Q factor analysis. In a loose sense, Q factor analysis reverses the roles of "variables" and "persons" in R factor analysis. In the Q technique, the k variables are the cases for analysis. Moreover, factors are no longer "unmeasured variables"; they are, in effect, "unmeasured persons." More technically, the factors are "linear combinations of the *persons*," and the factors can be used to determine factor scores for each *variable*. (Note that in Brown's chapter, each variable is a particular "*statement*," or more precisely, the extent to which an individual agrees or disagrees with a statement.) This means that each factor F takes can be expressed as

$$F_j = w_1X_{j1} + w_2X_{j2} + \ldots + w_nX_{jn} \qquad [1.7]$$

where F_j represents the score of variable X_j on factor F, and where w_1, w_2, . . . , w_n are the weights for the n persons in the linear combination. In contrast to the R technique, Q factor analyses are based on correlations among *persons*, as the data required to determine factors is the bivariate correlation—across the k variables—for all pairs of persons being analyzed.

This discussion of the technical differences between R and Q factor analysis should not make it appear that we believe the fundamental difference between the two should be viewed as whether the factor analysis is based on "correlations among variables" or "correlations among persons." The more important difference is conceptual, having to do with the different purposes for which Q and R factor analyses should be used, and the different types of theories that should underlie the use of the Q and R techniques. The editors share the view of Nunnally (1978: 426–429) who notes that in much social science literature, the theories presented "concern clusters of related variables." When factor analysis is used in such a research situation, the R technique is the appropriate one. Then factors can be interpreted as "hypothetical variables" (as they are indeed linear combinations of variables; see equation 1.6), and *loadings* are defined as correlations (across persons) between individual variables and individual factors. In contrast, Nunnally maintains that Q factor analysis is appropriate in a situation in which the theory being tested "concerns clusters of persons" (Nunnally, 1978: 429). Each factor derived then represents a "hypothetical" or "idealized type" of person, and a loading is a correlation (across variables) between an individual person and a specific factor. In one of Brown's illustrations of Q factor analysis in Chapter 3, the idealized types of persons conceptualized are based on Laswell's (1930) typology of political actors, which suggests three types: agitators, administrators, and theorists.

Brown does not share this view that the main distinction between Q and R factor analysis is whether the theory being tested concerns "clusters of persons" or "clusters of variables." Instead, he argues forcefully that *Q factor analysis* can only be used fruitfully when viewed as a part of a broader methodological approach called *Q methodology*. Although Brown devotes most of his attention to technical matters surrounding the use of Q factor analysis, he concludes his paper with a discussion of the philosophical and conceptual issues underlying Q methodology.

The data used most often in studies relying on Q factor analysis are derived from a specific technique used to "scale" or measure persons referred to as the Q-sort. In a Q-sort, persons are presented a set of cards each containing (what is typically called) a *stimulus*. The persons are then asked to sort the cards into a specified number of piles, in which the piles are designated in an ordinal fashion, for instance from "least preferred" to "most preferred." Brown uses Q-sorts to generate the data for the illustrations of Q factor analysis in Chapter 3; in his analyses, the stimuli are statements chosen to identify different points of view.

Readers should note that a Q-sort is different from the most frequently used form of scale in sociology, political science, and psychology—namely Likert scales. In a Likert (or summative) scale, the scale score for a person is obtained by adding the person's scores on each of a set of stimuli (or items).[7] One fundamental difference between a Q-sort scaling and Likert scaling is in the task required of individual respondents. When constructing a Likert scale, persons are asked to make *absolute* judgments about each stimuli (for example, whether the respondent (1) agrees with, (2) is neutral about, or (3) disagrees with a statement). In contrast, in a Q-sort, persons are asked to make *comparative* judgments about a set of stimuli (for example, ranking a set of statements into a fixed number of piles from "agree most" to "disagree most").

While the Q-sort technique presented by Brown (and the more commonly used Likert scaling technique) is used to scale (or measure) *people* by their responses to a set of stimuli, Chapter 4 presents a report by George Rabinowitz, "Nonmetric Multidimensional Scaling and Individual Difference Scaling," which describes a technique for scaling *stimuli* themselves: multidimensional scaling. In the illustrations he presents, the stimuli being scaled are the candidates running in a presidential election. In multidimensional scaling, the goal is to identify the positions of stimuli in a multidimensional geometric space, and interpret the "structure of the space." Generally, this is done by translating psychological notions of *similarity* between stimuli into *distance* in a geometric space. Most importantly, Rabinowitz shows how multidimensional scaling results (that is, the measured positions of stimuli) can be used to test hypotheses about the dimensions or criteria that underlie individuals' perceptions of the stimuli that have been scaled. For example, in his candidate illustration, Rabinowitz assesses the extent to which the party identification of political figures, and their ideological positions underlie the perceptions by the electorate of the candidates.

Rabinowitz looks at two specific types of multidimensional scaling: nonmetric multidimensional scaling and individual difference scaling. The former technique assumes that all persons judge the stimuli based on the same set of criteria and that the weight attached to each criterion is constant across persons and is likely the more familiar of the two to readers. More recently developed, individual difference scaling is a powerful modification of nonmetric multidimensional scaling that will often be more consistent with the real-world nature of individual perceptions. Specifically, individual difference scaling recognizes that different persons are likely to attach different degrees of importance to criteria in judging stimuli, and thus assumes that different respondents have different patterns of "weights" for a common set of evaluative dimensions.

NOTES

1. For a definition of random measurement error, see Carmines and Zeller (1979: 13-15, 30-32).

2. This "distinct stage" conception of the research process is reflected in the descriptions of the process found in major introductory textbooks such as those by Babbie (1979) and Williamson et al. (1982).

3. For a discussion of the general technique of causal modeling, see Asher (1983) and Duncan (1975: chaps. 3-4); for an introduction to the use of causal models containing unmeasured variables, consult Sullivan and Feldman (1979) and Duncan (1975: chaps. 9-10).

4. But note that this model is not *identified*, that is, data for a sample of individuals for the measured variables would not be sufficient to generate meaningful estimates of the coefficients of the model. Additional variables would have to be added to the model, and/or additional assumptions would have to be made about coefficients or error terms in order to "identify the model." For discussions of "identification" in causal modeling, see Berry (1984) and Chapter 2 of this volume.

5. Of course, in some analyses, states, nations, organizations, or other objects are used instead of persons.

6. For general discussions of R factor analysis, see Kim and Mueller (1981a, 1981b) and Nunnally (1978: chaps. 10-11).

7. See McIver and Carmines (1981: 22-40) for an introduction to Likert scales.

references

Asher, Herbert B. (1983) Causal Modeling. Beverly Hills, CA: Sage.

Babbie, Earl R. (1979) The Practice of Social Research. Belmont, CA: Wadsworth.

Berry, William D. (1984) Nonrecursive Causal Models. Beverly Hills, CA: Sage.

Blalock, Hubert M., Jr. (1968) "The measurement problem: a gap between the languages of theory and research." In H. M. Blalock, Jr., and A. B. Blalock (eds.) Methodology in Social Research. New York: McGraw-Hill.

Carmines, Edward G. and Richard A. Zeller (1979) Reliability and Validity Assessment. Beverly Hills, CA: Sage.

Duncan, Otis Dudley (1975) Introduction to Structural Equation Models. New York: Academic Press.

Kim, Jae-On and Charles W. Mueller (1981a) Factor Analysis: Statistical Methods and Practical Issues. Beverly Hills, CA: Sage.

———(1981b) Introduction to Factor Analysis. Beverly Hills, CA: Sage.

Laswell, Harold D. (1930) Psychopathology and Politics. Chicago: University of Chicago Press.

McIver, John and Edward Carmines (1981) Unidimensional Scaling. Beverly Hills, CA: Sage.

Nunnally, Jum (1978) Psychometric Theory. New York: McGraw-Hill.

Sullivan, John and Stanley Feldman (1979) Multiple Indicator Models. Beverly Hills, CA: Sage.

Williamson, John B., David A. Karp, John R. Dalphin, and Paul S. Gray (1982) The Research Craft. Boston: Little, Brown.

2

The Analysis of Covariance Structure Models

EDWARD G. CARMINES

Broadly speaking, there are two basic types of inferences that are relevant in the social sciences. The first is causal or *structural* in nature; in its most elementary form, it focuses on the causal relationship between a single independent (X) and dependent (Y) variable. The key question with respect to this inference is: Do changes in X produce changes in Y? To take a popular political example, does high socioeconomic status produce conservative political views? In order to make strong causal inferences, it is necessary to establish time precedence, functional relatedness, and nonspuriousness between cause and effect variables.

The second type of inference is concerned with *measurement*. Although this type of inference has received less attention from methodologists, it is no less central to social science research. Many of the most important variables in the social sciences cannot be directly observed. As a consequence, they can only be measured indirectly through the use of empirical (or measured) indicators that represent the unmeasured theoretical variables (or constructs). The fundamental question with regard to measurement inferences is how validly and reliably these indicators represent the unobserved theoretical constructs. In other words, do the measured indicators provide an accurate, consistent, and repeatable representation of their unmeasured theoretical constructs? To refer to our earlier example, do income, residential location, and/or education adequately represent socioeconomic status?

Although these two types of inferences are logically related and empirically interdependent, they have developed along separate methodologi-

---

AUTHOR'S NOTE: *The data analyzed in this chapter were collected with the financial assistance of the National Science Foundation, NSF SOC73-05801 A01. The principal investigator was Roberta S. Sigel, who kindly made the data available to me. The editors provided useful comments on an earlier draft of this chapter. I am also indebted to John McIver, who coauthored earlier papers on this topic.*

cal paths. Structural inferences have been studied most extensively by econometricians. In contrast, psychometricians have made the greatest contribution to understanding measurement inferences. They have developed a variety of factor analysis models that can be used to estimate the relationship between measured indicators and unobserved constructs.

Methods for estimating the parameters of structural equation systems and of factor-analytic models were developed in isolation from one another. Social scientists interested in examining causal relationships among unobserved variables found themselves in a methodological no-man's-land. The practical "solution" to this problem has usually involved a two-step sequential process in which (1) each set of measured variables is factor analyzed to obtain a single derived composite and (2) these factor-generated composites then serve as variables in the causal modeling process.

The problems with this approach, however, are severe and readily apparent. Theoretically, this procedure treats measurement and causal inferences as completely separate and distinct instead of intimately related to one another. Methodologically, the approach is essentially ad hoc and lacks an explicit statistical justification. As a result, the properties of the parameter estimates derived from this procedure are unknown.

Recognizing these difficulties, social science methodologists in the late 1960s began to formulate a more coherent strategy for dealing with these dual inferences. A general solution to this dual inference problem, however, was not forthcoming until the ground-breaking work completed by Karl G. Jöreskog and his collaborators (1967, 1969, 1970, 1973a, 1973b, 1974, 1977, 1978).

Over the past 10 years, Jöreskog has developed a general system for analyzing covariance structures. In its most general form, the approach provides for the efficient estimation of structural equation models containing both observed and unobserved variables. Specifically, his approach permits the simultaneous estimation of both the parameters linking empirical indicators to latent, unobserved variables (the measurement equations) as well as the parameters linking the unobserved variables to each other (the structural equations).

The purpose of this chapter is to present an introduction to this method for analyzing covariance structures; it is divided into four major sections. The first section deals with measurement inferences, focusing on factor analysis models linking empirically observed indicators to theoretically unobserved constructs. In the second part of the chapter we consider structural equation models without unmeasured variables—that is, models that assume that theoretical constructs have been measured without error. The third section integrates these two submodels into the gen-

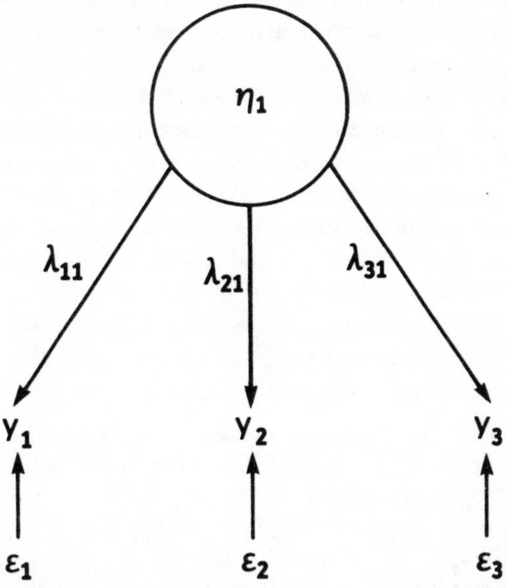

Figure 2.1: A Factor Analytic Model with Three Indicators of a Single Factor

eral model for analyzing covariance structures. This model, in particular, allows researchers to analyze structural equation models that contain unobserved variables. Finally, in the last section of the chapter, we illustrate this general method for analyzing covariance structures by examining the relationship between personality and political behavior.

FACTOR ANALYSIS MODELS

Factor analysis models in the social sciences have often been used to assess the relationship between measured indicators and unmeasured constructs. As noted above, most of the variables of interest to social scientists cannot be measured directly. Thus, for example, political interest, social status, and psychological adjustment cannot be measured directly—there is no simple, straightforward, unambiguous measure of any of these variables. Instead, there are a variety of specific measures that can be used to represent these unmeasured variables. For example, political interest might be indicated by the extent to which people read political stories in newspapers, watch television news programs, and discuss politics with their friends and family. None of these indicators would be a perfect measure of political interest, but together they might provide an adequate measure of this construct. Factor analysis can be used to evaluate how well a set of empirical indicators represents a given theoretical construct.

The simplest factor model is one in which there is a single unobserved variable with several indicators that are uncorrelated among themselves. Figure 2.1 presents an illustration of such a model containing three indicators of the unobserved variable. There are three measurement equations associated with this model:

$$\begin{aligned} y_1 &= \lambda_{11}\eta_1 + \varepsilon_1 \\ y_2 &= \lambda_{21}\eta_1 + \varepsilon_2 \\ y_3 &= \lambda_{31}\eta_1 + \varepsilon_3 \end{aligned} \qquad [2.1]$$

where y_i is an empirical indicator of the unobserved variable η_1, λ_{ij} is the factor loading of the empirical indicator on the unobserved variable, and ε_i is the error of measurement in y_i.

There are two basic types of factor analysis models: *exploratory* and *confirmatory*. Exploratory factor analysis is usually undertaken to answer the question, how many common factors are needed to adequately describe the covariation among a set of empirical indicators. Such analyses usually proceed on the basis of little prior knowledge about the phenomenon being examined.

Figure 2.2 provides an illustration of an exploratory factor model. The model presumes that

(1) all common factors are correlated with one another;
(2) all common factors affect all of the empirical indicators;
(3) errors of measurement of each of the empirical indicators are uncorrelated with each other;
(4) each empirical indicator is affected by a single measurement error; and
(5) all measurement errors are uncorrelated with all common factors.

The important point is that these assumptions are made irrespective of their substantive appropriateness. They are necessary in order to estimate the models. By contrast, the application of confirmatory factor analysis allows the researcher to examine more substantively realistic models by altering the above cited assumptions. For example, the researcher may impose a constraint that the common factors should be uncorrelated with one another, thus removing the curved arrow between η_1 and η_2 in Figure 2.2. Alternatively, the research may specify which common factors affect which measured indicators. This could be achieved by

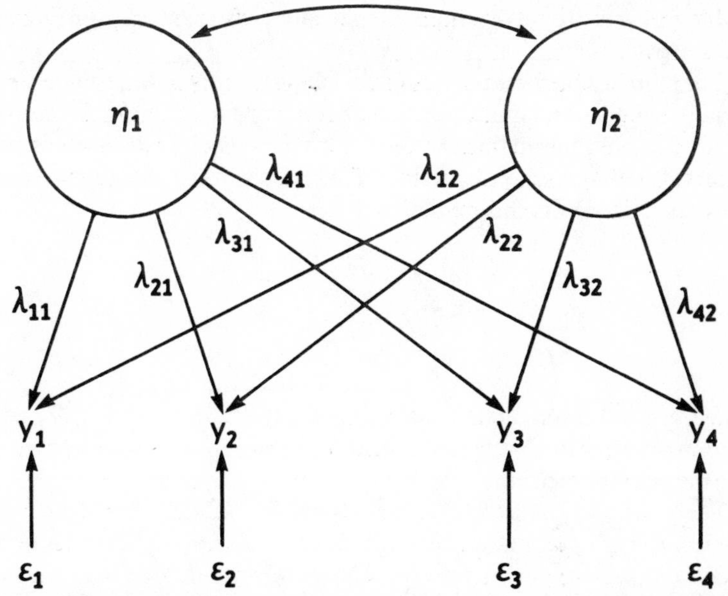

Figure 2.2: An Explanatory Factor Analytic Model with Four Indicators and Two Common Factors

allowing η_1 to affect only y_1 and y_2—and not y_3 and y_4—in Figure 2.2. These constraints imposed on the confirmatory factor model can be evaluated statistically to see if they are consistent with the sample data. It is easy to see that the confirmatory factor model is far more flexible and substantively relevant than its exploratory counterpart.

It is extremely convenient when analyzing confirmatory factor-analysis models to make use of matrix notation. The three measurement equations associated with Figure 2.1 were written in scalar form above (see equation system 2.1). These equations may be simplified in matrix notation as follows:

$$\begin{bmatrix} y_1 \\ y_2 \\ y_3 \end{bmatrix} = \begin{bmatrix} \lambda_{11} \\ \lambda_{21} \\ \lambda_{31} \end{bmatrix} [\eta_1] + \begin{bmatrix} \varepsilon_1 \\ \varepsilon_2 \\ \varepsilon_3 \end{bmatrix} \qquad [2.2]$$

or

$$\mathbf{y} = \boldsymbol{\Lambda} \quad \boldsymbol{\eta} + \boldsymbol{\epsilon} \qquad [2.3]$$

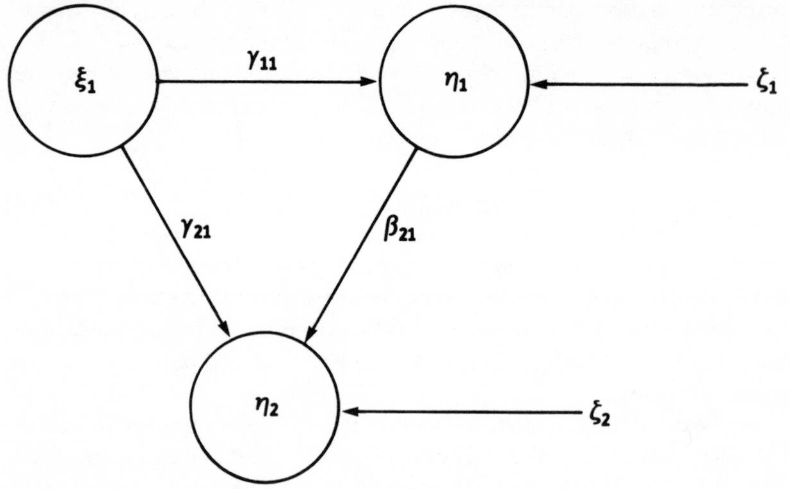

Figure 2.3: A Structural Equation Model with One Exogenous and Two Endogenous Variables

where **y** is a vector of empirical indicators, η is a vector of common factors, Λ is a matrix of factor loadings relating the empirical indicators to the common factors, and ϵ is a vector of measurement errors associated with the empirical indicators. Although the exploratory factor-analytic model specifies a set of essentially arbitrary assumptions, the major assumption associated with the confirmatory factor-analysis model is that all the common factors be uncorrelated with the errors of measurement of the observed indicators. That is, $E(\eta\epsilon) = 0$. In particular, it is *no longer* necessary to assume (1) that common factors are correlated with one another, (2) that all common factors affect all empirical indicators, (3) that errors of measurement are uncorrelated, and (4) that each empirical indicator is affected by only a single measurement error. By not imposing these assumptions, confirmatory factor-analysis is able to represent and analyze far more realistic and complex measurement models.

STRUCTURAL EQUATION MODELS

A structural equation model specifies the causal relationship among a set of variables. Structural equation models contain two types of variables. Exogenous variables are assumed to be caused by variables outside of the model. Endogenous variables are assumed to be explained within the context of the model. That is, they are presumed to be causally dependent upon other endogenous and/or exogenous variables.

The simplest structural equation model specifies the causal relationship between a single endogenous variable (η_1) and one exogenous variable (ξ_1):

$$\eta_1 = \gamma_{11}\,\xi_1 + \zeta_1 \qquad [2.4]$$

where γ_{11} is a parameter estimate signifying the relationship between η_1 and ξ_1—it may be thought of as the estimate of the regression of η_1 on ξ_1—and ζ_1 is error in the equation or disturbance term indicating that ξ_1 does not perfectly predict η_1. This is an example of an ordinary bivariate regression equation.

A slightly more complex structural model is illustrated in Figure 2.3. There are two endogenous variables (η_1 and η_2) and one exogenous variable (ξ_1) in this model. η_1 is determined by ξ_1, whereas η_2 is affected by both ξ_1 and η_1. The two equations associated with this model are as follows:

$$\begin{aligned} \eta_1 &= \gamma_{11}\,\xi_1 + \zeta_1 \\ \eta_2 &= \beta_{21}\,\eta_1 + \gamma_{21}\,\xi_1 + \zeta_2 \end{aligned} \qquad [2.5]$$

where γ_{ij} is a parameter describing the structural relationship between an endogenous variable η_i and an exogenous variable ξ_j and β_{ij} signifies the causal effect of endogenous variable η_j on η_i. This type of structural model is often referred to as a path model or path analysis model.

Again, it is quite useful to be able to present structural models in matrix form. With $\boldsymbol{\eta} = (\eta_1, \eta_2, \ldots, \eta_m)$ and $\boldsymbol{\xi} = (\xi_1, \xi_2, \ldots, \xi_n)$ representing random vectors of latent endogenous and exogenous variables, a general system of linear structural equations may be expressed as:

$$\boldsymbol{\beta\eta} = \boldsymbol{\Gamma\xi} + \boldsymbol{\zeta} \qquad [2.6]$$

where $\boldsymbol{\beta}$ (an m $\times$ m matrix) and $\boldsymbol{\Gamma}$ (m $\times$ n) are coefficient matrices relating the endogenous variables to one another and the exogenous variables to the endogenous variables, respectively, and $\boldsymbol{\zeta} = (\zeta_1, \zeta_2, \ldots, \zeta_m)$ is a vector of errors in equations.

Our two-equation system may be written in matrix form as follows: First, rearrange the equations in system 2.5 so that all endogenous variables are on the left side of the equals signs:

$$\eta_1 = \gamma_{11}\,\xi_1 + \zeta_1$$
$$-\beta_{21}\eta_1 + \eta_2 = \gamma_{21}\,\xi_1 + \zeta_2 \qquad [2.7]$$

Then the coefficient matrices $\boldsymbol{\beta}$ and $\boldsymbol{\Gamma}$ may be read from these rearranged equations. Combining these coefficient matrices with the three vectors of endogenous, exogenous, and error variables yields:

$$\begin{bmatrix} 1 & 0 \\ -\beta_{21} & 1 \end{bmatrix} \begin{bmatrix} \eta_1 \\ \eta_2 \end{bmatrix} = \begin{bmatrix} \gamma_{11} \\ \gamma_{21} \end{bmatrix} \begin{bmatrix} \xi_1 \end{bmatrix} + \begin{bmatrix} \zeta_1 \\ \zeta_2 \end{bmatrix} \qquad [2.8]$$

or

$$\boldsymbol{\beta} \quad \boldsymbol{\eta} \quad = \quad \boldsymbol{\Gamma} \quad \boldsymbol{\xi} \quad + \quad \boldsymbol{\zeta} \qquad [2.9]$$

Alternatively, to read any single equation from this system of matrices, one reads across the coefficient matrices ($\boldsymbol{\beta}$ and $\boldsymbol{\Gamma}$) and down the variable vectors ($\boldsymbol{\eta}$ and $\boldsymbol{\xi}$) and adds the disturbance term ($\boldsymbol{\zeta}$).

Just as there are two basic types of factor analysis models, there are also two types of structural models: recursive and nonrecursive. Very simply, recursive models have two defining characteristics. First, all endogenous variables in the structural model may be arrayed in an unambiguous causal ordering. Another way of stating this condition is that causal paths among the endogenous variables run in only one direction and no feedback loop exists. Second, the disturbances in recursive models are uncorrelated. These constraints mean that no reciprocal effects are possible in recursive models.

Nonrecursive causal systems exhibit the characteristics recursive equation systems do not. In particular, reciprocal relationships may exist among the endogenous variables and disturbances may be correlated. Ability to model reciprocal relationships and correlated disturbances is not without a price, however. Identification of the uniqueness of parameter estimates is not guaranteed (as it is for recursive models). On the contrary, a series of necessary and sufficient conditions for identification must be examined prior to estimation.

Earlier, it was noted that in order to estimate the general confirmatory factor-analytic model, it is necessary to assume that the common factors are uncorrelated with the errors of measurement of the observed indicators. There is a parallel assumption that is associated with structural equation models. Specifically, it is necessary to assume that the exogenous variables are uncorrelated with errors in the equations. That is, $E(\xi\zeta) = 0$. Figure 2.3 conforms to this assumption by the absence of arrows connecting the exogenous variable to the specific errors in the equations.

ANALYSIS OF COVARIANCE STRUCTURES: THE GENERAL MODEL

As has been seen, the general model for the analysis of covariance structures can be broken down into its two component submodels. One of these submodels uses factor analysis to examine the relationships between measured indicators and unmeasured theoretical constructs. This submodel leads to a set of measurement equations. The second submodel focuses on the causal relationships among the unobserved variables assuming that they are measured without error. This submodel leads to a set of structural equations. The great utility of the covariance structures approach, however, does not lie in its capacity to represent these submodels separately. Rather, its real advantage is that it can be used to analyze structural and measurement models simultaneously. That is, it can be used to examine structural relations among theoretical constructs presuming that they are measured by sets of imperfect indicators. The structural model without its measurement component makes the unrealistic assumption of perfect measurement. The measurement model without the structural component does not allow for causal relationships among the unobserved theoretical constructs. Only when the two submodels are fully integrated to form the general model for the analysis of covariance structures is it possible to analyze the most realistic case—a structural model with causal relationships among the unobserved theoretical constructs, recognizing that they are measured imperfectly. We shall first describe the covariance structures model informally before presenting it in a more formal manner, with special attention given to identification, estimation, and assessment.

Figure 2.4 is an illustration of a structural model that contains both causal relationships among the theoretical constructs (or the common factors) and measurement relationships between the unmeasured factors and their associated empirical indicators. The unmeasured theoretical constructs are represented in circles, and the measured indicators of the constructs are represented in squares. Essentially, this covariance structure model reflects a combination of the measurement and structural submodels discussed earlier. It is similar to the measurement model in that it provides a set of measurement equations linking the measured empirical

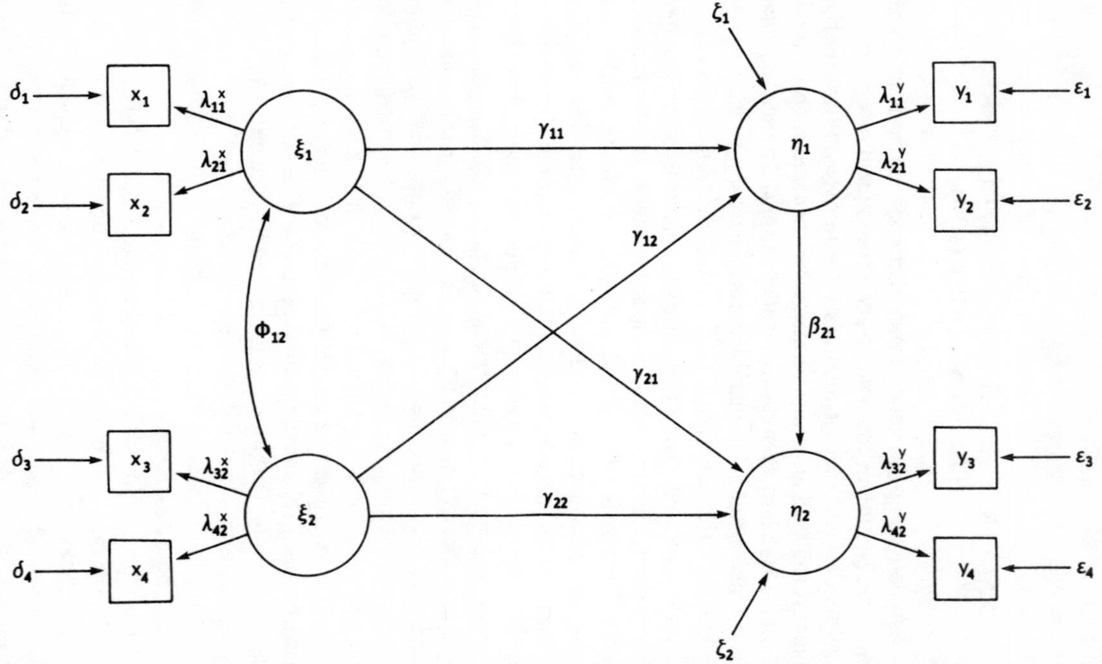

Figure 2.4: A Combined Measurement Component and Structural Component of the Covariance Structure Model

indicators to unobserved theoretical constructs. These equations are estimated within the confirmatory factor analysis model. The covariance model is similar to the structural equation model in that it postulates causal relationships among the theoretical constructs that are represented by structural equations. Specifically, Figure 2.4 specifies that endogenous variables η_1 is determined by exogenous variables ξ_1 and ξ_2, whereas η_2 is affected by ξ_1, ξ_2, and η_1. The model is recursive because it does not postulate any two-way causation or feedback causal loops between variables.

It is helpful to examine the measurement and structural components of the covariance structure model separately so that one can see how the general model is simply a combination of these two submodels. The measurement model itself is composed of two sets of equations. The first set specifies the linkages between the latent *exogenous* variables and their indicators. These equations may be written in scalar form as follows:

$$\begin{aligned} x_1 &= \lambda_{11}^{x} \xi_1 + \delta_1 \\ x_2 &= \lambda_{21}^{x} \xi_1 + \delta_2 \\ x_3 &= \lambda_{32}^{x} \xi_2 + \delta_3 \\ x_4 &= \lambda_{42}^{x} \xi_2 + \delta_4 \end{aligned} \qquad [2.10]$$

where x_i's are empirical indicators of the exogenous variables ξ_1 and ξ_2, λ_{ij}^{x}'s are the factor loadings of the empirical indicators on their specified unobserved exogenous variable, and δ_i's are the errors of measurement in the x_i's on the assumption that the factors do not fully account for the indicators.

The second set of measurement equations specifies the relationships between the latent *endogenous* variables and their indicators. With respect to Figure 2.4, these equations are

$$\begin{aligned} y_1 &= \lambda_{11}^{y} \eta_1 + \varepsilon_1 \\ y_2 &= \lambda_{21}^{y} \eta_1 + \varepsilon_2 \\ y_3 &= \lambda_{32}^{y} \eta_2 + \varepsilon_3 \\ y_4 &= \lambda_{42}^{y} \eta_2 + \varepsilon_4 \end{aligned} \qquad [2.11]$$

where y_i's are empirical indicators of the endogenous variables η_1 and η_2, λ_{ij}^{y}'s are the respective factor loadings, and ε_i's are the errors of measurement.

Both sets of measurement equations have the same form as those given in equation system 2.1 except that we now differentiate between exogenous and endogenous variables. This was not necessary in the confirmatory factor model because that model does not allow for causal relationships among the unobserved common factors.

These two sets of measurement equations can be written in matrix notation. For the relationship between the latent *exogenous* variables and their indicators, the matrix equation is

$$\mathbf{x} = \Lambda_x \, \xi + \delta \qquad [2.12]$$

and for the corresponding relationship between the latent *endogenous* variables and their indicators, the matrix equation is

$$\mathbf{y} = \Lambda_y \, \eta + \epsilon \qquad [2.13]$$

where Λ_x and Λ_y are factor matrices of x and y on ξ and η, respectively, and δ and ϵ are vectors of errors of measurement in **x** and **y**.

In discussing the confirmatory factor model shown above, it was noted that it is necessary to assume that common factors are uncorrelated with errors of measurement of the observed indicators. That is, $E(\eta\epsilon) = 0$. This same assumption applies when we consider the two sets of measurement equations associated with the latent exogenous and endogenous variables. In other words, common factors are assumed to be uncorrelated with errors of measurement not only in their own factor equation but in other equations as well. Thus $E(\eta\epsilon) = E(\eta\delta) = E(\xi\delta) = E(\xi\epsilon) = 0$.

A second important assumption is also made in the measurement component of the covariance structure model. Specifically, it is assumed that the δ's and ε's are uncorrelated—$E(\delta\epsilon) = 0$. That is, the errors of measurement of the indicators of the latent exogenous variables are presumed to be uncorrelated with the errors of measurement of the indicators of the latent endogenous variables. The δ's and ε's may be correlated among themselves but not across equations. Finally, it is assumed that the indicators of latent exogenous variables do not load on the latent endogenous variables and vice versa. Thus $E(x_i \, \eta_i) = 0$ and $E(y_i \, \xi_i) = 0$.

The structural component of the covariance structure model presented in Figure 2.4 is concerned with the causal relationships among the latent exogenous and endogenous variables ξ_1, ξ_2, η_1, and η_2. As noted earlier, the causal determinants of exogenous variables are not considered within structural models. Therefore, the curved doubleheaded arrow between ξ_1 and ξ_2 simply signifies the possible correlation between these exogenous variables. This parameter is represented by ϕ_{12}. There are two structural equations in Figure 2.4, one for each of the endogenous variables. They may be written in scalar form as follows:

$$\eta_1 = \gamma_{11}\xi_1 + \gamma_{12}\xi_2 + \zeta_1$$
$$\eta_2 = \gamma_{21}\xi_1 + \gamma_{22}\xi_2 + \beta_{21}\eta_1 + \zeta_2 \qquad [2.14]$$

These structural equations indicate that η_1 is causally determined by ξ_1 and ξ_2, and that η_2 is determined by ξ_1, ξ_2, and η_1. ζ_1 and ζ_2 are included to reflect the fact that the variables in these equations will not fully account for η_1 and η_2. Notice that these equations are identical to those discussed earlier in the structural equation section of the chapter except that we now explicitly recognize that the theoretical constructs are measured with error.

The measurement and structural components of the covariance structure model have now been established. The main advantage of this general model, however, is not that it can be used to analyze measurement and structural relationships separately. Rather, its main virtue is its capacity to represent and estimate these relationships simultaneously. In other words, the covariance structure model allows the researcher to examine simultaneously the relationships between unmeasured theoretical constructs and their observed indicators as well as the structural relations among the theoretical constructs. Having already presented the confirmatory factor model and the structural equation model, it is fairly simple to outline the full covariance structure model by combining and integrating these submodels. Specifically, by combining the matrix version of the structural and measurement equations 2.6, 2.12, and 2.13, one can represent the variance-covariance matrix of all measured variables as follows:

$$\Sigma = \left[\begin{array}{c|c} \Lambda_y\,(\beta^{-1}\Gamma\Phi\Gamma'\beta'^{-1} + \beta^{-1}\Psi\beta'^{-1})\,\Lambda_y' + \theta_\epsilon & \Lambda_y\beta^{-1}\,\Gamma\Phi\Lambda'_x \\ \hline \Lambda_x\Phi\Gamma'\beta'^{-1}\quad\Lambda_y' & \Lambda_x\Phi\Lambda_x' + \theta_\delta \end{array}\right] \qquad [2.15]$$

where the above new matrices are as follows: $\mathbf{\Phi}$ is the covariance matrix of the latent exogenous variables (ξ), $\mathbf{\Psi}$ is the covariance matrix of the errors in structural equations (ζ), θ_ϵ^2 is the covariance matrix of errors in measurement for the observed endogenous variables (ϵ), and θ_δ^2 is the covariance matrix of errors in measurement for the observed exogenous vari-

TABLE 2.1
Variables and Matrices Used in the Analysis of Covariance Structures

	Symbol	*Definition*
I. Observed variables	y	observed endogenous variable/ indicators of unobserved endogenous variable
	x	observed exogenous variable/ indicators of unobserved exogenous variable
II. Unobserved variables	η (eta)	unobserved endogenous variable
	ξ (xi)	unobserved exogenous variable
	ζ (zeta)	errors in structural equation
	ϵ (epsilon)	errors in measurement of endogenous variable
	δ (delta)	errors in measurement of exogenous variable
III. Coefficient Matrices	β (beta)	coefficient matrix of unobserved endogenous variables
	Γ (gamma)	coefficient matrix of unobserved exogenous variables
	Λ_y (lambda y)	factor matrix of **y** on η
	Λ_x (lambda x)	factor matrix of **x** on ξ
	ϕ (phi)	variance-covariance matrix of unobserved exogenous variables
	ψ (psi)	variance-covariance matrix of structural errors
	θ^2_ϵ (theta epsilon)	variance-covariance matrix of errors of measurements of observed endogenous variables
	θ^2_δ (theta delta)	variance-covariance matrix of errors of measurement of observed exogenous variables

ables (δ). In other words, the population variance-covariance matrix Σ can be represented completely by the functions of the elements of the parameter matrices Λ_y, Λ_x, β, Γ, Φ, Ψ, θ_ϵ, and θ_δ. The measurement and structural parameters must be estimated from the only information the researcher has—namely, the variances and covariances of the measured x and y indicators. This suggests that the population variance-covariance matrix may be partitioned into four submatrices. The upper-left-hand cluster of parameter matrices describes the variances and covariances among the y_i's (Σ_{yy}), the lower-left and upper-right sets of parameter matrices describe the interrelationships among the y_i's and x_i's (Σ_{yx}), and the lower-right-hand group of matrices delineates the variances and covariances of the x_i's (Σ_{xx}). Table 2.1 provides a summary of the variables and matrices used in the analysis of covariance structures.

Equation 2.15 may be simplified considerably in given research situations. For example, if the researcher is interested only in examining a particular factor analysis model, then equation 2.15 reduces to

$$\Sigma = \Lambda_y \psi \Lambda_y + \theta_\epsilon \qquad [2.16]$$

In this case, there is no $\boldsymbol{\xi}$, $\boldsymbol{\Gamma}$, $\boldsymbol{\delta}$, $\boldsymbol{\Lambda}_x$, $\boldsymbol{\phi}$, and $\boldsymbol{\theta}_\delta$. $\boldsymbol{\beta}$ must be set to $\mathbf{I}$, the identity matrix. Similarly, for structural equation models where all variables are assumed to be measured without error, the equation of interest is equation 2.6. In this case, $\mathbf{y} = \eta$ and $\mathbf{x} = \xi$. The model is specified by setting $\boldsymbol{\Lambda}_y$ and $\boldsymbol{\Lambda}_x$ to $\mathbf{I}$, the identity matrix. Both $\boldsymbol{\theta}_\epsilon$ and $\boldsymbol{\theta}_\delta$ are zero matrices. It is easy to see that the confirmatory factor model and the structural equation model are simply special cases of the covariance structure model.

Most of the assumptions that are necessary to estimate the general covariance structure model have already been mentioned in the earlier discussion of the measurement and structural submodels. However, for convenience, they are summarized here. First, exogenous variables are assumed to be uncorrelated with errors in equations. Second, common factors are presumed to be uncorrelated with errors in measurement both within and across equations. Finally, a key assumption linking the two models is that errors in measurement and errors in equations are uncorrelated across equations. In other words, it is assumed that the δ's, ε's and ζ's are mutually uncorrelated even though they may be correlated among themselves.

Identification

Basically, the identification status of any covariance structure model is determined by the correspondence between the amount of information contained in the observed data—specifically, the variance-covariance matrix of the observed indicators—and the total number of model parameters that need to be estimated. Models cannot be analyzed usefully if they are underidentified; meaning, generally, that Σ can be generated by more than one θ.[1] Under these circumstances there is no unique set of parameter estimates, that is, $\boldsymbol{\theta}$ is not uniquely determined by Σ. Rather, the parameters of the model can take on many values; hence the analysis is statistically indeterminate.

An exactly identified model is one that contains a unique set of parameters and a corresponding unique set of parameter estimates. That is, Σ is generated by one and only one $\boldsymbol{\theta}$. In other words, if the model is exactly identified, then the number of parameters to be estimated is equivalent to the number of observed variance and covariances. Although such a model can be estimated (that is, its parameters have unique values), it is not scientifically interesting because it can never be rejected. Instead, it can be fit to any sample data. The model has no discriminative power. For a model to be useful, it must be *overidentified*, meaning, loosely speaking, that the number of parameters to be estimated is smaller than the number of observed variances and covariances. In this situation, the proposed model can be rejected by discovering data that are inconsistent with it. This often takes the form of one or more covariances that are expected to be zero under the conditions of the model that turn out in actuality to have non-zero values. Although overidentified models can be rejected given certain data configurations, they cannot be considered valid merely because they are consistent with the sample data. This asymmetric situation arises because it is always possible that other models can also reproduce the variance-covariance matrix of the sample data, perhaps even providing a closer fit.

In sum, underidentified models cannot be estimated, exactly identified models can be estimated but not rejected, and overidentified models can be estimated and possibly rejected, but not confirmed. For this reason, overidentified models are the most interesting and useful from a theory-testing standpoint.[2]

Estimation

Assuming a model is identified, one is then in a position to estimate its parameters. It is presumed that the population variance-covariance matrix Σ is a function of the parameters contained in equation 2.15. In practice, at least some of the parameters are unknown and must be estimated from the sample variance-covariance matrix **S**. Three general methods for estimating the unknown parameters have been proposed, normally unweighted least squares (ULS), generalized least squares (GLS), and maximum likelihood (ML). We will confine our discussion to maximum likelihood estimation. ML is one of the methods used in LISREL6, a computer program written by Jöreskog and Sörbom (1983) to estimate covariance structure models.

In fitting Σ to **S**, maximum likelihood estimation minimizes a complex mathematical function with respect to the unknown parameters. Specifically, the loss function

$$L(\boldsymbol{\theta}) = \log |\boldsymbol{\Sigma}| - \log |\mathbf{S}| + \mathrm{tr}(\boldsymbol{\Sigma}^{-1}\mathbf{S}) - p \qquad [2.17]$$

is minimized with respect to $\boldsymbol{\theta}$, the parameter vector. Unfortunately, this function cannot be solved analytically, but it can minimized numerically by several methods (see Gruvaeus and Jöreskog, 1970). Basically, this estimation procedure operates as follows. $L(\boldsymbol{\theta})$ is a positive value that we are attempting to minimize. We start with a vector of initial parameter values that is used to generate a predicted covariance matrix $\boldsymbol{\Sigma}$. $\boldsymbol{\Sigma}$ is then compared to our sample covariance matrix in the above cited function. Assuming the initial set of parameter values does not reproduce $\mathbf{S}$ perfectly, we generate a second set of parameter estimates (based on certain mathematical properties of the $L(\boldsymbol{\theta})$ function) to provide us with a closer fit between $\boldsymbol{\Sigma}$ and $\mathbf{S}$. This process continues until we can no longer improve the fit between $\boldsymbol{\Sigma}$ and $\mathbf{S}$. We can see the logic of this process by examining the components of the loss function: As the predicted and sample covariance matrices become identical, $\log |\boldsymbol{\Sigma}| - \log |\mathbf{S}|$ goes to zero as does $\mathrm{tr}\,(\boldsymbol{\Sigma}^{-1}\mathbf{S}) - p$.

The parameter values that provide the lowest value of $L(\boldsymbol{\theta})$ are the maximum likelihood estimates. If the distribution of the observed variables is multivariate joint normal, then these parameter estimates are "consistent." That is, the parameter estimates approach the true parameter values as sample size increases. In addition, the parameter estimates are also "asymptotically efficient"; that is, these estimates have the minimum variance of any consistent estimator in large samples.

This maximum likelihood method provides standard errors for the specific parameter estimates as well as a likelihood ratio test for the entire model that is distributed in large samples as a χ^2 distribution with appropriate degrees of freedom.

Assessment

How can the researcher tell if the proposed model adequately fits the observed data?[3] A test of the overall goodness of fit between the proposed model and the sample variance-covariance matrix is provided by a chi-square or likelihood ratio test. This chi-square test may be regarded as a comparison of the specified model against the general alternative that it is any positive definite matrix, that is, that the observed variables, the x_i and y_i, are simply correlated to an arbitrary extent. The goodness-of-fit value is equal to $(N - 1)$ times the minimum value of the function L with

$$df = 1/2p\,(p + 1) - t \qquad [2.18]$$

degrees of freedom where p is the number of variables and t is the number of unknown parameters to be estimated under the specification of the model. Given comparable degrees of freedom, relatively small χ^2 values indicate that the model closely fits the observed data while relatively large χ^2 values show that the model is empirically inadequate.

It should be emphasized that this is just the opposite from typical use. Generally, the researcher wants to obtain high χ^2 values, thus indicating that the theoretical relationship differs from the null hypothesis of no relationship. But in this instance, a comparison is being made of the variance-covariance matrix implied by the theoretical model with the observed variance-covariance matrix, and hence, small χ^2 values indicate the close correspondence between the model and sample data.

In many situations, the researcher may be interested in evaluating several plausible models rather than a single hypothesis. If these models are nested (hierarchical), meaning that model M_o can be obtained by constraining one or more parameters of model M_1, then the models can be compared by examining differences in their χ^2 values; These differences in χ^2 are themselves distributed as χ^2. Thus a set of nested models can be evaluated by computing their likelihood ratio tests and comparing them as follows:

$$\chi^2_d = \chi^2_{M_1} - \chi^2_{M_o}$$

with [2.19]

$$df_d = df_{M_1} - df_{M_o}$$

Commenting on this strategy for evaluating competing models. Jöreskog (1978: 448) suggests that,

> if the drop in χ^2 is large compared to the difference in degrees of freedom, this is an indication that the change made in the model represents a real improvement. If, on the other hand, the drop in χ^2 is close to the difference in number of degrees of freedom, this is an indication that the improvement in fit is obtained by "capitalizing on chance" and the added parameters may not have any real significance or meaning.

The fact that the likelihood ratio test is sensitive to sample size (as are all chi-square statistics) proves to be something of a double-edged sword. If, on the one hand, the sample is too small, even an inadequate model is likely to fit the data. The more typical situation, however, especially in regard to mass survey studies, is that the sample will be so large that even reasonable theories will be rejected by using the chi-square test. Focusing specifically on factor analysis models, Burt (1973: 148) observes the following:

> For extremely large sample sizes . . . almost no theoretical structure will be adequate unless every possible factor is retained in the final structure (i.e., unless the number of unobserved variables equals the number of observed variables). In such a case, the factor analytic model loses its ability to make parsimonious statements based on the covariance of a set of observed variables.

Because of these difficulties in using the χ^2 test as a measure of goodness of fit, Wheaton et al. (1977) suggest that the researcher also compute a *relative* chi square (χ^2/df). As they indicate, this statistic takes sample size into consideration in assessing goodness of fit. They suggest that a ratio of approximately five or less "as beginning to be reasonable."

PERSONALITY AND POLITICAL BEHAVIOR: AN ILLUSTRATION

The focus now shifts to a substantive example that illustrates how the covariance structure model can estimate a structural model that contains theoretical constructs represented by empirical indicators. Focusing on a sample of high school seniors, the question to be addressed is as follows: What is the nature of the relationship between personality and political behavior? On the one hand, it is possible that political behavior is a mere extension of basic features of personality. As Mussen and Wyzenski (1952: 80) observe, "Political apathy and activity are specific manifestations of more deep-lying and pervasive passive and active orientations." In this case, one would expect to find a strong, direct effect of personality on political participation.

On the other hand, it is quite possible that instead of directly influencing political behavior, personality affects participation only through a series of intervening psychological processes. This would be consistent with McClosky's (1968: 258) observation that

> personality is so complex a phenomenon that the connection between any particular activity and any source trait is bound to be extremely tenuous. The "distance" between a basic personality trait and a specific manifestation of political activity is too great and the route between them too circuitous for one to be directly engaged by the other.

These alternative theoretical propositions concerning the relationship between personality and political participation can be evaluated within

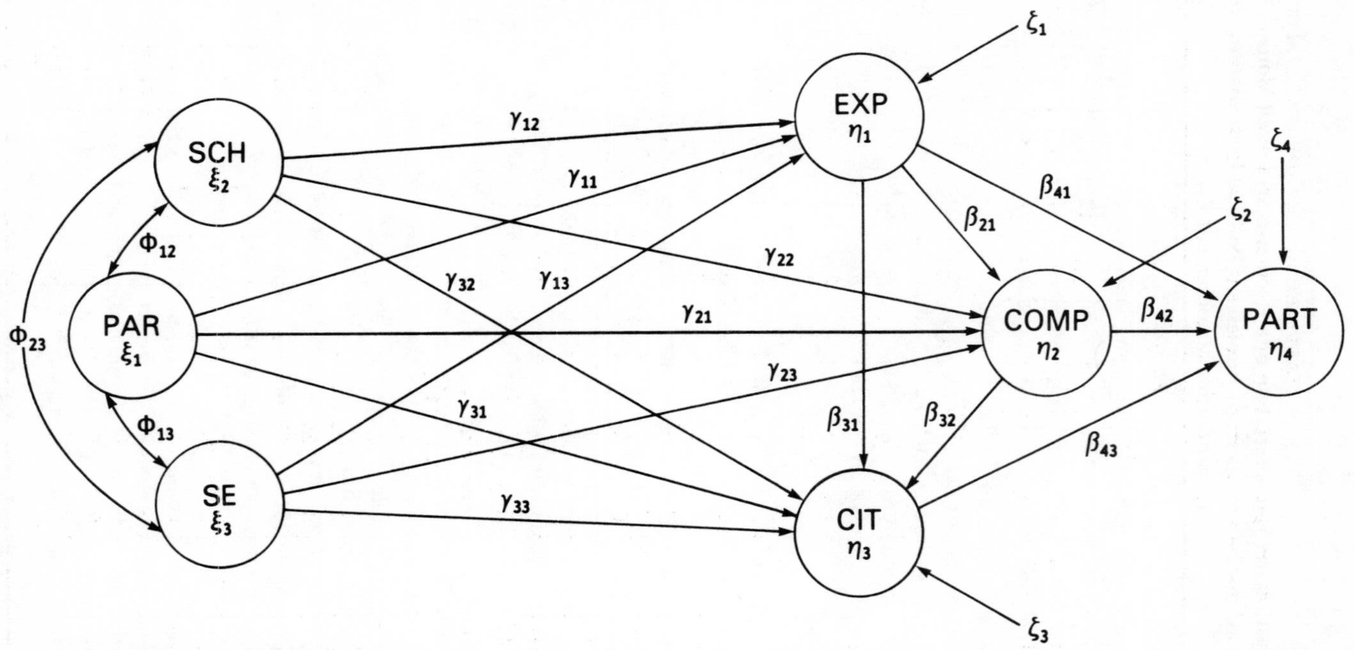

Figure 2.5: A Structural Model of the Determinants of Adolescent Political Participation

TABLE 2.2
A Matrix Representation of a Recursive Structural Model of the Determinants of Adolescent Political Participation Incorporating Measurement Error

$$\boldsymbol{\beta\eta} = \boldsymbol{\gamma\xi} + \boldsymbol{\zeta}$$

(a)

$$\begin{bmatrix} 1 & 0 & 0 & 0 \\ -\beta_{21} & 1 & 0 & 0 \\ -\beta_{31} & -\beta_{32} & 1 & 0 \\ -\beta_{41} & -\beta_{42} & -\beta_{43} & 1 \end{bmatrix} \begin{bmatrix} \eta_1 \\ \eta_2 \\ \eta_3 \\ \eta_4 \end{bmatrix} \begin{matrix} = \\ = \\ = \\ \end{matrix} \begin{bmatrix} \gamma_{11} & \gamma_{12} & \gamma_{13} \\ \gamma_{21} & \gamma_{22} & \gamma_{23} \\ \gamma_{31} & \gamma_{32} & \gamma_{33} \\ \gamma_{41} & \gamma_{42} & \gamma_{43} \end{bmatrix} \begin{bmatrix} \xi_1 \\ \xi_2 \\ \xi_3 \end{bmatrix} \begin{matrix} + \\ + \\ + \\ \end{matrix} \begin{bmatrix} \zeta_1 \\ \zeta_2 \\ \zeta_3 \\ \zeta_4 \end{bmatrix}$$

$$\mathbf{y} = \boldsymbol{\Lambda}_y \boldsymbol{\eta} + \boldsymbol{\epsilon}$$

(b)

$$\begin{bmatrix} y_1 \\ y_2 \\ y_3 \\ y_4 \\ y_5 \\ y_6 \\ y_7 \\ y_8 \\ y_9 \\ y_{10} \\ y_{11} \\ y_{12} \\ y_{13} \\ y_{14} \\ y_{15} \end{bmatrix} = \begin{bmatrix} \lambda_{11} & 0 & 0 & 0 \\ \lambda_{21} & 0 & 0 & 0 \\ \lambda_{31} & 0 & 0 & 0 \\ 0 & \lambda_{42} & 0 & 0 \\ 0 & \lambda_{52} & 0 & 0 \\ 0 & \lambda_{62} & 0 & 0 \\ 0 & 0 & \lambda_{73} & 0\;0 \\ 0 & 0 & \lambda_{83} & 0 \\ 0 & 0 & \lambda_{93} & 0 \\ 0 & 0 & 0 & \lambda_{10,\,4} \\ 0 & 0 & 0 & \lambda_{11,\,4} \\ 0 & 0 & 0 & \lambda_{12,\,4} \\ 0 & 0 & 0 & \lambda_{13,\,4} \\ 0 & 0 & 0 & \lambda_{14,\,4} \\ 0 & 0 & 0 & \lambda_{15,\,4} \end{bmatrix} \begin{bmatrix} \eta_1 \\ \eta_2 \\ \eta_3 \\ \eta_4 \end{bmatrix} + \begin{bmatrix} \epsilon_1 \\ \epsilon_2 \\ \epsilon_3 \\ \epsilon_4 \\ \epsilon_5 \\ \epsilon_6 \\ \epsilon_7 \\ \epsilon_8 \\ \epsilon_9 \\ \epsilon_{10} \\ \epsilon_{11} \\ \epsilon_{12} \\ \epsilon_{13} \\ \epsilon_{14} \\ \epsilon_{15} \end{bmatrix}$$

$$\mathbf{x} = \boldsymbol{\Lambda}_x \boldsymbol{\xi} + \boldsymbol{\delta}$$

(c)

$$\begin{bmatrix} x_1 \\ x_2 \\ x_3 \\ x_4 \\ x_5 \\ x_6 \\ x_7 \\ x_8 \\ x_9 \\ x_{10} \\ x_{11} \\ x_{12} \end{bmatrix} = \begin{bmatrix} \lambda_{11} & 0 & 0 \\ 0 & \lambda_{22} & 0 \\ 0 & \lambda_{32} & 0 \\ 0 & 0 & \lambda_{43} \\ 0 & 0 & \lambda_{53} \\ 0 & 0 & \lambda_{63} \\ 0 & 0 & \lambda_{73} \\ 0 & 0 & \lambda_{83} \\ 0 & 0 & \lambda_{93} \\ 0 & 0 & \lambda_{10,\,3} \\ 0 & 0 & \lambda_{11,\,3} \\ 0 & 0 & \lambda_{12,\,3} \end{bmatrix} \begin{bmatrix} \xi_1 \\ \xi_2 \\ \xi_3 \end{bmatrix} + \begin{bmatrix} 0 \\ \delta_2 \\ \delta_3 \\ \delta_4 \\ \delta_5 \\ \delta_6 \\ \delta_7 \\ \delta_8 \\ \delta_9 \\ \delta_{10} \\ \delta_{11} \\ \delta_{12} \end{bmatrix}$$

NOTE: In part a, the model of Figure 2.6 assumes that $\gamma_{41} = \gamma_{42} = \gamma_{43} = 0$; in part c, the model of Figure 2.6 assumes that $\lambda^{x}_{11} = 1.0$ (i.e., that ξ_1 is measured perfectly by x_1).

the context of the structural model represented in Figure 2.5. This model presumes that self-esteem (ξ_3) is linked to political participation (η_4) via three intervening variables: exposure to political stimuli (η_1), comprehension of political information (η_2), and orientation toward participant citizenship (η_3). That is, the model specifies that self-esteem does not affect participation directly but only indirectly through these mediating variables. These intervening variables are themselves postulated to be causally related to one another. Specifically, political exposure should directly affect both political comprehension and citizenship and comprehension should have a direct effect on citizenship. Finally, two additional exogenous variables—parental politics (ξ_1) and the political environment of the school (ξ_2)—are included to specify the model more fully and to control for possible spurious effects of self-esteem on the intervening variables. Both of these exogenous variables are postulated to have the same causal effects as self-esteem; that is, ξ_1 and ξ_2 are presumed to have direct causal effects on η_1, η_2, and η_3, but only indirect effects on η_4.

The four structural equations associated with the four endogenous variables in Figure 2.5 are as follows:

$$\begin{aligned}
\eta_1 &= \gamma_{11}\xi_1 + \gamma_{12}\xi_2 + \gamma_{13}\xi_3 + \zeta_1 \\
\eta_2 &= \beta_{21}\eta_1 + \gamma_{21}\xi_1 + \gamma_{22}\xi_2 + \gamma_{23}\xi_3 + \zeta_2 \\
\eta_3 &= \beta_{32}\eta_2 + \beta_{31}\eta_1 + \gamma_{31}\xi_1 + \gamma_{32}\xi_2 + \gamma_{33}\xi_3 + \zeta_3 \\
\eta_4 &= \beta_{43}\eta_3 + \beta_{42}\eta_2 + \beta_{41}\eta_1 + \zeta_4
\end{aligned} \qquad [2.20]$$

These structural equations may be summarized in more compact form through matrix notation as follows:

$$\boldsymbol{\beta\eta} = \boldsymbol{\Gamma\xi} + \boldsymbol{\zeta} \qquad [2.21]$$

where $\boldsymbol{\beta}$ is a coefficient matrix of the relationships among the endogenous variables, $\boldsymbol{\Gamma}$ is a matrix of causal effects of the exogenous variables on the endogenous variables, and $\boldsymbol{\zeta}$ is a residual vector for errors in equation.

Part a of Table 2.2 presents a matrix representation of the four equations relating the latent exogenous and endogenous variables. The parameters to be estimated are noted by their appropriate coefficients. The zero elements in the upper triangle of the $\boldsymbol{\beta}$ matrix indicate that the model is recursive.

Figure 2.5 assumes implicitly that the theoretical constructs have been measured without error. This is, of course, a highly unrealistic assumption as it is not possible to measure any of these theoretical constructs perfectly or exactly but only approximately. In this particular situation, we have tried to obtain approximate measures of these constructs by selecting appropriate items from a large survey. For example, one of the items used to measure political participation is whether or not the respondent had ever campaigned for a political candidate. We have tried to select the best possible measures of each of these theoretical constructs, realizing that there will at best only be a close—not a perfect—relationship between the theoretical constructs and their empirical indicators. In effect, the measurement and structural parameters of the model are estimated from the variances and covariances among the indicators. The result is a structural model that simultaneously expresses the relationships among the latent exogenous and endogenous variables as well as the relationships between the latent variables and their empirical indicators.

Figure 2.6 provides the structural model of Figure 2.5 together with its measurement component. The relationship between the latent exogenous variables ξ_1, ξ_2, and ξ_3 and their empirical indicators are represented by the matrix equation:

$$\mathbf{x} = \boldsymbol{\Lambda}_x \boldsymbol{\xi} + \boldsymbol{\delta} \qquad [2.22]$$

where $\boldsymbol{\Lambda}_x$ is the matrix of the factor loadings that relate the observed measures to the appropriate unobserved variable and $\boldsymbol{\delta}$ is a vector containing errors in measurement. There are twelve scalar equations described by matrix equation 2.22 because there are twelve indicators associated with these three exogenous variables. An example of one of these equations is the relationship between indicator 5 and latent exogenous variable 3, which takes the following form:

$$x_5 = \lambda^x_{53}\, \xi_3 + \delta_5 \qquad [2.23]$$

The relationship between the latent endogenous variables η_1, η_2, η_3, η_4 and their respective y indicators can be represented in the following matrix equation:

$$\mathbf{y} = \boldsymbol{\Lambda}_y \boldsymbol{\eta} + \boldsymbol{\epsilon} \qquad [2.24]$$

Fifteen individual equations are summarized in this matrix equation. For example, the relationship between indicator 9 and endogenous variable 3 takes the following form:

$$y_9 = \lambda^y_{93}\, \eta_3 + \epsilon_9 \qquad [2.25]$$

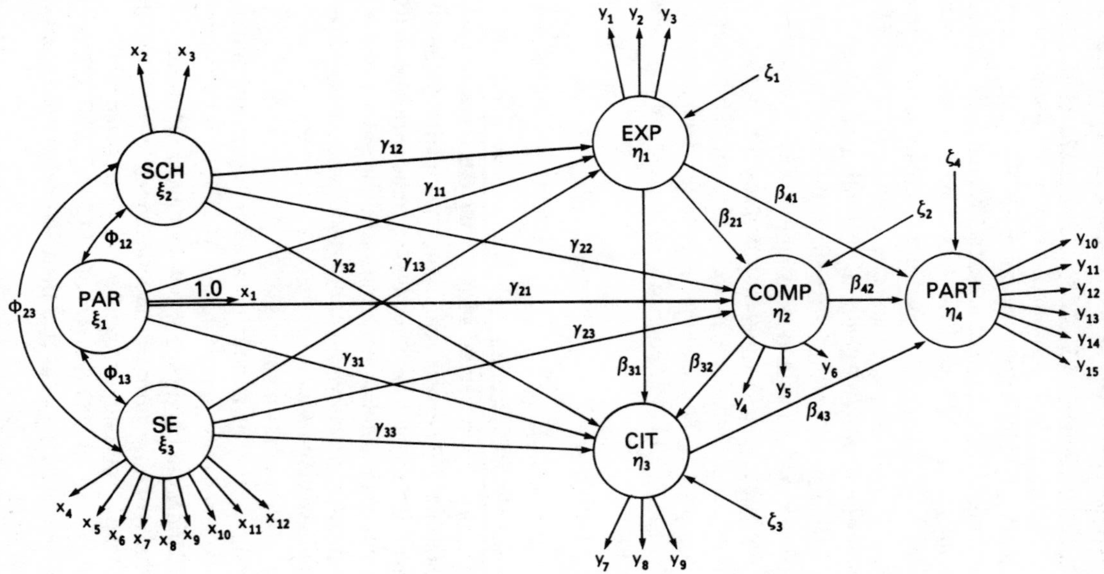

NOTE: The squares enclosing the measured x's and measured y's have been excluded for clarity of presentation. The error terms of these measured indicators have also been excluded for this purpose.

Figure 2.6: Determinants of Adolescent Political Participation: A Recursive Structural Model with Measurement Error

TABLE 2.3
A Comparison of Recursive Models of the Determinants of Adolescent Political Participation
(N = 776)

Model	χ^2 Likelihood Ratio	Degrees of Freedom	Relative (χ^2 / df) Fit
I. Null model No structural effects – 7 orthogonal factors	1343.067	322	4.171
II. No exogenous effects on participation $\gamma_{41} = 0,\ \gamma_{42} = 0,\ \gamma_{43} = 0;$ β lower triangular free	618.095	307	2.013
III. No exogenous effects on participation $\gamma_{41} = 0 \quad \gamma_{42} = 0$ $\gamma_{43} = 0, \quad \beta_{32} = 0,$ $\gamma_{32} = 0, \quad \gamma_{23} = 0,$ $\gamma_{21} = 0, \quad \gamma_{33} = 0;$ β lower triangular free	623.438	312	1.998
IV. Saturated structural model Γ free, β lower triangular free	612.121	304	2.014

Parts b and c of Table 2.2 present a matrix representation of the measurement equations relating the four latent endogenous variables to their fifteen indicators and the three latent exogenous variables to their twelve indicators, respectively. The parameters to be estimated are identified by their respective coefficients while the zeros in the columns indicate that each indicator loads on only a single factor.

Table 2.3 shows the fit of four covariance structures linking self-esteem to political behavior; one of these—Model II—is the model specified in Figure 2.6. Model I (shown in row 1) may be regarded as a test of the null hypothesis of no relationship among the seven latent variables. In this case we fit the 27 measured variables to 7 orthogonal factors. The fit is relatively poor: a χ^2 likelihood ratio of 1343.067 with 322 degrees of freedom. This evidence suggests that there are relationships among the seven latent variables.

The second model (Model IV) to be estimated (see row 4) is a fully saturated recursive model. By fully saturated it is meant that it allows for the estimation of all possible causal paths, but still retains the recursiveness of the system. This model, as expected, provides a much closer fit to the observed data. The χ^2 difference between the null model and the satu-

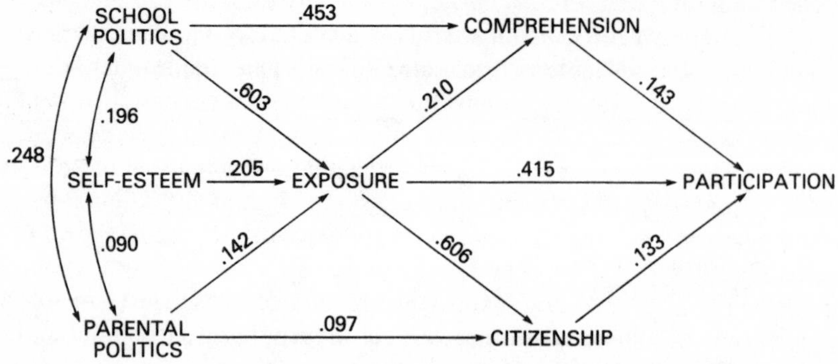

Figure 2.7: Model III: Standardized Structural Coefficients of the Determinants of Adolescent Political Participation (N = 776)

rated model equals 730.946 with 18 degrees of freedom, indicating a relatively better fit. However, the saturated model with 304 degrees of freedom yields overall an X^2 of 612.121, which is not statistically significant ($\geqslant .05$). Given the large sample size, this is not at all surprising; and the fit relative to degrees of freedom is impressive (2.014).

Is the saturated model, then, most appropriate for these data? Row 2 of Table 2.3 (Model II) suggests this may not be the case. In this model the direct paths between the exogenous variables and participation have been eliminated; they have been constrained to be zero. Thus under the conditions of the model, self-esteem (as well as the political environments of the home and school) only affects adolescent political behavior through its influence on the intervening variables. The X^2 difference between this indirect casual model and the saturated model is not significant. Moreover, their relative degrees of fit are almost identical. In other words, the three exogeneous variables, self-esteem, school politics, and parental politics, do not have a direct effect on adolescent political participation. The impact of these variables is medicated by three intervening endogenous variables, exposure to politics, comprehension, and citizenship.

The indirect causal model (Model III) contains several paths that are statistically insignificant β_{32}, γ_{21}, γ_{23}, γ_{32}, and γ_{33}. Constraining these paths to be zero leads to slight improvement in the relative fit of the model as seen in row 3 of Table 2.3 (Model III). In sum, based on this evidence, it can be concluded that the indirect causal model (Model III) provides a more appropriate representation of the process by which personality is linked to political participation. Not only does it fit the data as well as the saturated model, but it is more parsimonious and theoretically more reasonable.

The standardized structural coefficients for Model III are presented in Figure 2.7.[4] These coefficients are easily interpreted. A one standard deviation increase in self-esteem, for example, leads to a .205 standard deviation increase in exposure, controlling for all other variables affecting exposure (school politics and parental politics). A standard deviation increase in exposure leads to a .415 standard deviation increase in participation, all other variables being held constant. Similar interpretations can be given to the other structural coefficients in this model.[5] Self-esteem has its strongest impact on political participation via its effect on political exposure. Thus adolescents with higher levels of self-esteem are more likely to be exposed to politics which, in turn, has a substantial effect on actual participation.

CONCLUSION

There is a duality of language that characterizes theory and research in the social science. On the one hand, we refer to theoretical constructs such as party identification, class consciousness, and social isolation. Typically, we seek to place these theoretical constructs within an explicit causal structure—to understand the causal dynamics that surround them. But the attempt to examine the structural relations among these constructs systematically is severely hampered by our inability to observe and hence, directly measure them. As a consequence, the empirical exploration and testing of causal theories requires the use of empirical indicators, designed to represent given theoretical constructs.

If social scientists needed only to estimate structural relationships, they could simply rely on some type of regression-type analysis. If they needed only to examine measurement relationships, they could turn to a variety of factor analysis models. But typically, social scientists must make inferences about both types of relationships: the causal relationship among the latent theoretical constructs and the measurement relationships between the empirical indicators and their respective latent variables. And until quite recently no general statistical method for the simultaneous estimation of structural and measurement equations existed. Instead, researchers were forced to employ ad hoc procedures that provided neither efficient estimates of structural parameters nor an overall test of the adequacy of the model.

The general method for analyzing covariance structures outlined in this chapter provides a general solution to this dual inference problem. It provides for the efficient simultaneous estimation of structural and measurement parameters. Thus it allows the researcher to estimate structural models that explicitly allow for measurement error. The method provides an overall goodness-of-fit assessment of the entire model and allows nested models to be compared with one another. In sum, this method of analyzing covariance structure models combines the separate strengths of structural equation models and factor analysis models and overcomes their respective limitations. Because of its substantial flexibility and generality, it should play an increasingly prominent role in the social sciences.

APPENDIX: THE PENNSYLVANIA HIGH SCHOOL SURVEY

The data analyzed in this chapter come from a large-scale study of the political orientations, psychological predispositions, and sociological characteristics of adolescents. The data consist of a stratified random sample of 1,000 high school seniors attending 25 public schools in Pennsylvania. The students were interviewed during April and May 1974 by trained interviewers from the Institute for Survey Research at Temple University. Each interview lasted approximately 50 minutes. Three weeks later, 868 of the original sample completed a follow-up questionnaire administered by high school personnel. Both sources of data are used in the analysis.

The questions used as indicators of each of the latent variables in the model of the determinants of political participation are as follows:

ξ_1: Political Environment: Parents

- x_1: Do you hear your parents talk about politics? (very often, occasionally, not at all)

ξ_2: Political Environment: School

- x_2: Number of civics, social studies, or current events courses. (none, one, more than one)
- x_3: Watergate discussed in classes. (regularly, a few times, just once, never)

ξ_3: Respondent Self-Esteem (each coded almost always true, often true, sometimes true, seldom true, or never true)

- x_4: I feel that I have a number of good qualities.
- x_5: I feel I am a person of worth, at least on an equal plane with others.
- x_6: I feel I do not have much to be proud of.
- x_7: I take a positive attitude toward myself.
- x_8: I certainly feel useless at times.
- x_9: All in all, I am inclined to feel that I am a failure.
- x_{10}: I am able to do things as well as most other people.

x_{11}: At times I think I am no good at all.
x_{12}: On the whole, I am satisfied with myself.

η_1: Exposure to Politics

y_1: Some people think about what is going on in politics and public affairs very often and others are not that interested. How much of an interest do you take in such matters? (very great deal, a lot of interest, some interest, very little interest, no interest at all)

y_2: Thinking about the important political issues facing the country, how well do you understand these issues? (very well, moderately well, depends on the issue, not so well, not at all)

y_3: Do you follow current events in the news? (almost every day, maybe once or twice a week, very seldom, not at all)

η_2: Comprehension of Political World

y_4: Number of political leaders correctly identified. (0-7)

y_5: Number of international political affairs items correctly answered. (0-4)

y_6: Number of state political questions correctly answered. (0-5)

η_3: Citizenship Orientation to Politics (extremely important, important, no opinion, not very important, not at all important)

y_7: Voting in most elections.
y_8: Trying to influence government decisions.
y_9: Keeping informed about public affairs.

η_4: Participation Index (never, once, more than once)

y_{10}: Campaigned for a candidate.
y_{11}: Tried to convince people how to vote.
y_{12}: Wore a campaign button/bumper sticker on car.
y_{13}: Stopped a candidate to talk.
y_{14}: Complained to or made request of government official.
y_{15}: Participated in a political demonstration.

The sample correlation matrix and item standard deviations for these items are presented in Carmines and McIver (1981).

NOTES

1. For this discussion, Jöreskog's convention is being followed of letting $\boldsymbol{\theta}$ be a vector of all the unknown parameters that are to be estimated in the model.

2. For the general model, one necessary condition for identification of all parameters is that the number of parameters to be estimated (t) be less than the number of observed variances and covariances, that is, $t < 1/2(p + q)(p + q + 1)$, where p is the number of observed y variables and q is the number of observed x variables. If the data are scale-free, correlations rather than variances and covariances may be analyzed. In this case, the necessary condition for identification becomes $t < 1/2(p + q)(p + q - 1)$.

Beyond this very simple necessary condition, few additional guidelines exist for the identification of the general model. Consequently, Jöreskog and Sörbom (1983) provide a numerical method of determining whether or not a model is identified. After computing the maximum likelihood coefficients of a given model, LISREL computes the information matrix (the variance-covariance matrix of the parameter estimates) for all independent parameters. Following Silvey (1970), Jöreskog and Sörbom argue that if this information matrix is positive definite, it is "almost certain" the model is identified. But if it is singular, the model is not identified. This empirical approach to evaluating identification has been criticized by McDonald and Krane (1979), and Bentler (1980).

Although few guidelines exist for evaluating the identification of the general model, certain criteria have been outlined for identifying special cases of the general model. Jöreskog (1969, 1979), Dunn (1973), Jennrich (1978), and Algina (1980) discuss various criteria for computing unique factor analysis estimates. Wiley (1973), Werts, Jöreskog, and Linn (1973), Gerci (1976), Hsiao (1976), and Jöreskog (1977) provide examples of how structural equation models with imperfectly measured variables may be identified.

3. There are several alternative methods for assessing the goodness of fit of covariance structure models. A more comprehensive discussion is contained in Carmines and McIver (1983), and Long (1983).

4. A presentation and discussion of the estimates of the measurement parameters of Figure 2.6 are contained in Carmines and McIver (1983).

5. These coefficients of course indicate only the direct effects of the exogenous and endogenous variables on specified endogeneous variables. There are also indirect effects that need to be taken into consideration in assessing total effects. See Graff and Schmidt (1982) for a discussion of indirect effects in covariance structure models.

references

Algina, James (1980) "A note on identification in the oblique and orthogonal factor analysis." Psychometrika 45 (September): 393-397.

Alwin, Duane F. and David J. Jackson (1979) "Measurement models for response errors in surveys: issues and application," in K. F. Schuessler (ed.) Sociological Methodology. San Francisco: Jossey-Bass.

———(1981) "Application of simultaneous factor analysis to issues of factorial invariance," in D. J. Jackson and E. F. Borgatta (eds.) Factor Analysis and Measurement in Sociological Research. Beverly Hills, CA: Sage.

Bentler, Peter M. (1980) "Multivariate analysis with latent variables: causal modeling." Annual Review in Psychology 31: 419-456.

———and Douglas G. Bonett (1980) "Significance tests and goodness-of-fit in the analysis of covariance structures." Psychological Bulletin 88 (November): 588-606.

Bentler, Peter M. and David G. Weeks (1980) "Linear structural equations with latent variables." Psychometrika 45 (September): 298-308.

Boomsa, A. (1981) "The robustness of LISREL against small sample sizes in factor analysis models." in K. G. Jöreskog and H. Wold, (eds.) Systems Under Indirect Observation: Causality, Structure, Prediction. Amsterdam: North-Holland.

Browne, Michael W. (1974) "Generalized least-squared estimators in the analysis of covariance structures." South African Statistical Journal 8: 1-24.

Burt, Ronald S. (1973) "Confirmatory factor-analytic structures and the theory construction process." Sociological methods and research, 2 (November): 131-190.

———(1976) "Interpretational confounding of unobserved variables in structural equation models." Sociological Methods and Research, 5 (August): 3-52.

Carmines, Edward G. and John P. McIver (1981) "Analyzing models with unobserved variables: analysis of covariance structures." in George W. Bohrnstedt and Edgar F. Borgatta, eds. Social Measurement: Current Issues. Beverly Hills, CA: Sage.

———(1983) "An introduction to the analysis of models with unobserved variables." Political Methodology 5: 51-102.

Christoffersson, Andres (1975) "Factor analysis of dichotomised variables." Psychometrika 40 (March): 5-32.

Chubb, John E. (1978) "Multiple indicators and measurement error in panel data: an evaluation of summated scales, path analysis and confirmatory maximum likelihood factor analysis." Political Methodology 5: 413-444.

Dunn, James E. (1973) "A note on sufficiency condition for uniqueness of a restricted factor matrix." Psychometrika 38 (March): 141-143.

Geraci, Vincent J. (1976) "Identification of simultaneous equation models with measurement error." Journal of Econometrics 4: 262-283.

Gerweke, John F. and Kenneth J. Singleton (1980) "Interpreting the likelihood ratio statistic in factor models when sample size is small." Journal of the American Statistical Association 75: 133-137.

Gnanadesikan, R. (1977) Methods For Statistical Data Analysis of Multivariate Observations. New York: John Wiley.

Graff, J. and P. Schmidt (1982) "A general model for decomposition of effects," in K. G. Jöreskog and H. Wald (eds.) Systems Under Indirect Observation: Causality, Structure, Prediction. Amsterdam: North-Holland.

Hsaiao, Cheng (1976) "Identification and estimation of simultaneous equation models with measurement error." International Economics Review 17 (June): 319-339.

Jeenrich, Robert I. (1978) "Rotational equivalence of factor loading matrices with specified values." Psychometrika 43(September): 421-426.

Jöreskog, Karl G. (1967) "Some contributions to maximum likelihood factor analysis." Psychometrika 32 (December): 433-482.

———(1969) "A general approach to confirmatory maximum likelihood factor analysis." Psychometrika 34 (June): 183-202.

———(1970) "A general method for analysis of covariance structures." Biometrika 57: 239-251.

———(1971a) "Simultaneous factor analysis in several populations." Psychometrika 36 (December): 409-426.

———(1971b) "Statistical analysis of sets of congeneric tests." Psychometrika 36 (June): 109-133.

———(1973a) "A general method for estimating a linear structural equation system," in Arthur S. Goldberger and Otis Dudley Duncan (eds.) Structural Equation Models in the Social Sciences. New York: Seminar Press.

———(1973b) "Analysis of covariance structures," in P. R. Krishnaiah (ed.) Multivariate Analysis—III. New York: Academic Press.

———(1974) "Analyzing psychological data by structural analysis of covariance matrices," in R. C. Atkins et al. (eds.) Contemporary Developments in Mathematical Psychology—Volume II. San Francisco, CA: W. H. Freeman.

———(1976) "Factor analysis by least squares and maximum likelihood methods." in K. Enslein et al. (eds.) Statistical Methods for Digital Computers. New York: John Wiley.

———(1977) "Structural equation models in the social sciences: specification, estimation, and testing," in P. R. Krishnaiah (ed.) Application of Statistics. Amsterdam: North-Holland.

———(1978) "Structural analysis of covariance and correlations matrices." Psychometrika 43 (December): 443-477.

———(1979) Advances in Factor Analysis and Structural Equations Models. Cambridge, MA: Abt.

———and Dag Sörbom (1983) "LISREL VI: analysis of linear structural relationships by maximum likelihood and least squared methods." Uppsala, Sweden: University of Uppsala, Department of Statistics.

Krane, William R. and Roderick P. McDonald (1978) "Scale invariance and the factor analysis of correlation matrices." British Journal of Mathematical and Statistical Psychology 31(November): 218-228.

Long, J. Scott (1976) "Estimation and hypothesis testing in linear models containing measurement error: a review of Jöreskog's model for the analysis of covariance structures." Sociological Methods and Research, 5 (November): 157-206.

———(1983) Confirmatory Factory Analysis. Beverly Hills, CA: Sage.

———(1983) Covariance Structure Models. Beverly Hills, CA: Sage.

McClosky, Herbert (1968) "Political participation." International Encyclopedia of the Social Sciences. New York: Macmillan.

McDonald, Roderick P. and William R. Krane (1979) "A Monte Carlo study of local indentifiability and degrees of freedom in the asymptotic likelihood ratio test." British Journal of Mathematical and Statistical Psychology, 32 (May): 121-132.

McIver, John P., Edward G. Carmines, and Richard A. Zeller (1980) "Multiple indicators." in Richard A. Zeller and Edward G. Carmines (eds.) Measurement in the Social Sciences: The Link Between Theory and Data. New York: Cambridge University Press.

Mussen, Paul H. and Anne B. Wysznski (1952) "Personality and political participation." Human Relations, 5 (February): 65-82.

Muthen, Bengt (1978) "Contributions to factor analysis of dichotomous variables." Psychometrika, 43 (December): 551-560.

———(1979) "A structural probit model with latent variables." Journal of the American Statistical Association, 74 (December): 807-811.

———(1981) "Factor analysis of dichotomous variables: American attitudes toward abortion," in David J. Jackson and Edgar F. Borgatta (eds.) Factor Analysis and Measurement in Sociological Research. Beverly Hills, CA: Sage.

———and Anders Christoffersson (1981) "Simultaneous factor analysis of dichotomous variables in several groups." Psychometrika, 46 (December): 407-419.

Olsson, Ulf (1979a) "On the robustness of factor analysis against crude classification of the observations." Multivariate Behavior Research 14 (October): 485-500.

———(1979b) "Maximum likelihood estimation of the polychonic correlation coefficient." Psychometrika 44 (December): 443-460.

Rosenberg, Morris (1965) Society and the Adolescent Self-Image. Princeton, NJ: Princeton University Press.

Saris, W. E., W. M. DePijper, and P. Zegwaart (1978) "Detection of specification errors in linear structural equation models," in Karl F. Schuessler (ed.) Sociological Methodology 1979. San Francisco, CA: Jossey-Bass.

Silvey, S. D. (1970) Statistical Inference. Middlesex, England: Penguin.

Sörbom, Dag (1974) "A general method for studying differences in factor means and factor structure between groups." British Journal of Mathematical and Statistical Psychology 27 (November): 229-239.

———(1981) "The use of LISREL in sociological model building." in David J. Jackson and Edgar F. Borgatta (eds.) Factor Analysis and Measurement in Sociological Research. Beverly Hills, CA: Sage.

Tucker, L. R. and C. Lewis (1973) "A reliability coefficient for maximum likelihood analysis." Psychometrika 38 (March): 1-10.

Werts, C. E., Karl G. Jöreskog, and Robert Linn (1973) "Identification and estimation in path analysis with unmeasured variables." American Journal of Sociology, 78, (May): 1,469-1, 484.

Wheaton, Blair, Bengt Muthen, Duane F. Alwin, and Gene F. Summers (1977) "Assessing the reliability and stability in panel models." in David R. Heise (ed.) Sociological Methodology 1977. San Francisco, CA: Jossey-Bass.

Wiley, David E. (1973) "The identification problem for structural equation models with unmeasured variables," in Arthur S. Goldberger and Otis Dudley Duncan (eds.) Structural Equation Models in the Social Sciences. New York: Seminar Press.

———and James A. Wiley (1970) "The estimation of measurement error in panel data." American Sociological Review 35 (February): 112-117.

Wilson, Kenneth L. (1981) "On population comparisons using factor indexes or latent variables." Social Science Research 10 (December): 301-313.

Zeller, Richard A. and Edward G. Carmines (1980) Measurement in the Social Sciences: The Link Between Theory and Data. New York, NY: Cambridge University Press.

3

Q Technique and Method
Principles and Procedures

STEVEN R. BROWN

Q methodology is now a half-century old, having been introduced by William Stephenson (1935a, 1935b), and it may consequently seem odd to include a chapter on it in a volume devoted to *new* tools for social scientists. This can perhaps be justified by noting that, whereas most social scientists have at least heard of inverted or "Q" factor analysis (which predated Q methodology), fewer have incorporated Q technique into their bag of technical tools, and only a handful have attended seriously to the broader conceptual and methodological issues these technicalities were intended to subserve. In a sense, therefore, Q methodology may still qualify as new, and perhaps innovative, even by today's standards.

Broadly, Q *methodology* provides the foundation for a science of subjectivity, and was originally distinguished from R methodology, which provided and still provides the basis for a science of objectivity in psychology. The letter R in R methodology is a generalization of Pearson's product moment *r*, which has most often been used in the study of relationships among objective characteristics such as traits, attributes, abilities, and so forth. The most often-cited example is that of intelligence, the assessment of which involves responses to questions that have right answers; but what is essential to R methodology generalizes to any situation in which measurement is independent of the individual's self-reference. Q methodology, by way of contrast, operates within the "internal" frame of reference, not in the sense of a metaphysical subjectivism accessible only to introspection, but in the thoroughly empirical sense of subjective communicability (Stephenson, 1980a), of the world (political or otherwise) as it is experienced from "my own point of view." There is a "fundamental incommensurability" between objectivity and subjectivity (Brown, 1972)—the one lacking the self-referentiality contained in the other—and in scientific respects, Q subserves the latter as R does the former.

Broad philosophical principles are at issue in Q methodology, and there will be occasion to refer to these briefly at the end of this chapter, but it is also essential to clarify those more specific procedural and technical details upon which successful measurement depends (and which, in Q, are frequently regarded as controversial), and it will be to these matters that this chapter will primarily attend. In the course of exemplification, two studies will be presented, the first dealing with public opinion and the second with political roles. Before turning to these, however, a brief conceptual overview may be helpful.

CONCOURSES, Q SORTS, AND OPERANT FACTORS

Much of politics is talk, among ordinary citizens no less than among ward heelers, mayors, diplomats, and heads of state, and it is this communicability, primarily, that Q seeks to model. The volume of discussion on any topic is referred to as a *concourse* (from the Latin *concursus*, meaning "a running together"), and it is these statements of opinion, or ideas that run together in thought, that are the elements of a Q study (Stephenson, 1978). Hence, during the 1984 presidential campaign we might have overheard candidates, political commentators, or neighbors remarking that "Reagan deserves the chance to finish what he started," or that "the nomination of Geraldine Ferraro was just a ploy to get the women's vote," or that "Walter Mondale seems nice enough, but lacks leadership qualities." Statements of opinion such as these are clearly distinguishable from statements of fact (such as "Walter Mondale was Jimmy Carter's Vice President"): The former are of necessity synthetic and self-referential—it is the I, the subjective self, who believes (or not) that Mondale lacks leadership qualities—whereas the latter is analytic and self-evidential, hence without self-reference. Only subjective opinions are at issue in Q, and although they are typically unprovable, they can nonetheless be shown to have structure and form, and it is the task of Q technique to render this form manifest for purposes of observation and study.

Prior to the application of technique, however, it is necessary to reduce the number of statements to practical proportions, and for this purpose reliance is placed upon principles of experimental design, notably the factorial variant advanced by Fisher (1935). A simple illustration can be made using the statements mentioned above concerning the 1984 campaign in that they refer to candidates (Reagan-Bush, Mondale-Ferraro) and that each carries valence (positive, negative). This results in a 2×2 factorial arrangement, and four cells within which each statement finds a home: For example, the view that "Mondale lacks leadership qualities" may, as a first approximation, be judged to belong in the negative/Mondale-Ferraro category, and likewise for all other statements in the concourse. Several statements (usually equal in number) are then drawn from each of the four categories, and the result is referred to as a *Q sample*. A more detailed example is given later, but it is important to state at the outset that statements in a Q sample, unlike items in a conventional rating scale, are not regarded as having a priori meaning, or as being valid measures of a characteristic or trait: Their placement in this or that cell of the design is provisional, and their selection in terms of the structure of the design is for purposes of constructing a Q sample that has the same breadth as the concourse that generated it. It is always recognized that language in use can produce different meanings in singular situations: Hence Mondale's alleged lack of leadership qualities may be considered a plus from the standpoint of the person who values political amateurism over professionalism.

The statements of the Q sample, which typically range in number from 40 to 60, are next numbered randomly and printed one to a card. Each respondent then models his or her own point of view by ranking the statements along a continuum that is usually numbered (so as to aid the Q sorter) from +5 (most agree) to -5 (most disagree), with all other gradations in between, as shown in Figure 3.2. The result is called a *Q sort*. The Q sort statements are conventionally arrayed in a forced, quasi-normal distribution (see Figure 3.2), and this feature has attracted unnecessary notoriety (for example, Bolland, forthcoming). Suffice it to say, the normal distribution was never conceived as a statistical conclusion to be tested—that is, it has never been argued that people naturally sort statements in this form. Statistically, differences in scatter and distribution are of little import within the correlational and factor-analytic framework of Q method, as has been demonstrated on numerous occasions (for example, Cottle and McKeown, 1980). Even under free-choice conditions, significant deviations from normality are rare when the Q sample is sufficiently comprehensive in scope.

Q sorts are conventionally correlated using Pearson's r, although other coefficients can be utilized and produce essentially the same results. In this case, a high positive correlation between any two persons indicates that they have arranged the statements similarly as a reflection (it is initially presumed) of a commonly held viewpoint. Given N respondents, a correlation matrix of the order $N \times N$ is produced for factor analysis.

A Matrix of Q correlations can be factor analyzed by any of the conventional methods, although Q methodology is most frequently associated with the centroid method. (For the computations involved, see Brown, 1980: 208-224.) Generally, factor analysis is a procedure for determining the number of attitudinal groupings implicit in the correlation matrix: If all respondents are of the same mind regarding the topic under consideration (for example, the 1984 presidential campaign), then they will tend to rank the statements the same way, all correlations will be positive and high, and there will be only one factor; if there are two groups of people—members within each group highly correlated among themselves but uncorrelated with persons in the other group, and vice versa—then two factors will emerge, and so forth. The number of factors is therefore a purely empirical matter as determined by the extent to which the audience is actually divided on the issue. When attitudes are in diametric opposition, significantly negative correlations are in evidence and result in bipolar factors.

The centroid method is often preferred in Q methodology because of the indeterminacy of its solution, which thereby permits rotation according to theoretical considerations. The arguments in support of theoretical rotation are intricate and require considerable demonstration (see Brown, 1980: 224-239; Stephenson, 1953: 30-46; Thompson, 1962). Suffice it to say that rotation in Q methodology provides an opportunity for the investigator to pursue hunches and to examine the data from a theoretical standpoint, as will be demonstrated briefly below in the study of political roles.

Finally, at the end of the factoring process, factor scores are calculated for each of the statements in each of the factors. The result is a single Q sort (factor array) for each factor, with each factor array being a composite of those individual Q sorts constituting the factor. If ten persons share a common outlook, for example, then they will be highly intercorrelated, they will define a factor together, and the merger of their separate responses will result in a single Q sort representing the view they hold in common. With two factors, there would be two such Q sorts; and so forth. Ultimately, the task is to interpret and explain the similarities and differences among these factor arrays.

The factors in Q methodology are categories of *operant subjectivity* (Stephenson, 1977) that were inherent in the concourse originally, for it was these separate attitudes (the existence of which the factor analysis demonstrates) that gave rise to all the conversation initially. What begins as subjective communicability, therefore, is prepared for viewing through "the midwifery of Q methodology," as Barchak (1984: 118) has nicely put it, and is eventually manifested as operant factors, which, in turn, display the form and structure of the communicability at issue.

For persons unfamiliar with factor analysis in general and Q factor analysis in particular, the above matters may appear obscure; the following two illustrations are therefore designed to provide further clarification. Additional details can be found in Stephenson (1953) and Brown

(1980), and ongoing developments are reported in *Operant Subjectivity: The Q Methodology Newsletter,* which began quarterly publication in 1977.

PUBLIC OPINION: THE ARAB-ISRAELI CONTROVERSY

Among the most prevalent uses of Q methodology has been in the study of public opinion and political attitudes and beliefs (see, for examples, Casey, 1984; Conover and Feldman, 1984; Kerlinger, 1984), and in this regard a context for illustrating the principles and procedures involved was provided by the Israeli invasion of Lebanon on June 6, 1982, the chain of events having been ostensibly initiated by the assassination of Israel's ambassador to England.

The discussion that ensued dominated the public's attention for several weeks thereafter, and the volume of opinions expressed assumed large proportions. The conventional survey approach to such material was to determine whether the public generally supported or disapproved of Israel's actions, and then to examine those demographic correlates (religion, age, education, and so forth) associated with the various positions and that might be considered causally related to them. Pro and con are imputed categories, however, and whereas they may perhaps not be far from the truth in certain instances, they can be fruitfully preceded by a less committed line of inquiry that permits the public to demonstrate how it is in fact segmented with respect to the issue, and that facilitates a more detailed examination of the quality of thinking involved.

The following opinions from the Arab-Israeli concourse, drawn from public sources and private interviews, will serve as a reminder of the issues in controversy in mid-1982:

(1) "Israel has acted on its own initiative and not as a result of contacts with U.S. officials." (Comment made by Israeli Foreign Minister Yitzhak Shamir in broadcast interview.)

(2) "I hope there can be real peace between a free and independent Lebanon and the state of Israel." (Comment by Israeli Cabinet Secretary Dan Merridor in newspaper interview.)

(3) "What is required is a strong American role in a peace-keeping force to replace the Israeli army and keep Lebanon free from PLO and Syrian domination." (Comment by Israeli Prime Minister Menachem Begin in newspaper interview.)

(4) "The Israelis demolished quiet villages, pulverized crowded neighborhoods, and made Lebanon bleed once more." (From a privately conducted interview with a student.)

		Perspectives		
		Israel (a)	Arabs (b)	Other (c)
	bias (d)	ad	bd	cd
Elaborateness	notion (e)	ae	be	ce
	policy (f)	af	bf	cf

Figure 3.1: 3 X 3 Factorial Structure for the Arab-Israeli Q Sample

(5) "The PLO guerrilla forces will eventually teach Jerusalem a lesson." (Comment by Yasser Arafat, the leader of the Palestine Liberation Organization, as reported in *Time* magazine.)
(6) "If the Israeli forces do not withdraw from Lebanon, the United States should cut off all military aid to Israel." (From a privately conducted interview.)
(7) "Syria should reduce its military presence in Lebanon, and Israel should likewise yield the area which it dominates." (Comment by U.S. envoy Philip Habib, as reported in *Newsweek* magazine.)

And so on in large quantities. These kinds of comments were made in the press, on street corners, in beauty parlors, on the telephone, and elsewhere.

For pragmatic purposes, concourses are modeled theoretically, typically in balanced Fisherian designs of the kind shown in Figure 3.1. Manifestly, (a) Israeli and (b) Arab perspectives are at issue, as indicated in above cited statements 1-3 and 4-6, respectively, but there are also (c) other views, as statement 7 illustrates. Elaborateness is a theoretical term borrowed from George Carslake Thompson's schema (Stephenson, 1964): (d) Bias denotes an understanding and acceptance of facts from a particular standpoint, (e) notion refers to wishes for desired ends, and (f) policy is a recommended course of action that presupposes certain biases and wishes. Hence statement 1 is an Israeli bias (ad), 2 is an Israeli notion (ae), and 3 an Israeli policy position (af); and statements 4-6 are biases,

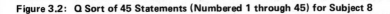

(disagree) -5	-4	-3	-2	-1	0	+1	+2	+3	+4	(agree) +5
12	2	28	6	7	3	5	9	1	4	21
15	16	36	8	23	18	10	14	13	11	25
42	17	39	31	26	24	20	30	19	32	40
	22	41	37	33	29	27	38	44	45	
				43	35	34				

Figure 3.2: Q Sort of 45 Statements (Numbered 1 through 45) for Subject 8

notions, and policies from the Arab perspective. Statement 7 is a policy recommendation that favors neither position. There are, therefore, nine combinations into which the statements of the concourse were fitted, and eventually 5 statements of each kind were selected, for a Q sample size of (9)(5) = 45. The statements were then randomly numbered and typed one to a card for subsequent administration.

The Q sorting procedure itself consists of each subject rank-ordering the set of statements according to some condition of instruction, in this case from agree (+5) to disagree (-5). The resulting Q sort for one of the subjects (number 8 in Table 3.1) is displayed in Figure 3.2. As can be seen from the right-most column in this Q sort, this individual (an Arab Moslem) agreed most with statements 21, 25, and 40, which are as follows:

(21) The PLO has no option other than to fight in self-defense regardless of the consequences.
(25) The U.S. should take a step toward the Palestinians, and help end the bloodshed.
(40) If the Israeli forces do not withdraw from Lebanon, the United States should cut off all military aid to Israel.

As is apparent, this person's sympathies are with the Palestinians rather than with the Israelis, and these feelings are equally obvious at the opposite end of the distribution:

(12) Israel is doing everyone a favor in this war. The PLO should have been kicked out long ago.
(15) The PLO is not and never has been a representative of the Palestinian people. It is a terrorist organization—nothing more, nothing less—and should be treated as such.
(42) Nuke Jerusalem! That would solve things. Don't let anyone live there, Jews or Arabs.

The Q sort is therefore schematic in the sense that a common feeling runs throughout, the ideas involved being welded together into a system of thought sustained by a preexistent organization of sentiment.

The structuring of *P sets,* or sets of persons to whom the Q sort is to be administered, proceeds in a fashion similar to the structuring of Q samples. (For details, see Brown, 1980: 191-194.) Ideally, according to Thompson's schema, we would include experts, such as Middle Eastern scholars; authorities, such as journalists, politicians, members of the clergy, and others who speak with authority; representatives of special (including class) interests, especially citizens of Lebanon, Israel, and other countries in the region; and the uninformed. Inasmuch as Q studies proceed typologically and reveal the qualitative segments that exist in a population, there is far less need to rely on large numbers of respondents—P sets of 30 to 50 are generally more than adequate for most studies of public opinion—and for illustrative purposes the sample of 15 used in this study is sufficient.

Q sorts are typically intercorrelated, eventuating in this instance in a 15×15 correlation matrix, and with coefficients indicating the degree of similarity between each Q sort and the others. Except on rare occasions, there is little reason to take much interest in the correlation matrix itself, which only serves to prepare the data for factor analysis.

The three-factor solution for this study is shown in Table 3.1 (The standard error for factor loadings is given by the expression $SE = 1 / \sqrt{n}$, where n = the number of statements; for $n = 45$ statements, $SE = 1/\sqrt{45} = 0.15$. Loadings in excess of $2.58(SE) = 0.39$ are significant at the .01 level and are placed in parentheses for convenience.) Factors A, B, and C point to three distinct outlooks with respect to the Israeli invasion, with persons 1–5 sharing one viewpoint, 6–9 a second, and 10–12 a third—that is, respondents 1–5 ranked the statements sufficiently alike so as to have demonstrated the existence of a like-minded group (factor A) distinguishable from respondents 6–9, who formed a second group (factor B): The factor analysis therefore reveals the number of distinct ways (three in this case) in which the statements were Q sorted. Individuals 13–15 are shown to have mixed views—that is, to have views in common with more than one of the primary factors—hence demonstrate that the attitudes involved in the public debate are to some extent compatible in the sense that they can be entertained simultaneously within individual minds.

Due to the nonrandom nature of person samples in Q technique studies, inferences concerning demographics must always be tentative, but suggestive relationships often appear. In Table 3.1, for instance, factor B is defined by non-American respondents, two of them from the Arab

TABLE 3.1
Factor Matrix: Arab-Israeli Controversy Study

	*Factor Loadings**			*Selected Characteristics*			
Subjects	*Factor A*	*Factor B*	*Factor C*	*Age*	*Sex*	*Religion*	*Nationality*
1	(.83)	–.09	.17	25	m	Prot	U.S.
2	(.73)	–.01	.32	32	m	Prot	Ethiopian
3	(.77)	.02	.09	41	m	Cath	U.S.
4	(.65)	.02	.30	26	f	Jew	U.S.
5	(.58)	.00	.11	24	m	Prot	Lebanese
6	–.31	(.65)	.27	38	m	–	Armenian
7	.00	(.65)	.07	23	f	Cath	Venezuelan
8	–.30	(.83)	.05	26	f	Moslem	Arabian
9	–.04	(.67)	–.18	23	m	Prot	Jordanian
10	.04	.05	(.49)	25	f	Prot	U.S.
11	–.17	.10	(.66)	50	m	Prot	U.S.
12	.21	.12	(.59)	21	f	Cath	U.S.
13	(.44)	.02	(.54)	46	f	Cath	U.S.
14	.26	(.44)	(.55)	42	m	–	U.S.
15	(.40)	(.42)	(.45)	23	m	Prot	U.S.

*Loadings in parentheses significant ($p < .01$).

world, but the significant loadings of subjects 14 and 15 preclude B from being considered a uniquely Arab or Third World view; factor C suggests the possibility of a uniquely American view; and the existence of American and non-American respondents on A indicates a view that crosses national boundaries and that we may initially suspect as being pro-Israel, given the existence on the factor of subject 4, a Jew.

But arguments in Q methodology are not based merely on the matrix of factor loadings, but more importantly on the factor scores, that is, on the scores (from +5 to –5) associated with each of the statements in each of the three factors. Space precludes detailed attention to the factor scores for each statement, but the following three statements, each distinguishing a factor from the other two, begin to give a taste of the divergent sentiments at issue (parenthetical scores following each statement are for factors A, B, and C, respectively):

(26) Israel demands and deserves a 25-mile guerrilla-free buffer zone along the southern Lebanese border. (+5 0 –4)

(40) If the Israeli forces do not withdraw from Lebanon, the United States should cut off all military aid to Israel. (–4 +5 –3)

(9) It would be unfortunate if an all-out clash between Israel and Syria were to spark a broader regional war and prompt the Soviets to intervene. (+2 0 +5)

The best strategy to follow when examining Q factors is usually to lay all of the statements out into a Q sort representing each factor, and then to apply "the Sontag rule," as Stephenson (1983a: 103) has referred to it, that is, to "*see* more, *hear* more, *feel* more" of what a factor expresses before attempting to interpret or explain the feelings that have given rise to it. But with the above as only a bare beginning, we can already see by the strong positive score on factor A of statement 26 that factor A is concerned with *security* (for Israel), that factor B identifies with the Arab cause and is (implicitly) *frustrated* with the United States's backing of Israel, and that factor C is thinking *strategically* in broader international and balance-of-power terms. (We should not be surprised to learn that two of the individuals significantly loaded on factor C are university professors, one of them a political scientist, and another an administrator in the Department of Defense.) In short, factors A and B are preoccupied with one another, whereas C takes a conciliatory and perhaps more detached stance, and views the situation in a wider context.

Questions are often raised concerning the small numbers of cases (persons) employed in Q studies and their connection to generalizability, and part of the answer resides in the fact that Q factors are already generalizations, being "composites" of those persons significantly loaded on them; therefore, the composite constructed to represent factor A, for example, reveals in a general way how people of that type think. (How many persons there are of a given type is another question, and one Q technique is not designed to answer.) What Q technique and its factors provide is a direct way to compare attitudes as attitudes, irrespective of the numbers of persons holding to each—for example, to show, through the factor scores, how the pro-Israeli point of view (factor A) compares with the pro-Arab standpoint (factor B), and how these two in turn relate to the unexpected factor C—and for this purpose only a handful of representatives of each of the operant categories is necessary.

Even with small numbers, however, Q studies can frequently cast light on configurations that turn up in mass data. De Boer (1983) notes, for example, that even before the September 18-19, 1982, massacres in the Palestinian refugee camps, significant segments of the American public felt that the United States should deal more directly with the Palestine Liberation Organization and that the United States should use military aid as a sanction against Israel. The results from this study give a hint as to the source of this emergent opinion segment (scores in parentheses for factors A, B, and C, respectively):

(19) The U.S. could exercise more control over Israel if it really wanted to—for example, by threatening to delay delivery of new F-16 fighters. (0 +1 +4)

(25) The U.S. should take a step toward the Palestinians, and help end the bloodshed. (–1 –5 +4)
(32) Palestinian autonomy is the key. Without it, all this fighting is simply stop-gap and of no lasting importance. (+3 0 +5)
(40) If the Israeli forces do not withdraw from Lebanon, the United States should cut off all military aid to Israel. (–4 +5 –3)

Persons from factor C have very likely been the source of the policy recommendations that have been detected in the polls de Boer reports, for it is factor C that is most sensitive (even more so than the pro-Palestinian factor B) to the importance of Palestinian autonomy and the role of the United States in fostering or impeding it (statements 25 and 32), and it is factor C that entertains the idea of using military aid as a lever in controlling Israel (statement 19). Note, however, that factor C's position is thoughtful rather than impulsive: It is one thing to bring pressure to bear (statement 19) and quite another to pull the rug from under an ally without warning (statement 40) simply because of policy differences, and factor C is quite opposed to the latter.

In sum, surveys and polls reveal bulges of proportions that exist in the aggregate, and Q can supplement this effort by showing, however tentatively, how these bulges can be understood and the nature of the intellectual reasoning that is producing them.

POLITICAL ROLES: LASSWELL'S TYPOLOGY

The previous example began with few preconceived notions other than the expectation that the public would be segmented in terms of the Arab-Israeli controversy—the intent was to discover what those segments were—but there are occasions when an investigator sets out to prove something, or at least to amass whatever evidence can be obtained in support of this or that contention, and under certain conditions Q methodology can be of assistance in this regard.

Take as an example Mayer's (1983) recent criticism of Davies's (1980) efforts to enhance the credibility of Lasswell's typology of political actors—agitators, administrators, and theorists. Lasswell (1930) drew on the psychoanalytic theory of his time in suggesting a new division of political thought into functional as opposed to conventional categories, and Davies sought to summarize Lasswell's ideas and substantiate his categories through additional case studies. Although Mayer is willing to acknowledge that Lasswell's work was seminal a half century ago, he wonders whether the imputation of oral fixations and oedipal complexes is adequate today, and complains that "Even with 50 years of hindsight,

Davies still is unable to offer unambiguous criteria for placing individuals in one category or another" (Mayer, 1983: 242).

Davies's credentials as a political psychologist are rather substantial, as are Lasswell's of course, and cannot be lightly regarded, but Mayer does have a point that relates to the principle of operationism, and his criticism is directed implicitly at psychodynamic theorists who apparently presume that they can see the world clearly and are capable of synthesizing all of the details of human behavior without the use of instrumentation. How, then, might a Davies convince someone like Mayer that Lasswell's theory is worthy of continued consideration?

The raw materials are already at hand for making at least a beginning, and they consist of the assertions and descriptive phrases that Lasswell and Davies have already produced while describing these types, as well as the self-descriptive statements of role actors themselves contained in the interviews that Lasswell and Davies report. The *agitator*, for example, is said to feel a special fitness to represent a public issue (Davies, 1980: 25), to eschew the morass of bureaucratic detail in favor of the roving freedom of the platform (Lasswell, 1930: 79), and to obtain pleasure from "rubbing the fur the wrong way" (Lasswell, p. 80), whereas the *administrator* is said to prefer working through a system of interlocking agreements (Davies, p. 71), to have a fondness for detail and accuracy (Lasswell, p. 142), and to be dominated by relationships with concrete individuals rather than abstractions (Lasswell, p. 135). Davies's major contribution was to provide evidence, lacking in Lasswell's account, concerning the skill base of the *theorist*, who is said to have a preference for ideas (Davies, p. 101) but to be otherwise detached (p. 101) and to have a distaste for gushiness (p. 108).

The above statements and many others like them were extracted from Lasswell's and Davies's volumes—their sum total representing a political skills concourse—and each was placed into one of the three role categories; ultimately, a Q sample of 45 statements (15 from each of the categories) was composed and administered in a Q sort to a sizable number of individuals in a variety of walks of life, including persons in political roles as conventionally defined (mayors, city council members, budget directors, candidates, county welfare and educational administrators, etc.), and especially philosophers and political theorists.

For illustrative purposes, 14 subjects were selected, and the original (unrotated) Q factor loadings that were produced are displayed as factors x, y, and z in Table 3.2. Unlike the previous study, this investigation was motivated in part by a desire to find individuals of a particular kind if they could be located, and so brief background information was obtained for some of the subjects to determine if they possessed some of the expected

TABLE 3.2
Factor Matrix: Political Role Study

	Original Factor Loadings				*Rotated Factor Loadings*		
Subjects	*Factor x*	*Factor y*	*Factor z*	*Factor z'*	*Factor Y*	*Factor X*	*Factor Z*
1	−.13	(.56)	(.46)	.19	(.70)	.03	−.23
2	.16	(.73)	.13	−.18	(.72)	−.01	.24
3	.07	(.57)	.01	−.22	(.53)	−.10	.21
4	.00	.32	.15	.01	.35	.01	−.01
5	(.74)	.15	−.19	−.23	.06	.38	(.67)
6	.26	.24	(−.52)	(−.57)	.01	−.20	(.59)
7	(.52)	−.18	−.24	−.15	−.26	.27	(.46)
8	(.57)	−.14	.28	.31	−.02	(.62)	.16
9	.24	−.22	(.56)	(.60)	.02	(.58)	−.28
10	(.78)	−.16	.17	.22	−.08	(.71)	.37
11	(.62)	−.02	.11	.11	.03	(.52)	.34
12	(.55)	.16	.16	.08	.21	(.45)	.31
13	(.67)	(.42)	.25	.06	(.48)	(.53)	(.41)
14	.26	−.03	.04	.05	−.01	.22	.14

NOTE: Loadings in parentheses are statistically significant ($p < .01$).

characteristics. Subjects 1 and 2 proved to be especially interesting: The first was a rather withdrawn individual who was more adept at manipulating technical gadgets than at joining in the flow of interpersonal relationships; the second expressed an interest in abstract political ideas. Davies had suggested something of this kind of introverted attitude in relation to the theorist type, and so the factors were rotated judgmentally with this working hypothesis in mind.

The initial rotation is shown in Figure 3.3, with the locations of each subject designated in terms of the original loadings on factors y and z from Table 3.2: Hence subject 1's location is specified by his loading of 0.56 on factor y and 0.46 on factor z. Due to a prior theoretical interest in subjects 1 and 2, vector y was rotated to position Y, midway between the two Q sorts, so that both subjects would load equally (and with high values) on the resulting factor. To retain orthogonality, z was then relocated to z'. Calculations were then made of the new loadings, which are reported in columns Y and z' of Table 3.2.

There was similar theoretical interest in subjects 5 and 8: The former was in the process of preparing herself for a business career, much like that of her executive father (suggestive of the administrative type); the latter was in the process of gaining professional skills for an anticipated lifetime of professional campaigning for liberal candidates and causes (reminiscent of the agitational type). In a second rotation not shown, therefore, the previously rotated factor z' was plotted against original un-

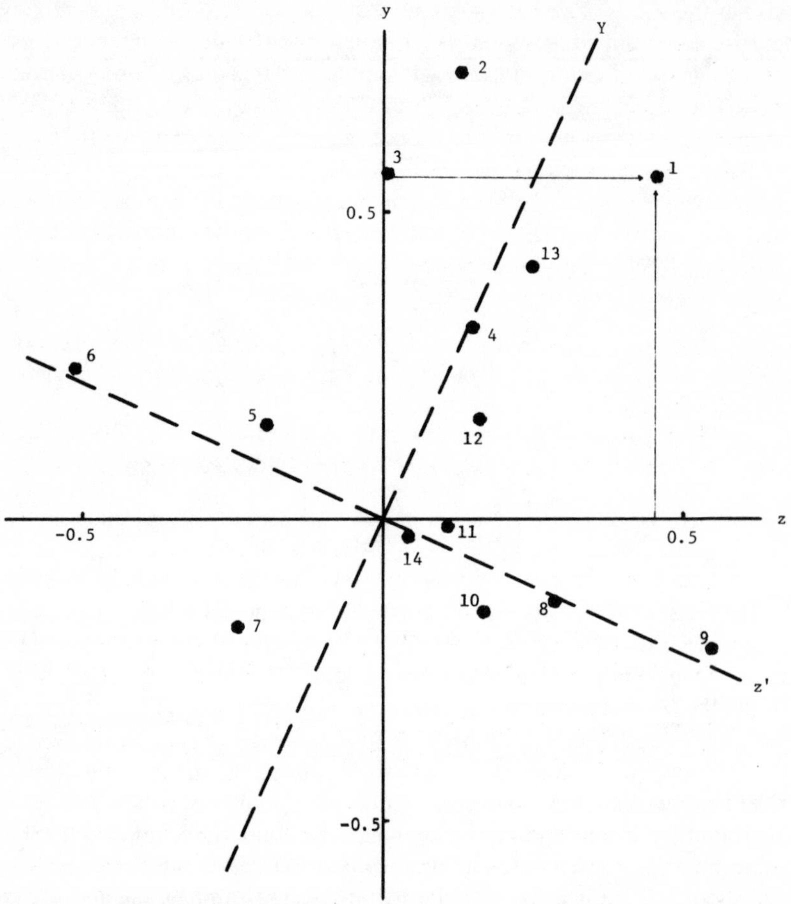

NOTE: The points represent subjects.

Figure 3.3: Graphical Representation of Q Factor Analysis Results in Table 3.2

rotated factor x, with the reference vectors relocated in an effort to place the suspected agitational subject on the one factor and the suspected administrative type on the other. The results of this rotation are displayed in columns X and Z of Table 3.2.

Final factors X, Y, and Z of Table 3.2 and the theoretical rotations that led up to them are simplified versions of what is typically involved, which is a concrete illustration of what Polanyi (1958: 131) refers to as the shifting back and forth between intuition and computation (compare Stephenson, 1980b). In conventional factor analyses, the investigator waits passively for what the factorial and varimax algorithms will produce and then proceeds to interpret the results, but in Q methodology factor analysis has the status of a probing device that enables the observer to actively pursue ideas and hunches that emerge in the course of inquiry, and to ask of the data whether or not they will support a particular theoretical position. The results are in no sense arbitrary as a consequence, but represent a slant on a phenomenon from a special vantage point (Brown, 1979).

Space again prohibits too much detail, but the factor scores clearly indicate the similarity between factor X and Lasswell's agitator, between factor Y and the theorist type, and between Z and the administrator, as indicated by the factor scores (in parentheses) for factors X, Y, and Z, respectively, for the following selected statements:

— I have been known to be forceful and aggressive, and my contentiousness is notorious. I am accustomed to distinguishing myself by bold opinions. (+3 -2 -3)
— When I get agitated and worked up about something, I want other people to get aroused, too. I like to communicate my excitement to those around me. (+3 -1 +1)
— I like to be close to the action, but also intellectually distanced enough to keep me above raw feeling and involvement. (0 +3 -1)
— I have the habit of doubting—my own judgment as well as everyone else's—and of regarding every question as open. (0 +3 0)
— On the whole I look up to superiors who support, direct, set goals, and are sympathetic: I try to cooperate and maintain good relations with them. (0 +1 +4)
— I derive a good deal of satisfaction from knowing how to get others to do things that I have decided are worth doing. (+1 -2 +3)

The first two statements receive significantly higher scores in factors X than in Y or Z and attest to the agitator's rambunctiousness and need to communicate excitement; similarly, the second pair of statements betrays the theorist's need to be detached from feelings and to live the life of doubt; and the final two statements show the administrative type's proclivity to yield to authority and get others to do his bidding, which Davies (1980: 65) regards as the underlying motive for choosing administrative over other kinds of work.

The focus until this point has been on pure types, but as the loadings in Table 3.2 indicate, composite and "null" types are also in evidence: Subject 13 is associated with all three types, much as Lasswell (1930: 54) indicated for Lenin; subject 14, in correlating with none of the factors, demonstrates the possibility of discovering roles not accounted for in Lasswell's and Davies's theorizing.

In sum, we would take issue with Mayer's (1983) criticism of Davies if he means to imply that Davies's conjectures are somehow beyond measurement. That they refer to complicated affairs cannot be doubted, and that they deal with aspects of behavior relatively untouched and untouchable by conventional methods should also be obvious. And although the preceding forays do not penetrate deeply into the phenomenon, it should be clear that the general strategy is quite capable of doing so.

METHODOLOGICAL CONCLUSION

The literature of Q technique and its methodology now exceeds 1500 entries (Brown, 1968, 1977), and there is hardly a corner of human endeavor to which it has not been applied. Space once again limits extensive treatment, but selective note can be made of recent applications in the policy sciences (Ascher, forthcoming; Brown, 1984; Brunner and Vivian, 1980; Greenberger et al., 1983; Pacho, 1981; Thomas and Sigelman, 1984), communication (Barchak, 1984; Cragan and Shields, 1981), and to various areas in political science (Carlson and Hyde, 1984; McKeown, 1984; Wattier, 1982, forthcoming), including political philosophy (Martin et al., 1984; Poole and Steuernagel, 1984). Moreover, its range of applicability has extended from the preschooler (Castaneda de Leon, 1983; Stephenson, 1980a: 24-26) to the elderly (Lieberman and Tobin, 1983), and from highly specialized NATO elites (Carlton, in progress) to illiterate Guatemalan Indians (Castaneda, 1974), and has included altered states of consciousness induced by hypnosis (McKeown, 1978) and drugs (Spotts and Shontz, 1980). It has, of course, been used to examine collections of persons, as in the two studies reported above, but also to focus intensively on single cases (Brown, 1981, 1982). Q samples have typically contained statements of opinion, but also propaganda posters (Brown, 1979), political cartoons (Kinsey and Taylor, 1982), and a variety of other materials. Additional applications are to be found in Brown (1980) and Stephenson (1953, 1967), and in the pages of *Operant Subjectivity: The Q Methodology Newsletter,* where coverage has been given to poetry, autobiography, advertising, philosophy of science, consumer preferences, political culture, foreign travel, psychoanalysis, imagery, movies, food policy, decision making, nurse-patient relationships, meta-ethics, and much else. The possibilities for application are boundless wherever subjectivity is implicated.

This is not to say that investigations in which the Q sort has been employed have always been well conceived. In their reviews of two recent studies, for example, Dennis (1984) and Rohrbaugh (1984) note that Q technique was applied in ways to a greater or lesser extent at variance with the broader epistemological concerns of Q methodology, and so it is perhaps fitting to end this primarily technological chapter by providing a brief vision of the wider context within which these technicalities have meaning.

Technology is of course important and makes its own contributions to the growth of knowledge: Where would astronomy be without the telescope, or physics without its giant accelerators and atom smashers? But the essence of Q methodology can no more be reduced to factor analysis and the Q-sort technique than the essence of medical science can to X-ray plates. These are mere technical accouterments that prepare phenomena for observation: In the same way that contingencies of reinforcement are not perceptible without the aid of a Skinner Box, so does a person's viewpoint remain implicit (that is, present but undetected) unless provided with some instrumental medium, such as a Q sort, for transforming it into a manifestation.

The first axiom of Q methodology is that it is the *subjective self* (a primitive and undefined term) that is at the center of all meaning. This is not the Kierkegaardian self (the only true reality), nor the Lasswellian self (the primary ego plus its symbols of identification), nor is it the Kohutian self of psychoanalytic self psychology: These are all logical categories, each with predefined traits and characteristics. Nor is the self a variable for which reliable measures and norms can be established, as in scaling theory. What these conceptions all share in common is a nineteenth-century presumption that what science measures are *observables* (including so-called "intervening variables"), which exist in certain states, and one need not look far to find many studies in which the Q sort has been used in precisely this way, that is, as if it were a scalar measure of some trait or attribute (for example, see Kerlinger, 1984).

What Q methodology deals with instead are *states of mind* (rather than observables in states), hence its connection to modern quantum theory (Stephenson, 1983b), which is concerned with states of matter. Whereas contemporary social science searches for reductionistic determinants, the factors of Q methodology are indeterminant: We can never predict with certainty, particularly at the level of the single case, exactly how many factors will emerge, nor what their form and structure will be.

The principles of measurement, to which the preceding pages have been devoted, flow as a matter of course from this indeterminacy: (1) The statements of a concourse, like particles in a liquid state, have no predetermined order or importance: That they condense into a particular order is due to the fact that meaning is projected onto them by a person in the course of Q sorting—hence, to reiterate, it is the subjective self that is at the center of all meaning. (2) There is no standard Q sample for a concourse: Any suitably comprehensive sample is adequate for purposes of experimentation. (3) The measure of a person's subjective point of view can only be given by the person; it cannot be gained from the external, "objective" standpoint. As Stephenson (1972: 17) has said, "objective measurements and observations can, in principle, be made by everyone (or by a piece of apparatus), whereas measurements and observations of a person's subjectivity can be made only by himself." (4) The forced-frequency Q-sort distribution is a theoretical expression of the law of error and not a statistical hypothesis for testing: "to give the distribution any prior empirical foundation would be to deny the fundamental premise of concourse—that nothing about it is normative" (Stephenson, 1980a: 10). (5) By the same token, there is no factor-analytic or related algorithm (for example, principal components, varimax) the mathematical and geometric formulations of which are valid across all problems—hence the value of the centroid method (the solution of which is indeterminate) and the problem-centeredness of theoretical rotation. (6) The fact that what statements mean can only be determined (by interpretation) after the factors are first found demonstrates that order precedes meaning. (In the scales of R methodology, by contrast, meanings precede order: Indeed, the meaning of the scales dictates how the responses will be ordered.)

This methodological conclusion, incomplete and unexemplified as it is, may read like the Book of Revelations to the casual reader of the literature of Q technique, and it is left, like Revelations, for thoughtful contemplation. Suffice it to say (at the risk of sounding redundant), Q methodology provides the basis for a science of subjectivity, and it does so by the simple expediency of replacing the metaphysics of consciousness with the empiricism of communicability. Among the consequences are genuine laws (for example, of transformations of form, of operant factors, and the like), a solution to Isaac Newton's fifth rule of reasoning (Stephenson, 1979), conformity with twentieth-century developments in science generally, and, not incidentally, flexible procedures for the careful examination of all aspects of social and political life that engage human attentiveness. Its primary use has been in these more procedural and Q-technological applications. The broader methodological principles have profound implications for political and social theory, but they have yet to be given close and extended scrutiny.

references

Ascher, William (forthcoming) "The moralism of attitudes supporting inter-group violence." Political Psychology.

Barchak, Leonard J. (1984) "Discovering communication paradigms with Q methodology: ferment or sour grapes?" Operant Subjectivity 7 (July): 115-130.

Bolland, John M. (forthcoming) "The search for structure: an alternative to the structured Q-sort technique." Political Methodology.

Brown, Steven R. (1968) "Bibliography on Q technique and its methodology." Perceptual and Motor Skills 26 (April): 587-613.

———(1972) "A fundamental incommensurability between objectivity and subjectivity," pp. 57-94 in Steven R. Brown and Donald J. Brenner (eds.) Science, Psychology, and Communication. New York: Teachers College Press.

———(1977) "Q bibliographic update: a continuation of 'Bibliography on Q technique and its methodology.'" Operant Subjectivity 1 (October): 17-26.

———(1979) Perspective, transfiguration, and equivalence in communication theory," pp. 51-66 in Dan Nimmo (ed.) Communication Yearbook 3. New Brunswick, NJ: Transaction Books.

———(1980) Political Subjectivity: Applications of Q Methodology in Political Science. New Haven, CT: Yale University Press.

———(1981) "Intensive analysis," pp. 627-649 in Dan D. Nimmo and Keith R. Sanders (eds.) Handbook of Political Communication. Beverly Hills, CA: Sage.

———(1982) "Imagery, mood, and the public expression of opinion." Micropolitics 2: 153-173.

———(1984) "Values, development, and character: appraising Korean experience." Korean Fulbright Forum 1: 33-66.

Brunner, Ronald D. and Weston E. Vivian (1980) "Citizen viewpoints on energy policy." Policy Sciences 12 (August): 147-174.

Carlson, James M. and Mark S. Hyde (1984) "Situations and party activist role orientations: a Q study." Micropolitics 3: 441-464.

Carlton, James R. (forthcoming) "The problem of NATO standardization decision-making." Ph.D. dissertation, Kent State University.

Casey, Gregory (1984) "Intensive analysis of a 'single' issue: attitudes on abortion." Political Methodology 10: 97-124.

Castaneda, Lucila (1974) "Media images for Guatemala's culture: a Q-study involving Indian subjects." M.A. thesis, University of Missouri—Columbia.

Castaneda de Leon, Lucila (1983) "Correlation between maternal deprivation and asocial behavior: Q methodology applied at the Healthy Child Clinic of the Roosevelt Hospital in Guatemala City." M.D. thesis, University of San Carlos of Guatemala.

Conover, Pamela Johnston and Stanley Feldman (1984) "Group identification, values, and the nature of political beliefs." American Politics Quarterly 12 (April): 151-175.

Cottle, Charles E. and Bruce F. McKeown (1980) "The forced-free distribution in Q technique: a note on unused categories in the Q sort continuum." Operant Subjectivity 3 (January): 58-63.

Cragan, John F. and Donald C. Shields [eds.] (1981) Applied Communication Research. Prospect Heights, IL: Waveland Press.

Davies, A. F. (1980) Skills, Outlooks and Passions. Cambridge: Cambridge University Press.

de Boer, Connie (1983) "The polls: attitudes toward the Arab-Israeli conflict." Public Opinion Quarterly 47 (Spring): 121-131.

Dennis, Karen E. (1984) "Review of 'Experience of Old Age,' by Morton A. Lieberman and Sheldon S. Tobin." Operant Subjectivity 7 (January): 67-69.

Fisher, R. A. (1935) The Design of Experiments. Edinburgh: Oliver & Boyd.

Greenberger, Martin, Garry D. Brewer, William Hogan, and Milton Russell (1983) Caught Unawares: The Energy Decade in Retrospect. Cambridge, MA: Ballinger.

Kerlinger, Fred N. (1984) Liberalism and Conservatism. Hillsdale, NJ: Lawrence Erlbaum.

Kinsey, Dennis and Richard W. Taylor (1982) "Some meanings of political cartoons." Operant Subjectivity 5 (April): 107-114.

Lasswell, Harold D. (1930) Psychopathology and Politics. Chicago: University of Chicago Press.

Lieberman, Morton A. and Sheldon S. Tobin (1983) The Experience of Old Age. New York: Basic Books.

McKeown, Bruce F. (1978) "Displacement effects of hypnotically-induced mood states upon perception of public symbols." Presented at the annual meeting of the Midwest Political Science Association, Chicago.

———(1984) "Q methodology in political psychology: theory and technique in psychoanalytic applications." Political Psychology 5 (September): 415-436.

Martin, Richard T., Eloise Ronay, and Richard W. Taylor (1984) "Obligation, equality, and a sense of fairness." Presented at the annual meeting of the Northeastern Political Science Association, Boston.

Mayer, Lawrence C. (1983) "Review of 'Skills, Outlooks, and Passions,' by A. F. Davies." Journal of Politics 45 (February): 241-243.

Pacho, Arturo G. (1981) "Policy concerns and priorities: ethnic Chinese in the Philippines." Philippine Journal of Public Administration 25 (April): 207-230.

Polanyi, Michael (1958) Personal Knowledge. Chicago: University of Chicago Press.

Poole, Barbara L. and Gertrude A. Steuernagel (1984) "A subjective evaluation of theories of justice." Presented at the meeting of the Southern Political Science Association, Savannah.

Rohrbaugh, Michael (1984) "Review of 'Black and White Identity Formation,' by Stuart T. Hauser and Eydie Kasendorf." Operant Subjectivity 7 (January): 70-72.

Spotts, James V. and Franklin C. Shontz (1980) Cocaine Users. New York: Free Press.

Stephenson, William (1935a) "Technique of factor analysis." Nature 136 (August 24): 297.

———(1935b) "Correlating persons instead of tests." Character and Personality 4 (September): 17-24.

———(1953) The Study of Behavior: Q-technique and its Methodology. Chicago: University of Chicago Press.

———(1964) "Application of the Thompson schema to the current controversy over Cuba." Psychological Record 14 (July): 275-290.

———(1967) The Play Theory of Mass Communication. Chicago: University of Chicago Press.

———(1972) "Applications of communication theory. I: the substructure of science." Psychological Record 22 (Winter): 17-36.

———(1977) "Factors as operant subjectivity." Operant Subjectivity 1 (October): 3-16.

———(1978) "Concourse theory of communication." Communication 3: 21-40.

———(1979) "Q methodology and Newton's fifth rule." American Psychologist 34 (April): 354-357.

———(1980a) "Consciring: a general theory for subjective communicability," pp. 7-36 in Dan Nimmo (ed.) Communication Yearbook 4. New Brunswick, NJ: Transaction Books.

———(1980b) "Michael Polanyi, science and belief." Ethics in Science & Medicine 7: 97-110.

———(1983a) "Against interpretation." Operant Subjectivity 6 (April/July): 73-103, 109-125.

———(1983b) "Quantum theory and Q-methodology: fictionalistic and probabilistic theories conjoined." Psychological Record 33 (Spring): 213-230.

Thomas, Dan B. and Lee Sigelman (1984) "Presidential identification and policy leadership: experimental evidence on the Reagan case." Policy Studies Journal 12 (June): 663-675.

Thompson, John W. (1962) "Meaningful and unmeaningful rotation of factors." Psychological Bulletin 59 (May): 211-223.

Wattier, Mark J. (1982) "Voter targeting using the Q-method." Campaigns & Elections 2 (Winter): 31-41.

———(forthcoming) "Discovering campaign themes: reinforcement with Q method." Election Politics.

4

Nonmetric Multidimensional Scaling and Individual Difference Scaling

GEORGE RABINOWITZ

Why do people perceive Ronald Reagan and George Bush to be similar and Ronald Reagan and Walter Mondale to be different? More generally, do people have structured views of candidates in terms of criteria such as party and ideology, or are their views more ad hoc, based on the styles and personalities of the candidates? If we believe that understanding how people perceive objects is critical to understanding their behavior toward those objects, then we need to have methodologies to address these types of perceptual questions. I will present two such methods in this chapter, nonmetric multidimensional scaling and individual difference scaling, and provide a substantive example in which each of the methods is used. My goal is to provide a feel for the methods and substantively meaningful examples, rather than a full technical treatment of either method.

Both nonmetric multidimensional scaling and individual difference scaling have their roots in psychology and, as we shall see, are closely related. They can be applied more broadly than just in terms of how people perceive objects. Indeed, they can be used to analyze problems as diverse as the structure underlying roll-call voting in a legislature and the pattern of international trade. These scaling methods are, however, most naturally discussed in terms of individual perceptions, because it was for problems of understanding perceptions that they were designed.

Scaling in General

Any procedure that scales or measures an attribute involves assigning numbers to objects so that the numerical assignments correspond to some real-world relationships. For example, when we talk about how much a person weighs, we use a number such as 143 pounds. The assumption is

---

AUTHOR'S NOTE: *I would like to thank Stuart Elaine Macdonald, Peter Galderisi, and the editors for their help with this project.*

that weight can be represented by a single abstract number and that real-world relationships among weights can be modeled effectively by relationships among those abstract numbers. Knowing someone weighs 143 pounds tells us immediately that that person is similar in weight to, but lighter than someone who weighs 147, but is significantly heavier than someone who weighs 110 pounds. This is because virtually all the relationships that hold among the abstract numbers 143, 147, and 110 (equality, greater than, less than, additivity, and so forth) hold with regard to the attribute "weight." Weight provides a simple illustration of the idea of measurement because the measurement is so straightforward and the interpretation of the numbers so direct.

NONMETRIC MULTIDIMENSIONAL SCALING

Nonmetric multidimensional scaling is based on a measurement model that assumes that the *relative similarity of pairs of objects* can be represented in terms of the *relative distance between pairs of points*. Hence the real-world relationship of "being perceived similar to" is modeled as the mathematical relationship "close to." That model is expressed by the equation:

$$d_{jk} = M(s_{jk}) \qquad [4.1]$$

Here s_{jk} is the similarity between objects j and k, while d_{jk} represents the distance between the points representing objects j and k. The M represents a monotonic function. If M is monotonic, then when one pair of objects is more similar than a second pair, the distance is less between the first pair than the second. Monotonic functions differ from linear functions in not insisting on a particular relationship between similarity and distance other than that it be order preserving. A linear function implies that for every fixed decrease in similarity we would expect to find a proportional increase in distance.

The advantage of using nonmetric rather than metric assumptions is that a wide variety of nonlinear relationships is allowed between the observed similarities and the recovered distances. Using a nonmetric method also allows the investigator to measure the similarity of object pairs with somewhat less concern about the level of measurement. A potential disadvantage is that nonmetric methods offer less constraint on solutions than do metric methods. But experience has shown that nonmetric multidimensional scaling solutions are usually highly constrained when the ratio of the number of objects to the number of dimensions is four or greater and when there are at least ten objects to be scaled.

Because distance is so important in multidimensional scaling, it is useful to know how distance is calculated. The Euclidean distance between two points j and k in a multidimensional space is

$$d_{jk} = \left[\sum_{t=1}^{r} (x_{jt} - x_{kt})^2 \right]^{1/2} \qquad [4.2]$$

where x_{jt} and x_{kt} are, respectively, the locations of point j and point k on dimension t, and r represents the number of dimensions in the space. One important reason to look at the distance formula by itself is that it makes clear what is actually being obtained in a nonmetric multidimensional scaling analysis: a set of x values for each object. Hence unlike weight in which only one number is associated with each object, the scaling associates a set of numbers with each object, and these numbers locate the objects in a multidimensional space.

A Simple Example

Let us now consider a practical problem. Suppose we are interested in constructing a map of fourteen of the larger cities east of the Mississippi River. Furthermore, suppose all we know (from bitter experience) is how long it takes to drive from city to city. Could we construct such a map?

A reasonable goal in constructing the map would be to have the distances between cities on the map correspond as closely as possible to the length of time it takes to drive between the cities. If we use intercity driving times as a measure of similarity between cities, it is appropriate to solve this problem using multidimensional scaling. The input to the multidimensional scaling program would be a matrix in which the labels for the rows and columns would be the names of the cities, and the values of the cells would be the driving times. So, for example, if New York were the first city in the matrix and Chicago the second, the value in row 1 column 2 would be the driving time between New York and Chicago. The output from the multidimensional scaling program would be a plot of city points, which should be the map we seek.

Figure 4.1A shows the map of cities constructed using a nonmetric multidimensional scaling procedure on the driving time data. Figure 4.1B shows an actual map of the eastern half of the United States with the city points marked, and Figure 4.1C shows the map in Figure 4.1A

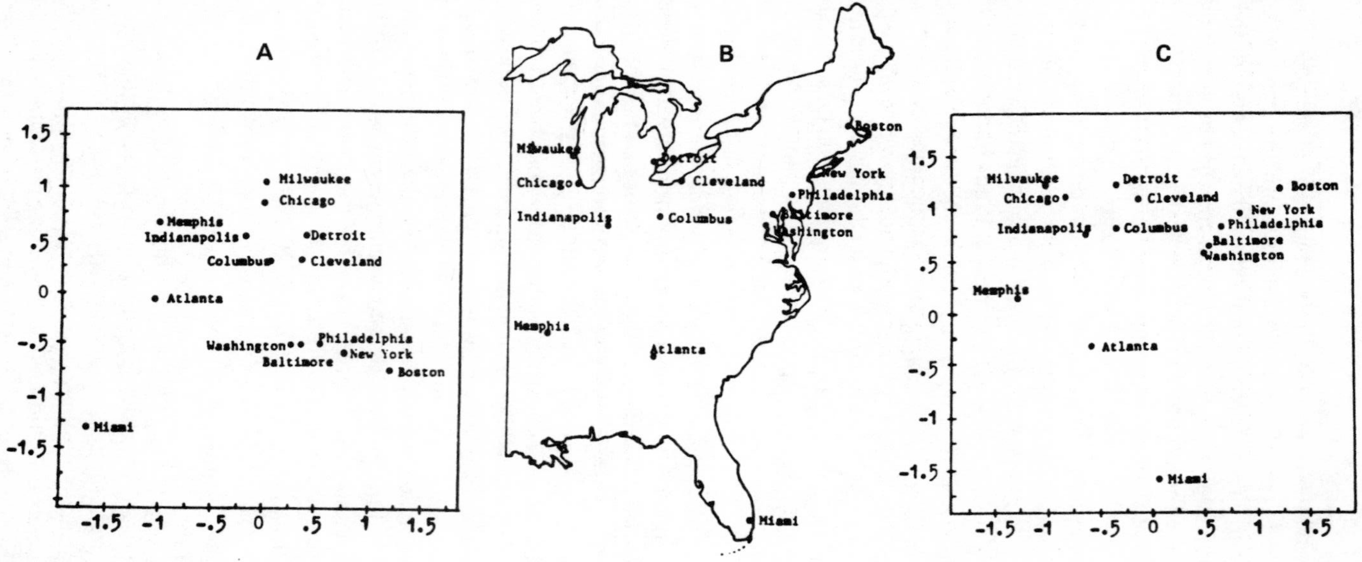

Figure 4.1: Nonmetric Multidimensional Scaling of Cities Based on Intercity Driving Time: Nonmetric Multidimensional Scaling Solution; (B) Actual Map Showing Locations of Cities; (C) Scaling Solution Rotated to the Same Orientation as the Map

rotated to match the orientation of the map in Figure 4.1B. The actual map of the cities and the map recovered from the driving times are almost identical. The differences that occur arise because of the impact of the Great Lakes and the Atlantic Ocean and the absence of interstate highways between certain cities. These cause driving times to be proportionally greater than distances and thus cause positions to be slightly distorted.

In recovering the position of each city point on our map, we are recovering two numbers. One number reflects the position of the point on the horizontal axis and the other reflects the position on the vertical axis. For example, the scale positions of New York in Figure 4.1A are 0.75 on the horizontal dimension and –0.56 on the vertical dimension, and those of Chicago are –0.01 and 0.84. By themselves the numbers have no meaning; neither would a weight of 110 if we did not know if it was measured in pounds, grams, or kilograms. So, in part, the lack of a unit makes the numbers less informative. But the difference between these numbers and weights is that even in comparing one value to another we do not learn much, because it is unclear (unless we use our independent knowledge of geography) what the specific dimensions represent. This contrasts with the weight example, in which the conceptual dimension is clear. The fact, however, that the specific dimensions are not conceptually clear does not mean that the scaling is invalid. The similarity between the map in Figure 4.1C and the standard road map shows the scale values are indeed quite meaningful.

Determining the conceptual meaning of dimensions is a problem that arises frequently in scaling phenomena that are multidimensional. In some cases there is no solution to the problem, either because there are no meaningful dimensions or because we cannot identify them. In other cases it is possible to identify conceptually meaningful dimensions in the multidimensional space. Indeed, the individual difference scaling procedure that we will discuss in the second half of the chapter is formulated to enhance a researcher's ability to identify conceptually meaningful dimensions, if any exist.

The Analytic Procedure

How does a nonmetric multidimensional scaling procedure actually locate the points corresponding to the objects being scaled? In the map illustration, a rather intuitive notion of how to proceed is to guess the location of cities and then adjust the positions to improve the fit with driving times. All nonmetric multidimensional scaling procedures actually operate on this rather intuitive sequential improvement principle. Indeed, solutions to many complicated mathematical problems are obtained in this iterative (moving from one estimate to a better estimate) fashion.

Initially, a decision is made as to the number of dimensions to use. This decision is not critical given that solutions are usually obtained in several different dimensionalities. Once that decision is made, the technical procedure can be thought of as operating in four stages. *First*, each object is represented by a point at some initial location. This collection of points is called the *starting configuration*. *Second*, for any given configuration of points a set of interpoint distances is calculated—one distance for each pair of objects. In the map example, these are the distances between the points representing the cities on the map. *Third*, a set of target values (or *disparities*) is constructed—one target value corresponding to the distance between each pair of objects. These target values are used both to guide the next move and to assess the goodness of fit of the solution. The values are constrained to be in the same order as (monotonic with) the similarities, while within that constraint as similar as possible (in a least squares sense) to the distances calculated in the second step.[1] *Fourth*, if there is a reason to expect that the (goodness of) fit can be significantly improved so as to make the distances more like the target values, the points are moved. Steps two, three, and four are then repeated until the procedure terminates.

Goodness-of-Fit Measures

The goodness-of-fit measure most commonly used in nonmetric multidimensional scaling is Kruskal's Stress Formula 1. The measure is

$$[\ \sum_{j<k}\sum(\text{Distance pair}_{jk}\ -\ \text{Target value pair}_{jk})^2\ /\ \sum_{j<k}\sum(\text{Distance pair}_{jk})^2]^{1/2} \quad [4.3]$$

where the summation is over all pairs of objects j and k. The numerator of the measure simply assesses how close the distances in the space are to the monotonic criterion. The denominator is inserted to make the measure insensitive to the unit (for example, inches, miles, and so forth) used to measure distance. Following standard convention, the squaring of units, which occurs in both the numerator and the denominator is reversed by calculating the square root of the ratio. The measure takes on relatively small values when the fit is good and relatively large values when the fit is poor—hence, the name "stress."

An alternate measure that has a somewhat easier interpretation for those familiar with regression analysis is Kruskal's Stress Formula 2. Formula 2 is identical to Formula 1 except for the denominator which is:

$$[\sum_{j<k}\sum(\text{Distance pair}_{jk} - \text{Mean distance over all pairs})^2] \qquad [4.4]$$

Thus the ratio calculated in Formula 2 is comparable to that between the "unexplained" and "total" variance in a regression analysis, and is interpretable as the percent of variance in the similarities *not* accounted for in the nonmetric multidimensional scaling solution.

Some useful "rule of thumb" criteria relating the quality of the fit to the stress values for both formulas are the following:

Quality of Solution	*Stress 1*	*Stress 2*
Perfect	0.000–0.025	0.00–0.05
Excellent	0.025–0.050	0.05–0.10
Good	0.050–0.100	0.10–0.20
Fair	0.100–0.200	0.20–0.40
Poor	0.200–0.400	0.40–1.00

However, these criteria should be used cautiously; they are most appropriate for situations in which the number of objects is between 10 and 30, the ratio of objects to dimensions is four or more, and the solution is in two or more dimensions. In general, research has shown that solutions in one dimension run slightly higher stress values for the same quality of fit than those of higher dimensionality.

Using Nonmetric Multidimensional Scaling Procedures in Research

I began this chapter raising questions of individual perceptions and then moved quickly to an example of intercity distances that had nothing to do with individual perceptions. The example did, however, have something to do with constructing a map based on information concerning the similarity of pairs of objects. Just as we constructed a physical representation of the cities based on information about the similarity of pairs of cities, so we can attempt to construct a cognitive map of how individuals perceive objects based on similarities data.

Whether the notion of a cognitive space is useful or not depends, of course, on the validity of this type of spatial model as a way to represent cognitive phenomena. We are used to thinking of intercity distance as distance on a two-dimensional plane, although in fact that model is not accurate. The Earth is, as we all know, basically spherical in shape and distance cannot be modeled exactly in terms of standard (Euclidean) distance in a two-dimensional space. The Euclidean distance model is, nevertheless, a pretty good approximation if we are not considering large distances compared to the size of the sphere. If our cities had been major, world capitals rather than those in the eastern United States, we would have been forced to abandon a simple two dimensional view of the world. Hence we made two modeling errors in this example. We assumed driving time was monotonically related to distance between cities, which is generally true but wrong when water bodies disrupt the land mass between cities or when there is a relatively poor highway link between cities. Also, we assumed that distance between cities is Euclidean when in fact it is not. Nevertheless, we recovered quite accurate locations for these cities. And, had we not already known where these cities were located (from other maps that exist), we would have learned a great deal of useful information from this scaling.

When we apply this type of distance model to understanding individual perceptions, or for that matter other phenomena such as alliance structures or legislative coalitions, we are in a situation similar to our map construction example. We are in a position to potentially learn a great deal about the underlying structure. We are, of course, very unlikely to reproduce exactly an individual's cognitive structure or the full structure underlying any phenomenon of empirical interest. The scaling will be useful to the extent that the particular abstraction of structure reasonably approximates the unknown structure of interest. Our map-making example shows both the usefulness and the limitations of this type of approach. In the final analysis, despite certain errors, the model was a sufficiently close approximation of reality to make the scaling quite informative.

MASS PERCEPTIONS OF POLITICAL CANDIDATES IN THE UNITED STATES IN 1980

I started the chapter by asking how people perceive political candidates. I will now address that question for the set of candidates that were salient in the 1980 election. Since 1968 the Center for Political Studies at the University of Michigan has asked people in their national election studies to evaluate sets of political figures in terms of how warmly they feel toward the figures in question. If people feel very warmly, they rate the candidate at the 100° point on a hypothetical thermometer. If people feel very cool toward a candidate, they rate the candidate at the 0° point. Those with lukewarm feelings are asked to rate the candidate at the 50° point. The 1980 pre-election interview schedule included twelve candidates and former candidates who were of sufficient interest to include in our analysis.

Graphic representations of mass perceptions of candidates in U.S. presidential elections have been constructed since 1968. Works in this area include Weisberg and Rusk (1970), Rabinowitz (1978), Cahoon et al. (1978), Enelow and Hinich (1984), and Poole and Rosenthal (1984). The basis of this work has been the unfolding (spatial choice) model (Coombs, 1964). In the context of candidate preference, the unfolding model assumes that each individual has an ideal candidate, and the *closer* some real-world candidate comes to that ideal, the more favorably the individual will evaluate the candidate. "Liking" is thus translated into spatial proximity. Implicit in this description is the assumption that each respondent shares a common perception of the candidates and that each respondent uses the same criteria in evaluating candidates. In mass samples these assumptions are very unlikely to be fully satisfied, but they may be sufficiently well satisfied to allow meaningful scaling to occur. The scaling I shall perform will operate in two steps. First, I will measure the similarity of candidate pairs; then I will scale the candidates based on their pairwise similarity.

The Line-of-Sight Similarity Measure

The line-of-sight measure will be used to assess the similarity of object pairs (Rabinowitz, 1976). This nonmetric measure is developed directly from the unfolding model. In addition to the standard unfolding assumptions, the line-of-sight measure assumes that individual ideal points are widely scattered in the object space. In terms of the candidate data, this assumption is satisfied if each candidate is favorably evaluated by at least some respondents. In addition to assessing the relative similarity of candidate pairs, the measure provides an independent assessment of the fit of the data to the measurement assumptions.

The line-of-sight measure is constructed from two separate measures of the similarity of candidate pairs. One of these is based on the evaluations of those who give relatively different evaluations to the candidates in a pair; the other is based on the evaluations of those who give relatively favorable responses to both candidates in a pair.[2] Each of the measures has been shown to be an unbiased measure of intercandidate similarity. The two are averaged to form the single line-of-sight measure.

The Spearman rho correlation between the two measures assesses the fit of the unfolding model to the data. If the full set of unfolding and distribution assumptions is satisfied, this correlation will be close to its maximum value of 1.0. As the correlation decreases, the unfolding assumptions become increasingly suspect. For example, a low correlation can occur when some individuals give systematically more extreme responses (both favorable and unfavorable) to well-known candidates, and others simply give systematically more favorable responses to well-known candidates. Although a low correlation is grounds for caution, scaling of data is still possible as reasonably accurate scaling can occur in the face of a wide range of behaviors that are incompatible with the unfolding model.

Analysis of the 1980 Election

In 1980 the estimated goodness of fit of the unfolding model was lower than that for any presidential election between 1968 and 1976, an abysmal -0.03. The comparable correlations for the 1968, 1972, and 1976 elections were 0.40, 0.45, and 0.15, respectively. Notice that the 1976 correlation was a distinct drop from those in 1968 and 1972 and the correlation in 1980 represents yet another drop. This suggests there is less coherence to mass perceptions of candidates in the two later elections as compared to the two earlier ones.

In each of the elections from 1968 through 1976 the perceptual space recovered from the multidimensional scaling of the thermometer data was two dimensional, with each of the configurations compatible with a party-ideology interpretation. Figures 4.2A through 4.2C show the spatial representation of each of those elections with the space divided into four quadrants by party and ideology axes. These axes have been inserted by me on the basis of my own interpretation of the spaces; later in the chapter we will discuss a more systematic method for placing axes in a multidimensional space.

The line-of-sight similarity matrix for the 1980 set of candidates was subjected to a nonmetric multidimensional scaling analysis in one, two, and three dimensions. In using multidimensional scaling procedures, we commonly perform solutions in several dimensionalities to assess the appropriate dimensionality. Solutions must improve as dimensionality increases because there are more degrees of freedom in higher dimensions. For example, even a perfect solution in one or two dimensions can be reproduced in three dimensions by simply holding the values of points on the third dimension at a constant value. Hence, one is not really interested in finding the solution with the lowest stress, but rather a solution such that adding a dimension does not substantially reduce the stress value.

For the 1980 election, the stress values for the one-, two-, and three-dimensional solutions are 0.422, 0.216, and 0.151, respectively. The decline in stress from the two- to three-dimensional solution (0.216 – 0.151 = 0.061) as compared to the decline in stress from the one- to the

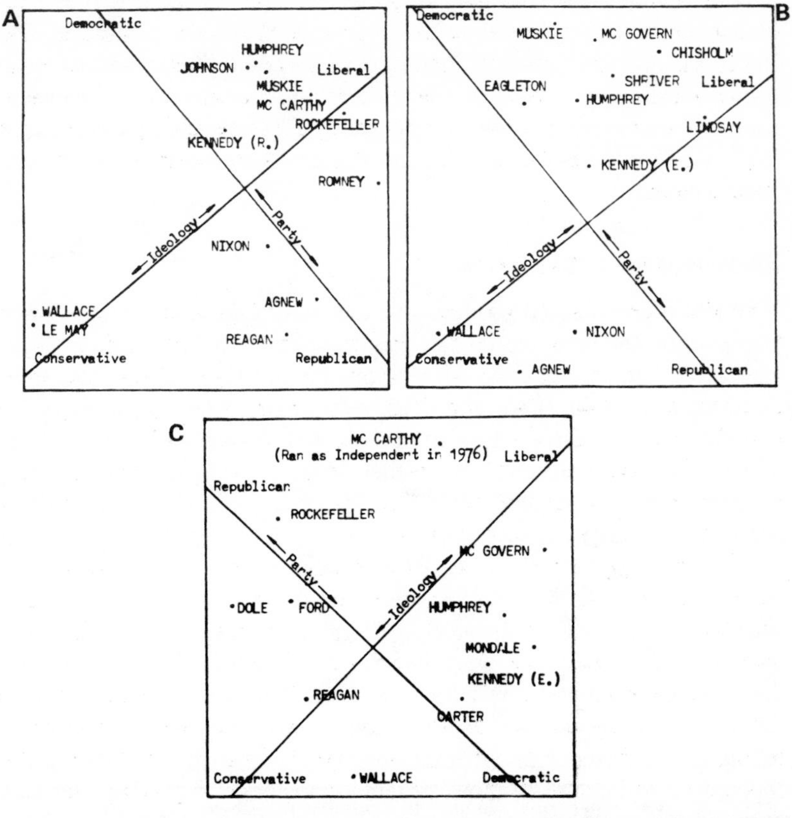

Figure 4.2: Nonmetric Multidimensional Scaling of Political Figures: (A) 1968, (B) 1972; and (C) 1976 Configurations

two-dimensional solution (0.422 − 0.216 = 0.206) is relatively modest. But the 0.061 drop-off is still substantial. Furthermore, the three-dimensional solution falls in the "good" range whereas the two-dimensional solution does not. Based on the magnitude of the drop-off and the relative quality of the solutions, the three-dimensional solution seems preferable. Given the poor general fit of the unfolding model, however, that preference might be suspect. We might be getting the typical two-dimensional solution with more noise than usual. Hence it is useful to examine the solutions in both two and three dimensions.

The two-dimensional solution appears in Figure 4.3. The only tight-knit clusters present are the Bush-Ford-Baker group of moderate Republicans and the Carter-Mondale link on the Democratic side. The rest of

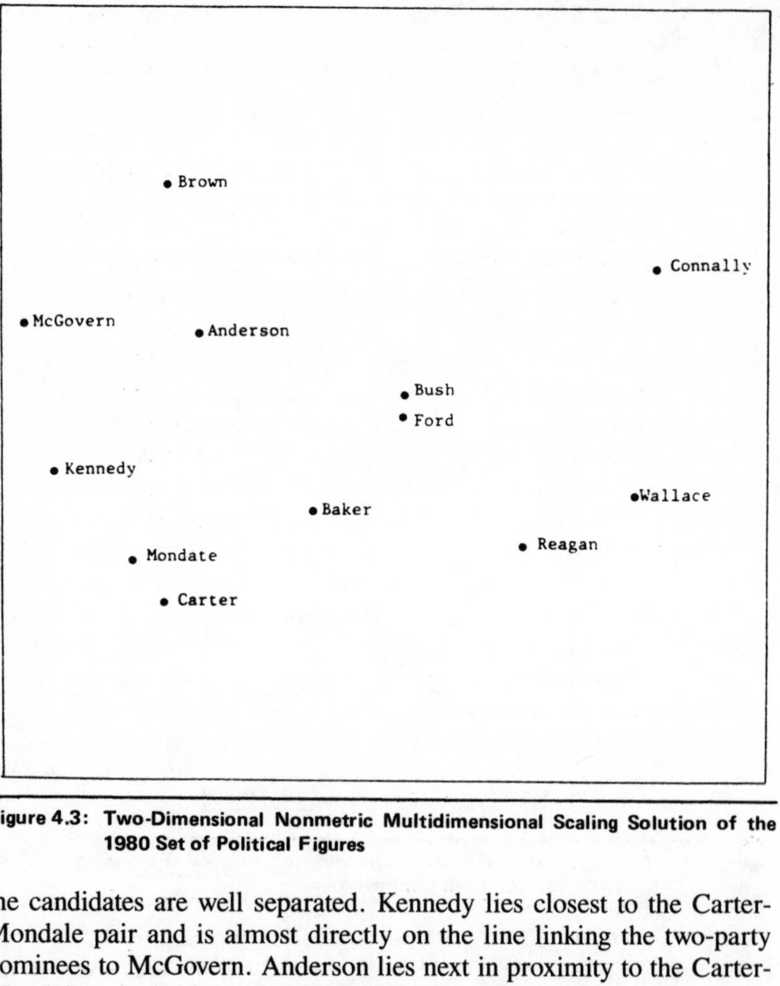

Figure 4.3: Two-Dimensional Nonmetric Multidimensional Scaling Solution of the 1980 Set of Political Figures

the candidates are well separated. Kennedy lies closest to the Carter-Mondale pair and is almost directly on the line linking the two-party nominees to McGovern. Anderson lies next in proximity to the Carter-Mondale pair and is almost equidistant from the various moderate and liberal Democrats. Reagan, the Republican nominee, lies closer to Wallace than he does to any of the Republican candidates, but closer to the various mainstream Republicans than to Connally. From the Downs (1957) spatial theory perspective, which emphasizes the importance of centrality in electoral competition, the most interesting feature of the result is the *non*centrality of Reagan as a candidate.

The solution does not display the clear party and ideology cleavages evident in the previous years' spatial configurations. Although an ideological axis seems to be present—one roughly analagous to the horizontal

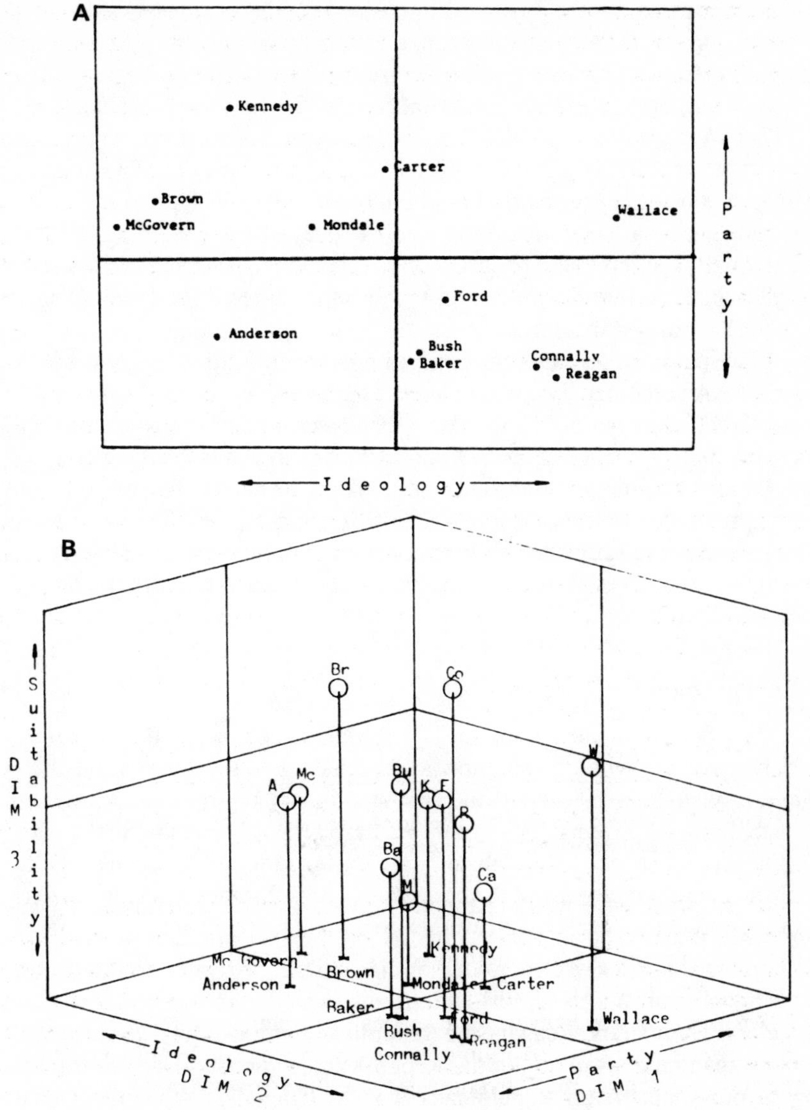

Figure 4.4: Three-Dimensional Configuration of the 1980 Set of Political Figures: (A) The Party and Ideology Plane; (B) Full Three-Dimensional Configuration

axis in the space—the vertical dimension, if it is associated with anything, appears to reflect some type of candidate personality (that is, personal suitability) dimension. Earlier studies have noted the presence of a candidate-personal-effectiveness influence on the space (Rabinowitz, 1978; Cahoon et al., 1978). The fact that this dimension is present in place of the normal party dimension is, however, unusual. The appearance of a personality dimension in the two-dimensional solution is consistent with the poor fit of the original data to the unfolding model. Personality judgments are inherently more idiosyncratic and less spatially coherent than judgments based on more explicit structural factors such as ideology and party.

The spatial structure of the three-dimensional solution, shown in Figures 4.4A and 4.4B, is more consistent with earlier studies. Figure 4.4A shows the view from directly above the three-dimensional space; hence the position of the points on the bottom plane is shown in that view. Figure 4.4B shows the three dimensional space from the perspective of someone looking at the configuration from the front-right corner. The two views provide a better overview of the configuration than would any single perspective. We have labeled the three axes in the space as Party, Ideology, and Suitability.

Interpretation

Any particular interpretation of a spatial structure can be controversial, especially when the solution is more than two-dimensional and difficult to visualize. Generally, the first step in any interpretation involves identifying the groups that cluster. We have already done that in the two-dimensional space, where clusters are easier to identify because of the physical ease of looking at the configuration. Substantive interpretations of specific dimensions require either general agreement among researchers on the meaning of a dimension or specific analysis performed to test the interpretation's credibility.

An excellent way to evaluate a dimensional interpretation is by assessing independently the position of object points on the hypothesized dimensions. For example, I hypothesize that the structure of the space is a function of party, ideology, and the personal suitability of candidates. In order to assess the reasonableness of this hypothesis, I need to assess independently the position of the candidates in terms of each of these factors.

A dummy variable where the nominal Republicans are assigned a zero and the nominal Democrats a one provides a reasonable measure of party affiliation—to be called PARTY. A measure of the ideology of the candidates is also straightforward. In the 1980 CPS Election Study respondents were asked to locate each of the candidates (with the exception of McGovern and Wallace) on a seven-point scale going from 1 = extremely liberal to 7 = extremely conservative. The mean placement of the candidates on the scale forms a natural measure of their ideological position—to be denoted IDEOLOGY. Candidate suitability is less readily measured than either party or ideology; we will, therefore, postpone the discussion of it until after we consider the party and ideology variables.

We can test hypotheses concerning the interpretation of structure by regressing the independently measured construct variables on the spatial locations of the points. For example, we can assess the fit of the ideology variable to the structure by analyzing the following regression model:

$$\text{IDEOLOGY} = a + b_1\text{DIM1} + b_2\text{DIM2} + b_3\text{DIM3} \qquad [4.5]$$

The independent variables in the equation are the values representing the position of points on the three axes [Party (DIM1), Ideology (DIM2), and Suitability (DIM3)] shown in Figure 4.4B. If the space has a potential dimension similar to the independently measured IDEOLOGY variable, then the coefficient of determination (the multiple R^2 value) for the regression will be high. Furthermore, the regression coefficients will indicate how such a dimension is oriented in the space.

Ideology appears to be an important determinant of the structure of the three-dimensional space. The coefficient of determination for equation 4.5 is 0.94, indicating a near perfect fit. The regression coefficients indicating where the best fitting ideology axis could be placed in the space are -0.88, 0.99, and 0.21 for DIM1, DIM2, and DIM3, respectively. Although it is hard to draw well in three dimensions, that axis could be inserted by locating the point (-0.88, 0.99, 0.21) in the space and drawing the line from the origin through that point. Notice that the axis we labeled "Ideology" is not the best fitting ideology axis. We could rotate the space so that the line from the origin to the (–0.88, 0.99, 0.21) point is one of the three reference axes. We did not do that in this case for reasons to be discussed below.

The regression of PARTY on the three dimensions supports the idea that party is also represented in the three-dimensional space. The coefficient of determination is a robust 0.85 and more importantly, given that party is a dichotomous variable, the parties are entirely separable in the three-space. This is evident in Figure 4.4A, where all the Republicans lie on the lower half of the Party axis and all the Democrats lie on the upper half. Of additional note is the fact that the line (or the vertical plane, to be more technically accurate) between Anderson and Wallace, the two political figures who ran as independent candidates for the presidency, would still separate the remaining Republicans and Democrats perfectly. Hence if we assigned those two candidates nonparty status, the party-based structure is still perfectly represented in the space. The regression coefficients using PARTY as the dependent variable are 1.2, 0.0, and 0.0 for the Party (DIM1), Ideology (DIM2) and Suitability (DIM3) dimensions, respectively.

The fact that the point (1.2, 0, 0) lies exactly on the Party axis is not accidental. The particular rotation of the space that appears in Figures 4.4A and 4.4B is the one in which the Party axis best matches the separately measured party variable. The Ideology axis in the figures, although not the one that best matches the ideology variable, *is* the best match to the ideology variable under the constraint that the axis be orthogonal (at right angles) to the Party axis. In the context of this example orthogonality implies that party and ideology are independent sources of judgment about the candidates. This is different from the implications in factor analysis, in which orthogonality implies that the two concepts (party and ideology) are uncorrelated. Hence, both for theoretical and practical (ease of plotting) reasons it is desirable to have these reference axes be orthogonal. The Ideology axis, although not as good a match to the ideology variable as the line going through the point (–0.88, 0.99, 0.21) would be, is quite a good match to the ideology variable. The correlation between values of candidates on the Ideology axis and the ideology variable is a substantial 0.90.

This particular rotation of the space was selected because it provided an easy way to check whether the solution could be partitioned into ideological and party quadrants, as had the earlier 1968-1976 structures. Quite clearly it can be. Of course, other rotations of the space are possible and these might be consistent with other plausible interpretations of spatial structure. Interpretations that are very rotationally dependent are somewhat suspect, because a rotation is arbitrary from a mathematical standpoint. That is why the correlational fit between the independently measured construct variables and the spatial structure, which is entirely unaffected by rotation, is important to evaluate. A nice discussion of the use of external criteria to interpret multidimensional scaling solutions appears in Cliff and Young (1968) and a discussion of some potential vulnerabilities appears in Berry (1979).

Independent evidence to support the hypothesis that the third dimension is related to candidate "personal suitability" is far more tenuous. The 1980 election study did include questions that asked respondents to assess some of the personal characteristics of candidates. But these questions were asked about relatively few candidates; more significantly, the work I did with them did *not* suggest that the qualities that were assessed with those questions were particularly well represented in the space.

Consequently, I performed one additional ad hoc analysis. I divided the candidates into three groups. One group included those I felt were the personally *unflawed* candidates. This group included Reagan, Baker, Bush, Carter, and Mondale. A second group included those I saw as *moderately flawed* candidates: Anderson, Kennedy, McGovern, and Wallace. Anderson and Wallace were included in this group because of their third-party runs, McGovern because of his extremely poor showing against Nixon in 1972, and Kennedy because of the Chappaquidick incident. The third group of *flawed candidates* included Brown and Connally, because of the generally conceded personal weakness of each as candidates in the 1980 primaries. I then assigned a 1 to candidates in the first group, a 2 to those in the second, and a 3 to those in the third.

When that constructed variable was regressed on DIM1, DIM2, and DIM3 the coefficient of determination was a respectable 0.82. The regression coefficients for this variable were -0.66, 0.53 and 1.27 for the Party, Ideology, and Suitability dimensions, respectively. The orientation of the Suitability dimension in the three-dimensional space was determined by the placement of the Party and Ideology axes; it was simply the only axis possible that was orthogonal to the other two. The correlation between the values of candidates on the suitability variable and the Suitability dimension is 0.64. Given the arbitrary way in which the independent measure of candidate suitability was constructed, any conclusions based on that measure should be drawn cautiously. Nevertheless, some personality effects do seem apparent in the perceptual map of these candidates.

Summary

My intent in this section of the chapter was to assess the way in which political candidates were perceived by the American mass public in the 1980 campaign period. We found that party, ideology, and some personality characteristics all seemed relevant to mass perceptions of these political figures. This result is similar to that obtained in analyses of other elections.

The evidence suggests that the 1980 set of candidates was, however, discriminated more markedly on nonstructural (personality) grounds than were candidates in past campaigns. This could well be caused by the fact that many of the candidates had marked personality weaknesses, rather than a fundamental reemphasis in the criteria people use to evaluate candidates. Certainly for Kennedy, Brown, and Connally negative personality judgments were made with some regularity in the media. Hence the change we observe could be caused by the fact that there was simply more variation in the personal attractiveness of candidates in 1980. On the other hand, as politics is increasingly a media phenomenon, personality (or other nonstructural) assessments might become generically more important. If this is the case, we could well see the trend established in 1980 continued into future campaigns.

INDIVIDUAL DIFFERENCE SCALING

For an individual to whom ideology was the only significant factor in evaluating candidates, the differences between Jimmy Carter and John Anderson in 1980 would likely have been relatively minor. For an individual strongly attached to the Democratic party, the differences between the Republican/Independent Anderson and the Democrat Carter would probably have been substantial. Individual difference scaling is an attempt to incorporate in a multidimensional scaling procedure the explicit recognition that individuals differ in terms of the importance they attach to criteria in making judgments about objects.

Figure 4.5A shows a series of circles each of which differs from the others in terms of size and/or striation pattern. Imagine taking each of the 36 (9 × 8/2) pairs of figures and presenting them to a set of respondents and asking each respondent to judge each pair based on the similarity of the two objects in the pair. Would we expect the individuals to rate the pairs in exactly the same way, or would we expect differences? If there are differences, how would we explain them? My suspicion is that individuals would differ and that the differences would be based on whether the individuals react more to the size or to the striation pattern of the circles.

The results from two hypothetical scalings of similarity judgments obtained from two different subjects appear in Figures 4.5B and 4.5C. Notice that for the first subject, the size of the circle is more important. If two objects differ in size, they are located quite far apart in that person's mind. For the second subject, striation pattern is more important. Here two objects with different striation are placed quite far from each other, and size has decidedly less importance. The spatial impact of the importance of a dimension is to magnify or stretch that dimension and thus increase the relevance of distinctions made on that dimension; the effect of being unimportant is to reduce or shrink a dimension and thus decrease the relevance of distinctions made on that dimension. If a dimension were irrelevant to a subject, that dimension would shrink so that all objects

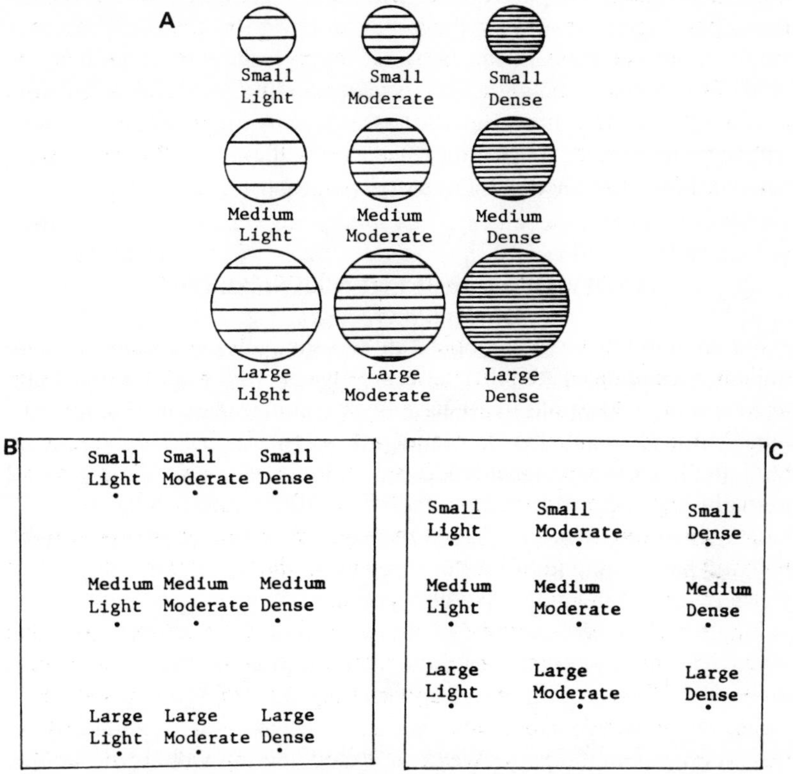

Figure 4.5: Illustration of the Model Underlying Individual Difference Scaling: (A) Set of 9 Objects to be Evaluated in Terms of the Similarity of Object Pairs; (B) Configuration from the Perspective of an Individual Who Placed More Emphasis on *Size* than Striation Pattern; (C) Configuration from the Perspective of the Individual Who Placed More Emphasis on *Striation Pattern* than on Size

would be collapsed to a single point, and no discrimination on that dimension would occur.

Recall that nonmetric multidimensional scaling is based on the mathematical model:

$$d_{jk} = M(s_{jk}) \qquad [4.5]$$

where M is an arbitrary monotonic function, d_{jk} is the distance between points j and k in the recovered space, and s_{jk} is the similarity between objects j and k. In individual difference scaling the model is the following:

$$d^i_{jk} = L(s^i_{jk}) \qquad [4.6]$$

where L stands for a linear transformation, s and d stand, respectively, for the similarities and the distances (as they do in the nonmetric multidimensional scaling procedures), the i superscript refers to a specific individual, and the j and k subscripts refer to objects. Notice that the function relating distance to similarity judgment is linear, rather than any monotonic function as in nonmetric multidimensional scaling. This change reflects the fact that most individual difference analyses use the stronger linear assumption. This is because experience with the technique suggests that the monotonicity (nonmetric) assumption often does not provide adequate constraint for the scaling. One can, however, do an individual difference analysis nonmetrically using many of the existing scaling packages.

The key to the specification of the individual difference model is the distance term which is defined as follows:

$$d^i_{jk} = \left[\sum_{t=1}^{r} w_{it} (x_{jt} - x_{kt})^2 \right]^{1/2} \qquad [4.7]$$

Here r stands for the number of dimensions in the space and x_{jt} stands for the location of object j on dimension t. The formula is exactly the same as the standard formula for calculating the Euclidean distance between two points in a space of r dimensions that appears in equation 4.2 except for the w_{it} term. That term weights the dimension by its salience for individual i. Notice that the formula attaches no i subscript to the coordinates for the object point locations (the x values). This implies that every individual agrees on the relative location of the objects on each dimension. In terms of the circle example, all individuals are assumed to see identical size and striation differences among the circles, such that if one asked them to place the circles on a scale based just on their size or just on their striation, they would produce identical unidimensional scales. Individuals are expected to differ in how similar they perceive the circles to be because the size and striation are differentially important to them.

In an individual difference analysis the differential importance of dimensions is estimated by the w values. The fact that the individual difference model allows for this differential weighting of dimensions is what distinguishes it from conventional multidimensional scaling. One significant consequence of this change is that unlike conventional multidimensional scaling, the particular rotation of axes is important in the model itself. For example, if our assumption that striation and size will be differentially important is true, then only a solution in which one dimension corresponds *directly* to striation and the other corresponds *directly* to size will correctly represent the data. This is an important property of the model, for it means that when the scaling is performed, the particular rotation recovered is *not* arbitrary, but rather, that the set of axes recovered is rigidly determined.

Hence unlike conventional multidimensional scaling or factor analysis, there is no ambiguity as to the "correct" rotation to represent a particular spatial structure. When I drew the hypothetical recovered spaces based on the shaded circles, I drew them so that the objects were perfectly oriented on the two underlying dimensions. This is exactly what should be recovered from an individual difference scaling. In emphasizing the rigidity of the rotation, I should also offer the important caveat that in order for the rotation to be meaningful there must be real variation across individuals in the salience of the underlying dimensions. If no such variation occurs, then the rotation is not really fixed because the variance in weighting schemes is the information used to establish the rotation. There must also be a sufficient number of individuals to constrain the solution.

Estimation, Goodness of Fit, and Other Considerations

The solution to the individual difference model is obtained using an alternating least-squares method. This approach requires first converting the original similarities data to make it compatible with a scalar product rather than a distance-based algorithm. This technical feature need not be of concern to most users, but is still useful to know. The impact of the conversion is to have the model estimate a three-way interaction term that is structured as follows:

$$b^{i}_{jk} = \sum_{t=1}^{r} w_{it}\, x_{jt}\, x_{kt} \qquad [4.8]$$

where the b^{i}_{jk} is the converted similarity score, and the w and x terms are defined as they were earlier. Alternating least-squares operates by alternately fixing two of the three values and then estimating the third, until the estimates stabilize.

The output of an individual difference scaling procedure is two sets of values: (1) the coordinate location of each of the object points (the value of each of the points on each of the dimensions) and (2) the set of individual weights (the values that indicate the importance of each dimension in the individual's judgment). This contrasts with nonmetric multidimensional scaling in which only the object point locations are estimated. In the course of our substantive example we will examine the results of an individual difference scaling analysis and discuss them in more detail.

Because the most widely used version of the individual difference scaling model is interval, a natural goodness-of-fit measure is the correlation between the (converted) similarities data and the similarities predicted by the individual difference analysis. This correlation is computed across all pairs of objects for all subjects, and is the fit optimized by the Carroll and Chang INDSCAL procedure. What is especially pleasing about the use of the correlation coefficient as the fit measure is its easy interpretability. Different algorithms optimize slightly different functions. The most general of the multidimensional scaling program packages now available is the ALSCAL program developed by Forrest Young and his associates; this program is available as part of the SAS set of supplemental statistical procedures. In ALSCAL, a function similar to Kruskal's stress is optimized; however, both the correlational fit and Kruskal's Stress Formula 1 are reported with each solution obtained.

STATE DIFFERENCES IN PERCEPTIONS OF POLITICAL CANDIDATES IN 1968

I am interested in investigating the extent to which the American polity is nationalized. This question has been cast in terms of either how similarly people in various regions stand on different issues (for example, Key, 1963; Hamilton, 1972; Nie et al., 1976) or how uniformly electoral tides sweep the country (Stokes, 1967; Katz, 1973). I will address this issue from a different perspective—how people in thirteen states perceived a set of presidential candidates in 1968. In particular I will consider two questions: (1) Do some state electorates respond to candidates in a more structured manner than others? (2) Do people in different states have similar or different perceptions of the candidates? By examining how structured state electorates are in evaluating candidates, I will be able to analyze factors that encourage structured competition among candidates in different states. By examining whether or not candidates are perceived similarly across states, I will be able to determine the extent to which candidate competition in the United States takes place within a common framework.

The principal data source for this analysis is the Comparative State Elections Project (CSEP). Interviewing for this project took place immediately following the 1968 presidential election with probability samples drawn from each of thirteen states. The study provides a rich and unique data source for comparative state analysis. Unfortunately no study since the CSEP project has replicated its interesting design.

The 1968 election was a rather unusual one from a comparative state perspective because George Wallace ran an effective third-party candidacy and was clearly a regional candidate. That the 1968 election had an unusual subnational character, however, is not a disadvantage. If we find little variation in perceptions of candidates in 1968, there seems to be virtually no chance that variation in perceptions occurs in modern presidential elections. If we do find variations in 1968, it will suggest that perceptual variation is likely at least under some circumstances.

The CSEP study included a question that is comparable to the thermometer question we analyzed in the first half of the chapter. The question asked respondents to rate each of thirteen political figures in terms of how good a president (or in a few instances, vice president) each would be. Based on the responses to these questions, I calculated a line-of-sight similarity matrix and a line-of-sight consistency measure for each of the states. Thus I had thirteen consistency measures and thirteen separate similarity matrices.

Cognitive Consistency

Do some state electorates respond to candidates in a more structured manner than others? My initial hypothesis is that we should see meaningful differences among states and that these differences should be related to levels of education and partisan competitiveness within the state. High levels of interparty competition should tend to add structure to the political climate of the state, while the presence of high education levels should tend to increase the sophistication of the political discourse in the state. One might imagine both of these factors working on an individual level. But one can imagine them working contextually on the state level as well. For example, respondents who have attained a relatively low level of education and who live in an environment in which politics is cast in relatively ideological or issue terms are more likely to respond to politics in those terms. In contrast, in environments in which politics tends to be of the "friends and neighbors" variety, people at all education levels are likely to respond to candidates in a more idiosyncratic fashion.

TABLE 4.1
Interstate Differences in Cognitive Constraint: Data Used in Analysis

	Line-of-sight Consistency	*Percentage of Males Over 25 Who Have Completed High School*	*[% Str Dem + % Str Rep] – |% Str Dem – % Str Rep|*
Alabama	0.10	42	10
California	0.57	63	30
Florida	0.33	52	24
Illinois	0.38	53	38
Louisiana	0.21	43	6
Massachusetts	0.27	57	20
Minnesota	0.29	54	34
New York	0.29	53	34
North Carolina	0.27	37	22
Ohio	0.31	52	28
Pennsylvania	0.40	50	46
South Dakota	0.20	48	30
Texas	0.16	48	10

The line-of-sight consistency measure (the Spearman rho correlation) provides a suitable measure of the cognitive consistency of the electorate in each of the states. The measure, as we noted previously, will be high if people within a state use the same systematic framework to evaluate candidates and will tend to be low if they do not. The line-of-sight consistency measure for each of the states appears in Table 4.1 along with the percentage of those over 25 years old who have completed high school (based on the 1970 census), and a measure of the partisan competitiveness of each state.

The competitiveness measure is based on the percentage of strong party identifiers in the states. The CSEP study included the conventional seven-point party identification question in which respondents were scaled from "Strong Democrat" at one extreme to "Strong Republican" at the other. The competitiveness measure is simply the percentage of respondents who were strong identifiers less the absolute difference between the percentage of Strong Democrats and the percentage of Strong Republicans. This measure would equal 100 if half the population were Strong Democrats and half were Strong Republicans; the measure would equal 0 if either there were no strong identifiers or all the strong identifiers were of the same party.

In order to test the hypothesis two regressions were performed using education and competitiveness to predict cognitive consistency. One regression was based on the entire thirteen-state sample; the other was based on just the eight nonsouthern states. I performed the nonsouthern

TABLE 4.2
Summary of Regression Results with Consistency as the Dependent Variable and Education and Partisan Competitiveness as the Independent Variables

	Regression Using All 13 States as Cases	*Regression Using Only 8 Nonsouthern States as Cases*
Multiple correlation	0.880	0.917
Unadjusted percentage variance explained	77.4	84.1
Adjusted percentage variance explained	72.9	77.0
Unstandardized and [standardized] weight for education	0.0138 [0.71]	0.0235 [0.97]
F value for education	17.5*	23.9*
Unstandardized and [standardized] weight for competitiveness	0.0031 [0.28]	0.0104 [0.70]
F value for competitiveness	2.8	12.6*
Intercept	–0.50	–1.27

*Significant at the .01 level.

regression for two reasons. The South is sufficiently unusual as a region that I did not want to attribute influence to specific variables when the results might have been due to the contrast between the South and the non-South. Second, the danger of misestimation because of multicollinearity effects is greater when the southern states are included, given that residents of the southern states are among the least well educated and the least competitive of the people living in the thirteen states included in the study.

The regressions are similar in showing a positive impact for both variables, although more strongly for education than for competitiveness. The results are reported in Table 4.2. The effect of education is significant at the .01 level in both regressions; in the non-South regression, competitiveness is also significant at the .01 level. Overall, these results are consistent with the view that the better educated the populace and the more competitive and partisan the political conflict within a state, the more coherently individuals within the state evaluate national candidates.

Differential Perception

In order to assess how the candidates were perceived in each of the states, I performed an individual difference scaling of the thirteen line-of-sight matrices. Based on the previous work with the 1968 election, I as-

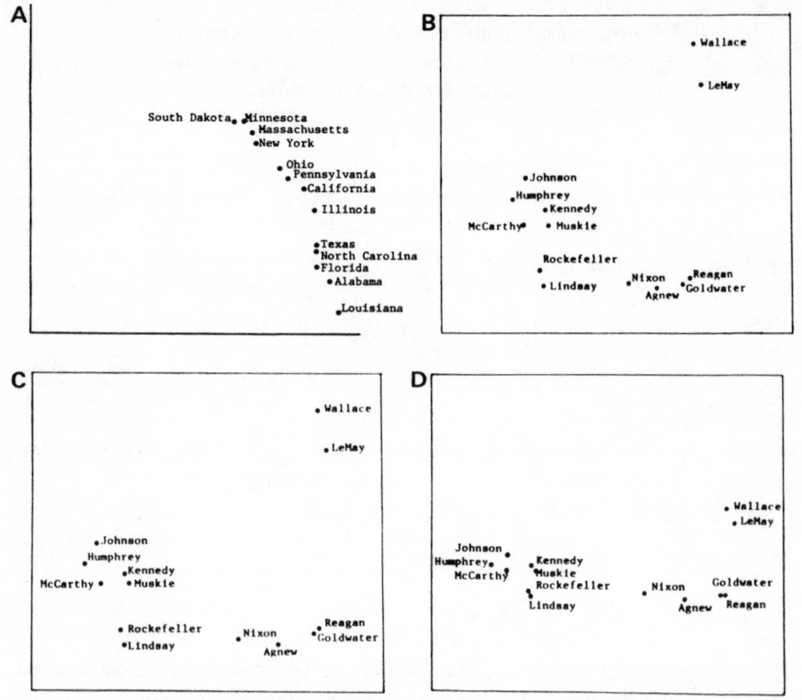

Figure 4.6: Analysis of 1968 Candidate Perception Using Individual Difference Scaling: (A) Relative Weighting of Axes by States; (B) South Dakota Configuration; (C) California Configuration; (D) Louisiana Configuration

sumed that the scaling should occur in two dimensions. This appears to be correct, as the thirteen states were all scaled effectively in the two-dimensional space. The correlation across pairs of candidates between the (converted) state similarity ratings and the predicted similarities range from 0.94 for Illinois and California to 0.89 for South Dakota. Quite substantial differences occur in the relative weighting of the dimensions across the states. The ratio of weights (weight of the horizontal dimension / weight of the vertical dimension) ranges from a high of 12.82 for Louisiana to a low of 0.97 for the state of South Dakota.

Figure 4.6A shows the relative weight of the dimensions for each state from the individual difference analysis. This figure not only shows the relative weighting of the two axes but also the relative success (correlational fit) of the scaling for each of the states. The further the weight point is from the origin, the more successfully the state similarity judgments have been explained by the analysis. We should also note that the three state configurations were constructed by multiplying each x_{jt} candidate coordinate by the *square root* of the w_{it} estimate for the state, rather than the weight coefficient itself. This occurs because the weight coefficient in the distance formula multiplies the squared difference in coordinate locations, rather than the unsquared difference.

Figure 4.6B shows the actual configuration recovered from the perspective of South Dakota, the state in which individuals appear to place the greatest emphasis on the vertical dimension. Figure 4.6C shows the configuration from the perspective of California, the state with the median weighting pattern. Figure 4.6D shows the configuration from the perspective of Louisiana, the state in which individuals place the greatest emphasis on the horizontal dimension. Remember that the *relative* position of candidate points on either the horizontal or the vertical dimension is identical in each of the state configurations; what differs is the importance of the dimensions in the various states. Hence in interpreting the results any of the three object configurations can be used.

The horizontal dimension of the object configurations seems to be an ideology axis. Indeed the ideological placement of Wallace, Reagan, and Kennedy appears remarkably similar to that observed in the 1980 mapping examined earlier. The vertical dimension appears to be an unusual party dimension. The Republicans are all located at the bottom of the axis and the conventional Democrats are located together in the middle. The American Independent candidates Wallace and LeMay are located together at the top of that axis. The American Independents give the appearance of being a deviant offshoot of the Democratic party, but one that is quite distinct from either major party.

The assumption underlying the individual difference model is that candidates are located differently for each state because of the differential importance of the underlying dimensions for citizens of the different states. The citizens of the different states do appear to have markedly different views of the candidates. How can these differences be explained?

My initial hypothesis is that the differential weighting scheme should be explained by the level of interparty competition in each state. I expect that the greater the level of interparty competition, the more influential the vertical "party" dimension is in determining perceptions of candidates. To test this hypothesis, I computed the correlation between the log of the weight ratio (weight of vertical dimension / weight of horizontal dimension) and the state competitiveness variable.[3] This correlation is a robust 0.852. Yet this relationship is not as strong as it first appears. When the five southern states are removed to check on the stability of the relationship, the correlation not only declines but changes sign: The new correlation is –0.20. Hence I feel this hypothesis should be rejected.

An alternate hypothesis is that the differential weighting should be associated with the percentage of black population in each of the states. This is based on the fact that Wallace and LeMay lie in an extreme position on the party dimension. Their candidacies rested largely on the racial issue, and it seems plausible that in states with low percentages of blacks Wallace and LeMay would be seen as more distinct—in a sense more atypical—than in states where the racial issue was a more natural part of the political dialogue. This hypothesis is well supported by the data. The correlation between percentage black in the state and the log of the weight ratios is 0.927; when we exclude the five southern states, it remains a substantial 0.736.

That percentage black accounts so well for the ratios suggests the results are strongly influenced by the presence of Wallace and LeMay. The Wallace-LeMay candidacy represented a third-party movement rooted in the South and was so clearly out of the ordinary that I felt the analysis should be repeated excluding these two candidates. When I did this, I found that once again each of the states was well explained by the analysis; the correlation between the original similarities and those predicted from the individual difference scaling analysis ranged from a low of 0.90 to a high of 0.96. Differential use of axes by the states markedly declined, suggesting a more national politics. The most extreme ratio in the weights given to the two dimensions was that of Louisiana, which had a weight ratio of 2.13. On the opposite extreme was Pennsylvania with a ratio of 0.64. The rotational structure was also quite different, although given the general similarity of the weights across states, the rotation is not likely to be particularly meaningful. Consistent with this I found that the ratio in weighting patterns was not strongly related to any state characteristic that I thought might explain differential perception (for example, party competition, percentage black, education). In short, with the regional candidates Wallace and LeMay excluded, perceptions of candidates were nationalized in character.

Summary

The cognitive consistency displayed by state aggregates in 1968 seemed to depend on both the education levels and levels of interparty competition within the states. Mass perceptions of candidates varied from state to state when Wallace and LeMay were included as political actors; without these two candidates only modest differences in perceptions occurred. The generality of these findings based on a single election must not be overstated. Nevertheless, these results should sensitize us to the possibility that differences exist in the manner in which state electorates respond to candidates, and that quite different perceptions of candidates can occur across states.

CONCLUSION

In this chapter I have attempted to expose readers to two methods for scaling similarities data. My intent has been to provide a feel for the methods and to undertake two substantive analyses to illustrate how the methods can be applied in social science research. Those interested in applying these methods in their own research should read more extensively about them. A useful general text is Schiffman et al. (1981). Rabinowitz (1975) is an article-length introduction to nonmetric multidimensional scaling; Carroll (1972) provides a concise overview of individual difference scaling as well as a discussion about a set of related scaling models. The Kruskal and Wish (1978) monograph provides an introduction to both nonmetric multidimensional and individual difference scaling.

NOTES

1. The calculation of the target values is not very difficult to understand. A very simple example illustrates the idea. Suppose we have three pairs, AB, AC, and BC, where AB is the most similar pair, AC next most similar, and BC least similar. Further suppose that the distances among AB, AC, and BC are 2, 4, and 3 units, respectively. The target value would be 2 for the AB pair and 3.5 for both the AC and BC pairs. In general, target values are identical to distances when distances are in the correct order, and averages of distances when the distances are out of order.

2. To obtain a sense of the logic underlying the line-of-sight measure imagine playing the following party game. The idea of the game is for a blindfolded player to guess who is close to whom in a room filled with people. The people must stay in one place, but the player is allowed to position himself in several different places (for example, in the center of the room and in each of the four corners). Once positioned, the player gets to find out how far from him each of the people is.

What the player learns about a pair will depend on his position in the room. For example, if the player is in the center of the room, and he finds out that two people are both eight feet from him, he would know very little about how far apart the pair is. They could be standing right next to each other or they could be sixteen feet apart on opposite ends of the room. However, suppose that at one corner of the room he finds he is one foot from one of the players and fourteen feet from the other. Then he would know that they are quite far apart, because they are at such different distances from him. If the player finds that another pair is roughly the same distance from him wherever he is in the room, he would guess they are quite close together. Hence one tactic a player could use is to remember if two people ever have a large difference in their distances from him.

Another tactic the player could use to assess the closeness of pairs is simply to add the distance the two people are from him. If two people are close together and he gets near them, then the sum of their distances from him would be quite small. However, if two people are far apart, whenever he is near one, he would be far from the other, and the sum of the distances would always be large. Thus the player could *either* concentrate on whether difference in distance from himself to each of two people ever becomes large, *or* whether the sum of distances from him to each of two people ever becomes small, in order to make his guess.

The different positions of the player in the party game are analogous to the locations of individual ideal points, and the positions of the people in the room are analogous to the locations of points representing candidates. The ratings individual respondents give candidates are similar to the distance information given the player. The two tactics used in playing the party game correspond to the strategies used in constructing the two measures that are averaged to form the single line-of-sight measure.

3. The log of the ratio was used rather than the ratio itself because ratios behave poorly as analytic variables in linear models. For example, a ratio of 1/5 is the mirror image of 5/1 and both should be equally different from the 1/1 ratio. Using the ratios directly, however, we get values of 0.2 (1/5), 1, and 5. Linearly 0.2 is quite a bit closer to 1 than is 5. By taking the log of the ratios, this problem is resolved. The log of 1/5 is -0.6990, the log of 1 is 0, and the log of 5 is 0.6990. Problems of very extreme ratios that occur if the denominator of the ratio is a small value are also obviated by the use of logs. Hence in general, log transformed ratios are preferable to the ratios themselves.

references

Berry, William D. (1979) "On the use of external criteria to interpret spatial structure: a note of caution but encouragement." Political Methodology 6 (August): 425-436.

Cahoon, Lawrence S., Melvin J. Hinich, and Peter C. Ordeshook (1978) "A statistical multidimensional scaling method based on the spatial theory of voting," pp. 243-278 in P. J. Wang (ed.) Graphical Representation of Multivariate Data. New York: Academic Press.

Carroll, J. Douglas (1972) "Individual differences and multidimensional scaling," pp. 105-155 in A. Kimball Romney et al. (eds.) Multidimensional Scaling, Vol. I: Theory. New York: Seminar.

Cliff, Norman and Forrest W. Young (1968) "On the relationship between unidimensional judgments and multidimensional scaling." Organizational Behavior and Human Performance 3 (August): 269-285.

Coombs, Clyde H. (1964) A Theory of Data. New York: John Wiley.

Downs, Anthony (1957) An Economic Theory of Democracy. New York: Harper & Row.

Enelow, James M. and Melvin J. Hinich (1984) The Spatial Theory of Voting: An Introduction. New York: Cambridge University Press.

Hamilton, Richard F. (1972) Class and Politics in the United States. New York: John Wiley.

Katz, Richard S. (1973) "The attribution of variance in electoral returns: an alternative measurement technique." American Political Science Review 67 (September): 817-828.

Key, V. O. (1963) Public Opinion and American Democracy. New York: Knopf.

Kruskal, Joseph B. and Myron Wish (1978) Multidimensional Scaling. Beverly Hills, CA: Sage.

Nie, Norman H., Sidney Verba, and John Petrocik (1976) The Changing American Voter. Cambridge, MA: Harvard Press.

Poole, Keith and Howard Rosenthal (1984) "U.S. presidential elections 1968-1980: a spatial analysis." American Journal of Political Science 28 (May): 282-312.

Rabinowitz, George (1975) "An introduction to nonmetric multidimensional scaling." American Journal of Political Science 19 (May): 343-390.

———(1976) "A procedure for ordering object pairs consistent with the multidimensional unfolding model." Psychometrika 41 (September): 349-373.

———(1978) "On the nature of political issues: insights from a spatial analysis." American Journal of Political Science 22 (November): 793-817.

Schiffman, Susan S., M. Lance Reynolds, and Forrest W. Young (1981) Introduction to Multidimensional Scaling: Theory, Methods, and Applications. New York: Academic Press.

Stokes, Donald E. (1967) "Parties and the nationalization of electoral forces," in William N. Chambers and Walter D. Burnham (eds.) The American Party System: Stages of Development. New York: Oxford Press.

Weisberg, Herbert F. and Jerrold G. Rusk (1970) "Dimensions of candidate evaluations." American Political Science Review 64 (December): 1167-1185.

II

TECHNIQUES FOR NONINTERVAL DATA

5

Introduction

WILLIAM D. BERRY
MICHAEL S. LEWIS-BECK

Social scientists would prefer to conduct their research using interval-level data, for example, dollars of income, years of education, but they must usually settle for less numeric precision. Ordinal measures of attitudes and nominal measures of attributes, for example, are common fare. Still, weak data have not prevented ambitious efforts at multivariate analysis, of which there are two standard approaches: tabular controls and multiple regression. Each will be illustrated through a modest example. Professor Jones, utilizing responses in a local social survey (N = 250), has constructed the following variables: political participation (active = 1, not active = 0), income (low = 1, medium = 2, high = 3), race (white = 1, nonwhite = 0), and neighborhood (urban = 1, suburban = 2, rural = 3). He hypothesizes that race is related to participation. Also, he believes participation to be influenced by an individual's income. In addition, he suspects participation varies according to the character of the neighborhood where one resides. His guess is that high-income, urban whites are the most politically active group in his sample. To explore these possibilities, Professor Jones, mindful of his noninterval measures, turns to contingency table analysis and imposes controls. First, he cross-tabulates race and participation, controlling for the three income categories and the three neighborhood types, which generates nine 2 × 2 tables, for example, the cross-tab of race and participation for urban, middle-income respondents.

Already, the analysis problems are apparent. The sample size, although initially large (N = 250), is reduced to a statistically unreliable magnitude in several of the nine tables. Indeed, for some tables there are empty cells (perhaps rural high-income nonwhites), which leaves no variance to study there. Further, ignoring these sample difficulties, formidable obstacles to meaningful generalization of the findings are imposed.

Across the nine distinct tables, the relationship between race and participation is bound to differ, for example, it may be statistically significant in some and not others. Moreover, even if the pattern of significance is consistent, what about the general impact of race on participation? Each table will give a somewhat different answer, for example, the tau-b's will vary from table to table. Finally, what is to be said concerning the participation effects of the other independent variables, income and neighborhood, that have yet to be evaluated?

Because of these frustrations, Professor Jones turns to multiple regression (ordinary least squares—OLS). Thus using his survey data, he estimates the following equation:

$$Y = b_0 + b_1X_1 + b_2X_2 + b_3X_3 + e \qquad [5.1]$$

where Y = participation (0 = not active, 1 = active); X_1 = race (0 = nonwhite, 1 = white); X_2 = income (1 = low, 2 = medium, 3 = high); X_3 = neighborhood type (1 = rural, 2 = suburban, 3 = urban).

The advantages of this multiple regression approach over a traditional contingency table approach are clear. First, the overall sample size is maintained, thereby strengthening statistical inference. Second, easy generalizations about the relationship between Y and the independent variables are possible. For instance, "race is significantly related to participation." Or, perhaps, "a white respondent has a b_1 (say .13) greater probability of participating than a nonwhite." Third, the effect of X_1 can be directly compared to the effect of X_2, under a condition of statistical control. These strengths of OLS would seem to make it the preferred analytic tool for multivariate analysis. But, of course, its Achilles' heel is the assumption of interval-level measures. Key variables of interest to Professor Jones are measured only at the ordinal or nominal levels, as is true of most social science data. What to do? Until recently, the practicing multivariate researcher either chose to swallow the interval assumption and apply OLS, or stick to tables and face the frustrations of tabular control. Fortunately, these troubled solutions are no longer necessary, in part because of the analysis techniques explicated in the chapters of this section.

These estimation difficulties, which arise with a dichotomous dependent variable, are explicated in Chapter 6 by John Aldrich and Forrest Nelson, and then overcome in the solutions proposed. They offer logit and probit models that, because of the nonlinear specification, render maximum likelihood the standard estimation procedure, rather than least squares. Given the assumptions are met, either probit or logit produces estimates that are consistent, asymptotically efficient, and asymptotically normal. Thus the coefficient estimates can be properly tested for significance, and inferences about the effect of, say, income on political participation can be drawn safely. (Of course, the techniques are not entirely without difficulties. For example, an ideal goodness-of-fit measure is lacking. Further, the interpretation of the coefficients is sometimes tricky.) Finally, as Aldrich and Nelson note, while their focus is on the dichotomous dependent variable, the techniques can be extended to ordered or nonordered polytomous variables, with probit preferred in the former case, logit in the latter.

The effort by Herbert Kritzer in Chapter 7 elaborates what he labels "categorical regression," an approach to the analysis of multivariate contingency tables based on work by Grizzle, Starmer, and Koch (GSK). The technique combines the usual tools of contingency table analysis—chi-square, difference of proportions, cross-product ratios—with regression analysis. The critical difference between categorical regression and ordinary regression concerns the dependent variables. In the latter, the dependent variable is a measure on individual observations, for example, a respondent in a survey. With categorical regression, however, the dependent variable is a probability estimate, a function of the proportions derived from a sample of individual observations. Hence when predicting an individual observation one must refer to the probability that it will place itself in one category or other of the dependent variable. To illustrate the procedure, he examines multivariate contingency table data relating federal district judge decisions (liberal, conservative) to political party affiliation (Democrat, Republican), case subject area (civil rights, criminal justice, economics), and the time period (1933–1953, 1954–1968, 1969–1977). An important feature of categorical regression is that the effects of variables, as well as their significance, can be assessed. For example, the coefficient for the party variable (.04) can be used to calculate the difference in the proportion of liberal decisions for Democrats compared to Republicans.

The Kritzer chapter brings statistical elegance to contingency table analysis, a research approach that has its deepest roots in sociology. However, suppose the investigator has the problem of noninterval data but comes out of a discipline, such as economics, habituated to equations rather than tables. The first impulse might be to solve the measurement problem by converting all the variables to dichotomous dummies. In Professor Jones's example, cited above, this would mean the income (X_2) of respondents could be captured by two dummies, D_2 ($0 =$ not low, $1 =$ low), and D_3 ($0 =$ not middle, $1 =$ middle). Similarly, the type-of-neighborhood variable (X_3) could be measured by D_4 ($0 =$ not rural, $1 =$ rural) and D_5 ($0 =$ not suburban, $1 =$ suburban). (Recall that, when a variable is "dummied up," we must always have G – 1 dummies, where G equals the number of categories of the original variable, in order to avoid the trap of perfect multicollinearity). This procedure yields the following equation:

$$Y = b_0 + b_1X_1 + b_2D_2 + b_3D_3 + b_4D_4 + b_5D_5 + e \quad [5.2]$$

where Y = participation (0 = not active, 1 = active); X_1 = race (0 = nonwhite, 1 = white); D_2 = dummy variable (0 = not low income, 1 = low income); D_3 = dummy variable (0 = not middle income, 1 = middle income); D_4 = dummy variable (0 = not rural, 1 = rural); D_5 = dummy variable (0 = not suburban, 1 = suburban).

In this equation, each variable is necessarily an interval measure, because it is a dichotomy. Can OLS now yield the best linear unbiased estimates (BLUE) of the coefficients for this political participation model? No. BLUE status still cannot be achieved, precisely because of the dichotomous nature of the dependent variable. A binary dependent variable causes the error term to be heteroskedastic, which means that the OLS parameter estimates will not be efficient (although they remain unbiased). Further, such a dependent variable guarantees that the error term is not normally distributed, which invalidates the significant tests. Also, the OLS coefficients, which generate predictions of the occurrence of Y, may yield impossible probability estimates, for example, the estimated probability of being a political activist might exceed 1.00 for some types of persons. Finally, especially if one or more of the independent variables is fully an interval variable (for example, income measured in dollars), then its relationship to the dependent variable may be inherently nonlinear, implying that a linear model will yield biased estimates.

6

Logit and Probit Models for Multivariate Analysis with Qualitative Dependent Variables

JOHN H. ALDRICH
FORREST D. NELSON

INTRODUCTION

The general linear model plays a central role in the methods of statistical inference used in the social sciences. Perhaps the most prominent of all such inferential procedures drawn from the linear model is regression. Ordinary least-squares regression, which we denote as "OLS," has much to recommend it, so long as the associated Gauss-Markov assumptions are met by the data at hand. It could be argued, however, that the linear model and the associated OLS estimator are particularly unsuitable for many of the research problems in the behavioral sciences. If that argument, to be briefly outlined below, is accepted, then what is needed is some alternative model and/or estimator that will preserve as much as possible of the flexibility (for example, easy extension to the multivariate case), statistical justification (such as unbiasedness, consistency, and efficiency properties), and ease of interpretation of the linear model. Two models, logit and probit, and associated methods analysis that achieve this goal for a certain class of problems are considered here. The linear model is considered in some detail as well to demonstrate its limitations and to serve as a benchmark against which logit and probit may be compared.

The central problem with OLS in the behavioral sciences is just this: OLS implicitly requires a continuous, interval-level, and unbounded dependent variable. In principle, that is, the dependent variable of OLS should be able to take on any value from negative to positive infinity. No finite, real-world case can logically satisfy those requirements, of course. The real questions, then, are the following: How badly do the data deviate from the assumption and what are the consequences of such deviations? In the social and behavioral sciences, many variables that, in principle, might occur in sufficiently large numbers of distinct values to be a reasonable approximation of a continuous dependent variable (for example, income) in practice may be measured in only a small number of categories (surveys asking about income typically measure it only as being in one of a few very broad categories). In other cases, not only is the set of distinct possible behaviors finite *in principle*, but also the finite number is very small, frequently just two. For example, the variable of interest may represent a person's choice of buying or not buying something, of marrying or remaining single, or of voting for or against a bill. In short, studies of behavioral measures, especially, regularly entail extreme departures from an unbounded interval-level variable. The extreme opposite, the two-category case, is often encountered.

Variables that can assume only two distinct values are called dichotomous. The dichotomous case will be the focus of this chapter. It is chosen because it is very common, it is especially far from that assumed in OLS, and it is easy to explain and follow. Furthermore, rather more can be done with this case than with the more general polytomous variable; it makes no difference whether the two possible outcomes of a dichotomous variable are ordered or unordered, for example.

The dichotomous dependent variable will be denoted as Y and will be assumed to take on the two values, 0 and 1, although any two distinct values would serve as well. Analogous to OLS, it is further assumed that Y is related to or influenced by a set of K other variables. These variables will be distinguished from the "dependent" variable Y by the descriptor "independent" and will be labeled as X_1 through X_K.[1] Specific details of the relationship between Y and X, for example the values of parameters that measure the extent or even the direction of the relationship between each X_k and Y, are in general unknown and, indeed, are the objective of statistical analysis. But analysis will require, as a first step, a precise statement about the general form of the relationship, that is, it requires a specification of the model. Thus the distinction between the linear model and other models considered here amounts to a difference in the a priori specification of the form of the relationship between Y and X.

Whether the relationship of interest is a presumed "causal" one from X to Y or merely a description of their association, it is not, strictly speaking, correct to suggest that changes in X are associated, literally, with changes in Y. (For example, it may be quite consistent with the presumed relationship to have two observations with the same value for X but different values for Y.) Thus the relationship will be carefully stated as between the value of X and the *likelihood* of an outcome, $Y = 1$. Let $P(Y = 1)$, or simply $P(Y)$, represent this likelihood or probability, and note that P(Y) ranges from zero to one inclusively, with a value of zero indicating that Y will be zero for certain, and a value of one indicating the corresponding certainty of a value of one for Y. There is nothing unique about the focus on probabilities. If Y were a continuous variable, models for it would not specify the value of each observation. Rather, they would dictate the behavior of Y *on average*. Thus the standard linear model specifies that the *expected value* of Y, denoted by E(Y), is a linear function of the associated independent variables, X. It just so happens that when Y is a dichotomous variable its expectation is simply the probability of a positive response:

$$E(Y) = P(Y = 1)1 + P(Y = 0)0 = P(Y = 1)$$

What is needed, then, is some statistical procedure that will allow assessment of the nature and extent of the relationship between P(Y) and X. Because the choice of procedures depends in large measure on the specification of the model under consideration, it is necessary to consider first the merits and demerits of alternative models. It might help to do that in the context of a particular problem. In the following pages such an example is introduced, with the discussion focusing on its substantive aspects and their implications for theoretical models. Further ahead, four distinct probability models are identified from the substantive modeling considerations described. The four models include the linear probability model (which is the implicit specification when OLS is applied to dichotomous dependent variables), a truncated version of the linear probability model, the probit model, and the logit model. Salient features of each of the four, including similarities as well as differences, are summarized. The statistical issues of estimation and inference appropriate for each of the models will be examined. In addition, the limitations and necessary extensions of the OLS procedure as applied to the linear probability model are described, and this analysis is illustrated with a numerical example. The statistical roadblocks to analysis of the truncated model, maximum likelihood estimation of the probit and logit models, and an alternative estimation procedure for the logit model under special conditions are discussed also. Finally, a numerical illustration of these estimators for logit and probit, and summary comments are given.

This treatment of the various models is necessarily brief. A more extensive analysis of the same material can be found in Aldrich and Nelson (1984). Amemiya (1981) provides a more advanced survey of analysis methods for qualitative variables, and Maddala (1983) covers this topic as well as a number of related models and methods. The first standard econometrics textbook to treat the problems of interest here was Goldberger (1964). Several contemporary texts now include this material; among them are Pindyck and Rubinfeld (1976), Maddala (1977), and Judge et al. (1985).

AN EXAMPLE: REPRESENTATION, OR THE RELATIONSHIP BETWEEN POLICY BELIEFS OF CITIZENS AND LEADERS

Recently Powell and Powell (1978) proposed a quite clever analysis of what they called the "representation structure." Democratic theories of representation assert that there ought to be a relationship between the proportion of citizens in favor of some position on an important issue and the likelihood that their leader would favor that same position. Just what form that relationship might take is the empirical question they examine. They consider two "ideal" relationships, one based on majority rule, the other on proportionality. The data they use are issue preferences of mayors and residents of 48 cities in Austria, and they consider issues involving two sides, a "for" and an "against" position.

The dependent variable in the relationships they consider is the position taken by the mayor. Accordingly, let $Y_i = 1$ indicate that the mayor in city i supports the issue in question and $Y_i = 0$ indicate that he does not support it. At this stage in the example there is a single independent variable; an observation on it, say X_{i1}, is measured as the fraction of the constituency in city i supporting the issue. We consider below several specific formulations of the theoretical relationship between P(Y) and X_1. Our point is neither to expound a particular substantive theory nor to accurately summarize the analysis of Powell and Powell but rather to suggest the variety of forms that might arise in practice.

A possible null model would assert that elections provide no particular linkage between citizens and elites, at least in terms of policy. What "no linkage" means must be that the likelihood a mayor supports an issue is the same no matter what proportion of the constituency favors that issue. This verbal description can be written in equation form quite simply as

$$P(Y_i) = \beta_0 \qquad [6.1a]$$

and its graph appears in Figure 6.1. Because the likelihood of a mayor's support for the issue does not depend on the preferences of the constituency, $P(Y_i)$ is a constant β_0 (it does not vary with X_{i1}), and its graph is a horizontal line. The only unknown in this null model is the value of the "parameter," β_0. Although it is quite obvious here, it is worth noting

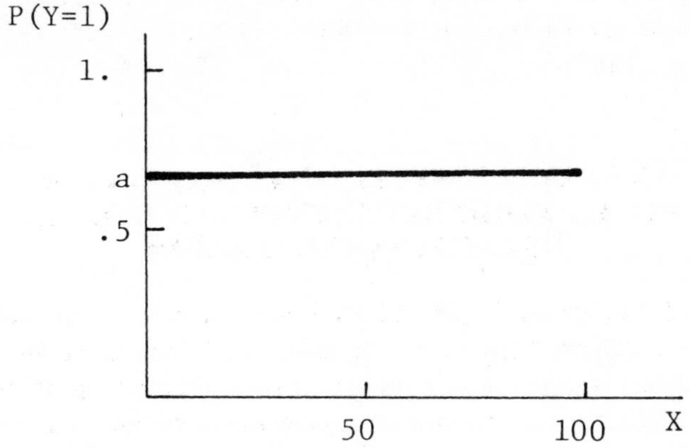

NOTE: Model: P(Y = 1) = a; Y: 1 if Mayor supports the issue, otherwise 0; X: percentage of citizens supporting the issue.

Figure 6.1: Null Model

explicitly that β_0 cannot take on any arbitrary value. Rather it must satisfy the following constraint:

$$0 \leqslant \beta_0 \leqslant 1 \qquad [6.1b]$$

The numbering of these two relations as 6.1a and 6.1b serves to emphasize that the constraint in 6.1b is, as a logical necessity, a part of the model. Subsequent reference to equation 6.1 will imply the full model 6.1a and 6.1b, and this convention will be followed in other relations below.

One of the alternative models considered by Powell and Powell is proportional representation (or PR). In this model, it is asserted that, for example, a party that receives x% of the popular vote ought to receive x% of the seats in Parliament. The extension of the model to votes on issues would be that the probability a mayor favors a position ought to reflect the proportion of people in his/her city who favor that position. This is captured in the equation

$$P(Y_i) = X_{i1}$$

and the graph, as in Figure 6.2, is a straight line extending from the origin to the northeast at a 45° angle. Note that this pure PR model involves no unknowns. Note too the similarity between the null and PR models; each is a special case of the following more general model:

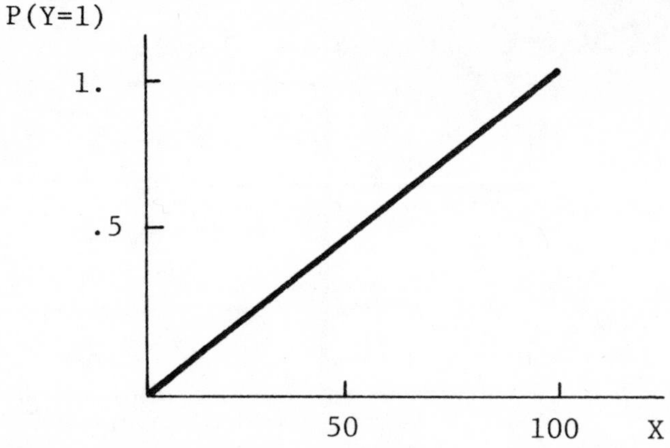

NOTE: P(Y = 1) = .01X; Y: 1 if Mayor supports the issue, otherwise 0; X: percentage of citizens supporting the issue.

Figure 6.2: Pure Proportional Representation Model

$$P(Y_i) = \beta_0 + \beta_1 X_{i1} \tag{6.2a}$$

For the null model, β_1 is zero and β_o is a number between zero and one, and for the pure PR model, β_0 equals zero and β_1 is one. We could imagine, in fact, a continuum of PR models ranging from no relationship between X and P(Y) as in the null model to a strong one as in the pure PR model. Equation 6.2a represents this continuum, but note that some constraint must be appended to it to make the specification logically consistent, that is, to guarantee that the right-hand side lies between zero and one as the equality suggests it must. The following such constraint presumes a positive relationship:

$$0 \leqslant \beta_0 \leqslant (1 - \beta_1) \text{ and } 0 \leqslant \beta_1 \leqslant 1 \tag{6.2b}$$

The other model discussed by Powell and Powell is majority rule (MR). Under it, the mayor favors an issue when, and only when, a majority of the citizenry favors the issue. A graph of such a relationship appears in Figure 6.3. In terms of the definitions and models described above, this situation may be approximated by equation 6.2a if β_0 tends toward negative infinity and β_1 tends toward positive infinity with $P(Y_i)$ constrained to be between zero and one. A more precise description is obtained by defining a second independent variable according to

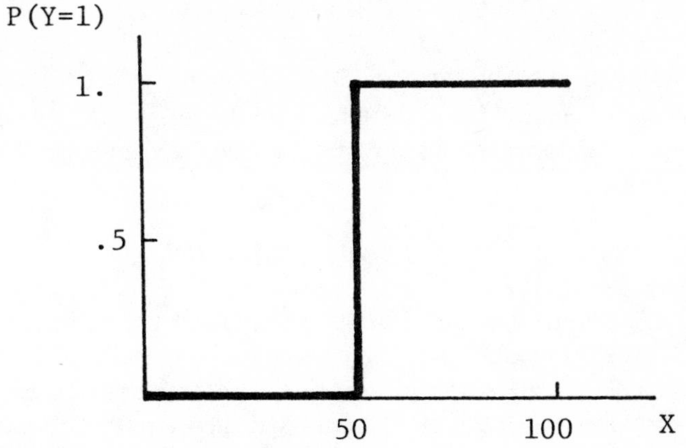

NOTE: Model P(Y = 1) = 0 if X ⩽ 50, 1 if X > 50; Y: 1 if Mayor supports the issue, otherwise 0; X: percentage of citizens supporting the issue.

Figure 6.3: Pure Majority Rule Model

$$X_{i2} = \begin{cases} 1 & \text{if } X_{i1} > .5 \\ 0 & \text{if } X_{i1} \leqslant .5 \end{cases}$$

and then writing the pure MR model as

$$P(Y_i) = X_{i2}$$

Analogous to equation 6.2a, the null and MR models can be nested in a single equation as

$$P(Y_i) = \beta_0 + \beta_2 X_{i2} \qquad [6.3a]$$

This formulation represents the null model, if β_2 is zero and β_o is between zero and one, or the pure MR model, if β_o is zero and β_1 is one. And if the constraint

$$0 \leqslant \beta_o \leqslant (\beta_o + \beta_2) \leqslant 1 \qquad [6.3b]$$

is appended, it represents an interesting generalization of the MR specification.

Proceeding one step further, it is clearly possible to nest all three models in a single one:

$$P(Y_i) = \beta_o + \beta_1 X_{i1} + \beta_2 X_{i2} \quad [6.4a]$$

Values of the three parameters (β_o, β_1, β_2) given by (p, 0, 0), (0, 1, 0) or (0, 0, 1) would correspond to the null, pure PR, or pure MR models respectively, where p represents any value between zero and one. And with the constraints

$$0 \leqslant \beta_o \leqslant (\beta_o + \beta_2) \leqslant (1 - \beta_1) \text{ and } 0 \leqslant \beta_1 \leqslant 1 \quad [6.4b]$$

the pair of relations 6.4a and 6.4b represent a full generalization of the null, PR, and MR models. This model, and the models given by equation pairs 6.2 and 6.3, might be criticized on the grounds that they are rather ad hoc extensions of the null, PR, and MR theories. Furthermore, although they may appear quite general, they lack complete flexibility in the degree of effect from X_1 to P(Y): except for a step increase of size β_2 in P(Y) at the point $X_1 = .5$, no increase in X_1 can lead to more than a proportional increase in P(Y). Still, they may be quite reasonable and interesting formulations; certainly they are for the purposes here, and in other applications models very similar to them may be direct derivations from the relevant theory.

In an alternative generalization that avoids the two criticisms addressed above, Powell and Powell noted that three models in their pure forms are excessively stringent. Because the mayor is also a citizen, the requirement of the null model that $\beta_1 = 0$ is surely too extreme; slopes (values of β_1) only slightly different from one should hardly be taken as a rejection of the PR model; and inaccuracies in assessing the magnitude of X, or even nearly neutral voters who may switch positions from one day to the next, will cause the MR model to be "tilted" at least a little bit in the direction of the PR model. Indeed, one might expect that both logics, PR and MR, might exert some force, so that a hybrid model that allows elements of all three might well best describe the data. In this direction, Powell and Powell suggest a "mixed" model, three forms of which are illustrated in figure 6.4. Part A of that figure reflects a situation in which a near majority is required before any mayor dare offer support. Apparently in part B, a majority demands adherence from the mayor, but even a strong minority impacts heavily. And part C suggests a simple compromise between PR and MR forces. In all three illustrations, the effect of PR is seen in the increase in P(Y) as X_1 increases, so the slope is not zero. And while the threshold of 50% citizenry support does not cause a step increase in P(Y) as in the pure MR model and its generalizations, the effect of MR is seen in the detail that all three figures indicate a slope steeper than one.

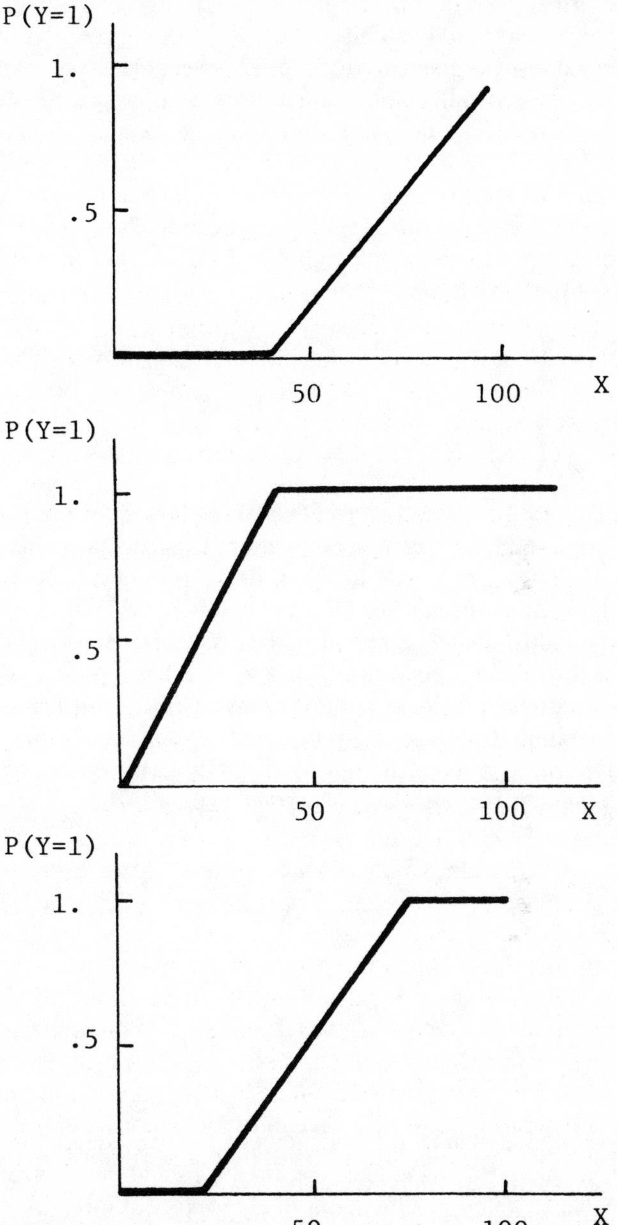

NOTE: Y: 1 if Mayor supports the issue, otherwise 0; X: percentage of citizens supporting the issues.

Figure 6.4: Three Mixed PR-MR Models

To describe this mixed model in equation form, note that all three illustrations of Figure 6.4 exhibit a positively sloping relationship of the same general form as given in equation 6.2a over at least part of the range on X_1. But note too that all three illustrations as drawn violate the condition 6.2b, so model 6.2 does not describe the mixed model suggested by Powell and Powell. And, as suggested above, equation 6.2a without constraints does not specify a logically consistent model of probabilities. A precise statement of the mixed model in equation form must be written with explicit constraints on the right hand side, rather than on the parameters of the model:

$$P(Y_i) = \begin{cases} 0 & \text{if } (\beta_o + \beta_1 X_{i1}) < 0 \\ \beta_o + \beta_1 X_{i1} & \text{if } 0 \leqslant (\beta_o + \beta_1 X_{i1}) < 1 \\ 1 & \text{if } 1 \leqslant (\beta_o + \beta_1 X_{i1}) \end{cases} \qquad [6.5]$$

Proceeding with the reasoning of Powell and Powell, even equation 6.5 appears to be a rather stringent specification. In particular, as seen in Figure 6.4, it allows for the possibility of limiting values on X_1, above or below which the position taken by the mayor is known with certainty. In the situation illustrated by Figure 6.4, for example, the model appears to deny even the remotest possibility that a maverick mayor will oppose the issue in question if a majority of the citizens favor it. A further relaxation or generalization that avoids such stringent assumptions is illustrated by the sigmoid curve graphed in Figure 6.5. Of the many equations exhibiting this general form, we will concentrate on only two,

$$P(Y_i) = \frac{\exp(\beta_o + \beta_1 X_{i1})}{1 + \exp(\beta_o + \beta_1 X_{i1})} \overset{(def)}{=} \Lambda(\beta_o + \beta_1 X_{i1}) \qquad [6.6]$$

and

$$P(Y_i) = \int_{-\infty}^{\beta_o + \beta_1 X_{i1}} \frac{1}{\sqrt{2\Pi}} \exp \frac{-u^2}{2} \, du \overset{(def)}{=} \Phi(\beta_o + \beta_1 X_{i1}) \qquad [6.7]$$

Equation 6.6 is known as the logistic equation and equation 6.7 is the familiar cumulative distribution function for a standard-normal random variable. They are the specifications of choice probabilities used in logit and probit analysis, respectively.[2] Details of the behavior of these two forms will be discussed shortly.

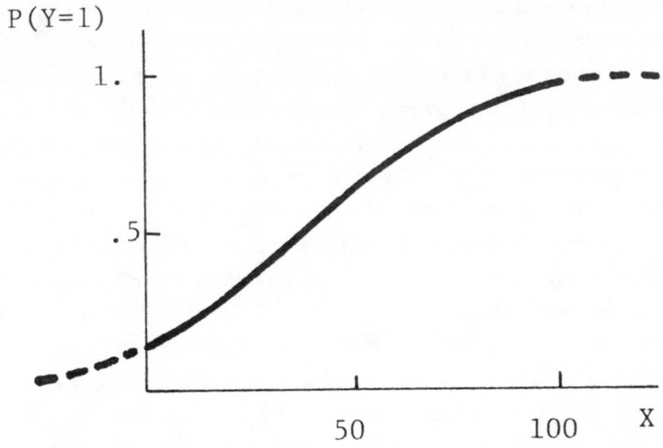

NOTE: Y: 1 if Mayor supports the issue, otherwise 0; X: percentage of citizens supporting the issue.

Figure 6.5: Nonlinear Model

Although the particular expressions in equations 6.6 and 6.7 may seem to have been chosen arbitrarily, they can be derived rigorously from a more detailed description of choice behavior. (See Luce and Suppes, 1965; and McFadden, 1973.) Let the variable A_i denote the (unmeasured) attitude of the mayor in city i toward the issue in question, and suppose it depends on a great many measurable and unmeasurable factors. Of the former we might be most interested in the expressed attitude of the citizenry, X_1; accordingly specify

$$A_i = \alpha_o + \alpha_1 X_{i1} - e_i$$

where e_i represents all factors which affect A_i except X_{i1}. Observed behavior is explained by

$$Y_i = \begin{cases} 1 & \text{if } A_i > 0 \\ 0 & \text{if } A_i \leqslant 0 \end{cases}$$

Next note that the sign of A, and thus the value of Y, is not changed if A is multiplied by a positive constant, say c. Define $\beta_0 = c\,\alpha_0$ and $\beta_1 = c\,\alpha_1$. Then the needed expression for P(Y) is given by

$$\begin{aligned} P(Y_i = 1) &= P(A_i > 0) = P(cA_i > 0) \\ &= P(c\alpha_o + c\alpha_1 X_{i1} - ce_i > 0) = P(\beta_0 + \beta_1 X_{i1} > ce_i) \end{aligned}$$

The last expression on the right in the equation shown above is a familiar one in statistics: It is the cumulative distribution function (cdf) of the random variable ce_i, evaluated at the point ($\beta_o + \beta_1 X_{i1}$). If the probability distribution of ce_i is known, then the functional form of this cdf, and thus of $P(Y_i)$, is also known. In particular, if ce_i follows the "standard normal" distribution, then the correct form is given by equation 6.7 and if the distribution of ce_i is the "standardized logistic," then equation 6.6 is the correct form. Because the expression just above for P(Y) holds for any positive value of c, the original and relevant variable e_i can have any variance; c is simply the reciprocal of the standard deviation of e_i, and it is apparent that the choice of "standardized" distributions involves no loss of generality. (Note that the standard deviations of the standardized normal and standardized logistic are one and 1.814, respectively, suggesting that parameters from the probit and logit models should differ by a factor of about 1.8, a detail expanded upon in the next section.) Of course the variance of e_i, like the original parameters α_0 and α_1, can never be estimated: Information can be obtained only on the scaled parameters β_o and β_1. This diminishes, somewhat, the interpretability of numerical values of the parameters of logit and probit models. Finally, an important implicit assumption in the above derivation is that e_i can be treated as a random variable which is independent of X_i.

CLASSIFICATION OF PROBABILITY MODELS

Thus far, three distinct forms for the relationship between the likelihood of outcomes on a dichotomous dependent variable, Y, and a set of independent variables, X, were derived for a particular substantive problem, the linkage between attitudes of elites and citizens. This section of the chapter will focus on isolating and identifying those three models. Except for model 6.4, all the relations described above involved a single independent variable. The extension to models with several, say K, independent variables is straightforward in all three cases. It requires merely that the expression $\beta_o + \beta_1 X_1$ be replaced by the expanded form $\beta_o + \beta_1 X_1 + \beta_2 X_2 + \ldots + \beta_K X_K$, or simply $\Sigma \beta_k X_k$, where the summation is across $k = 0, 1, \ldots K$, and X_o is taken to be the constant 1.

The first of the three forms is represented by the equation pairs 6.2, 6.3, and 6.4. Each involves a simple linear relationship (for example, equation 6.2a) between the outcome probability and the exogenous variables. Accordingly, this form is called the *linear probability model*, and will be denoted LPM in what follows. It is important to note that the LPM also involves an inherent constraint on the parameters of the relationship (for example, equation 6.2b), which simply guarantees that P(Y) will lie in the zero-one interval no matter what values the independent variables assume. In some cases this constraint is of no particular concern, for example, 6.3b is quite innocuous. In other cases it may be an effective one that has important substantive interpretations: Relation 6.2b implies that an increase in the likelihood of support by the mayor cannot be greater than the accompanying increase in support by the citizenry, for example. In still other cases the constraint might well render this particular form uninteresting. In the representation example, X_1 was constrained to the zero-one interval, so β_1 could range from zero to one. In a different problem, if X_1 could assume values from, say, zero to 1000, then β_1 could not be larger than .001. And if X_1 is, in principle, unlimited, then β_1 is implicitly zero! Note that even writing down the constraint may be difficult for the general case with K independent variables, each of which can assume values in some particular range. Estimation of the LPM will be discussed shortly. It will be shown, for example, that OLS is not an appropriate estimator, in spite of the linearity of the model.

The second form is represented by equation 6.5. It also involves a linear specification of the choice probability, but unlike the LPM, it imposes no constraints on its parameters. Rather, it achieves consistency as a probability model by direct truncation of the linear form. Accordingly, we call it the *truncated linear probability model*, or TLPM. Its drawbacks are the implications of, first, the sharp kinks in the linear relationship at zero on the left and one on the right, and, second, the strong statement of certainty of outcomes on Y over potentially wide ranges of the data. But the biggest limitation of the TLPM is that there is no appropriate and convenient estimator for this model. As will be discussed, neither OLS nor any simple variant serves as an appropriate procedure.

The third form consists of two distinct specifications that we group together because of their similar sigmoid shapes and other characteristics. They are the *logit* specification, given by equation 6.6, and the *probit* model, represented by equation 6.7. Estimation of these models by two different procedures, methods termed "maximum likelihood" and "minimum chi-square," will be examined later.

Because the logistic and normal curves of equations 6.6 and 6.7 play a significant role in the discussion of this paper, it is worth considering their properties in greater detail at this stage. Although not all of the previous models were strictly linear, for example, equation 6.5 was only "piecewise" linear, these two specifications are distinctly nonlinear in that the magnitude of the effect from X_1 to P(Y) varies throughout the range of X_1. The linear function of X_{i1}, namely $\beta_o + \beta_1 X_{i1}$, appears as the argument in both functions. The role of β_o in both cases is to shift the sigmoid curve to the right (as β_0 increases) or left (as β_0 decreases) without changing its shape. And the role of β_1 in both is to make the curves sharper or flatter. As β_1 approaches zero, both sigmoid curves become horizontal lines as in Figure 6.1, and as it gets very large, both curves approach the step function illustrated in Figure 6.3. (Negative values of β_1 would simply reverse the direction of the sigmoid curve.) Thus both curves are seen to approach the null and pure MR models as limiting cases, the former when β_1 is very small and the latter when β_1 is very large. For intermediate values, P(Y) simply rises with X as per the PR model. But note that no set of values for the two parameters will yield the pure PR model even as a limiting case. And the nonlinearity of both models even masks the interpretation of specific numerical values of β_1: A value of one for β_1 in equations 6.6 and 6.7 does not represent the PR model.

As noted above, the curves depend on X_i only through the imbedded linear function. And, as with the other models, the logit and probit forms are readily generalized to include additional explanatory variables. Thus it is convenient to define $Z = \Sigma\beta_k X_k$ so that the curves can be written in abbreviated form as $\Lambda(Z)$ and $\Phi(Z)$. Clearly, changes in any X_k induce changes in Z that in turn induce changes in Λ and Φ. Table 6.1 illustrates the behavior of both curves. Note that both $\Lambda(Z)$ and $\Phi(Z)$ are exactly one-half at $Z = 0$. As Z increases from zero, both get larger but at increasingly slower rates, so that the curves approach, but never quite reach, the value one as Z gets infinitely large. (Values of 0.0000 and 1.0000 for $\phi(z)$ appear in the table only because of rounding.) The behavior for negative values of Z is symmetric: As Z decreases from zero the curves both decrease from one-half toward zero, approaching zero asymptotically as Z approaches negative infinity.

Although the two curves are described as being very similar, it is not true that $\Lambda(Z) = \Phi(Z)$ for all values of Z. Indeed, the curves cross at no more than three points, $Z = 0$ and perhaps at one point on either side of $Z = 0$, so that $\Lambda(Z)$ is steeper near $Z = 0$ and has "thicker tails" (is closer to one-half at extreme values of Z). But it is true that a constant, say c, can be found such that $\Lambda(cZ)$ is very close to $\Phi(Z)$ for all values of Z. Choice of that constant c depends on how "closeness of two curves" is defined and measured: A value $c = 1.6$ makes the curves agree very well near the center, $Z = 0$, and a value $c = 1.8$ improves the agreement further out in the tails. What this means is that if Logistic and Normal curves are both "fitted" to the same data, the values of all parameters, β_0, β_1, β_2, and so on will be larger for the logistic curve by roughly the same factor, c, in the range 1.5 to 2; the value of the factor will be close to 1.5 if the data are centered near $P(Y) = .5$ and it will be

TABLE 6.1
Illustrative Values of the Probit and Logit Curves

Z	ϕ (Z)	Λ (Z)	Z	ϕ (Z)	Λ (Z)
−6.0	0.0000	0.0025	0.0	0.5000	0.5000
−5.8	0.0000	0.0030	0.2	0.5793	0.5498
−5.6	0.0000	0.0037	0.4	0.6554	0.5987
−5.4	0.0000	0.0045	0.6	0.7257	0.6457
−5.2	0.0000	0.0055	0.8	0.7881	0.6900
−5.0	0.0000	0.0067	1.0	0.8413	0.7311
−4.8	0.0000	0.0082	1.2	0.8849	0.7685
−4.6	0.0000	0.0100	1.4	0.9192	0.8022
−4.4	0.0000	0.0121	1.6	0.9452	0.8320
−4.2	0.0000	0.0148	1.8	0.9641	0.8581
−4.0	0.0000	0.0180	2.0	0.9772	0.8808
−3.8	0.0001	0.0219	2.2	0.9861	0.9002
−3.6	0.0002	0.0266	2.4	0.9918	0.9168
−3.4	0.0003	0.0323	2.6	0.9953	0.9309
−3.2	0.0007	0.0392	2.8	0.9974	0.9427
−3.0	0.0013	0.0474	3.0	0.9987	0.9526
−2.8	0.0026	0.0573	3.2	0.9993	0.9608
−2.6	0.0047	0.0691	3.4	0.9997	0.9677
−2.4	0.0082	0.0832	3.6	0.9998	0.9734
−2.2	0.0139	0.0998	3.8	0.9999	0.9781
−2.0	0.0228	0.1192	4.0	1.0000	0.9820
−1.8	0.0359	0.1419	4.2	1.0000	0.9852
−1.6	0.0548	0.1680	4.4	1.0000	0.9879
−1.4	0.0808	0.1978	4.6	1.0000	0.9900
−1.2	0.1151	0.2315	4.8	1.0000	0.9918
−1.0	0.1587	0.2689	5.0	1.0000	0.9933
−0.8	0.2119	0.3100	5.2	1.0000	0.9945
−0.6	0.2743	0.3543	5.4	1.0000	0.9955
−0.4	0.3446	0.4013	5.6	1.0000	0.9963
−0.2	0.4207	0.4502	5.8	1.0000	0.9970
0.0	0.5000	0.5000	6.0	1.0000	0.9975

NOTE: ϕ is the normal CDF of the Probit Model and Λ is the logistic equation of the Logit Model. Z is the ordinate of both ϕ and Λ.

closer to 2 if the data are distributed further out in the tails (large positive or negative values of Z so that P(Y) is near 1 or 0 respectively).

ESTIMATION OF THE LINEAR PROBABILITY MODEL

This section treats methods for estimating the parameters of the first of the three probability forms, the LPM. It will be demonstrated that the obvious estimator, ordinary least squares (OLS), has certain disadvantages that can be overcome, to some extent, with a weighted least-squares (WLS) alternative. The analysis developed here will ignore the side constraint on the parameters, apparently in violation of the full specification of the model under consideration. But although it is true that taking the constraints into account could lead to an improved estimator, doing so is by no means easy. And failure to account for that constraint does not greatly affect the quality of the estimates obtained by the OLS and WLS procedures discussed here. A particular set of estimates may violate the constraints, but, if the specification of the model is correct, that occurs by chance alone and the violations can be essentially ignored without major consequence.

For ease of reference, the linear portion of the specification is repeated here in general form:

$$\begin{aligned} P(Y_i) &= \beta_o + \beta_1 X_{i1} + \ldots + \beta_K X_{iK} \\ &= \Sigma \beta_k X_{ik} \end{aligned} \quad [6.8]$$

(The implicit side constraint is that the β_k satisfy $0 \leqslant \Sigma\beta_k X_{ik} \leqslant 1$ for all possible values of the X_{ik}.) Recall that the expected value of a dichotomous (0,1) variable is its probability of a positive response. Thus,

$$E(Y_i) = P(Y_i = 1) = \Sigma\beta_k X_{ik}$$

Defining the "disturbance" term ε_i as the difference between an observation on Y and its expected value yields the "regression" equation

$$Y_i = \Sigma\beta_k X_{ik} + \varepsilon_i \quad [6.9]$$

Equation 6.9 is nothing more than a restatement of equation 6.8. But writing it in this form makes it apparent that OLS might serve as an estimation procedure for the parameters β_k.[3]

Although OLS may be a viable estimation technique, whether it is also a good estimator depends on certain conditions. Take all the values X_{ik}, for i ranging from 1 up to the sample size N and for k from 1 to the number of independent variables K, to be a set of fixed numbers.[4] Then those conditions can be stated as follows:

(1) Nonsingularity: Each X_{ik} exhibits variation across observations i, and the K independent variables are not perfectly collinear.
(2) Specification: The ε_i have zero expectation ($E(\varepsilon_i) = 0$).

(3) Homoscedasticity: The variance of ε_i is the same across all observations ($V(\varepsilon_i) = \sigma^2$).
(4) Independence: The covariance between any two observations on ε is zero ($Cov(\varepsilon_i,\varepsilon_j) = 0$ for i not equal to j).
(5) Normality: The ε_i are independently and identically distributed as Gaussian-normal random variates ($\varepsilon_i \sim IN(0,\sigma^2)$).

The first four of these constitute the standard "Gauss-Markov" assumptions and are conditions under which OLS yields estimates that are best, linear, and unbiased (BLUE). The purposes here are threefold. The first is to argue that the homoscedasticity and normality assumptions necessarily fail when the dependent variable is dichotomous. The second is to consider the consequences of this heteroscedasticity and nonnormality, namely that the estimates, though still unbiased, are unduly "noisy," and that standard methods of drawing inferences such as hypothesis tests are invalid. And the third is to suggest an alternative estimator, namely WLS, which dominates OLS for these problems.

It should be noted that the nonsingularity, specification, and independence assumptions are not an issue here; although they may or may not hold in a particular problem, there is nothing inherent in dichotomous dependent variable problems to make them particularly suspect.[5] Still, the specification assumption warrants brief discussion. If, as is assumed here, equation 6.8 is taken as the theoretical model, then the zero expectation of the disturbance term necessarily follows from its definition and equation 6.8. This does not suggest that the specification assumption can be taken lightly: It is indeed the key assumption of the model, and its failure will invalidate all of the results discussed here. In addition to linearity, equation 6.8 implies that the chosen set of K independent variables must be uncorrelated with any and all other factors affecting the outcome probabilities P(Y). This rules out the use of independent variables that are themselves the dependent variables in other, and related, equations (the simultaneous equations problem); it presumes that all independent variables are correctly measured (the errors in variables problem); and it presupposes that all relevant independent variables have been accounted for (the specification error problem).

The other two assumptions, homoscedasticity and normality, are not so easily dismissed. That both must fail is seen from observing the implicit dichotomous nature of the disturbance term. If Y_i can take on only two values, then, for given X_i, ε_i can likewise assume only two values:

$$\varepsilon_i = Y_i - \Sigma\beta_k X_{ik} = \begin{cases} 1 - \Sigma\beta_k X_{ik} & \text{if } Y_i = 1 \\ 0 - \Sigma\beta_k X_{ik} & \text{if } Y_i = 0 \end{cases}$$

Clearly, then, ε_i cannot be normally distributed, for a normal random variable can take on not just two values but any value on the real-number line. Less obviously, but just as certainly, ε_i is heteroscedastic. For notational ease, let $P_i = P(Y_i = 1)$ and $Q_i = P(Y_i = 0)$. Then,

$$P(\varepsilon_i = 1 - \Sigma\beta_k X_{ik}) = P_i = \Sigma\beta_k X_{ik}$$

and

$$P(\varepsilon_i = -\Sigma\beta_k X_{ik}) = Q_i = 1 - P_i = 1 - \Sigma\beta_k X_{ik}$$

From the definition of variance and because ε_i has a mean of zero, we obtain

$$\begin{aligned} V(\varepsilon_i) &= (1 - \Sigma\beta_k X_{ik})^2 P_i + (-\Sigma\beta_k X_{ik})^2 Q_i \\ &= Q_i^2 P_i + (-P_i)^2 Q_i = Q_i P_i (Q_i + P_i) \\ &= Q_i P_i (1 - P_i + P_i) = Q_i P_i. \end{aligned}$$

Thus

$$V(\varepsilon_i) = \Sigma\beta_k X_{ik}(1 - \Sigma\beta_k X_{ik}) \qquad [6.10]$$

Because $V(\varepsilon_i)$ varies with X_i and, by the nonsingularity assumption, X_i must indeed vary between observations, the variance is not constant.

It should be emphasized that failure of these two conditions is a direct consequence of the dichotomous nature of the dependent variable and cannot be avoided. Thus the Gauss-Markov result that OLS is efficient need not hold for these problems and the consequences must be examined. It happens that the OLS estimator is still linear and unbiased: Those characteristics follow from the definition of OLS and from the nonsingularity and specification assumptions alone. But failure of the homoscedasticity assumption means that OLS is not "best": Other estimators that exhibit smaller sampling variation are available. Furthermore, the standard formulas (that is, the formulas used in OLS computer packages) for computing estimates of the sampling variance are incorrect. Because those variance estimates are the ones used in the standard inference procedures of confidence intervals and hypothesis tests, the only useful result of the OLS procedure is the set of point estimates. Recall that the normality assumption is not required for OLS to be BLUE: The property gained by this assumption is the distributional result on the estimates that justifies the use of the standard t and F tests, and so forth. Because these tests are rendered invalid by the bias in OLS estimates of variance, no additional consequences follow from the failure of the normality assumption.

The serious disadvantages of OLS prompt a search for a better estimator. Multiply equation 6.9 by arbitrary constants, say W_i, i = 1, . . . , N, to obtain

$$(W_iY_i) = \Sigma\beta_k(W_iX_{ik}) + (W_i\varepsilon_i)$$

or, with the implicit redefinition of variables Y^*, X^* and ε^*,

$$Y_i^* = \Sigma\beta_kX_{ik}^* + \varepsilon_i^* \qquad [6.11]$$

The variance of ε_i^* is given by the variance of ε_i multiplied by the square of W_i. Thus if W_i is chosen as the reciprocal of the standard deviation of ε_i, then ε_i^* has a variance that is equal to one and, more importantly, that is constant across observations. Apparently, then, one could apply OLS to this transformed equation and the result, given that all of the Gauss-Markov assumptions are now satisfied, would be an estimator that is BLUE. This estimation procedure is called weighted least-squares (WLS).[6]

The difficulty with the suggestion given above is that the required standard deviation of ε_i depends on the β_k (see equation 6.10), which are unknown. But recall that OLS provides unbiased estimates of the β_k. So one could apply least squares as a first step to obtain estimates of the β_k, use these to compute the needed values of W_i, and then proceed as directed above.[7] The statistical consequence of using estimated weights is of some concern. In this case, the variance of ε_i^* will not be precisely one and the WLS correction will not be totally effective. Although at an intuitive level one would presume the WLS procedure, even with estimated weights, would outperform OLS, the only analytic result on this issue involves "large sample" approximations. If the estimates of β_k, which are used in the construction of W_i, have the statistical property of consistency (and the OLS estimates in this case do) then BLUE results hold but only as an approximation that assumes (and gets better in) large samples. Experience with the WLS estimator in these problems suggests the results are actually better than that—so long as the LPM specification is correct, the WLS procedure does seem to outperform OLS and the inferences drawn using standard procedures seem appropriate even in moderately sized samples of, say, N = 50.

Note that the WLS procedure does not correct for nonnormality, so such things as t and F statistics are not guaranteed to behave the way theory says they would under normality, and inferences are still questionable. But a version of the central limit theorem shows that inferences based on the normality assumption will still hold as approximations that tend to be quite good when the sample is large. Coincidentally, that is precisely the case when the use of estimated weights is justified. It is thus the case that WLS does overcome the limitations associated with OLS, with the added proviso that it should be used with due caution when the sample size is quite small.[8]

It is convenient to summarize the application of WLS to the linear probability model at this stage (the steps will be illustrated in detail). First note that three of the conditions listed above must hold for WLS to yield useful results. They are the nonsingularity, specification and independence assumptions. Estimation proceeds as follows:

Step 1: Regress Y_i on the K independent variables X_{i1} through X_{ik} to obtain the OLS estimates, say, b_o through b_K.

Step 2: Form the "weight" W_i according to $W_i = [(\Sigma b_k X_{ik})(1 - \Sigma b_k X_{ik})]^{-1/2}$. Note that this weight is the reciprocal of the square root of the estimate of the variance of ε_i given in equation 6.10. Because OLS estimates b_k may violate the side constraint on the parameter by chance even if the specification is correct, some computed values of $\Sigma b_k X_{ik}$ may be outside the interval from zero to one. That means W_i cannot be computed for those observations from the above formula cited above. A solution often used in practice is to simply truncate $\Sigma b_k X_{ik}$ at, say, .99 and .01, yielding $W_i = 10.05$, for the problematic observations. Of course frequent occurrence of the problem should lead one to question the specification of the model.

Step 3: Multiply each variable in the model, including the constant term, X_{io}, by W_i to create "transformed" variables, viz. $Y_i^* = W_i Y_i$ and $X_{ik}^* = W_i X_{ik}$ for $k = 0, 1, \ldots, K$.

Step 4: Regress Y_i^* on the set of $(K + 1)$ independent variables X_{io}^* through X_{ik}^* with the intercept suppressed. Note that the coefficient of the variable X_{io}^* is to be interpreted as the estimate of the constant term.[9]

Step 5: Inference now proceeds as in OLS. For example, the t-ratios formed as the ratio of coefficient estimates to their standard errors serve for testing hypotheses regarding the effect of the corresponding independent variables on P(Y). Note, however, that the coefficient of determination (R^2) obtained in the final step is of limited use: It measures the proportion of the variance of the transformed variable, Y^*, which is explained by the independent variables, but the variable of interest is the original Y.[10]

Empirical Example of the Linear Probability Model

The discussion returns to the problem posed by Powell and Powell to present estimates of the LPM for two different issues. The two issues considered are whether housing subsidies should be increased and whether farm price supports should be increased. Note that the estimates presented here are original; Powell and Powell relied on descriptive measures of the data to draw conclusions regarding the role of proportional representation. By these means, they argued that the farm issue was a nearly perfect PR-type issue, but they suggest a modified PR rule for housing subsidies. The PR issue is reexamined here by fitting the LPM to their data.

The independent variable X_1 (the proportion of the citizenry supporting the issue) is reported as a ten-point scale, collapsing the support of the electorate into deciles. (Thus $X_{i1} = 4$ means that between 40% and 49% of the citizens support the issue in city i.) The dependent variable is dichotomous; $Y_i = 0$ if the mayor in city i does not support the issue and $Y_i = 1$ if (s)he does. Columns 1, 2, and 3 of Table 6.4 contain the data in crosstabular form. (Other columns in that table will be explained below.) Note that preparation for entry in a standard computer package would require "stretching" the data out as 48 observations, even though sets of observations are identical in all respects.

Table 6.2 contains estimates of an assumed linear relationship (the LPM) between the position of the mayor and support by the electorate on the two issues. Results for each issue include estimates by two different procedures (OLS and WLS) for each of two different specifications (with $K = 1$ and $K = 2$).

OLS as applied to the LPM yields estimates that are of some interest in their own right, but its primary role here is as the first stage of the WLS procedure. OLS coefficient estimates are used to form the weights as described in Step 2 above. For example, in the one independent variable specification for the farm price support issue, the weights are computed as

$$W_i = \left\{[.097 + .113X_{i1}][1 - (.097 + .113X_{i1})]\right\}^{-1/2}.$$

Y_i and X_{i1} are then multiplied by W_i to yield Y_i^* and X_{i1}^* of step 3, and Y_i^* is regressed on W_i and X_{i1}^* with no intercept in step 4. The resulting WLS estimates, an intercept of .132 and an X_{i1} coefficient of .108 in this example, appear below the corresponding OLS estimates in Table 6.2.

Several features alluded to in the previous discussion are worth noting. First, these estimates rely heavily on the LPM specification: If it fails,

TABLE 6.2
OLS and WLS Estimates of the Linear Probability Model for Proportional Representation Data

A. *Farm Price Supports:*

(1) Two-Independent Variable Specification

		Constant		X_1		X_2		u	F
OLS:	Y =	.105	+	.108 X_1	+	.025 X_2	+	u	F (2,45) = 6.17
(st. error)		(.154)		(.058)		(.263)		(.457)	
(t ratio)		(0.68)		(1.86)		(0.10)			
WLS:	Y =	.144	+	.097 X_1	+	.077 X_2	+	u	F (2,45) = 24.4
(st. error)		(.114)		(.043)		(.261)		(1.02)	
(t ratio)		(1.26)		(2.26)		(0.29)			

(2) One-Independent Variable Specification

		Constant		X_1		u	F
OLS:	Y =	.097	+	.113 X_1	+	u	F (1,46) = 12.6
(st. error)		(.126)		(.032)		(.452)	
(t ratio)		(0.77)		(3.55)			
WLS:	Y =	.132	+	.108 X_1	+	u	F (1,46) = 49.7
(st. error)		(.099)		(.015)		(1.00)	
(t ratio)		(1.34)		(7.05)			

$H_0: \beta_0 = 0\ \beta_1 = .1,$ F (2,46) = 8.41

B. *Housing Subsidies:*

(1) Two-Independent Variable Specification

		Constant		X_1		X_2		u	F
OLS:	Y =	.089	+	.127 X_1	+	.150 X_2	+	u	F (2,45) = 17.4
(st. error)		(.078)		(.036)		(.227)		(.375)	
(t ratio)		(0.68)		(1.86)		(0.10)			
WLS:	Y =	.126	+	.081 X_1	+	.361 X_2	+	u	F (2,45) = 71.4
(st. error)		(.059)		(.033)		(.196)		(1.00)	
(t ratio)		(2.13)		(2.48)		(1.84)			

(2) One-Independent Variable Specification

		Constant		X_1		u	F
OLS:	Y =	.074	+	.144 X_1	+	u	F (1,46) = 34.8
(st. error)		(.074)		(.025)		(.373)	
(t ratio)		(0.99)		(5.90)			
WLS:	Y =	.105	+	.124 X_1	+	u	F (1,46) = 86.1
(st. error)		(.057)		(.013)		(1.03)	
(t ratio)		(1.86)		(9.28)			

$H_0: \beta_0 = 0\ \beta_1 = .1,$ F (2,46) = 9.60

NOTE: Y is support of the issue by the mayor (1 = yes, 2 = no), X_1 is support by the citizens (on a scale from 0 to 10), and X_2 is 0 when X_1 is less than 5 and 1 when X_1 is 5 or greater. The sample size is 48.

then the estimates are of questionable use. Evidence on this matter will be discussed below. Second, there should not be large differences between OLS and WLS coefficient estimates, given that both are unbiased under the LPM assumptions, and indeed the differences are uniformly small. It is somewhat surprising that the coefficient of X_1 is always smaller under WLS than under OLS: This point will also be expanded upon below. Third, the heteroscedasticity of the error term makes the standard errors and t and F ratios associated with the OLS estimates all biased and thus of little interest. They are reported here only for the sake of comparison. In contrasting OLS estimates with the adjacent WLS estimates on the same model, note that the standard errors of WLS estimates are always smaller, as expected.[11] Fourth, the entry in parentheses under the error term u is the "root mean square error" (RMSE) and is an estimate of the standard deviation of the disturbance term. The interpretation of this term is unclear under OLS, because it amounts to using a constant to estimate a nonconstant variance. Under WLS, each observation has been weighted by an estimate of the reciprocal of the disturbance's standard error, so the resulting weighted disturbance has a standard deviation of approximately 1. Thus to observe that all RMSE entries reported for WLS are approximately 1 is comforting: A value dramatically different from one would add to suspicions of the specification of the model. Finally, because R^2 is of questionable use in these models, it is not reported here (see footnote 10). Instead, the table contains the F-ratio for testing the overall fit of the model, and of course it is of use for only the WLS equations.

Examination of Table 6.2 reveals the following substantive points, in line with Step 5 of the WLS procedure outlined above. Positive signs on all coefficients of X_1 and X_2 support the claim of a positive relationship between support of the citizenry and the position of the mayor. In comparing the PR and MR theories, the first set of estimates (involving both X_1 and X_2) for each issue is the relevant one. The pure MR hypothesis is clearly rejected by the data for both issues. Under it, the coefficient pattern should be (0, 0, 1). But in both issues the estimate of β_1 (.097 and .081) is significantly different from zero, and in the farm issue the WLS estimate of the X_2 coefficient is only .077, far below one and not even significantly different from zero. In the housing issue, there is more evidence of a majority-rule effect, but it is still small, and the contradiction between the inferences one would draw from OLS and WLS is peculiar. Because of the questionable role of MR as measured by X_2, each relationship was reestimated with X_2 omitted. The PR hypothesis fares somewhat better than MR, though again the pure model is rejected. The hypothesized pure PR model is $Y = 0 + .1X_1 + u$. Under both issues the estimated intercept and slope coefficients are significantly larger than 0 and .1 respectively: As reported in Table 6.2, the F statistics for this hypothesis are 8.41 and 9.6.

Of more interest for the purposes here is the question of whether the LPM serves to explain the data well. The answer is no. The most disturbing result is that coefficient estimates place the predicted probability of a mayor's support above one for a significant range on X_1. Columns 5 and 6 of Table 6.4 (below) contain the relevant probability estimates ($P(Y_i) = \Sigma b_k X_{ik}$, where b_k is the OLS and WLS estimate, respectively, of β_k) from the LPM specification with one independent variable. For both issues, note the implication that whenever the degree of public support exceeds about 80% the estimated probability of the mayor's support is *greater than one*. This is because the side constraint on the coefficients, which is an inherent part of the LPM, is violated by the reported estimates for both issues. (In the one-independent variable specification with X_1 ranging from 0 to 10, that constraint is $0 \leqslant \beta_0 \leqslant 1$ and $0 \leqslant \beta_0 + 10\beta_1 \leqslant 1$.) As noted earlier, small violations would be of little concern, for they might well arise as a chance occurrence due to sampling error: The paucity of observations at high values of X_1 would contribute to the suggested sampling error in these examples. But the violations in the cases here are large, and the fact that the same pattern arises with both issues makes it harder to dismiss as random chance.

The conclusions we draw from the results discussed here are as follows. First, in a qualitative sense only, the pattern of the relationship is reasonably well captured by OLS estimation: Increases in support of the citizenry for an issue tend to be associated with increases in support of the mayor, and most of that effect exhausts itself over low levels of citizenry support (10%–60%). Second, stronger quantitative statements cannot be gleaned from this linear model. Evidence contrary to the LPM specification is too strong for firm reliance on it, meaning that rigorous statistical statements regarding the relationship and quantitative predictions of probabilities are not justified. Related remarks on this issue will be offered later in the chapter.

Estimation of Truncated Linear Probability Models

The second form for probability specifications depicted earlier, the "truncated linear probability model" (TLPM), is written in general form as

$$P(Y_i = 1) = \begin{cases} 0 & \text{if} \quad \Sigma\beta_k X_{ik} < 0 \\ \Sigma\beta_k X_{ik} & \text{if} \quad 0 \leqslant \Sigma\beta_k X_{ik} < 1 \\ 1 & \text{if} \quad 1 \leqslant \Sigma\beta_k X_{ik} \end{cases} \qquad [6.12]$$

Our discussion of it will be short and mostly negative. The linearity of the intermediate segment of $P(Y_i)$ makes it appear that OLS might serve as a viable estimator, just as it did in the previous LPM. But careful reflection reveals an important difference between the LPM and the TLPM in terms of the implicit regression equation. In the LPM, $P(Y_i)$ is equal to $\Sigma\beta_k X_{ik}$ across the entire range on X. Thus $\Sigma\beta_k X_{ik}$ is everywhere interpreted as $E(Y_i)$ and the definition of ε_i as $(Y_i - \Sigma\beta_k X_{ik})$ guarantees that assumption ii (specification) must hold:

$$E(\varepsilon_i) = E(Y_i - \Sigma\beta_k X_{ik}) = E(Y_i - E(Y_i)) = E(Y_i) - E(Y_i) = 0$$

In the TLPM, however, $P(Y_i)$ equals $\Sigma\beta_k X_{ik}$ over only a limited range on X. When $\Sigma\beta_k X_{ik}$ exceeds one, then $P(Y_i) = 1$, so $E(Y_i) = 1 < \Sigma\beta_k X_{ik}$, and for such observations $E(\varepsilon_i)$ is necessarily negative:

$$E(\varepsilon_i) = E(Y_i - \Sigma\beta_k X_{ik}) = E(Y_i) - E(\Sigma\beta_k X_{ik}) = 1 - \Sigma\beta_k X_{ik} < 0$$

And when $\Sigma\beta_k X_{ik}$ is negative a symmetric argument shows that $E(\varepsilon_i)$ is greater than zero. So a necessary implication of the TLPM is that the disturbance term in the regression equation as usually defined must necessarily violate the specification assumption of OLS.

The consequence of a failure of the specification assumption is that OLS estimates will be biased: Estimates of the β_k will not be "centered" about the true values. In this case, it is easy to find the direction of the bias. When the "true" $\Sigma\beta_k X_{ik}$ exceeds one, Y_i will be 1 (for certain), which is less than $\Sigma\beta_k X_{ik}$, so OLS will attempt to better fit this data by pulling the estimate of $\Sigma\beta_k X_{ik}$ down. And when $\Sigma\beta_k X_{ik}$ is negative, Y_i will be zero (for certain), so OLS will pull the estimate of $\Sigma\beta_k X_{ik}$ up. Thus the estimate of $\Sigma\beta_k X_{ik}$ will be closer to zero than the true value at either extreme; in turn, this means that each individual coefficient estimate (except perhaps the intercept term) will "tend" to be closer to zero than the true value.

This problem of biased coefficient estimates is generally of considerably more concern than the consequences of heteroscedasticity and nonnormality encountered in the LPM. But note that those same two problems arise in the TLPM as well, for similar reasons. That is, the

TLPM *inherently* violates three of the standard assumptions of OLS, specification, homoscedasticity and normality. And there is no easy correction for this combination of problems. In particular, if one applied WLS to correct for heteroscedasticity, the bias caused by the violation of the specification assumption would become more severe! The reason is that WLS applies the most weight to observations with extreme values of $\Sigma \beta_k X_{ik}$, and these are the values that cause the distortion described above. See Step 2 of the WLS procedure description given earlier, and note that values of $\Sigma b_k X_{ik}$ above one or below zero would be due to more than chance occurrence.

The OLS and WLS results on the LPM in Table 6.2 illustrate the problems discussed above. Suppose that a TLPM is a better description of the true relationship between elite and citizen support than is the LPM. Then coefficients of X_1 greater than .1 would not be unexpected. But as noted above, the true TLPM coefficient values would be underestimated by OLS, and, more to the point, WLS would make the downward bias even more severe. That is, under the TLPM scenario, WLS estimates are expected to be lower than OLS estimates, exactly as observed in both of the issues reported in Table 6.2. This evidence, along with the severe violation of the parameter constraint, would seem to suggest that the true relationship is better reflected by the TLPM specification than by the LPM. But the earlier noted substantive objections to the TLPM and the lack of a feasible estimation procedure for it lead us to reject both forms in favor of the probit and logit models to be illustrated in the next section.

Maximum Likelihood Estimation of the Nonlinear Probability Specifications

Here, a method is considered for estimating the two nonlinear specifications for probabilities introduced earlier, namely the logit and probit models described by equations 6.6 and 6.7, respectively. Because the procedures are identical in nearly all respects for both models except for the specification of choice probabilities, they are here treated in parallel, with any essential differences noted.

Estimation requires a sample of observations on Y and X. Suppose there are N observations in the sample, that the observations on X can be regarded as fixed numbers (nonrandom), and that the sample is random. Then observations on the N values of Y_i, $i = 1, 2, \ldots, N$, are independent, and the joint probability of observing this set of N values is given by the product of the N individual probabilities, $P(Y_i)$. According to either of the models, these individual probabilities depend on the values of the parameters β_k, for $k = 1, \ldots, K$, so the joint probability of the entire sample also depends on these parameters. One might ask the question: "What values of these parameters would have made the realized observations on Y_i the most likely?"

Posing and answering the question asked above in a very careful and rigorous way leads to the method of estimation called "Maximum Likelihood" (ML). Specifically, it amounts to specifying the "Likelihood Function," which is simply the joint probability described immediately above but interpreted as being a function of the unknown parameters. The form of this likelihood function depends on the a priori assumption regarding the form of probabilities of outcomes on the dependent variable Y: The logistic form of equation 6.6 leads to one likelihood function and the unit normal cdf of equation 6.7 leads to another. For a given sample of data, the value of the likelihood function will depend on only the values of the parameters of that function, namely the parameters β_k in the cases considered here. The ML estimates are those values of the K parameters that yield the largest value of the likelihood function.[12]

Details of the ML estimator are beyond the scope of this chapter. But it is important to note that, because of the degree of nonlinearity of the probit and logit specifications, the procedure does not lead to a simple formula for expressing the estimates as a function of the observed data, as does OLS in the linear model. Rather, computation of the estimates requires an "iterative maximization algorithm." Such a procedure (two of many procedures are Newton-Rapheson and Davidon-Fletcher-Powell) starts with an initial guess about the parameter values and cycles (iterates) through a repetitive series of steps to make improvements in the guess until no further improvements are possible (the iterations converge). These calculations are too lengthy to make hand-calculation feasible. But, just as there exist a number of computer programs for computing OLS estimates, computer routines for obtaining ML estimates by these iterative procedures for the two specifications of interest here are widely available. And though they do involve more computation, seldom do the costs (in machine time or dollars) for ML estimation of probit or logit exceed the costs of a comparably sized OLS problem by more than a factor of two or three.

Not surprisingly, certain assumptions are required for ML to yield acceptable answers in logit and probit.[13] Those assumptions are as follows:

(1) Nonsingularity: Each X_{ik} exhibits variation across observations i, $i = 1, \ldots, N$, and the K independent variables are not perfectly collinear.

(2) Specification: The probability that the dependent variable Y_i takes on the value 1 is given by the logit model of equation (6.6) (or the probit model of equation 6.7) for each $i = 1, 2, \ldots, N$.

(3) Independence: The realizations on Y_i are independent across observations.

Careful inspection will reveal an exact analogy between these assumptions and those required for WLS estimation of the linear probability model. The nonsingularity assumption is identical; the specification assumption reflects the appropriate substitution for the hypothesized model; and the independence assumption is essentially the same in both procedures. A difference that is purely superficial is that the assumptions for the LPM are conveniently stated in terms of the disturbance term. But in ML there is no need to define a disturbance (the procedure involves maximizing a likelihood rather than minimizing a sum of squared disturbances), so the assumptions are phrased in terms of Y_i itself.

Under assumptions 1–3, ML on either a logit or a probit model yields estimates with the statistical properties of consistency, asymptotic efficiency, and asymptotic normality. As with WLS on the LPM (and use of OLS whenever the normality assumption does not hold), these properties are "large sample" ones. What this means is that, so long as the sample is reasonably large, the estimator is approximately unbiased, no other unbiased estimator has smaller sampling variance, and the usual results of normal sampling theory (behavior of t and F ratios, and so forth) apply reasonably well. As an answer to the question of when is a sample large enough, we suggest 25 or more observations per coefficient as a rule of thumb.[14]

When the assumptions do not hold, these properties are not guaranteed; the consequences are similar to those for OLS in the linear model. Failure of the nonsingularity assumption means that estimates cannot be computed, and "near" singularity leads to the same multicollinearity problems of instable estimates and large sampling variances as in OLS. The specification assumption is of course crucial and its violation will generally lead to biased estimates. As in OLS, it will be violated when variables are measured with error, relevant exogenous variables are omitted, or when the "exogenous" variables include one or more that is in fact endogenous as in a simultaneous equations model. Robinson (1982) has demonstrated that the estimators considered here remain consistent when the independence assumption is violated, but efficiency is lost (though the efficient alternative is not tractible) and the usual formulas for estimates of estimator variance are incorrect. Robinson et al. (1984) provide a test for independence in the probit model.

Given the availability of appropriate computer software, implementation of ML on logit or probit problems is very similar to use of regression packages. And the nature of the output from those packages is quite similar. The package should produce estimates of the coefficients, standard errors for those coefficient estimates, and various other statistics. As in regression, the ratio of the coefficient estimate to its standard error can be interpreted as a t statistic, under the hypothesis that the true value of that coefficient is zero. As an example of its use, to test the (null) hypothesis that an exogenous variable has no effect on Y, one would compare the t-ratio of its coefficient to a critical value of t chosen from a table of the t-distribution, rejecting the null when the computed t exceeds the critical value.

Other means of drawing particular inferences are likewise similar to OLS. In particular, the analogue of the F tests of regression (for testing the overall fit of the model or for joint hypotheses on sets of coefficients) is the likelihood ratio test. Most logit and probit programs will report the overall χ^2 statistic, which follows a chi-square distribution with K degrees of freedom under the null hypothesis that all K coefficients (not counting the intercept) are zero. To implement the test for arbitrary hypotheses, the model is estimated twice, once with the constraints of the null hypothesis imposed (for example, the relevant subset of independent variables omitted) and once without these constraints (for example, with all variables included). Let L_0 be the reported value of the logarithm of the likelihood from the first of these estimation passes (that is, under the null hypothesis, H_0) and let L_a be its value from the second (under H_a). Then $C = [-2(L_0 - L_a)]$ is the required statistic and it follows a chi-square distribution with degrees of freedom equal to the number of constraints on coefficients implied by the null hypothesis (relative to the alternative). (See Maddala, 1977: 43-44, 179-180 and Aldrich and Nelson, 1984: 54-60 for more details.) Although the range of test statistics parallels those available for the linear model, attempts to construct goodness-of-fit measures have not been so successful. Several formulas for pseudo-R^2 have been proposed (see Aldrich and Nelson, 1984: 56-59), but they suffer serious disadvantages. There is no consensus on which of the several measures to use, and given that the distribution of values assumed by the measures varies across definitions and differs from the familiar regression case, interpretation is difficult. Accordingly, we recommend against heavy reliance on such descriptive statistics and suggest instead greater use of t and chi-square statistics to assess the goodness of fit of the model to the data.

The major difference between the estimates obtained from these models and from the LPM is in interpretation. As noted earlier, the quantitative interpretation of the coefficients is more delicate. In practice it is often helpful to present the results in tabular form, listing computed probabilities for various values of the exogenous variables.

An Alternative Estimation Procedure for Logit with Repeated Observations

When the sample available for a particular problem contains no replications, that is, when for each distinct observation on X there is a single (or very few) observation on the dependent variable Y, then the only readily available estimation procedure for probit and logit models is maximum likelihood, as discussed in the last section. But when the data are "replicated," that is when for each distinct observation on X there are several (say more than five) observations on Y, then an alternative and computationally easier estimator is available. It is described here for the case of the logit model. A probit version is available as well but, mostly for historical reasons, is seldom employed.

Define Z_i as $Z_i = \Sigma\beta_k X_{ik}$ so that equation 6.6 may be rewritten as

$$P(Y_i = 1) = \exp(Z_i)/[1 + \exp(Z_i)]$$

and note that $P(Y_i = 0)$ is then given by

$$P(Y_i = 0) = 1 - P(Y_i = 1) = 1/[1 + \exp(Z_i)]$$

Then the natural logarithm of the "odds ratio" is seen to be

$$\log\left[\frac{P(Y_i = 1)}{P(Y_i = 0)}\right] = \log\left[\frac{\exp(Z_i)/[1 + \exp(Z_i)]}{1/[1 + \exp(Z_i)]}\right] = \log[\exp(Z_i)] = Z_i$$

So this log-odds has a particularly simple form that can be used to great advantage.

Let M be the number of distinct values of X, so the observation index, i, runs from 1 to M. With replicated data there will be several, say n_i, readings (replications) on Y at each observation i. Let n_{1i} represent the number of these that correspond to positive observations ($Y = 1$) and n_{oi} be the number corresponding to negative observations ($Y = 0$), so $n_{1i} + n_{oi} = n_i$. Define p_i and q_i as the relative frequency of positive and negative observations respectively ($p_i = n_{1i}/n_i$ and $q_i = 1 - p_i = n_{oi}/n_i$). Then the "observed logit" can be defined as

$$\ell_i = \log[p_i/q_i] = \log[n_{1i}/n_{oi}] \qquad [6.13]$$

Since p_i is an estimate of $P(Y = 1)$, and q_i is an estimate of $P(Y = 0)$, this observed logit is an estimate of the "true logit" or log-odds defined above.[15] Let the difference between the two be represented by the error term ε_i. Then the relationship can be written as

$$\ell_i = Z_i + \varepsilon_i = \Sigma \beta_k X_{ik} + \varepsilon_i \qquad [6.14]$$

Equation 6.14 reveals the advantage of the log-odds transformation. It expresses a simple transformation of the dependent variable as a linear function of the independent variables. One is tempted to apply least squares to this model to estimate the β_k. Unfortunately, the error term ε_i does not have constant variance, so OLS is not the most efficient estimator. It can be shown that for large n_i the variance of ε_i is closely approximated by the reciprocal of the quantity $n_i P(Y = 1)P(Y = 0)$. Given that n_i is observed, and the other two factors are estimated by p_i and q_i, it is easy to form an estimate of this variance. That suggests the possibility of applying weighted least squares, and indeed this is the estimator that was the goal of this section. It has come to be known by two different names, "Berkson-Theil WLS" after its earliest proponents,[16] and "Minimum Chi-Square Logit." The latter name, abbreviated as min-χ^2 below, follows from the fact that the estimator can be derived from a quite different estimation principle, one based on minimization of a statistic that, under certain conditions, follows a chi-square distribution.

It is useful to summarize the assumptions required of this estimation procedure and the details of its implementation. The three basic assumptions have been encountered before. They are nonsingularity, specification, and independence. The specification assumption refers specifically to the functional form of the choice probabilities as given by equation 6.6; the other two are self explanatory. In addition to these assumptions, the method requires a large number of replications. Although M, the number of distinct observations on X, can be small (but no smaller than K + 2), n_i, the number of replications on Y corresponding to X_i, should be large for *each* $i = 1, \ldots, M$.

Implementation proceeds as follows:

Step 1: Compute the dependent variable ℓ_i as per equation 6.13 shown above. Note that these observed logits cannot be computed if either n_{1i} or n_{oi} are zero (p_i or q_i are zero), so use of this procedure requires a large number of replications at each observation to insure against this outcome. As a practical solution, replacing zero values of p_i and q_i by a small number, say .0001, will often allow effective use of the estimator, provided those zero values are infrequent.

Step 2: Compute the weights according to:[17]

$$W_i = (n_i p_i q_i)^{1/2}$$

Step 3: Estimate the coefficients by applying weighted least squares to the model given by equation 6.14. That is, regress $(W_i \ell_i)$ on W_i and

(W_iX_{ik}), for k = 1, . . . , K, with no intercept term. The coefficient of W_i is to be interpreted as the intercept, β_0.

Step 4: Conduct statistical inference as one would in regression analysis. In particular, t and F ratios are used just as they are in OLS. If predicted probabilities are needed, they must be computed from equation 6.6, after replacing the β_k by their estimated values. Note that, as above, the R^2 obtained from this regression will be of limited use. We continue to suggest ignoring it.

Empirical Examples of Probit and Logit Model Estimation

Once again, the data of Powell and Powell are used to illustrate the proposed estimation techniques for probit and logit. Table 6.3 contains results for both of the issues, farm price supports and housing subsidies, and includes ML estimates for the probit model and both ML and min-χ^2 estimates of the logit model. There are four relations represented in the table: For each of two issues there are two specifications, one with both X_1 and X_2 included as independent variables (K = 2) and one with only X_1 (K = 1). Thus equation A-1 in Table 6.3, for example, is for farm price supports using two independent variables. As in Table 6.2, the reported results include the coefficient estimates in equation form, the associated standard errors and t-ratios, and a test statistic for the overall fit of the model. For each of the four relations in the table, the three sets of results are written in different formats to emphasize the difference in techniques and models. The ML procedure maximizes a probability, so results for probit and logit ML are written in probability form with Φ and Λ (see equations 6.7 and 6.6, respectively) reflecting the difference in functional form. The min-χ^2 estimator, on the other hand, utilizes a log-odds transformation to produce a regression equation, so it is written in regression form.

The original data and estimates of the probabilities based on coefficient estimates for the various models appear in Table 6.4. These estimated probabilities are obtained as follows, using the farm price support issue and X_1 = 1 (citizen support between 10% and 19%) as an example. From Table 6.3, the probit coefficients for the one independent variable model of farm price supports are −1.19 and .340. Inserting these values into equation 6.7 yields

$$P(Y) = \Phi(-1.19 + .340X_1) = \Phi(-1.19 + .340(1)) = \Phi(-.85) = .198$$

(The number −.85 is a z-score, i.e., a value of a standardized normal variable. Use of a table for cumulative standard normal probabilities

TABLE 6.3
Estimates of Logit and Probit Models for Proportional Representation Data

A. *Farm Price Supports:* (N = 48, M = 8)						
(1) Two-Variable Specification						
Probit ML:	$P(Y) = \phi$ (	−1.20	$+ .348X_1$	$- .039X_2$)		χ^2 (2) = 11.49
(st. error)		(.507)	(.188)	(.767)		
(t ratio)		(−2.37)	(1.85)	(−.505)		
Logit ML:	$P(Y) = \Lambda$ (	−2.03	$+ .594X_1$	$- .132X_2$)		χ^2 (2) = 11.48
(st. error)		(.920)	(.333)	(1.29)		
(t ratio)		(2.21)	(1.78)	(−.102)		
Logit Min $-\chi^2$:	$l =$	−1.11	$+ .287X_1$	$.466X_2$	+ u	F (2, 5) = 3.28
(st. error)		(.689)	(.257)	(.949)	(.721)	
(t ratio)		(−1.61)	(1.12)	(0.49)		
(2) One-Variable Specification						
Probit ML:	$P(Y) = \phi$ (	−1.19	$+ .340X_1$)			χ^2 (1) = 11.49
(st. error)		(.408)	(.111)			
(t ratio)		(−2.74)	(3.07)			
Logit ML:	$P(Y) = \Lambda$ (	−1.98	$+ .565X_1$)			χ^2 (2) = 11.47
(st. error)		(.720)	(.197)			
(t ratio)		(−2.74)	(2.87)			
Logit Min $-\chi^2$:	$l =$	−1.31	$+ .387X_1$	+ u		F (2, 6) = 7.08
(st. error)		(5.18)	(.146)	(.681)		
(t ratio)		(−2.53)	(2.66)			
B. *Housing Subsidies:* (N = 48, M = 7)						
(1) Two-Variable Specification						
Probit ML:	$P(Y) = \phi$ (	−1.34	$+ .427X_1$	$+ 3.50X_2$)		χ^2 (2) = 25.07
(st. error)		(.357)	(.148)	(28.8)		
(t ratio)		(−3.75)	(2.88)	(0.12)		
Logit ML:	$P(Y) = \Lambda$ (	−2.30	$+ .730X_1$	$+ 9.36X_2$)		χ^2 (2) = 25.11
(st. error)		(.686)	(.265)	(63.6)		
(t ratio)		(−3.36)	(2.75)	(0.15)		
Logit Min $-\chi^2$:	$l =$	−2.19	$+ .712X_1$	$+ 2.52X_2$	+ u	F (2, 4) = 17.77
(st. error)		(.340)	(.135)	(1.99)	(.501)	
(t ratio)		(−6.44)	(5.26)	(1.26)		
(2) One-Variable Specification						
Probit ML:	$P(Y) = \phi$ (	−1.44	$+ .508X_1$)			χ^2 (1) = 23.68
(st. error)		(.352)	(.126)			
(t ratio)		(−4.09)	(4.03)			
Logit ML:	$P(Y) = \Lambda$ (	−2.51	$+ .868X_1$)			χ^2 (2) = 23.66
(st. error)		(.693)	(.237)			
(t ratio)		(−3.62)	(3.66)			
Logit Min $-\chi^2$:	$l =$	−2.26	$+ .758X_1$	+ u		F (1, 5) = 30.86
(st. error)		(.353)	(.136)	(.525)		
(t ratio)		(−6.40)	(5.55)			

NOTE: Y is support of the issue by the mayor (1 = yes, 0 = no), X_1 is support by the citizens (on a scale from 0 to 10), and X_2 is 0 when X_1 is less than 5 and 1 when X_1 is 5 or greater.

yields the probability of .198 corresponding to this z-score.) Similarly, the logit ML coefficients of −1.98 and .565 from Table 6.3, when inserted into equation 6.6, yield the column 8 entry for $X_1 = 1$:

$$P(Y) = \exp(-1.98 + .565X_1)/[1 + \exp(-1.98 + .565X_1)] = .195$$

And the logit min-χ^2 coefficients of −1.31 and .387, likewise inserted into equation 6.6, yield the column 9 entry of

$$P(Y) = \exp(-1.31 + .387X_1)/[1 + \exp(-1.31 + .387X_1)] = .284$$

Earlier it was noted that, when probit and logit are both fitted to the same data, the fits should be nearly the same, and the corresponding coefficients should differ by a constant factor the value of which is between 1.6 and 2.0. Table 6.3 reveals this to be the case when the same technique, ML, is used for both models. That is, in equation A-1 the ratio of the logit and probit intercepts (−2.03/−1.20 = 1.69) is about the same as the ratio of the estimates of β_1 (.592/.348 = 1.70). (The ratio of the estimates of β_2 violate the rule, but the very large standard errors suggest that this coefficient is estimated unreliably in both cases.) The corresponding two ratios are both about 1.66 in equation A-2. In equation B-1 they are 1.72 and 1.71 (again the estimates of β_2 disagree considerably more for the same reason), and in B-2 they are 1.74 and 1.71. The fit statistics likewise suggest close agreement between logit and probit ML estimates: The relevant chi-square statistics for the two models are very nearly the same in all four cases, never differing by more than .04 between probit and logit on the same equation, and the corresponding t-ratios on individual coefficients, though differing somewhat more between logit and probit, all lead to precisely the same inferences. Columns 7 and 8 of Table 6.4 contain predicted probabilities from ML estimation of equation A-2 (K = 1) for both issues. Here again one sees the very close agreement between probit and logit ML estimates: Never do the predicted probabilities differ by more than .02. All of these observations support the assertion made earlier that the choice between probit and logit is of little importance. They are different models, to be sure, and at most one of them can be the "true" model. But the two are so similar as to yield nearly identical inferences, and a formal test of which is correct would require a very large sample size.

The logit ML and logit min-χ^2 procedures are two estimators for the same model, and they have the same statistical properties. So one might expect to see coefficient estimates that are very close. As seen in Table 6.3, the pattern of inferences suggested by the two estimators is the same.

TABLE 6.4

Comparison of Observed and Predicted Probabilities for Proportional Representation Data

Observed Data				*Estimated Probability of Mayoral Support*				
X_1	n	n_1	(n_1/n)	*LPM (OLS)*	*LPM (WLS)*	*Probit (ML)*	*Logit (ML)*	*Logit (Min X^2)*
Farm Price Supports								
(0)	3	1	0.333	0.097	0.132	0.117	0.121	0.212
(1)	5	0	0.000	0.223	0.240	0.198	0.195	0.284
(2)	9	4	0.444	0.349	0.348	0.305	0.299	0.369
(3)	13	4	0.308	0.475	0.456	0.433	0.429	0.463
(4)	4	3	0.750	0.601	0.564	0.567	0.570	0.559
(5)	6	4	0.667	0.726	0.672	0.695	0.700	0.651
(6)	4	3	0.750	0.852	0.780	0.802	0.804	0.733
(7)	1	1	1.000	0.978	0.888	0.883	0.878	0.802
(8)	3	3	1.000	1.104	0.996	0.937	0.927	0.856
(9)	0	na	na	1.230	1.104	0.969	0.957	0.898
(10)	0	na	na	1.356	1.212	0.986	0.975	0.928
Housing Subsidies								
(0)	20	2	0.100	0.074	0.105	0.075	0.075	0.094
(1)	2	0	0.000	0.218	0.229	0.176	0.162	0.182
(2)	8	3	0.375	0.363	0.353	0.336	0.316	0.322
(3)	4	1	0.250	0.508	0.477	0.533	0.523	0.503
(4)	7	5	0.714	0.652	0.601	0.723	0.724	0.684
(5)	2	2	1.000	0.797	0.725	0.864	0.862	0.822
(6)	4	4	1.000	0.941	0.849	0.946	0.937	0.908
(7)	0	na	na	1.086	0.973	0.983	0.973	0.955
(8)	1	1	1.000	1.231	1.097	0.996	0.988	0.978
(9)	0	na	na	1.375	1.221	0.999	0.995	0.990
(10)	0	na	na	1.520	1.345	1.000	0.998	0.995

NOTE: X_1 is the decile support level of the populace, n is the number of towns with that support level, n_1 is the number in which the mayor supported the issue, and n_1/n is the observed proportion of mayoral support. Predicted probabilities are for specifications with one independent variable.

(As revealed by the t-ratios, whenever a coefficient would be judged significantly different from zero according to one of the estimators, it would be for the other estimator as well.) And in no case do estimates of the same coefficient differ by as much as one-and-a-half standard deviations across the two procedures. For example, in equation A-2 the estimate of β_1 is .565 by ML and .387 by min-χ^2. But both are significantly different from zero, and a two standard-error confidence band about either one would easily contain the other. Still, the differences are surprisingly large. This could be taken as evidence against the logit specification, and there is other evidence as well. As in an earlier WLS estimation of the LPM, the weights employed in the min-χ^2 procedure should make the weighted disturbance term have a standard deviation of one. Thus the RMSEs (which appear under the term "u") should be estimates of one, but the largest is only .721 and they range downward to .501. (Even this smallest value is not statistically significantly different from one, however.) But the small sample size makes both pieces of evidence very weak. The min-χ^2 estimator requires a large number of observations (replications) at each distinct value of X. In the problem at hand, for each issue there was only one case, out of seven or eight, of more than ten replications ($n_4 = 13$ for price supports and $n_1 = 20$ for housing subsidies). And in three of the eight cases for farm price supports ($X = 1, 7,$ and 8) and four of seven for housing subsidies ($X = 1, 5, 6,$ and 8), the observed proportion had to be artificially truncated (the values .01 and .99 were chosen, arbitrarily, as the truncation points) to even define the observed logit and the weight.

The considerations above suggest that the min-χ^2 results are not to be trusted because of the small sample size, but they still serve the purpose of illustration here. Interpretation of these results proceeds just as in OLS regression. The reported F statistic serves as an overall test of fit of the equation, namely that all coefficients except the intercept are zero. Its degrees of freedom are determined as the number of parameters being tested (K) for the numerator and the sample size less the total number of coefficients estimated ($M - K - 1$) for the denominator. Note that in this estimation procedure, the relevant sample size, M, is given by the number of distinct values of X; in the case at hand $M = 8$ for the farm issue and $M = 7$ for the housing issue. The t-ratios are the ratios of the coefficient estimates to their standard errors, just as in OLS, and can be used to test the hypothesis that the corresponding coefficient is zero. Their degrees of freedom are determined by $M - K - 1$, as is the denominator degrees-of-freedom for the F statistic. In all equations except A-1, the reported F statistics are significant at the 5% level, as are the t-ratios for the coefficient β_1, suggesting that the position of the mayor is indeed related to the level of popular support. The t ratio for β_2, on the other hand, suggests that this coefficient is not significantly different from zero in either issue. Calculation of the predicted choice probabilities from this procedure employs equation 6.6, with the coefficients β_k replaced by their respective estimates. Column 9 of Table 6.4 contains such calculations. If the model were correct and the sample size sufficient, entries in this column would agree well with those in the column 8 for logit estimated by ML.

As noted previously, the probit and logit results are so close as to make a choice between them quite arbitrary. And the method of interpretation is the same for both. The reported fit statistic in this case is computed from the likelihood ratio principle and follows a chi-square distribution with K degrees of freedom under the null hypothesis that none of the independent variables have any effect on Y. Comparing the reported values with critical values from a table of the chi-square distribution suggests rejecting that null hypothesis at a confidence level of at least 99% (a 1% level of significance) for both issues: Clearly there is some relationship between support of the citizenry and of the elites. The t ratios, again computed as the ratios of coefficients to standard errors, follow Student's t distribution, with N − K degrees of freedom, when the true coefficient is zero. (The sample size, N, is 48 for both issues.) These statistics tell the same story as before: X_2 appears not to have any explanatory power after controlling for X_1, and X_1 does have a statistically significant effect. (In the farm issue, X_1 is significant only at about the 10% level when X_2 is included in the model, but that level changes to 1% when X_2 is omitted.)

SUMMARY

This chapter is meant as an introduction to the use of probit and logit analysis to investigate multivariate relationships involving a dichotomous dependent variable. Because these methods are commonly viewed as alternatives to ordinary least squares, considerable attention was also devoted to the linear model to which OLS applies. Specification of the model is a prerequisite to estimation, so the chapter began with a careful derivation of theoretical models for dichotomous dependent variables. Both linear (LPM and TLPM) and nonlinear (probit and logit) forms were proposed, and salient features of each were discussed. Particular emphasis was placed on the restrictions, either on the parameters of the model (as in the LPM) or on the linear form itself (the TLPM), which are inherent but easily overlooked parts of the linear models. These restrictions belie the apparent simplicity and generality of application of those linear models.

The chapter then considered estimation methods for each of the models. For the LPM, a weighted least-squares estimator was shown to be preferable to ordinary least squares. Although the TLPM may appear to be a more attractive specification because it avoids the constraints on underlying parameters of interest, there are no well developed and widely known estimation procedures for it. An explanation of why the least squares procedures are inappropriate was provided; for the logit and probit models, two estimators were proposed. The first, maximum likelihood, is appropriate regardless of the nature of the data, provided certain assumptions are met. The second, minimum chi-square, imposes those same assumptions but in addition is applicable only when the data are in replicated form, and only the logit case was considered.

A wide variety of extensions to these simple dichotomous variable models are available. See Aldrich and Nelson (1984), Amemiya (1981), and Maddala (1983) for discussion of, or references to, extensions involving polytomous variables, ordered polytomous variables, simultaneous equations, and mixtures of continuous and discrete endogenous variables. These references also note the relationships to discriminant analysis and log-linear models. Examples of application of these models can be found in Kohn et al. (1976), Ostrom and Aldrich (1978), and Spector and Mazzeo (1980).

NOTES

1. The symbol X with no subscript will refer to the full set of K variables. When the reference is to the variable itself, no observation subscript is needed and the notation Y, X, X_1, X_k, etc. will be used. But at times, clarity will require an observation subscript, usually i, to make it clear that the reference is to an observation on the variable. Thus you will also see notation such as Y_i, X_i and X_{ik}.

2. As a historical footnote, C. R. Bliss coined the term probit as an abbreviation of "probability unit." Following this lead, Berkson (1944) used "logit" to refer to "logistic probability unit." Other authors suggested different models and corresponding "its," such as "Gompit" and "Burrit," and some chose to rename probit as "normit," emphasizing the use of the normal distribution in that model. Originally, those terms were applied to the arguments of the functions, rather than to the functional forms themselves. In contemporary usage, they refer to the argument, the model, or the method of analysis interchangeably.

3. Among the many good references on OLS regression are Lewis-Beck (1980), Maddala (1977), Pindyck and Rubinfeld (1976), and Goldberger (1964). Goldberger includes a discussion of the application to the LPM (pp. 248-250).

4. Alternatively, interpret all expectations as conditional on X_i.

5. The validity of the independence assumption depends on the nature of the sample. If it is random and cross-sectional, the assumption is innocuous. If the data represent a time series, or if observations are selected nonrandomly, then the assumption must be checked. Methods of testing and correcting for serial dependence in dichotomous variable problems are beyond the scope of this chapter, but it is worth noting that the special implied nature of the disturbance term, to be discussed below, would seem to rule out the standard autoregressive structure often taken as the alternative hypothesis in the linear model. Failure of the nonsingularity assumption means that the estimators discussed here will not work: They will entail division by zero. And near singularity is the problem of multicollinearity. These problems are neither more nor less severe than in the usual continuous-variable case.

6. This procedure of transforming the data in a regression model so that the transformed data satisfy the conditions necessary for effective estimation is a common one in regression analysis: The term applied to it is "generalized least squares" (GLS). (Some authors refer to the procedure as the "Aitken estimator" after one of its earlier proponents. See Aitken, 1934.) This generalization of OLS is indeed quite general in that with the appropriate transformation it can be used to correct for certain forms of serial correlation as well as for heteroscedasticity. In the heteroscedasticity correction, the transformation is the simple one of multiplying, or weighting, each observation by the appropriate value. Thus this special form of GLS is often denoted "weighted least squares" (WLS).

7. Because this amended procedure employs estimated weights, W_i, some authors prefix the label GLS with feasible-, approximate-, or pseudo- to distinguish it from the true generalized least-squares estimator. Curiously, the label WLS is not so amended.

8. Although it is not often admitted, nearly all of the statistical analysis tools employed in the social sciences should carry exactly the same disclaimer.

9. Some computer programs permit direct estimation using WLS. These simply ask for the name of the weight variable and the specification of the original model, thereby collapsing Steps 3 and 4 into a single one. Note, however, that various programs use different definitions of the weight variable, so caution is called for.

10. An appropriate R^2 can be computed as the square of the simple (Pearson) correlation coefficient between the unweighted observed and predicted values of Y. The latter is computed as $\Sigma\tilde{\beta}_k X_k$ using the estimates from Step 4 and the unweighted independent variables. Note that this R^2 will be smaller than that obtained from OLS, because OLS yields the largest possible R^2; maximizing R^2 is not always a good thing. Moreover, with a dichotomous dependent variable and a linear specification, a perfect fit is generally impossible: The regression line cannot go through all the data points no matter how good the fit. The upper limit on R^2 depends on the range of data in the sample and could be well below one. So a value of R^2 of .2, for example, could be very high. This uncertainty about the interpretation of R^2 greatly diminishes its usefulness. Accordingly, the authors recommend avoiding its use.

11. Of course, it is known only that the *true* standard errors of the OLS estimates exceed those of WLS, and the standard errors reported here are *estimated* ones. Thus to find the reverse ordering would be surprising but not alarming.

12. Instead of introducing the ML estimation procedure, the analysis could proceed as before with least squares. Defining ε_i as the deviation between Y_i and its expected value (recall that $E(Y_i) = P(Y_i)$) yields the regression equations

$$Y_i = \Lambda(\Sigma\beta_k X_{ik}) + \varepsilon_i$$

for the logit model (with Λ defined by equation (6.6)) or

$$Y_i = \Phi(\Sigma\beta_k X_{ik}) + \varepsilon_i$$

for probit (with Φ defined by equation 6.7). But these equations are clearly not linear in the β_ks, so although the "least squares" procedure is still feasible the estimator so obtained is not OLS; rather it is "Nonlinear Least Squares." As with the LPM, a "weighted nonlinear least squares" estimator dominates the unweighted version, and the weighted nonlinear least squares estimator can be shown to be equivalent to ML procedures discussed here. Because the literature favors the ML derivation, that approach is followed in the text.

13. As in the earlier discussion (note 4), take the exogenous variables to be fixed numbers; alternatively, take the results to follow as being conditional on the observed values of X in the sample.

14. That number should be increased if the sample is not approximately balanced between observations Y = 0 and Y = 1, and, of course, the more the better is always a good rule. In addition to making the applicability of asymptotic properties suspect, small sample sizes may lead to serious computational problems. Suppose that in a particular sample there is some value of X above which Y is always 1 and below which Y is always 0. Then perfect prediction is possible, and it manifests itself in the probit and logit models with a very large (infinite) coefficient on X and very small (negatively infinite) intercept: For such values the sigmoid curve of Figure 6.5 is made to look like the step function of Figure 6.3 with the step located at the critical value of X. The iterative estimation procedure described above will "diverge" as it tries to find these values. The problem is the same, though more complicated, when the (near) perfect prediction is based on several exogenous variables. As the sample size grows, the chances of such perfect predictability diminishes.

15. As observed in note 2, the term logit was originally applied to the argument (Z_i) of the logistic function. The usage is now broader, but it is still convenient to use it as a label for the log-odds, with the qualifiers "observed" and "true" appended to indicate the logarithms of the ratios of observed and theoretical probabilities respectively.

16. Berkson (1944) advocated this estimator for Bio-Assay problems, and Theil (1967) introduced it in the social science literature.

17. Note that this weight is the reciprocal of that used in the LPM. (In an earlier discussion, n_i was taken to be 1.) This estimator gives most weight to observations near the center, P(Y) = .5, not to those at either extreme as does WLS in the LPM.

references

Aitken, A. C. (1934) "On least squares and linear combinations of observations." Proceedings of the Royal Society of Edinburgh 55: 42-48.

Aldrich, J. H. and F. D. Nelson (1984) Linear Probability, Logit and Probit Models. Beverly Hills, CA: Sage.

Amemiya, T. (1981) "Qualitative response models: a survey." Journal of Economic Literature 19: 1483-1536.

Berkson, J. (1944) "Application of the logistic function to bio-assay." Journal of the American Statistical Association 39: 357-365.

Goldberger, A. S. (1964) Econometric Theory. New York: John Wiley.

Judge, G. G., W. E. Griffiths, R. C. Hill, H. Lutkepohl, and T. C. Lee (1985) The Theory and Practice of Econometrics. New York: John Wiley.

Kohn, M. G., C. F. Manski, and D. S. Mundel (1976) "An empirical investigation of factors which influence college-going behavior." Annals of Economic and Social Measurement 5: 391-420.

Lewis-Beck, M. S. (1980) Applied Regression: An Introduction. Beverly Hills, CA: Sage.

Luce, R. D. and P. Suppes (1965) "Preference, utility, and subjective probability," in R. D. Luce et al. (eds.) Handbook of Mathematical Psychology. New York: John Wiley.

Maddala, G. S. (1977) Econometrics. New York: McGraw-Hill.

———(1983) Limited-Dependent and Qualitative Variables in Econometrics. Cambridge: Cambridge University Press.

McFadden, D. (1973) "Conditional logit analysis of qualitative choice behavior," in P. Zarembka (ed.) Frontiers in Econometrics. New York: Academic Press.

Ostrom, C. W., Jr., and J. H. Aldrich (1978) "The relationship between size and stability in the major power international system." American Journal of Political Science 22: 743-771.

Pindyck, R. S. and D. L. Rubinfeld (1976) Econometric Models and Economic Forecasts. New York: McGraw-Hill.

Powell, G. B. with L. W. Powell (1978) "The analysis of citizen-elite linkages: representation by Austrian local elites," in S. Verba and L. Pye (ed.) The Citizen and Politics. Greylock.

Robinson, R. M. (1982) "On the asymptotic properties of estimators with limited dependent variables." Econometrica 50: 27-42.

Robinson, P. M., A. K. Berra, and C. M. Jarque (forthcoming) "Tests for serial dependence in limited dependent variable models." International Economic Review.

Spector, L. and M. Mazzeo (1980) "Probit analysis and economic education." Journal of Economic Education 11: 37-44.

Theil, H. (1967) Economics and Information Theory. Chicago: Rand McNally.

7

Using Categorical Regression to Analyze Multivariate Contingency Tables

HERBERT M. KRITZER

INTRODUCTION

Much of the data that political scientists deal with are qualitative in nature, and most of the rest are at best ordinal. How can we appropriately analyze such data with currently available techniques? Political scientists often analyze data as though they met the criteria of an interval scale, even though they fail to meet the assumption required for the methods used. With the methods now available for analyzing qualitative data, one need not make the kinds of questionable assumptions that are typically made. This chapter provides an introduction to those techniques that rely upon a regression focus. The first section reviews hypothesis testing for simple contingency tables; the next section presents a sketch of how such techniques might be extended to more complex situations; the method of "categorical regression" (Grizzle et al., 1969) is then introduced; the chapter closes by showing the link between categorical regression and log-linear models as described by Goodman (1972a) and Bishop et al. (1975).

AUTHOR'S NOTE: *This chapter is based on "An Introduction to Multivariate Contingency Table Analysis,"* American Journal of Political Science *(1978) 22: 187-226. I would like to thank the University of Texas Press for permission to reprint material from that earlier article. I would also like to thank Gary King for his valuable comments on the first draft of this chapter. Computer time and secretarial services were provided by the University of Wisconsin—Madison.*

THE ANALYSIS OF SIMPLE CONTINGENCY TABLES

Pearson Chi-Square

The simplest contingency table involves two dichotomous variables. Table 7.1A is an example of such a table taken from a recent book on decision making in the federal district courts (Carp and Rowland, 1983: 33). This table, which is based on data derived from opinions by federal district judges published in the Federal Supplement between 1933 and 1977, shows the simple relationship between the party affiliation of the judges (prior to going on the bench) and the direction of the decisions contained in the published opinions. From the frequencies in the table, one can see that 45.6% of the decisions published by Democratic judges were in the liberal direction, compared to 38.7% for Republican judges.

One may test for a significant relationship between the two variables by comparing the actual frequencies to the frequencies one would expect if the two variables were completely independent of one another. When computing the expected frequencies one constrains the marginal frequencies in the expected table to be equal to the marginal frequencies in the observed table (for example, one assumes, using the example of Table 7.1, that the overall numbers of decisions by Republican and Democratic judges is fixed and that the overall numbers of liberal and conservative decisions is fixed). One then determines the probability that the actual cell frequencies simply reflect random variations from the frequencies that would be present if there were absolutely no relationship between the two variables, assuming either that the "liberal" cases were randomly assigned to Republican and Democratic judges, or that the cases published in the *Federal Supplement* represent a random sample of judges' decisions drawn from a population in which there is no relationship between party affiliation and decisional direction.[1]

The statistic commonly used to test this relationship is Pearson's chi-square:

$$\chi^2 = \Sigma \frac{(O - E)^2}{E} \qquad [7.1]$$

where O refers to the *o*bserved frequencies, and E refers to the frequencies *e*xpected under the null hypothesis being tested. In this case the expected frequencies are obtained by multiplying the marginal column proportions shown in Table 7.1b (that is, .428 and .572) times the mar-

TABLE 7.1a
Decisional Direction by Judges' Party

	Frequencies		
	Decision		
Party	*Liberal*	*Conservative*	*Totals*
Democrat	7,152	8,541	15,693
Republican	4,131	6,548	10,679
Total	11,283	15,089	26,372

NOTE: $\chi^2 = 123.3$

TABLE 7.1b
Proportions: Decision by Party

	Decision		
Party	*Liberal*	*Conservative*	*Totals*
Democrat	.456	.544	1.000
Republican	.387	.613	1.000
Totals	.428	.572	1.000

NOTE: $Z = 11.11$; $\sigma_{p_1 - p_2} = .00621$.

ginal row totals in Table 7.1a (that is, 15693 and 10679). If the value of this statistic could not occur by chance more often than some predetermined proportion of the time (what is called "significance level"), we conclude that the observed frequencies differ significantly from the expected frequencies. This indicates that there is a significant relationship between the two variables in the table. We can draw this conclusion because the only difference between the expected table and the observed table is that the expected table hypothesizes that there is no relationship between the two variables; if the expected table involved any additional hypotheses, we would not be able to draw that conclusion. For this test to be valid, there must be a sufficient number of cases to obtain reliable estimates of the expected frequencies; a common rule of thumb is that none of the *expected* frequencies should be less than five.[2] Thus, the chi-square test may be said to be asymptotic; it relies upon large sample theory to be valid. The same approach can be used with bivariate tables involving polytomous variables.

The chi-square test for the data in Table 7.1a yields a test statistic with a value of 123.3; associated with this chi-square is one "degree of freedom." That is, given that we take the marginals as fixed (that is, there are 11283 liberal decisions, 15089 conservative decisions, and so forth), once we specify a frequency for one of the cells, the remaining cells are fixed. At the .05 level with one degree of freedom, the critical region of chi-square is 3.84 and above. Thus because the frequencies in the table are much greater than the minimum required for the test, we can conclude that the table provides evidence that there is a relationship between party and decisions.

Difference of Proportions

Another approach to testing for a relationship between two nominal variables is the difference of proportions test. Although the procedure for carrying out this test is completely different from the familiar chi-square test given above, it involves a statistical test that is actually mathematically identical to the chi-square test. The difference-of-proportions test is based upon a corollary of the central limit theorem:

> If independent random samples of sizes N_1 and N_2, respectively, are drawn from populations, one with a mean μ_1 and a variance σ^2_1, and the other mean μ_2 and a variance σ^2_2, as the sample sizes N_1 and N_2 become large, the sampling distribution of the difference between the two means will approach normality with a mean of $\mu_1 - \mu_2$, and a variance of $(\sigma^2_1/N_1 + \sigma^2_2/N_2)$, *regardless of the distribution of the two original populations.*

A proportion can be viewed as a type of mean and according to this theorem, it does not matter that the data are dichotomous and thus not from a normal distribution. To apply this theorem to proportions, one must obtain the variance of the proportion. Given a dichotomous variable, let us assume that all cases have a value of either one or zero, that the proportion of cases in the population having a value of 1 is π, and that there are M cases in the entire population. In that case πM cases will have a value of one and $(1 - \pi)$M cases will have a value of zero. Then, we can easily show that the mean μ is equal to π:

$$\mu = \frac{\sum_{i=1}^{M} X_i}{M} = \frac{\pi \cdot M \cdot 1 + (1-\pi)M \cdot 0}{M} = \frac{\pi M}{M} = \pi \qquad [7.2]$$

Similarly we can show that the variance of π is equal to $\pi(1 - \pi)$ (Blalock, 1972: 194-195):

$$\sigma^2 = \frac{\sum_{i=1}^{M} (X_i - \mu)^2}{M} \qquad \frac{\sum_{i=1}^{m} (X_i - \pi)^2}{M} \qquad [7.3]$$

Because X_i must be equal to 1 for πM cases and to 0 for $(1 - \pi)M$ cases, we may rewrite 7.3 as

$$\sigma^2 = \frac{M\pi(1-\pi)^2 + M(1-\pi)(0-\pi)^2}{M} \qquad [7.4]$$

rewriting

$$\sigma^2 = \frac{M\pi(1-\pi)^2 + M\pi^2(1-\pi)^2}{M} \qquad [7.5]$$

Factoring $M\pi(1 - \pi)$ from each term of the numerator yields

$$\sigma^2 = \frac{M\pi(1-\pi)(1-\pi+\pi)}{M} = \pi(1-\pi) \qquad [7.6]$$

Based upon this derivation, one can compute a Z-score and use the normal distribution to test for significant differences of proportions:

$$Z = \frac{(p_1 - p_2) - (\pi_1 - \pi_2)}{\sqrt{\frac{{}_1(1-\pi_1)}{N_1} + \frac{\pi_2(1-\pi_2)}{N_2}}} \qquad [7.7]$$

where p_i refers to the *i*th sample proportion and N_i refers to the number of cases in the *i*th sample. If the null hypothesis is that there is no difference between the population proportions π_1 and π_2, then $\pi_1 = \pi_2 = \pi$. In that case, we may simplify equation 7.7 to:

$$Z = \frac{p_1 - p_2}{\sqrt{\pi(1-\pi)}\sqrt{\frac{N_1 + N_2}{N_1 \cdot N_2}}} \qquad [7.8]$$

In applying this method to a two-by-two contingency table, the null hypothesis is that the two variables are independent of one another. This is equivalent to hypothesizing that

$$\pi_1 = \pi_2 \qquad [7.9]$$

Given that we are concerned with only this one null hypothesis, we may assume that π is equal to the proportion for the entire table. Obviously, in a contingency table, one may compute the proportions two different ways; however, this choice will not affect the results of the difference of proportions test. Using decision Table 7.1, we obtain a Z statistic of 11.11 (based on either row proportions or column proportions). From standard statistical theory, we know (see Hays, 1963: 337-338) that χ^2 for one degree of freedom is equal to Z^2; consequently we may rewrite equation 7.8 as:

$$\pi^2 = \frac{(p_1 - p_2)^2}{\pi(1-\pi)\dfrac{(N_1 + N_2)}{(N_1 \quad N_2)}} = \frac{(p_1 - p_2)^2}{\sigma^2_{p_1 - p_2}} \qquad [7.10]$$

If one squares the Z statistic for Table 7.1b, the result, 123.4, is the same as the χ^2 obtained for Table 7.1a (allowing for rounding error). Thus for a table involving two dichotomous variables, Pearson chi-square analysis and the simple difference-of-proportions test are equivalent. As we will see below, the difference-of-proportions test may be extended to polytomous variables.

One advantage of the difference-of-proportions approach over the chi-square approach is that the difference used in the test provides a direct description of the relationship that can be reexpressed in terms of percentage differences. In this case, we can say that Democrats are 6.9 percentage points more likely to make a liberal decision than are Republicans. I do not want to make too much of this advantage of the proportions test because it is a trivial exercise to convert the frequency table to percentages and then make exactly the same statement. The important point is that it would seem more direct to be able to test hypotheses directly about the descriptive measures given that those measures provide the vehicle for interpreting the results of the analysis.

The Cross-Product Ratio

With this last point in mind, let us look at one other measure that can be easily derived from a two-by-two contingency table. For any two-by-two table one can calculate the cross products, that is, the product of the two main diagonal cells and the product of the two secondary diagonal cells. In the case of Table 7.1a, these products would be 7152 × 6548 and 4131 × 8541. If we label the two cells in the first row of the table, cell *a* and cell *b*, and the cells in the second row cell *c* and cell *d*, we can write the two general cross products as *ad* and *bc*. Political scientists are probably most familiar with the cross products as the components of Yule's Q,

$$Q = \frac{ab - bc}{ad + bc} \qquad [7.11]$$

a statistic that is frequently used in roll-call analysis (see MacRae, 1970: 49-56; Clausen, 1977).

In the statistical literature, a more common application of the cross products is to form the cross-product ratio (α):

$$\alpha = \frac{ab}{bc} \qquad [7.12]$$

Because we are in fact obtaining an estimate of a parameter, we should designate the quantity in equation 7.12, as $\hat{\alpha}$. The cross-product ratio has the interesting property that it is invariant under row or column multiplication. This means that we could compute the cross-product ratio from the raw frequencies (Table 7.1a), the proportions (Table 7.1b), or percentages, and we would get exactly the same result: 1.33.

The cross-product ratio has a particularly nice interpretation. If, instead of taking cross products, we form the odds associated with each row, a/b and c/d, and then take the ratio of those odds (which we could call the odds of the odds), we have

$$\frac{a/b}{c/d} = \frac{ad}{bc} = \hat{\alpha} \qquad [7.13]$$

Thus the cross-product ratio is also the ratio of the odds (and, hence is also known as the "odds ratio"). If there is no relationship between the two variables used to form the two tables we would expect the odds to be equal; in this case the ratio of the two odds would be 1.0. For our example, this would mean that the odds of a Democrat making a liberal decision would be the same as the odds of a Republican making a liberal decision. In fact, the odds of a Democrat making a liberal decision are .84 to 1.00 compared to .63 to 1.00 for Republicans; the ratio of the odds for Democrats to odds for Republicans is equal to $\hat{\alpha}$, 1.33.

The odds ratio is analogous to the difference in proportions: It provides a comparison of two measures of relative frequency; in this case the measure of relative frequency is odds, and for the difference of proportions the measure was proportions. One problem with the odds ratio is that it appears to depend on the selection of the numerator and denominator; if we take the ratio of the Republican odds to the Democratic odds the result is .75 rather than 1.33. In fact, 1.33 and .75 are "symmetric" around 1.0; they are the inverse of one another (that is, $\frac{1}{1.33} = .75$). We can eliminate the apparent asymmetry by simply taking natural logarithms:

$$\log_e(\hat{\alpha}) = \hat{\alpha}^* = \log\left(\frac{ab}{bc}\right) \quad [7.14]$$

For our example these yield a value of .29 if we use Democratic to Republican, or –.29 if we use Republican to Democrat.

The log form has three advantages. First, we can see that $\hat{\alpha}^*$ is directly analogous to the difference of proportions:

$$\hat{\alpha}^* = \log\left(\frac{ad}{bc}\right) = \log\left(\frac{a/b}{c/d}\right) = \log\left(\frac{a}{b}\right) - \log\left(\frac{c}{d}\right) \quad [7.15]$$

Thus the log-odds ratio is, in fact, the difference of the log odds.[3] Second, as should be readily apparent from equation 7.15, the log-odds ratio will be zero if the two log odds are identical, which will occur if there is no relationship between the two variables. Third, if we can identify the sampling distribution of the log-odds ratio, and the parameters of the distribution, we can carry out statistical tests equivalent to those for the difference of proportions.

In fact, the log-odds ratio, $\hat{\alpha}^*$, has a normal sampling distribution with a mean equal to $\hat{\alpha}^*$, and a standard error that can be estimated by (Fienberg, 1977: 15) the following:

$$\hat{\sigma}_{\hat{\alpha}^*} = \sqrt{\frac{1}{a} + \frac{1}{b} + \frac{1}{c} + \frac{1}{d}} \quad [7.16]$$

In our example, $\sigma_{\hat{\alpha}^*}$ is .0255, and we can obtain a Z statistic on α^* of 11.36 or a χ^2 129.2; these values are very close to the earlier Z and χ^2 values we obtained. Thus the two approaches yield similar, though not identical tests of the same hypotheses.

Both the difference-of-proportions test and the test of significance for the log-odds ratio (log cross product) provide a direct test of significance on a measure that describes the relationship between the two variables. One disadvantage of the log odds is that the metric of the measure is not one that has intuitive meaning for many persons; this problem can be dealt with by returning the measure to its original odds-ratio metric. As will be seen as methods are developed for analyzing multivariate contingency tables, the two main approaches can be thought of as being generalizations of either the difference-of-proportions test or the log-odds ratio test.

EXTENSIONS TO MORE COMPLEX TABLES

In the example discussed so far, only the simplest of all tables has been considered, in which there are only two variables, each with two categories. The approaches can be extended either to tables with variables having more than two categories, or to tables involving more than two variables.

Extension to more than two variables is accomplished by what has been called the difference of difference-of-proportions test (Blalock, 1972: 231), or the equivalent for log odds. For purposes of discussion, the data in Table 7.2 will be used. This table is a further breakdown of judicial decisions drawn from the work of Carp and Rowland (1983: 106);[4] it shows the relationship among decisions, party, and subject area.[5]

The difference-of-difference test examines the question of whether or not there is an *interaction* between the two variables: That is, is the variation in the dependent variable related to the joint variation in the predictor variables, or simply of each independent variable taken in turn? One way of thinking about the example being used here is to consider whether or not the impact of party varies depending on subject matter: That is, is the party effect for civil rights and liberties greater than the effect for criminal justice? Using proportions, this is tested in the following equation (Blalock, 1972: 231):

$$\chi^2 = \frac{[(p_{11} - p_{21}) - (p_{31} - p_{41})]^2}{\frac{p_{11}(1 - p_{21})}{n_1} + \frac{p_{21}(1 - p_{21})}{n_2} + \frac{p_{31}(1 - p_{31})}{n_3} + \frac{p_{41}(1 - p_{41})}{n_4}} \quad [7.17]$$

The numerator consists of the difference of two differences and the denominator consists of the sum of a set of standard errors (the form of each term is the same as that of the denominator in equation 7.7). If we apply this formula to the data in Table 7.2 we obtain

$$\chi^2 = \frac{[(.31 - .24) - (.51 - .40)]^2}{\frac{.31 \times .69}{5729} \quad \frac{.24 \times .76}{4223} \quad \frac{.51 \times .49}{4479} \quad \frac{.40 \times .60}{3072}} = \frac{(-0.04)^2}{.00216} = 7.42 \quad [7.18]$$

which tells us that party has a larger impact for civil rights and liberties than for criminal justice. However, the magnitude of the difference, .04 ($|[.31 - .24] - [.5 - .40]|$), is not particularly large.

TABLE 7.2
Decisions by Party and Subject

		Decision			
Subject	*Party*	*Liberal*	*Conservative*	*Proportion Liberal*	*Log Odds Liberal*
Criminal justice	Democrat	1775	3954	.31	−.80
	Republican	1030	3193	.24	−1.13
Civil rights liberties	Democrat	2285	2194	.51	0.04
	Republican	1222	1800	.40	−0.39

We could accomplish the same test by using log odds in place of proportions. In doing so, we replace the differences of proportions in the numerator with differences of log odds, and we replace the standard errors in the denominator with the standard errors for the log odds (Theil, 1970: 109):

$$\sigma = \sqrt{\frac{1}{n\pi\,(1 - \pi)}} \qquad [7.19]$$

This yields

$$\chi^2 = \frac{\{[(\ln(p_{11} / p_{12}) - \ln(p_{21} / p_{22})] - [\ln(p_{31} / p_{32}) - \ln(p_{41} / p_{42})]\}}{1/n_1\, p_{11}\, p_{12} + 1/n_2\, p_{21}\, p_{22} + 1/n_3\, p_{31}\, p_{32} + 1/n_4\, p_{41}\, p_{42}} \qquad [7.20]$$

The resulting χ^2 for the data in Table 7.2 is 2.28, which is *not* statistically significant. This inconsistency between the two tests seems surprising, given that for the simple two-variable example the log-odds and proportions tests produced virtually identical results. In fact, the difference is extremely important for understanding the choice between log odds and proportions for analysis.

Table 7.3 shows proportions and the corresponding log odds across the range of proportions in .05 steps. Although the steps in the proportions scale are constant, the steps in the log-odds scale are not, and the difference becomes increasingly large as one moves out beyond proportions in the range .3 to .7. For example, the "distance" from .50 to .45 and from .10 to .15 is equal (.05) on the proportions scale but the latter "distance" is more than twice as large as the former on the log-odds scale (.47 versus .20). The difference in scaling can be seen visually in Figure 7.1; although the rate of change in the proportions is constant, the log odds is s-shaped (flatter in the middle of the range and steeper at the ex-

TABLE 7.3
Proportions, Odds, and Log Odds

Proportions	*Odds*	*Log Odds*
0.05	0.05	−2.94
0.10	0.11	−2.20
0.15	0.18	−1.73
0.20	0.25	−1.39
0.25	0.33	−1.00
0.30	0.43	−0.85
0.35	0.54	−0.62
0.40	0.67	−0.41
0.45	0.88	−0.20
0.50	1.00	0.00
0.55	1.22	0.20
0.60	1.50	0.41
0.65	1.86	0.62
0.70	2.33	0.85
0.75	3.00	1.00
0.80	4.00	1.39
0.85	5.68	1.73
0.90	9.00	2.20
0.95	19.00	2.94

tremes). If we look at the figures in Table 7.2, we see that the difference in proportions for civil rights and liberties is a little over one and a half times (1.57) the difference for criminal justice, and the difference of log odds for civil rights and liberties is only a little less than one and a third (1.30) times that for criminal justice. This difference is sufficient to push the difference of differences of log odds into the range of nonsignificance, even though we are working with very large N's.

This leaves the fundamental question: Which approach is "right"? The simple answer to that question is that "it depends." It depends on the substantive question: Does it make substantive sense to stretch out the scale at the extremes? Elsewhere, I have argued that it probably does not (Kritzer 1979a); I would back off from that argument now and suggest that the question of which scale to use is really one of researcher judgment and the more extreme the values the researcher is working with the more likely it is that the log-odds scale is the one that should be used. As we will see below, one can do exactly the same analysis regardless of the scale that is used, and the analyst should choose the scale that seems most appropriate for the task at hand.

Let us turn to the second type of extension: a bivariate table where one (or both) of the variables has more than two categories. The simplest extension is the standard bivariate contingency table test that involves com-

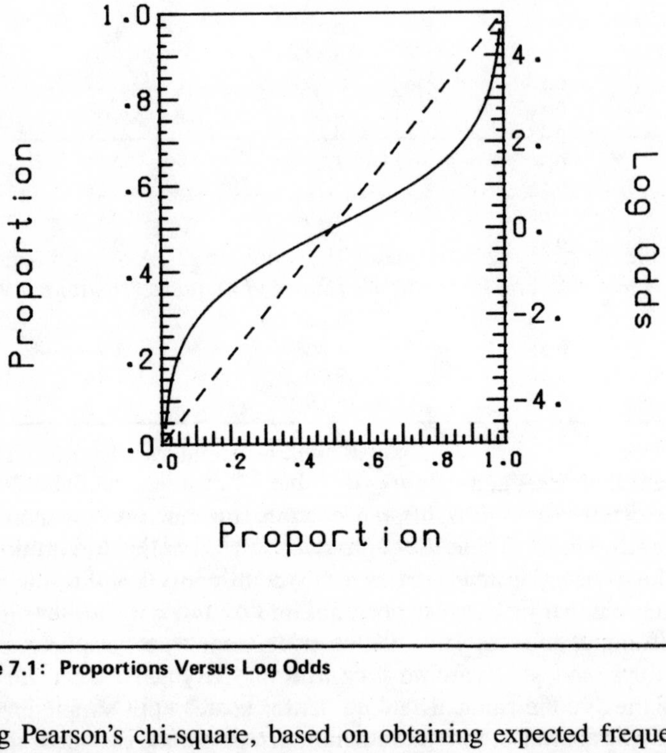

Figure 7.1: Proportions Versus Log Odds

puting Pearson's chi-square, based on obtaining expected frequencies from the table marginals in exactly the same way as was shown for the two-by-two table. If we use Table 7.4, which shows decision by subject (using three categories), we obtain a Pearson chi-square of 1785 (two degrees of freedom). It is useful at this point to introduce two alternative chi-square statistics that are typically used in multivariate contingency table analysis. The first of these statistics has the desirable property of additivity; that is, the sum of this statistic from independent tests will be equal to a single, overall test for an equivalent, combined analysis. This statistic is the likelihood ratio chi-square (Reynolds, 1977: 8):

$$\chi^2_{\text{L.R.}} = 2\,\Sigma\,\text{O} \quad \log_e \left(\frac{\text{O}}{\text{E}}\right) \qquad [7.21]$$

TABLE 7.4
Decisions by Subject

Subject	*Decision* *Liberal*	*Conservative*	*Proportion Liberal*	*Log Odds Liberal*
Criminal justice	2805	7147	.28	−0.94
	(4336)[a]	(5616)		
Civil rights and liberties	3507	3994	.47	−0.13
	(3268)	(4233)		
Economics	5014	3526	.59	0.35
	(3721)	(4818)		

NOTE: χ^2_p = 1785 (2 degrees of freedom).

a. Figures in parentheses are the expected value for each cell.

For Table 7.4, this statistic yields the value 1822. A second statistic, which is less well known, is the Neyman's chi-square (Neyman, 1949):

$$\chi^2_N = \Sigma \frac{(O + E)^2}{O} \qquad [7.22]$$

χ^2 for Table 7.4 is 2001. This statistic will be useful for a later discussion of categorical regression.

We can also carry out a difference-of-proportions test or a difference of log-odds test for Table 7.4. Intuitively, the simplest way to do this would be to select one category as a "base" category, contrast the other two categories to that base category, and add the test statistics for the two contrasts together to get a two degree of freedom χ^2; for example, using proportions, we could sum the χ^2 contrasting .28 (the base category) to .47 and the χ^2 contrasting .28 to .59. Unfortunately, this simple process will not work because, by using a common base for the two tests, the resulting χ^2's are not independent, and hence cannot be added together to yield a joint χ^2. In order to do a "joint" difference test, we must find two independent tests within the table. This is done through a process of partitioning the table: We select one pair of categories for the initial contrast and then combine those categories to contrast to the third category; the result is two independent χ^2's that can be added together.

To illustrate this process, Table 7.4 has been partitioned into two tables as shown in Table 7.5. Each of the three chi-squares for these tables has been computed (shown under each table); note that the two $\chi^2_{L.R.}$ add to 1821 (which differs from the overall $\chi^2_{L.R.}$ only because of the rounding we have done). We can now do the two difference tests for each of the tables; the results are shown as $\chi^2_{L.O.}$ (for log odds) and χ^2_{pr} (for propor-

TABLE 7.5a
Partitioning Decisions by Subject

Subject	Decision: Liberal	Decision: Conservative	Proportion Liberal	Log Odds Liberal
Criminal justice	2805 (3599)[a]	7147 (6353)	.28	−.94
Civil rights liberties	3507 (2713)	3994 (4788)	.47	−.13

NOTE: $\chi^2_P = 634$; $\chi^2_{L.R.} = 637$; $\chi^2_N = 651$.

a. Figures in parentheses are expected frequencies.

TABLE 7.5b
Partitioning Decisions by Subject

Subject	Decision: Liberal	Decision: Conservative	Proportion Liberal	Log Odds Liberal
Criminal justice and civil liberties	6312 (7605)[a]	11141 (9848)	.36	−.57
Economics	5014 (3721)	3526 (4819)	.59	.35

NOTE: $\chi^2_P = 1186$; $\chi^2_{L.R.} = 1184$; $\chi^2_N = 1223$; $\chi^2_{Pr} = 1222$; $\chi^2_{L.O.} = 1158$.

a. Figures in parentheses are expected frequencies.

tion) under the respective tables. Notice the similarity among all of the χ^2's. We could get an estimate of the joint χ^2 by adding together the appropriate pairs of χ^2's for each of the tests; in this example, we would end up with identical conclusions regardless of the particular statistic we were working with.

We could extend this approach to multivariate tables or to polytomous dependent variables very easily. However, given our ultimate goal, this would serve no useful purpose at this time. The important point is that various forms of contingency table analysis that are typically treated in elementary textbooks, Pearson χ^2, difference of proportions, and cross-product (or log odds) ratios, are all closely related. The focus now turns to an approach to contingency table analysis that combines these ideas with regression analysis to produce a very general and extremely powerful technique for examining the relationships represented in multivariate contingency table analysis.

CATEGORICAL REGRESSION

Introduction

The common feature of all of the tests discussed above is their orientation toward hypothesis testing. The only item of information they provide is the probability that the observed relationship or difference simply reflects the normal variations that arise from the process of drawing random samples. There are many other questions one might want to ask about a complex contingency table, such as Table 7.2, that do not necessarily lend themselves to hypothesis testing; for example: What is the *effect* of party upon decisions controlling for subject matter?

Rather than simply testing hypotheses about the differences among a set of proportions or log odds, we can seek to *explain* those differences; that is, we may view the variation among the proportions or log odds as being attributable to a combination of explanatory variables. This suggests the use of the general linear model with the table proportions or log odds as the dependent variable.

Let us develop this approach using the data arrayed in Table 7.6. This table shows decision by party, subject area, and time period. The only new variable here is the last one, and it consists of three categories:

1933–1953
1954–1968
1969–1977

On the right side of the table we show both the proportion liberal and the log odds of liberal versus conservative. For now let us focus on only the proportions; we will return later to the log odds. As suggested in the previous paragraph, what we want to do is to take the proportions as the dependent variable in a regression analysis.

Before proceeding, let us look at this dependent variable a bit more. If we were to replace all of the cells in the body of Table 7.6 with their respective "row conditional" proportions (that is, the proportions formed by dividing each cell count by its respective row total), we would have a total of 36 proportions. For our dependent variable, the proportion liberal, we have selected a subset of these 36 proportions. In a general sense we could think of each one of the proportions we are using as a function of the set of proportions for its corresponding row. In this case, the function is trivial, simply the weighted sum with the weight for the liberal column

TABLE 7.6
Decisions by Party, Period, and Subject

Subject	*Period*	*Party*	*Liberal*	*Conservative*	*Proportion Liberal*	*Log-Odds Liberal*
Criminal justice	Early	Democrat	144	409	.26	−1.05
	Early	Republican	98	369	.21	−1.32
	Middle	Democrat	609	1647	.27	−0.99
	Middle	Republican	386	1291	.23	−1.21
	Late	Democrat	1022	1898	.35	−0.62
	Late	Republican	546	1533	.26	−1.05
Civil rights and liberties	Early	Democrat	226	287	.44	−0.24
	Early	Republican	158	209	.43	−0.28
	Middle	Democrat	537	711	.43	−0.28
	Middle	Republican	314	511	.38	−0.49
	Late	Democrat	1522	1196	.56	0.24
	Late	Republican	750	1080	.41	−0.36
Economics	Early	Democrat	854	671	.56	0.24
	Early	Republican	486	547	.47	−0.12
	Middle	Democrat	1150	767	.60	0.41
	Middle	Republican	833	555	.60	0.41
	Late	Democrat	1049	541	.66	0.66
	Late	Republican	642	643	.50	0.00

equal to 1 and the weight for the conservative column equal to 0;[6] however, this notion of function of proportions, f(p) or f, for short, is useful, and we will denote our generalized dependent variable for the *i*th row of the table f_i.[7] We will refer to f_i as the *dependent variable function*.

We are now ready to apply the general linear model to the proportions in Table 7.6. The proportion of liberal decisions in the *i*th row can be viewed as a linear combination of a set of coefficients and dummy variables, plus an error term:

$$f_i = b_0 + b_1X_{i1} + b_2X_{i2} \ldots + e_i \qquad [7.23]$$

This is nothing more than the familiar regression equation with some minor (yet important) changes. The most important change has to do with the dependent variable; where ordinary case-level regression seeks to predict the value of a dependent variable for an individual "case," *categorical* regression uses as its dependent variable some function of the proportions (that is, a probability estimate) based upon a sample of cases. Thus with regard to individual cases, we will only be able to speak of the probability it will fall into one class or another on the actual categorical dependent variable.

The second change from ordinary regression concerns the error term, e. In ordinary regression, e is assumed to consist of three components: measurement error (on the dependent variable), specification error (error arising from the omission of variables from the model), and pure randomness. In categorical regression we effectively assume that the error term consists solely of specification error. We can make this assumption because the variation in the dependent variable function is defined by the table categories; if we were to change the table categories, we would change the nature of the variation in the function. Furthermore, because the variation is created by our specification of table categories, we can completely account for that variation by including in our regression model dummy variables for each of the table categories. Consequently, specification error in the model shown in equation 7.23 can only arise from the omission from the model of variables used in defining the table from which f is obtained.

For the example shown in Table 7.6, we will have a total of eighteen "observations" in the categorical regression analysis, one corresponding to each of the rows in the table. Thus we can include a maximum of eighteen predictor variables in the set of dummy variables; these predictors must correspond in some way to the independent variables that define the table (in this case party, period, and subject area). In the most common type of model, the possible regression terms include a constant (or "mean") effect, "main" effects for each of the independent variables, plus first- and second-order interactions for those variables; this is the hierarchical, complete factorial model. It is said to be "hierarchical" because the inclusion of an interaction term of order k presumes the inclusion of all possible terms of order less than k that can be factored out of the included term; that is, if we include a second order interaction among variables A, B, and C, we must include the three first-order interactions (AB, AC, and BC), plus the three main effects for A, B, and C. Models that include all eighteen possible terms are said to be "saturated," because they consume all available degrees of freedom and preclude a test for specification error; saturated models will perfectly recreate the original proportions.

A variety of other models may be used. The simplest models to interpret are those in which interactions are not present; such models are called "main effects models." However, before relying on a main effects model, we must determine whether or not the omission of interaction terms creates specification error in our model. If significant interactions are present, there are ways of representing those interactions in a substantively understandable and intuitively pleasing way; these nonhierarchical models, which are discussed below, are called "conditional models" (see

Wright, 1976). If interactions are not significant, the main effects for the independent variables represent the actual effect of that variable upon our dependent variable function which, in the case of our example, is the probability of liberal decisions; if more than one predictor variable is included in the regression model, we will obtain the effect of each predictor *controlling for the other variables in the equations*. Finally, it is possible to create specific dummy variables so that the resulting parameter estimates (i.e., $\hat{b}$'s), will actually be the change in the dependent variable function as we go from one category of the corresponding predictor variable to another category, controlling for the changes attributable to the other variables in the equation.

Before turning to the actual estimating procedure, it would be useful to summarize the basic approach of categorical regression. Categorical regression of contingency table data involves two separate aspects. First we must select a function of the proportions that correspond to the original frequency table to be used as the dependent variable in the regression analysis. Two common forms involve a subset of either the actual proportions or of the log odds; more complex functions such as Yule's Q measure of association (see Forthofer and Koch, 1973; and Kritzer, 1977, 1980) may also be used. The second part of categorical regression is the specification of an appropriate dummy variable model to be used to explain the variation in the dependent variable function, f. If there is no significant specification error in the model selected (which will be determined by means of a goodness-of-fit test to be described below), or if the model is saturated (that is, it consumes all available degrees of freedom and perfectly replicates the dependent variable function), we may test specific hypotheses concerning either the statistical significance of individual-model parameter estimates or differences among individual-model parameter estimates. Thus what we want to do for Table 7.6 is to identify a function of party, period, and subject area that will account for the variation in the proportion of liberal decisions; once this task is completed, we will repeat it for the log-odds dependent variable function.

Parameter Estimation and Significance Tests

Let us assume for the moment that we have selected our dependent variable function and specified a model (a set of dummy variables, or *X*'s) that we believe will "fit the data." We now would like to obtain estimates of the model parameters, or *b*'s. The estimating procedure suggested by Grizzle et al. is a form of weighted least squares (WLS); an alternate method of parameter estimation that could be used is maximum likelihood (ML). For practical purposes, particularly with large samples, the choice between ML estimation and WLS estimation has no effect on the results we will obtain. Because of the simpler mathematics involved, we will use WLS.[8]

The simplest form of least-squares estimation is ordinary least squares (OLS). To use OLS, we must be able to make a number of assumptions, including two assumptions regarding the error terms: homoscedasticity (equal variances) and independence. In Table 7.6 the problem of correlated (nonindependent) errors does not arise, because we have only one dependent variable for each row and the rows are independent of one another; if our actual dependent variable were polytomous rather than dichotomous, we might have more than one variable per row and the assumption of independence would be violated.[9] There are a variety of ways of explicating the meaning of homoscedasticity. Perhaps the easiest interpretation to grasp is the idea that it means all of the observations on our dependent variable are equally reliable; that is, the sampling error or variance of estimate is equal for all observations on the dependent variable. In general, with aggregate measures such as means or proportions this can be true only if each observation is based upon approximately the same number of actual cases; furthermore, in the case of proportions, the variance of estimate is directly related to the value of the underlying probability itself (as well as to the number of cases upon which the proportion estimate is based):

$$\sigma_p^2 = \frac{\pi(1 - \pi)}{n} \qquad [7.24]$$

This formula is simply an application of the central limit theorem to the variance of a proportion (equation 7.6 above); assuming a constant n, the variance of estimate is at a maximum when π equals .5 and decreases as π approaches either one or zero. Thus, rather than meeting the requirement of homoscedasticity, we must find a means of coping with the problem of heteroscedasticity.[10]

An extension of ordinary least squares, weighted least squares (see for example, Draper and Smith, 1967: 77-81), can be used to overcome the problem of homoscedasticity. With WLS (which is a particular form of GLS, or generalized least squares), each observation is weighted by the inverse of its known variance of estimate; thus the more reliable observations are counted more heavily. In most applications, the major stumbling block of WLS is determining the variance of estimate of each observation. In categorical regression, we can obtain an estimate of this variance by substituting the sample estimate of π, p, for π in equation 7.24 above;

only in rare cases will the difference between p and π be sufficient to greatly affect our estimate.[11] WLS can also be used to adjust for correlated errors such as those that occur with polytomous dependent variables; this is done by including in our least squares calculations a measure of the covariance of estimate. The actual computational differences between OLS and WLS are best understood in terms of matrix algebra; this is shown in Appendix 7A for those who are interested.

With categorical regression there are two basic types of significance tests that may be computed: goodness-of-fit tests, and hypothesis or contrast tests. Categorical regression uses the chi-square distribution for statistical inference because it is concerned with tests regarding proportions. As with ordinary chi-square tests and difference of proportion tests, the significance tests used with categorical regression are asymptotic. The goodness-of-fit test compares the difference between the observed f's and the f_i's predicted based upon the estimates of the parameters of our regression equation; given that *e* consists only of specification error this test tells us whether or not anything of significance has been omitted from the model. Thus if the goodness-of-fit test is statistically significant, we know that specification error is present in our dummy variable model, and we need to locate its source and include dummy variables to account for it. If significant specification error is present in our model, the parameter estimates we have obtained for that model are technically "biased" (see Deegan, 1974), and hypothesis testing based upon those estimates may be suspect. However, after examining the statistically significant effects we may decide to omit them if (1) they are substantively unimportant and (2) their omission has no meaningful effect on the estimates of the remaining parameters. The actual goodness-of-fit chi-square is equal to the difference between the total variance in our dependent variable functions and the variance explained by our model. This statistic, which is known as the Wald statistic, is equal to Neyman's chi-square (equation 7.22); Appendix 7A describes the actual computations involved.

There are three types of hypothesis tests that may be computed based upon the parameter estimates (assuming no specification error is present). The simplest of these is the test of individual parameter estimates; for example, is $\hat{b}_i$ significantly different from zero? This test is given by

$$\chi^2 = \frac{\hat{b}_i^2}{\sigma^2_{\hat{b}_i}} \qquad [7.25a]$$

or

$$Z = \frac{\hat{b}_i}{\sigma_{\hat{b}_i}} \qquad [7.25b]$$

$\sigma^2_{\hat{b}_i}$ is the variance of estimate of $\hat{b}_i$ and is taken from the diagonal of matrix **V** shown in equation 7.A19. A second type of test involves the simultaneous test of two or more parameter estimates; if this test includes all $\hat{\mathbf{b}}$ parameters except the constant term, a test of the entire equation results. This test is given by

$$\chi^2 = \sum_i^k \sum_j^k \hat{b}_i \hat{b}_j w_{ij} \qquad [7.26]$$

where k is the number of $\hat{b}$'s to be tested and w_{ij} is from the inverse of $\mathbf{V}_b$ (see Appendix 7A). The final type of hypothesis test involves complex hypotheses of the form

$$\hat{h}_i = \hat{b}_j - \hat{b}_k \qquad [7.27]$$

where the question of interest is whether $\hat{h}_i$ is significantly different from zero (that is, is $\hat{b}_j$ significantly different from $\hat{b}_k$). The test of a single hypothesis of the form shown in equation 7.27 is given by

$$\chi^2 = \frac{\hat{h}_i}{\sigma^2_{\hat{h}_i}} \qquad [7.28]$$

where $\sigma^2_{\hat{h}_i}$ is the variance of estimate of the hypothesis to be tested, which is taken from equation 7.A12 in Appendix 7A. The simultaneous test test of several hypotheses of this type can be performed using a test resembling equation 7.26 above; these tests are directly equivalent to the Chow test (Hanushek and Jackson, 1977: 128) used in ordinary regression, and could be performed in the same way as the Chow test is carried (that is, by fitting models with and without the parameters of interest, and computing the difference between the two goodness-of-fit statistics). In actual practice, these tests are computed as a series of matrix multiplications that are shown in Appendix 7A.[11]

Example I

The discussion now turns to an analysis of the dependent variable function, proportion liberal, from Table 7.6.[12] We must now select a suitable regression model for that dependent variable function; the next question then is how to determine which of the many possible dummy variable models to use. If one has a theoretically derived model of specific interest, it is best to start with that model. If this is not the case, one may start either with a model that includes only the constant term and the main effects for the independent variables that define the table, or with a hierarchical, saturated model (that is, a complete factorial model) that includes all main effects and all possible interaction terms. If one starts with a main effects model and finds that the goodness-of-fit test is nonsignificant, one may safely proceed to reduce the main effects model (by eliminating nonsignificant parameters) and to interpret the results.[13] For purposes of illustration we will start with a main effects model even though we know from the difference-of-differences test discussed earlier that significant interactions are likely to be present.

In the exposition below the sets of dummy variables corresponding to each model will be shown; these sets of variables can be thought of as a matrix we will call the **X** matrix (in ordinary regression, the **X** matrix is simply the data matrix of the independent variables). As stated above, we will start with the main effects model:

$$\mathbf{X}_{\text{Main}} = \begin{bmatrix} 1 & 1 & 0 & 1 & 0 & 1 \\ 1 & 1 & 0 & 1 & 0 & -1 \\ 1 & 1 & 0 & 0 & 1 & 1 \\ 1 & 1 & 0 & 0 & 1 & -1 \\ 1 & 1 & 0 & -1 & -1 & 1 \\ 1 & 1 & 0 & -1 & -1 & -1 \\ 1 & 0 & 1 & 1 & 0 & 1 \\ 1 & 0 & 1 & 1 & 0 & -1 \\ 1 & 0 & 1 & 0 & 1 & 1 \\ 1 & 0 & 1 & 0 & 1 & -1 \\ 1 & 0 & 1 & -1 & -1 & 1 \\ 1 & 0 & 1 & -1 & -1 & -1 \\ 1 & -1 & -1 & 1 & 0 & 1 \\ 1 & -1 & -1 & 1 & 0 & -1 \\ 1 & -1 & -1 & 0 & 1 & 1 \\ 1 & -1 & -1 & 0 & 1 & -1 \\ 1 & -1 & -1 & -1 & -1 & 1 \\ 1 & -1 & -1 & -1 & -1 & -1 \end{bmatrix} \qquad [7.29]$$

Each column of the **X** matrix consists of a single dummy variable. The second column is a dummy variable contrasting criminal justice cases to economics cases; the third column contrasts civil rights and liberties to economics cases. The second and third columns taken together represent the effect of subject area (a contrast for criminal justice versus civil rights and liberties can be obtained by taking the difference between columns 2 and 3). Each row consists of the set of dummy variables for one row of the original table being analyzed (for example, row three is the set of dummy variables for criminal justice cases decided in the middle period by Democratic judges).[14] In creating each of these dummy variables, we have assigned a value of +1.0 to the rows corresponding to one category for the relevant independent variables (for example, those rows that involve Democratic judges) and a value of −1.0 to those rows corresponding to a contrasting category of the same independent variable (for example, those rows that involve Republican judges). This type of dummy variable, which is normally associated with analysis of variance (see Fennessey, 1968), is called "effect coding." It may be contrasted to the type of dummy variables associated with regression that use ones and zeros (see Miller and Erickson, 1974); this latter type is called "dummy coding." Effect coding will be used throughout this chapter because it is customarily used for contingency table analysis. Note that there can be important differences in the results obtained with the two types of coding, particularly in the presence of interactions (see Kritzer, 1978a: 219-224).

Fitting the model shown in matrix 7.28 by means of weighted least squares produces a significant goodness-of-fit test (see Table 7.7) indicating that significant effects have been omitted from the model. This is consistent with our earlier analysis because model **X** did not include any interactions among the predictor variables. The best procedure when interactions are present is to fit a saturated, complete factorial model including all main effects and all interactions among those main effects. The interaction terms are formed by taking the product of the dummies for the variables that are believed to be interacting. The mechanics involved are to multiply together all intervariable combinations (for example, each dummy variable for period is multiplied in turn by each dummy variable for subject, for a total for four terms); one does not include "intravariable" combinations (that is, no term is created by multiplying together the two dummies for period). The resulting matrix, $\mathbf{X}_{SAT}$, contains a total of eighteen columns: the original six from $\mathbf{X}_{Main}$, four terms representing the interaction of period and subject, two representing period by party, two representing matrix 7.30:

$$
\mathbf{X}_{\mathrm{SAT}} = \begin{bmatrix}
1 & 1 & 0 & 1 & 0 & 1 & 1 & 0 & 0 & 0 & 1 & 0 & 1 & 0 & 1 & 0 & 0 & 0 \\
1 & 1 & 0 & 1 & 0 & -1 & 1 & 0 & 0 & 0 & -1 & 0 & -1 & 0 & -1 & 0 & 0 & 0 \\
1 & 1 & 0 & 0 & 1 & 1 & 0 & 1 & 0 & 0 & 1 & 0 & 0 & 1 & 0 & 1 & 0 & 0 \\
1 & 1 & 0 & 0 & 1 & -1 & 0 & 1 & 0 & 0 & -1 & 0 & 0 & -1 & 0 & -1 & 0 & 0 \\
1 & 1 & 0 & -1 & -1 & 1 & -1 & -1 & 0 & 0 & 1 & 0 & -1 & -1 & -1 & -1 & 0 & 0 \\
1 & 1 & 0 & -1 & -1 & -1 & -1 & -1 & 0 & 0 & -1 & 0 & 1 & 1 & 1 & 1 & 0 & 0 \\
1 & 0 & 1 & 1 & 0 & 1 & 0 & 0 & 1 & 0 & 0 & 1 & 1 & 0 & 0 & 0 & 1 & 0 \\
1 & 0 & 1 & 1 & 0 & -1 & 0 & 0 & 1 & 0 & 0 & -1 & -1 & 0 & 0 & 0 & -1 & 0 \\
1 & 0 & 1 & 0 & 1 & 1 & 0 & 0 & 0 & 1 & 0 & 1 & 0 & 1 & 0 & 0 & 0 & 1 \\
1 & 0 & 1 & 0 & 1 & -1 & 0 & 0 & 0 & 1 & 0 & -1 & 0 & -1 & 0 & 0 & 0 & -1 \\
1 & 0 & 1 & -1 & -1 & 1 & 0 & 0 & -1 & -1 & 0 & 1 & -1 & -1 & 0 & 0 & -1 & -1 \\
1 & 0 & 1 & -1 & -1 & -1 & 0 & 0 & -1 & -1 & 0 & -1 & 1 & 1 & 0 & 0 & 1 & 1 \\
1 & -1 & -1 & 1 & 0 & 1 & -1 & 0 & -1 & 0 & -1 & -1 & 1 & 0 & -1 & 0 & -1 & 0 \\
1 & -1 & -1 & 1 & 0 & -1 & -1 & 0 & -1 & 0 & 1 & 1 & -1 & 0 & 1 & 0 & 1 & 0 \\
1 & -1 & -1 & 0 & 1 & 1 & 0 & -1 & 0 & -1 & -1 & -1 & 0 & 1 & 0 & -1 & 0 & -1 \\
1 & -1 & -1 & 0 & 1 & -1 & 0 & -1 & 0 & -1 & 1 & 1 & 0 & -1 & 0 & 1 & 0 & 1 \\
1 & -1 & -1 & -1 & -1 & 1 & 1 & 1 & 1 & 1 & -1 & -1 & -1 & -1 & 1 & 1 & 1 & 1 \\
1 & -1 & -1 & -1 & -1 & -1 & 1 & 1 & 1 & 1 & 1 & 1 & 1 & 1 & -1 & -1 & -1 & -1
\end{bmatrix} \qquad [7.30]
$$

Because the second-order interaction is significant, we cannot reduce the saturated model (even though one of the first-order interactions is insignificant) if the model is to remain hierarchical (that is, all lower-order effects included in a significant effect are retained in the model). This is because the nonsignificance of lower-order effects may be an artifact of coding decisions (see Kritzer, 1978a: 219-224).

How do we substantively interpret the results shown in Table 7.7? Let us proceed as though the main effects model had produced a nonsignificant goodness-of-fit test. The estimate of the party effect is one-half of the difference between the proportion of liberal decisions by Democratic judges and the proportion of liberal decisions by Republican judges, *controlling for period and subject matter*;[16] thus, given that the b for party is .04, twice this, .08, represents the difference in the proportion of liberal decisions for Democratic compared to that for Republican judges. Thus, substantively, we can say that the *b* for party is the *effect* of party, in much the same sense that a b in OLS corresponds to the effect of the variable it represents; here, however, the effect refers to changes in proportions as we move from one category to another. The effects for period and subject matter can be interpreted in the same way, except that each coefficient represents a contrast between a specific pair of categories and it is the set of coefficients, two coefficients for each of the variables in this example, that represents the "effect" of the independent variable on the dependent variable function.

TABLE 7.7
Hierarchical Models for Conditional Probabilities and Log Odds

Model	*Conditional Probabilities*						*Log Odds*							
	X_{Main}			X_{SAT}			X_{Main}				X_{SAT}			
	b	*df*	χ^2	*b*	*df*	χ^2	*b*	τ	*df*	χ^2	*b*	τ	*df*	χ^2
Mean	.42	1	–	.42	1	–	–.34	.71	1	–	–.34	.71	1	–
Subject	–	2	1979.14	–	2	1567.21	–	–	2	1675.87	–	–	2	1239.07
Criminal justice vs. economics	–.16	1	1667.09	–.16	1	1159.94	–.70	.50	1	1420.50	–.70	.50	1	908.08
Criminal rights vs. economics	.02	1	15.02	.02	1	11.67	.04	1.09	1	22.45	.10	1.11	1	19.06
Period	–	2	99.95	–	2	103.42	–	–	2	97.74	–	–	2	54.02
Early vs. late	–.04	1	46.55	–.03	1	24.21	–.16	.85	1	46.56	–.13	.88	1	22.67
Middle vs. late	.00	1	[1.36] [a]	–.00	1	[1.15]	–.02	.98	1	[1.22]	–.02	.98	1	[1.30]
Party	.04	1	181.69	.04	1	103.42	.18	1.20	1	186.80	.16	1.17	1	96.86
Subject × period				–	4	42.63						–	4	41.30
Subject × party				–	2	2.30						–	2	[0.63]
Period × party				–	2	61.55					–	–	2	53.56
Subject × party × party				–	4	17.99					–	–	4	15.08
χ^2 GOF		12	116.43		0	–			12	190.31			0	–

a. Bracketed chi-squares are not statistically significant.

The presence of significant interactions complicates the interpretation of the results. As was noted above, the interaction terms in matrix 7.30 are multiplicative combinations of the main effects (Bottenberg and Ward, 1963: 69-74). Because there are significant interactions, the results for the main effects model are biased due to specification error, and we cannot speak of the party effect; rather, we must somehow distinguish between party effects (or period effects, or subject effects) for different subgroups. In other words, if an interaction exists between two variables, we cannot base an explanation of the effect of those variables upon the simple main effects, because the joint effect of the two variables is not simply the sum of their individual effects (see Kritzer, 1978a: 219-224).

In order to handle these interactions in a more substantively meaningful way, we turn to what can be called "conditional" or "nested" models. By nesting one effect inside of another, we can create separate effects for different subgroups. In deciding how to nest effects, the best guide is substantive theory, although actual analyses can provide some help. In this case common sense suggests that period should be the controlling variable. Consequently, the first conditional model that was fitted had a main effect for period and nested effects for party and subject, plus their interaction, within period:

$$\mathbf{X}_{CSAT} = \begin{bmatrix}
1 & 0 & 0 & 1 & 0 & 0 & 0 & 0 & 0 & 1 & 0 & 0 & 1 & 0 & 0 & 0 & 0 & 0 \\
1 & 1 & 0 & 1 & 0 & 0 & 0 & 0 & 0 & -1 & 0 & 0 & -1 & 0 & 0 & 0 & 0 & 0 \\
1 & 0 & 1 & 0 & 1 & 0 & 0 & 0 & 0 & 0 & 1 & 0 & 0 & 1 & 0 & 0 & 0 & 0 \\
1 & 0 & 1 & 0 & 1 & 0 & 0 & 0 & 0 & 0 & -1 & 0 & 0 & 1 & 0 & 0 & 0 & 0 \\
1 & -1 & -1 & 0 & 0 & 1 & 0 & 0 & 0 & 0 & 0 & 1 & 0 & 0 & 1 & 0 & 0 & 0 \\
1 & -1 & -1 & 0 & 0 & 1 & 0 & 0 & 0 & 0 & 0 & -1 & 0 & 0 & -1 & 0 & 0 & 0 \\
1 & 1 & 0 & 0 & 0 & 0 & 1 & 0 & 0 & 1 & 0 & 0 & 0 & 0 & 0 & 1 & 0 & 0 \\
1 & 1 & 0 & 0 & 0 & 0 & 1 & 0 & 0 & -1 & 0 & 0 & 0 & 0 & 0 & -1 & 0 & 0 \\
1 & 0 & 1 & 0 & 0 & 0 & 0 & 1 & 0 & 0 & 1 & 0 & 0 & 0 & 0 & 0 & 1 & 0 \\
1 & 0 & 1 & 0 & 0 & 0 & 0 & 1 & 0 & 0 & -1 & 0 & 0 & 0 & 0 & 0 & -1 & 0 \\
1 & -1 & -1 & 0 & 0 & 0 & 0 & 0 & 1 & 0 & 0 & 1 & 0 & 0 & 0 & 0 & 0 & 1 \\
1 & -1 & -1 & 0 & 0 & 0 & 0 & 0 & 1 & 0 & 0 & -1 & 0 & 0 & 0 & 0 & 0 & -1 \\
1 & 1 & 0 & -1 & 0 & 0 & -1 & 0 & 0 & 1 & 0 & 0 & -1 & 0 & 0 & -1 & 0 & 0 \\
1 & 1 & 0 & -1 & 0 & 0 & -1 & 0 & 0 & -1 & 0 & 0 & 1 & 0 & 0 & 1 & 0 & 0 \\
1 & 0 & 1 & 0 & -1 & 0 & 0 & -1 & 0 & 0 & 1 & 0 & 0 & -1 & 0 & 0 & -1 & 0 \\
1 & 0 & 1 & 0 & -1 & 0 & 0 & -1 & 0 & 0 & -1 & 0 & 0 & 1 & 0 & 0 & 1 & 0 \\
1 & -1 & -1 & 0 & 0 & -1 & 0 & 0 & -1 & 0 & 0 & 1 & 0 & 0 & -1 & 0 & 0 & -1 \\
1 & -1 & -1 & 0 & 0 & -1 & 0 & 0 & -1 & 0 & 0 & -1 & 0 & 0 & 1 & 0 & 0 & 1
\end{bmatrix} \qquad [7.31]$$

From the results for $\mathbf{X}_{CSAT}$ shown in Table 7.8 we see that this formulation takes care of most of the interactions in the model; the only significant interaction that remains unaccounted for is that between subject and party for the later time period. The second panel shows a slightly reduced model that eliminates the insignificant interaction terms; the χ^2_{GOF} (at the bottom of the table) indicates that this model fits the table. Can we further specify this remaining interaction?[17] One might argue that the impact of party depends on subject matter, or that the impact of subject matter depends on party. Which formulation is "correct" would depend upon the substantive theory guiding the research; for purposes of illustration, we will assume that subject is the controlling variable and nest party within subject. This model is shown in equation 7.32 and differs from the model with the multiplicative interaction term only by the replacement of the late party effect and the two interaction terms with three party dummies for the late period (one for each subject matter).

$$\mathbf{X}_{COND} = \begin{bmatrix} 1 & 1 & 0 & 1 & 0 & 0 & 0 & 0 & 0 & 1 & 0 & 0 & 0 & 0 \\ 1 & 1 & 0 & 1 & 0 & 0 & 0 & 0 & 0 & -1 & 0 & 0 & 0 & 0 \\ 1 & 0 & 1 & 0 & 1 & 0 & 0 & 0 & 0 & 0 & 1 & 0 & 0 & 0 \\ 1 & 0 & 1 & 0 & 1 & 0 & 0 & 0 & 0 & 0 & -1 & 0 & 0 & 0 \\ 1 & -1 & -1 & 0 & 0 & 1 & 0 & 0 & 0 & 0 & 0 & 1 & 0 & 0 \\ 1 & -1 & -1 & 0 & 0 & 1 & 0 & 0 & 0 & 0 & 0 & -1 & 0 & 0 \\ 1 & 1 & 0 & 0 & 0 & 0 & 1 & 0 & 0 & 1 & 0 & 0 & 0 & 0 \\ 1 & 1 & 0 & 0 & 0 & 0 & 1 & 0 & 0 & -1 & 0 & 0 & 0 & 0 \\ 1 & 0 & 1 & 0 & 0 & 0 & 0 & 1 & 0 & 0 & 1 & 0 & 0 & 0 \\ 1 & 0 & 1 & 0 & 0 & 0 & 0 & 1 & 0 & 0 & -1 & 0 & 0 & 0 \\ 1 & -1 & -1 & 0 & 0 & 0 & 0 & 0 & 1 & 0 & 0 & 0 & 1 & 0 \\ 1 & -1 & -1 & 0 & 0 & 0 & 0 & 0 & 1 & 0 & 0 & 0 & -1 & 0 \\ 1 & 1 & 0 & -1 & 0 & 0 & -1 & 0 & 0 & 1 & 0 & 0 & 0 & 0 \\ 1 & 1 & 0 & -1 & 0 & 0 & -1 & 0 & 0 & -1 & 0 & 0 & 0 & 0 \\ 1 & 0 & 1 & 0 & -1 & 0 & 0 & -1 & 0 & 0 & 1 & 0 & 0 & 0 \\ 1 & 0 & 1 & 0 & -1 & 0 & 0 & -1 & 0 & 0 & -1 & 0 & 0 & 0 \\ 1 & -1 & -1 & 0 & 0 & -1 & 0 & 0 & -1 & 0 & 0 & 0 & 0 & 1 \\ 1 & -1 & -1 & 0 & 0 & -1 & 0 & 0 & -1 & 0 & 0 & 0 & 0 & -1 \end{bmatrix} \qquad [7.32]$$

Because this model accounts for exactly the same variance as the previous model, the other terms are unchanged, and the χ^2_{GOF} is unchanged.

Interpretation of this model proceeds in exactly the same way as the earlier, main effects model. For purposes of discussion, the focus will be on the effect of party, controlling for the other variables in the model.

TABLE 7.8
Conditional Models for Conditional Probabilities and Log Odds

Model	Conditional Probabilities						Log Odds							
	X_{CSAT}			X_{COND}			X_{CSAT}				X_{COND}			
	b	*df*	χ^2	*b*	*df*	χ^2	*b*	τ	*df*	χ^2	*b*	τ	*df*	χ^2
Mean	.42	1	–	.42	1	–	–.34	.71	1	–	–.34	.71	1	–
Period	–	2	58.36	–	2	59.35	–		2	59.02	–		2	59.67
Early vs. late	–.03	1	24.21	–.03	1	25.12	–.13	.88	1	22.67	–.13	.88	1	24.11
Middle vs. late	–.00	1	[1.15][a]	–.00	1	[1.05]	–.02	.98	1	[1.30]	–.02	.98	1	[1.00]
Subject	–	6	1974.05	–	6	1983.09	–		6	1665.40	–		6	1680.77
Early	–	2	284.41	–	2	291.12	–		2	215.01	–		2	224.17
Criminal vs. economics	–.16	1	211.24	–.16	1	210.85	–.72	.46	1	164.11	–.72	.46	1	166.52
Civil rights vs. economics	.04	1	10.30	.04	1	8.67	.20	1.22	1	14.02	.19	1.21	1	12.23
Middle	–	2	999.63	–	2	1001.96	–		2	843.13	–		2	849.32
Criminal vs. economics	–.17	1	658.04	–.17	1	666.66	–.74	.48	1	548.88	–.74	.84	1	562.25
Civil rights vs. economics	–.01	1	[2.54]	–.01	1	[1.92]	.02	.98	1	[0.47]	–.02	.98	1	[0.26]
Late	–	2	690.01	–	2	690.01	–		2	607.27	–		2	607.27
Criminal vs. economics	–.15	1	669.01	–.15	1	669.01	–.64	.53	2	584.92	–.64	.53	2	584.92
Civil rights vs. economics	.03	1	20.54	.03	1	20.54	.13	1.14	1	22.79	.13	1.44	1	22.79
Party	–	3	237.33	–	3	247.52	–		3	228.83	–		3	237.54
Early	.03	1	10.12	.03	1	19.52	.11	1.12	1	9.82	.14	1.15	1	19.74
Middle	.01	1	8.18	.01	1	8.96	.07	1.07	1	9.09	.06	1.06	1	7.88
Late	.07	1	219.04	(.07)[b]	(1)	(219.04)	.28	1.32	1	209.91	(.28)	(1.32)	(1)	(209.91)
Party Conditional on Subject for Late Period[b]														
Criminal				*.04*	*1*	*47.63*					*.21*	*1.23*	*1*	*46.65*
Civil rights				*.08*	*1*	*101.16*					*.30*	*1.35*	*1*	*97.74*
Economics				*.08*	*1*	*75.64*					*.33*	*1.39*	*1*	*73.79*
Subject X party	–	6	22.51											
Early	–	2	[4.53]				–		2	[4.06]				
Middle	–	2	[4.36]				–		2	[5.22]				
Later	–	2	13.62	–	(2)	(13.62)	–		0	6.73	–		(2)	(6.73)
χ^2_{GOF}	–	0	–	–	4	8.89	–		0	–	–		4	9.28

a. Bracketed chi-squares are not significant at the .05 level.
b. The italicized entries replace the parenthesized effects; see the text.

During the early period, Democrats were six percentage points more likely to make a liberal decision than were Republicans; the gap was only two percentage points during the middle period. During the last period, the effect of party varies with subject matter, with criminal justice cases having a gap of only eight points compared to sixteen-point gaps for civil rights and economics.

Example II

The same table will now be examined, but a log-odds dependent variable function will be used. The only change in how the analysis is carried out is that the dependent variable vector now contains log odds (the last column of Table 7.6);[18] to distinguish the log odds function from conditional probabilities, we will denote it as f^*. The major change in the analysis comes at the interpretation stage.

Let us start this analysis with the same two hierarchical models we looked at previously, the main effects model and the saturated model. As Table 7.7 shows, in the log-odds analysis the same effects are significant as in the conditional probability analysis, and the χ^2_{GOF} for the main effects model is very close to the value we found for that earlier analysis. This is not always true: In the same way that the dependent variable metric can stretch or compress distances in the difference of proportions or difference of log-odds analysis, one formulation can lead to significant effects even though the other does not; this in turn can lead to differing substantive conclusions.

That can be illustrated here by carrying out categorical regression analyses on Table 7.2, which was used in the "differences" analysis. Note that although we cannot directly compare the values of parameter estimates for the two models, we can compare the results of significance tests. The results of this analysis are shown in Table 7.9. As can be seen in the table, the interaction term, which has a value of –.01 for the conditional probability model and a value of –.02 for the log-odds model, is statistically significant for the former but not for the latter. The results for the three variable tabulation are used (Table 7.2) to illustrate the process of interpretation for log-odds models. The last panel of Table 7.9 shows the results for a reduced model containing only main effects.[19] The following equation represents this model:

$$f_i^* = b_0 + b_1 X_1 + b_2 X_2 \qquad [7.33]$$

where variable 1 is subject area and variable 2 is party (b_0 is the mean). As noted above, the b's are interpreted in much the same way as ordinary regression, and we can get predicted values of f in the same fashion using the estimated b's and the dummy variables. As with conditional probabilities, the b's represent one-half the difference in the dependent variable attributable to the term corresponding to the coefficient, controlling for the other variables in the model.

Thus the log-odds b for party tells us that the log odds of a Democrat rendering a liberal decision is .38 (twice .19) greater than that for a Republican, controlling for subject. We might understand this a bit better by adding and subtracting .19 to b_0 (−.57), yielding a predicted log-odds of −.38 for Democrats and −.76 for Republicans; for the moment we have ignored the control variable *subject*. The problem with this approach is that the log-odds metric is not intuitively meaningful to most persons. This is one disadvantage of log odds in comparison to conditional probabilities, which can be interpreted in terms of percentage differences.

There are two approaches to shifting log-odds results to a more meaningful metric. The first is to translate the results back to probabilities. The predicted log odds of −.38 and −.76 can be converted to conditional probabilities. The log odds (f^*) can be obtained from the probabilities:

$$f^* = \log\left(\frac{n_1/n}{n_2/n}\right) = \log\left(\frac{n_1/n}{(n - n_1)/n}\right) \qquad [7.34]$$

where

$$n = n_1 + n_2 \qquad [7.35]$$

Therefore

$$f^* = \log\left(\frac{p}{1 - p}\right) \qquad [7.36]$$

given that

$$p = n_1/n \qquad [7.37]$$

We can now reverse the process

$$\frac{p}{1 - p} = e^{f^*} \qquad [7.38]$$

TABLE 7.9
Categorical Regression Results for Decision by Party and Subject

	Conditional Probabilities		Log Odds					
						Main Effects Only[b]		
Effect	*b*	χ^2	*b*	τ	χ^2	*b*	τ	χ^2
Mean	.37	–	–.57	.57	–	–.57	.57	–
Subject	–.09	601.30	–.40	.67	575.68	–.40	.67	620.38
Party	.04	136.20	.19	1.21	131.69	.19	1.21	130.59
Subject by party	–.01	7.34	–.02	.98	[2.17][a]	–	–	–

NOTE: All chi-squares have one degree of freedom.
a. Bracketed chi-squares are not statistically significant.
b. The χ^2 GOF for this model is exactly equal to the χ^2 for the omitted interaction term; in this case this value is 2.17 (with one degree of freedom).

and through simple algebra, we get

$$p = \frac{e^{f^*}}{1 + e^{f^*}} \qquad [7.39]$$

For our example, equation 5.39 yields a predicted probability (ignoring subject) of .41 for Democrats and .32 for Republicans; this is a gap of nine percentage points compared to a gap of about eight if we had worked directly with probabilities (ignoring the problem of the significant interaction term[20]). The problem of this approach is that it depends upon the baseline we choose to start from (in this case we use the mean as the baseline). The gap for the two subject areas will be looked at but first the calculations must be completed for equation 7.33 by adding in the subject effect. Doing this yields predicted log odds of –.78 and –1.16 for criminal justice, and +.02 and –.36 for civil rights; applying equation 7.39 yields predicted probabilities of .31, .24, .50, and .41, respectively. We now have two different percentage point gaps, one of seven and one of nine. Which is "correct"? Which one do we talk about? It is interesting that the original gap is not an average of these two, because the particular gap depends upon how far toward the extremes of the probability scale we have gone.

The alternative, and probably easier, way to interpret log-odds results is to forget about the probabilities and work instead with odds. If f^* (equations 7.34 and 7.36) is the log odds, then e^{f^*} is the odds (F^+). We can take the predictive equation for the general dependent variable function, f, and rewrite it for f^*:

$$f^* = b_0 + b_1 X_1 + b_2 X_2 \quad [7.40]$$

We can convert both sides to odds

$$f^+ = e^{f^*} = e^{[b_0 + b_1 X_1 + b_2 X_2]} \quad [7.41]$$

Because

$$e^{[b_0 + b_1 X_1 + b_2 X_2]} = e^{[b_0]} + e^{[b_1 X_1]} + e^{[b_2 X_2]} \quad [7.42]$$

we can let

$$\tau_i = e^{[b_i]} \quad [7.43]$$

and obtain

$$e^{[b_0 + b_1 X_1 + b_2 X_2]} = \tau_0 \, \tau_1^{X_1} \tau_2^{X_2} \quad [7.44]$$

We now can substitute in equation 7.41:

$$F^+ = \tau_0 \, \tau_1^{X_1} \, \tau_2^{X_2} \quad [7.45]$$

This shows we can think of the odds as arising from a multiplicative model in τ. Also note that X_1 and X_2 take on only one of two values in this example, +1 or −1, which as a power of τ means that we either multiply by τ or divide by τ; if we work with a polytomous predictor, X_i would also have the potential value of 0, which reduces the corresponding τ to 1 (because anything to the zero power is 1), which has no effect on the product obtained from the model.

Thus we can interpret the parameters of the categorical regression, suitably transformed to τ's by equation 7.43, as affecting the odds in a multiplicative fashion. Thus we can calculate the odds of a liberal decision for Democrats and Republicans, ignoring subject, by

$$F^+ = \tau_0 \, \tau_2^{X_2} \quad [7.46]$$

yielding .69 and .47, respectively. We could talk about there being a .22 gap in the odds, but because we are thinking in multiplicative terms, it probably makes more sense to say that the odds for Democrats is 1.47 times that of the Republicans; this figure is nothing more than an odds ratio. (That is, the ratio of two odds). More importantly, it is equal to the square of the τ that we multiplied by to get the odds (the minor discrepancy here simply reflects rounding error). We can see this by noting the following (using α to represent an odds ratio as we did earlier):

$$\alpha = \frac{\tau_0 \bullet \tau_2^1}{\tau_0 \bullet \tau_2^{-1}} = \frac{\tau_2}{1/\tau_2} = \tau_2^2 \qquad [7.47]$$

By using equation 7.45 in place of equation 7.46 we can now see that including the τ for subject in the calculation would have no effect on α:

$$\alpha = \frac{\tau_0 \bullet \tau_1^{X_i} \tau_2^1}{\tau_0 \bullet \tau_1^{X_i} \tau_2^1} = \frac{\tau_2}{1/\tau_2} = \tau_2^2 \qquad [7.48]$$

Thus, where for conditional probabilities we could double the values of the b estimates and use those figures to describe results in terms of percentage differences, for log odds we convert to odds by exponentiation and square the values of the τ estimates and describe results in terms of odds ratios.

Let me close this section by completing the discussion of the log odds dependent variable function model for Table 7.6. Given that the results for the hierarchical model paralleled those for the conditional probability function, the next logical step is to replicate the conditional models discussed previously. The results for these models are shown in Table 7.8. The results for the conditional models also paralleled those for the probability function. Whereas earlier I commented that Democrats were six percentage points more likely to make a liberal decision during the early period and two percentage points more likely during the middle period, one would now say that the odds ratio for the early period was 1.32 versus only 1.12 for the middle period. For the last period, the effect of party still varies with subject matter, with odds ratios of 1.51, 1.82, and 1.92 for criminal, civil rights, and economics, respectively.

Assumptions and Missing Data

The primary assumption of categorical regression is that one can obtain a valid estimate of the sampling variance of the individual proportions in the table. For this assumption to be met the number of cases upon which the proportions are based must be sufficient for the central limit theorem to hold. A good rule of thumb is that each row of the table should contain at least ten observations; in a large table if one or two rows fail to meet this criterion, it is probably still safe to proceed with the analysis. The second requirement that must be met in order to obtain valid variance estimates is that the data reflect an underlying multinomial or product multinomial distribution; usually, if the sampling design under which the data were collected is a random sample (or a good approximation of a random sample), this assumption will in practice be met. Strictly speaking, if a stratified random sample is used, the strata must be incorporated into the table (or appropriately weighted to remove the effect of stratification) and the variances should be adjusted to reflect differences in sampling rates among strata; however, if the sampling rates are very small, as is the case in national survey samples, these adjustments are so minimal that they can be ignored.[21]

In a large table it is not unusual for some cells to be vacant, or even for some subpopulations to be missing entirely (for example, Black Jews). If individual, scattered cells are vacant, a small value should be placed in the cell; as an arbitrary choice, a good value to use is $1/c$ where c is the number of columns in the table. If entire subpopulations are missing (that is, the data are not "complete factorial"), one can proceed without problems except that some of the interactions involving the missing subpopulations cannot be included in the model. Also, if one has a number of very small rows with small N's that represent groups with similar characteristics, one can collapse those rows and work with them as a single group (see Lehnen and Koch, 1974a: 293-300). With this approach to small N rows, the only problem is that, as with missing rows, interactions involving the collapsed rows cannot be represented in the model.

LOG-LINEAR MODELS

What is the relationship between the models I have developed above and log-linear models for contingency tables (Reynolds, 1977; Fienberg, 1977; Goodman 1971, 1972a, 1972b)? A log-linear model is most often described as a linear transformation of a multiplicative model for the cell frequencies. This multiplicative model is written as a set of terms that will be called gammas (γ). The example will be used of a three-variable table with the variables labeled "A," "B," and "C"; each cell frequency of this table is denoted as N_{ijk}, with each subscript corresponding to one of the three variables. As normally presented, the general log-linear models do not identify one variable as a dependent variable.

The saturated multiplicative model can now be written:

$$N_{ijk} = \gamma\gamma_i^A \gamma_j^B \gamma_k^C \gamma_{ij}^{AB} \gamma_{ik}^{AC} \gamma_{jk}^{BC} \gamma_{ijk}^{ABC} \qquad [7.50]$$

The most common procedure for obtaining estimates for the Υ's is to obtain a set of expected frequencies based on the model chosen, and then to calculate the estimates from those expected frequencies. Details of the procedure can be found in the sources cited above (see also Davis, 1974). For our purposes, we do not need to be concerned about the details of estimation; we are interested only in the relationship to the log-odds model described above.

One of the properties of the Υ's for a given variable (or interaction) is that their product must be equal to 1; for a dichotomous variable this means that (for an arbitrary variable denoted as *)

$$\Upsilon^{*}_{2} = 1/\Upsilon^{*}_{1} \qquad [7.51]$$

With this in mind, let us treat variable C in model 7.50 as a dependent variable, and form the odds:

$$F^{+} = \frac{N_{ij1}}{N_{ij2}} = \frac{\Upsilon\,\Upsilon^{A}_{i}\;\Upsilon^{B}_{j}\;\Upsilon^{C}_{1}\;\Upsilon^{AB}_{ij}\;\;\Upsilon^{AC}_{i1}\;\;\Upsilon^{BC}_{j1}\;\;\Upsilon^{ABC}_{ij1}}{\Upsilon\,\Upsilon^{A}_{i}\;\Upsilon^{B}_{j}\;\Upsilon^{C}_{2}\;\Upsilon^{AB}_{ij}\;\;\Upsilon^{AC}_{i2}\;\;\Upsilon^{BC}_{j2}\;\;\Upsilon^{ABC}_{ij2}} \qquad [7.52]$$

Assuming all variables are dichotomous we can substitute using equation 7.51 and simplify by dropping terms that cancel:

$$F^{+} = \frac{\Upsilon^{C}_{1}\;\;\Upsilon^{AC}_{i1}\;\;\Upsilon^{BC}_{ji}\;\;\Upsilon^{ABC}_{ij1}}{1/\Upsilon^{C}_{1}\;\;1/\Upsilon^{AC}_{i1}\;\;1/\Upsilon^{BC}_{ji}\;\;1/\Upsilon^{AC}_{ij1}} \qquad [7.53]$$

Further simplification yields

$$F^{+} = (\Upsilon^{C}_{1})^{2}\;(\Upsilon^{AC}_{il})^{2}\;(\Upsilon^{BC}_{ji})^{2}\;(\Upsilon^{ABC}_{ijk})^{2} \qquad [7.54]$$

Notice that all terms contain C as an identifying superscript and 1 as an identifying subscript; omitting these yields:

$$F = (\Upsilon)^{2}\,(\Upsilon^{A}{}_{i})^{2}\,(\Upsilon^{B}{}_{j)})^{2}\,(\Upsilon^{A}{}_{i}{}^{C}{}_{j})^{2} \qquad [7.55]$$

We now have a model that looks very much like the multiplicative odds model in equation 7.47; it would be identical in form if we let

$$\tau = \Upsilon^{2} \qquad [7.56]$$

Thus what we have shown is that for a given dependent variable, log-linear model parameters containing that variable's identifier are simply the square root of the corresponding log-odds parameter. That is, the log-odds model is nothing more than the log-linear model with one of the variables designated as a dependent variable. The general log-linear model can sometimes be used to test hypotheses that cannot be formulated in terms of independent and dependent variables (see Reynolds, 1977: 166–179), but where a dependent variable is identifiable, a log-odds formulation is most useful, whether that approach is used by means of categorical regression or by use of log-linear models.

CONCLUSIONS

The purpose of this chapter has been to outline one of the approaches to complex contingency table analysis. This discussion has been limited to relatively simple analytic problems. We have limited our discussion to dichotomous dependent variables; extensions to polytomies are both straightforward and interesting (see Lehnen and Koch, 1974a, for an example). Additionally, the categorical regression approach described here can be used in much more complex situations including those involving multiple dependent variables (Kritzer, 1977b; Lehnen and Koch, 1974b; Forthoter and Lehnen, 1981), cohort tables (Fienberg and Mason, 1979; Kritzer, 1983), and correlation coefficients, both ordinal and nominal (Forthofer and Koch, 1973; Kritzer, 1977, 1980).

The major advantage of this approach is its direct relationship to linear regression. Anyone who is versed in that common technique can quickly learn and use categorical regression: The mathematics are essentially the same and the mode of interpretation parallel to that of dummy variable regression. One other advantage of categorical regression is that it lends itself to interactive analysis: Once the table is defined one can quickly identify an appropriate model and carry out hypothesis tests. There are several computer programs available for categorical regression, including the FUNCAT procedure in SAS, and the stand-alone programs NONMET (Kritzer, 1976) and GLIM (Nelder, 1975). If neither of these programs is available, log-odds models can be examined by using the log-linear model programs in the $SPSS^X$ and BMDP packages. Lastly, because the entire process of categorical regression involves a series of matrix manipulations (see the Appendix), it is possible to perform the analysis using a matrix "language" (for example, MATLAB or Gauss) or using a matrix procedure in a larger package (for example, SAS or Minitab).

Appendix 7A: The Matrix Representation of Categorical Regression

The OLS matrix solution is

$$\hat{\mathbf{b}} = (\mathbf{X}'\mathbf{X})^{-1}\mathbf{X}'\mathbf{y} \qquad [7.A1]$$

where $\hat{\mathbf{b}}$ is the regression weights. $\mathbf{X}$ is the data matrix of independent variables, and $\mathbf{y}$ is the vector of dependent variables. The formula for weighted least squares is

$$\hat{\mathbf{b}} = (\mathbf{X}'\mathbf{V}^{-1}\mathbf{X})^{-1}\mathbf{X}'\mathbf{V}^{-1}\mathbf{y} \qquad [7.A2]$$

The usual problem in employing WLS is obtaining an estimate of $\mathbf{V}$. For this application, we may obtain an estimate of $\mathbf{V}$ by selecting appropriate elements of matrix $\mathbf{V}_p$ below:

$$\underset{(rs \ x \ rs)}{\mathbf{V}} = \begin{bmatrix} \mathbf{V}_1 & \mathbf{O} \cdot \cdot \cdot & \mathbf{O} \\ \mathbf{O} & \mathbf{V}_2 \cdot \cdot \cdot & \mathbf{O} \\ \cdot \cdot \cdot & & \cdot \cdot \cdot \\ \mathbf{O} & \mathbf{O} & \mathbf{V}_s \end{bmatrix} \qquad [7.A3]$$

where

$$\underset{(rxr)}{\mathbf{V}_i} = \frac{1}{n_i} \begin{bmatrix} p_{i1}(1 - p_{i1}) & -p_{i1}p_{i2} & \cdot \cdot \cdot & -p_{i1}p_{ir} \\ -p_{i1}p_{i2} & p_{i2}(1 - p_{i2}) & \cdot \cdot \cdot & -p_{i2}p_{ir} \\ \cdot \cdot \cdot & \cdot \cdot \cdot & & \cdot \cdot \cdot \\ -p_{i1}p_{ir} & -p_{i2}p_{ir} & \cdot \cdot \cdot & p_{ir}(i - p_{ir}) \end{bmatrix} \qquad [7.A4]$$

and r is the number of columns in the table and s is the number of rows. To distinguish categorical regression from ordinary regression, we will express the general linear model as

$$\mathbf{f} = \mathbf{X}\mathbf{b} + \mathbf{e} \qquad [7.A5]$$

and the WLS solution as

$$\hat{\mathbf{b}} = (\mathbf{X}\ \mathbf{V}_f^{-1}\mathbf{X})^{-1}\mathbf{X}'\mathbf{V}_f^{-1}\mathbf{f} \qquad [7.A6]$$

We may estimate the variance-covariance matrix of the estimated model parameters ($\hat{b}$'s) by

$$\mathbf{V}_b = (\mathbf{X}'\mathbf{V}_f^{-1}\mathbf{X})^{-1} \qquad [7.A7]$$

To test how well the set of dummy variables ("the model") recreates the observed proportions, we use a chi-square goodness-of-fit test:

$$\chi^2_{GOF} = [\mathbf{f}'\mathbf{V}_f^{-1}\mathbf{f}] - [\hat{\mathbf{b}}'\hat{\mathbf{V}}_b^{-1}\mathbf{b}] \qquad [7.A8]$$

Note that the two parts of equation 7.A8 correspond to the total variation and the explained variation; thus chi-square goodness-of-fit is equal to the unexplained variation. Hypothesis testing is done by means of the general linear hypothesis:

$$\hat{\mathbf{C}}\mathbf{b} = \mathbf{0} \qquad [7.A9]$$

where **C** is a contrast matrix that specifies the hypothesis to be tested. **C** can be such that it specifies any of the types of hypotheses discussed previously. The test of this hypothesis is given by

$$\chi^2 = (\mathbf{C}\hat{\mathbf{b}})'(\mathbf{C}\mathbf{V}_{\hat{b}}\mathbf{C}')^{-1}(\mathbf{C}\hat{\mathbf{b}}) \qquad [7.A10]$$

Note that if we allow

$$\mathbf{h} = \mathbf{C}\hat{\mathbf{b}} \qquad [7.A11]$$

and

$$\mathbf{V}_h = \mathbf{C}\mathbf{V}_{\hat{b}}\mathbf{C}' \qquad [7.A12]$$

Equation 7.A10 becomes

$$\chi^2 = \mathbf{h}'\mathbf{V}_h^{-1}\mathbf{h} \qquad [7.A13]$$

We could also obtain the predicted **f** based on the regression equation:

$$\hat{\mathbf{f}} = \mathbf{X}\hat{\mathbf{b}} \qquad [7.A14]$$

and its covariance matrix

$$\mathbf{V}_{\hat{f}} = \mathbf{X}\,\mathbf{V}_{\hat{b}}\,\mathbf{X} \qquad [7.A15]$$

Using **f**, we could compute residuals

$$\mathbf{f}_r = \mathbf{f} - \hat{\mathbf{f}} \qquad [7.A16]$$

In its simplest application, this approach could be used to test hypotheses about differences among proportions. If we let

$$\mathbf{X} = \mathbf{I} \qquad [7.A17]$$

(**I** is an identity matrix), we find that

$$\mathbf{f} = \mathbf{X}\hat{\mathbf{b}} = \mathbf{I}\hat{\mathbf{b}} = \hat{\mathbf{b}} \qquad [7.A18]$$

and

$$\mathbf{V}_{\hat{b}} = (\mathbf{X}'\,\mathbf{V}^{-1}\mathbf{X})^{-1} = (\mathbf{I}'\,\mathbf{V}_f^{-1}\mathbf{I})^{-1} = (\mathbf{V}_f^{-1})^{-1} = \mathbf{V}_f \qquad [7.A19]$$

We may then simply apply the general linear hypothesis (equation 7.A9) to test hypotheses about **f**. Using the data in Table 7.2:

$$\mathbf{f}' = \mathbf{b}' = [p_{11}\, p_{21}\, p_{31}\, p_{41}] \qquad [7.A20]$$

If we wish to test the hypothesis in equation 7.17:

$$H_0 : (p_{11} - p_{21}) - (p_{31} - p_{41}) = 0 \qquad [7.A21]$$

We specify the appropriate **C** matrix

$$\mathbf{C} = [1\ -1\ -1\ 1] \qquad [7.A22]$$

and compute the chi square by equation 7.A10.

The dependent variable function, **f**, is also created through a series of matrix manipulations. The probability table may be referred to as a matrix **P**; this matrix may be rewritten as a column vector (here shown as its transpose) **p**:

$$\mathbf{p}' = [p_{11}\, p_{12}\, .\ .\ p_{1r}\, p_{21}\, .\ .\ p_{sr}] \qquad [7.A23]$$

The dependent variable function (also called the response function) is formally defined as

$$\mathbf{f} = \mathbf{A}\,\mathbf{p} \qquad [7.A24]$$

where **A** is a matrix that is said to "define" the dependent variable function. In the case of Table 7.2, the **A** matrix would be

$$\mathbf{A} = \begin{bmatrix} 1 & 0 & 0 & 0 & 0 & 0 & 0 & 0 \\ 0 & 0 & 1 & 0 & 0 & 0 & 0 & 0 \\ 0 & 0 & 0 & 0 & 1 & 0 & 0 & 0 \\ 0 & 0 & 0 & 0 & 0 & 0 & 1 & 0 \end{bmatrix} \qquad [7.A25]$$

Multiplying out equation 7.A24 using the **p** vector corresponding to Table 7.2 and the **A** matrix in 7.A25, produces

$$\mathbf{f} = [.31\ .24\ .51\ .40] \qquad [7.A26]$$

which is the probability of liberal decisions for each row. In most cases, the expression of the **A** matrix may be simplified so that one must supply only a small part of it:

$$\mathbf{A} = \begin{bmatrix} \mathbf{A}^* & 0 & \cdots\cdot & 0 \\ 0 & \mathbf{A}^* & \cdots & 0 \\ \cdots & \cdots & \cdots & \cdots \\ 0 & 0 & \cdots & \mathbf{A}^* \end{bmatrix} \qquad [7.A27]$$

where in the case of matrix 7.A25

$$\mathbf{A}^* = [1\,0] \qquad [7.A28]$$

and

$$\mathbf{0} = [0\,0] \qquad [7.A29]$$

$\mathbf{A}^*$ is referred to as the block of the block diagonal **A** matrix. Given the variance-covariance matrix of **p** (equation 7.A3 above), we may simply derive the variance-covariance matrix of **f**:

$$\mathbf{V}_f = \mathbf{A}\,\mathbf{V}_p\,\mathbf{A}' \qquad [7.A30]$$

If we wish to use a log-odds response function we simply extend equations A24 and A30 by adding an additional matrix **K**:

$$\mathbf{f} = \mathbf{K}\log_e(\mathbf{A}\,\mathbf{p}) \qquad [7.A31]$$

and

$$V_f = \mathbf{K}\,\mathbf{D}^{-1}\,\mathbf{A}\,\mathbf{V}_f\,\mathbf{A}'\,\mathbf{D}^{-1}\,\mathbf{K}' \qquad [7.A32]$$

where **K** is a matrix defining the nature of the log function to be created and **D** is a diagonal matrix containing the elements of the vector **Ap** on the diagonal. If we desire to obtain a logit function for the data in Table 7.2, **A** and **K** are defined as

$$\mathbf{A} = \mathbf{I} \qquad [7.A33]$$

(I is a 8 × 8 identity matrix) and

$$\mathbf{K} = \begin{bmatrix} 1 & -1 & 0 & 0 & 0 & 0 & 0 & 0 \\ 0 & 0 & 1 & -1 & 0 & 0 & 0 & 0 \\ 0 & 0 & 0 & 0 & 1 & -1 & 0 & 0 \\ 0 & 0 & 0 & 0 & 0 & 0 & 1 & -1 \end{bmatrix} \qquad [7.A34]$$

The resulting **f** vector will be

$$\mathbf{f} = \begin{bmatrix} \log(p_{11}/p_{12}) \\ \log(p_{21}/p_{22}) \\ \log(p_{31}/p_{32}) \\ \log(p_{41}/p_{42}) \end{bmatrix} = \begin{bmatrix} \log(p_{11}) - \log(p_{12}) \\ \log(p_{21}) - \log(p_{22}) \\ \log(p_{31}) - \log(p_{32}) \\ \log(p_{41}) - \log(p_{42}) \end{bmatrix} \qquad [7.A35]$$

One can extend this approach by adding additional "operator" matrices and additional exponentiations and logarithmic operations; by doing so it is possible to build up complex functions of the simple proportions such as measures of association (see Forthofer and Koch, 1973; Kritzer, 1977, 1980).

NOTES

1. This rather convoluted statement reflects the uncertainty of whether the data in Table 1 should be considered a sample or a population. There is an ongoing debate over the appropriateness of tests of statistical significance with populations (see, for example, Henkel, 1976: 85-86; or Blalock, 1972: 238–239). This is not the place to get into a discussion over the merits of that debate; because I subscribe to the position that statistical tests *should* be used with populations in order to determine whether or not the *process* generating the observed data is a *random* process, I have posed the questions in the text to take into account that position. In the balance of this chapter, I will not consider which of the possible interpretations is appropriate.

2. The standard solution for small n's is to apply a "correction for continuity" (see Blalock, 1972: 285-387). However, recent evidence (see Fienberg, 1977: 21-22) indicates that this correction is excessively conservative and that the chi-square test is highly robust, even when the n's are small.

3. In fact, we should note that the log-odds ratio can be seen as the difference of two differences of log frequencies:

$$\hat{\alpha}^* = \log\left(\frac{a}{b}\right) - \log\left(\frac{c}{d}\right) = [\log(a) - \log(b)] - [\log(c) - \log(d)]$$

4. The totals in this table and the other raw data tables were generated by converting Carp and Rowland's percentage table back to frequency tables; consequently, frequencies may not add up exactly from table to table because of rounding.

5. The data in Table 7.1 include three subject areas; Table 7.2 involves only two.

6. If we had selected as the dependent variable proportion conservative the only change would have been in the signs of the parameters we will ultimately estimate.

7. We should also note here that we are assuming that the rows of the table constitute independent subsamples each selected from independent subpopulations. For independent random sampling this assumption is true by definition; it is possible to apply categorical regression in situations where this assumption is not met, though the "set up" is more involved.

8. One simple way to obtain ML estimates is to iterate the WLS solution; that is, one can use the estimates at each stage to update the weights and then repeat the WLS procedure (see Nelder and Wedderburn, 1972).

9. Because we have computed row conditional proportions, proportions from the same row (subpopulation) will not be independent of one another. However, because we can easily obtain the covariance of estimate (see Kritzer, 1978a: 214-215), this does not create major problems.

10. Strictly speaking, we are interested in the variance of the error term. However, because the independent variables in our regression model are all assumed to be nonstochastic, the variance of the error term is equal to the variance of the dependent variable (Theil, 1970: 138).

11. One can also compute a summary statistic, roughly analogous to R^2:

$$W^2 = \frac{\chi^2_{\text{equation}}}{\chi^2_{\text{GOF}} + \chi^2_{\text{equation}}}$$

This measure will always be very high in a correctly specified model, given the requirement that χ^2_{GOF} be nonsignificant.

12. The NONMET II computer program (see Kritzer, 1976) was used for this analysis.

13. Strictly speaking, it is possible to have a nonsignificant goodness-of-fit test even if a significant interaction term has been omitted. For example, if the χ^2_{GOF} is 15.37 with eight degrees of freedom, the eight omitted terms have an average chi-square of 1.92. Such a chi-square might obscure significant effects: One term may actually have a chi-square of 8.37, and the remaining terms have an average chi-square of 1.0. The only way to be sure that no significant terms have been omitted is to check a saturated model. Nonetheless, even if a significant term is hidden in a large nonsignificant goodness-of-fit chi-square, it is very unlikely that the omission of that term will result in important specification error (that is, bias in the other terms in the model).

14. If the dependent variable were polytomous, this interpretation would change slightly.

15. If we were to try to reduce the model, it would be advisable to do so in a "stepwise" fashion, starting with the highest-order interactions. For example, in a saturated model involving five independent variables, it may appear that none of the second-, third-, or fourth-order interactions are significant; however, if the third- and fourth-order interactions are removed, some of the second-order interactions may turn out to be significant after all. An example in which this was probably not done and as a result some significant effects were omitted is the analysis reported by Giles et al. (1976).

16. If we wanted the *b*'s to represent the actual differences rather than one-half the difference, we would simply use 1/2's and -1/2's for the main effects in $\mathbf{X}_{main}$. The interactions in $\mathbf{X}_{SAT}$ would still be formed by multiplying terms together yielding 1/4's and -1/4's for first-order interactions and 1/8's and -1/8's for second-order interactions.

17. One cautionary note is in order. As with many techniques, there are many conditional models in categorical regression that will "fit" a given set of data. The statistical analysis in no way proves which model is the "correct" one (although it may show some models to be probably incorrect); this is a problem for the substantive theory that should guide the selection of appropriate models.

18. The variance-covariance matrix for the dependent variable function will be changed accordingly, now being based on the logit variance (equation 7.19) rather than the proportion variance (equation 7.6).

19. The set of dummy variables for this model is

$$\mathbf{X} = \begin{bmatrix} 1 & 1 & 1 \\ 1 & 1 & -1 \\ 1 & -1 & 1 \\ 1 & -1 & -1 \end{bmatrix}$$

20. A main effects model fitted to the conditional probabilities in Table 2 yields b's of −.09 for subject and .04 for party.

21. In some types of sampling schemes (for example, multi-stage designs), the variance of estimate is greater than in normal random samples. For such samples, significance tests should be adjusted to be more conservative. Certain types of sample designs, such as those used in some types of experiments, may affect the type of dummy variable regression models that may be applied to the data; because these types of designs are not typically found in the work of political scientists, readers interested in such problems should consult the extensive work of Grizzle et al. (and their students) in the biometrics literature.

references

Bishop, Yvonne, Stephen Fienberg, and Paul Holland (1975) Discrete Multivariate Analysis: Theory and Practice. Cambridge, MA: MIT Press.

Blalock, Hubert M. (1972) Social Statistics. New York. McGraw-Hill.

Bottenberg, Robert A. and Joe H. Ward (1963) Applied Multiple Linear Regression. Springfield, VA: National Technical Information Service.

Carp, Robert A. and C. K. Rowland (1983) Policymaking in the Federal District Courts. Knoxville: University of Tennessee Press.

Clausen, Aage R. (1973) How Congressmen Decide: A Policy Focus. New York: St. Martin's Press.

David, James W. (1974) "Hierarchical models for significance tests in multivariate contingency tables: an exegesis of Goodman's recent papers," pp. 189-231 in H. Costner (ed.) Sociological Methodology 1973-74. San Francisco: Jossey-Bass.

Deegan, John (1974) "Specification error in causal models." Social Science Research 3 (September): 235-259.

Draper, N. and H. Smith (1967) Applied Regression Analysis. New York: John Wiley.

Fennessey, James (1968) The general linear model: a new perspective on some familiar topics. American Journal of Sociology 74 (July): 1-27.

Fienberg, Stephen E. (1977) The analysis of cross-classified categorical data. Cambridge: MIT Press.

Feinberg, Stephen E. and William M. Mason (1979) "Identification and estimation of age-period-cohort models in the analysis of discrete archival data," pp. 1-67 in K. F. Schuessler (ed.) Sociological Methodology 1979. San Francisco: Jossey-Bass.

Forthofer, Ronald N. and Gary G. Koch (1973) "An analysis for compounded functions of categorical data by linear models." Biometrics 29 (March): 143-157.

Forthofer, Ronald N. and Ronald G. Lehnen (1981) Public Program Analysis: A New Categorical Data Approach. Belmont, CA: Wadsworth.

Giles, Michael W., Douglas S. Gatlin, and Everett F. Catlado (1976) "Racial and class prejudice: their relative effects on protest against school desegregation." American Sociological Review 41 (April): 280-288.

Goodman, Leo A. (1971) "The analysis of multidimensional contingency tables." Technometrics 13 (February): 33-61.

———(1972a) "A modified multiple regression approach to the analysis of dichotomous variables." American Sociological Review 37 (February): 28-47.

———(1972b) "A general model for the analysis of surveys." American Journal of Sociology 77 (May): 1035-1086.

Grizzle, James E., C. Frank Starmer, and Gary G. Koch (1969) "Analysis of categorical data by linear models." Biometrics 25 (September): 489-504.

Hanushek, Eric A. and John E. Jackson (1977) Statistical Methods for Social Scientists. New York: Academic Press.

Henkel, Ramon E (1976) Tests of Significance. Beverly Hills, CA: Sage.

Kritzer, Herbert M. (1976) "NONMET II: a program for analyzing contingency tables by weighted least squares." Behavior Research Methods and Instrumentation 8 (June): 320-321.

———(1977) "Analyzing measures of association derived from contingency tables." Sociological Methods and Research 5 (May): 387-418.

———(1978a) "An introduction to multivariate contingency table analysis." American Journal of Political Science 22 (February): 187-226.

———(1978b) "Analyzing contingency tables by weighted least squares: an alternative to the Goodman approach." Political Methodology 5: 277-326.

———(1979) "Approaches to the analysis of complex contingency tables: a guide for the perplexed." Sociological Methods and Research 7 (February): 305-329.

———(1980) "Comparing partial rank order correlation coefficients from contingency table data." Sociological Methods and Research 8 (May): 420-433.

———(1983) "The identification problem in cohort analysis." Political Methodology 9: 35-50.

Lehnen, Robert G. and Gary G. Koch (1974a) "A general linear approach to the analysis of non-metric data: applications for political science." American Journal of Political Science 18 (May): 283-313.

———(1974b) "The analysis of categorical data from repeated measurement designs." Political Methodology 1: 103-123.

———(1974c) "Analyzing panel data with attrition." Public Opinion Quarterly 38 (Spring): 40-56.

MacRae, Duncan (1970) Issues and Parties in Legislative Voting: Methods of Statistical Analysis. New York: Harper & Row.

Miller, J. and M. Erickson (1974) "On dummy variable regression analysis: a description and illustration of the method." Sociological Methods and Research 2: (May): 409-430.

Nelder, J. A. (1975) General Linear Interactive Modelling (GLIM). Harpenden, England: Ruthamsted Experimental Station.

———and R.W.M. Wedderburn (1972) "Generalized linear models." Journal of The Royal Statistical Society (Series A) 135: 370-384.

Neyman, J. (1949) "Contribution to the theory of the χ^2 text." Proceedings of the Berkeley symposium on mathematical statistics and probability. Berkeley: University of California Press, pp. 239-273.

Reynolds, Henry T. (1977) The Analysis of Cross-Classifications. New York: Free Press.

Theil, Henri (1970) "On the estimation of relationships involving qualitative variables." American Journal of Sociology 76 (July): 103-154.

Wright, Gerald C. (1976) "Linear models for evaluating conditional relationships." American Journal of Political Science 20 (May): 349-373.

III

DYNAMIC ANALYSIS

8

Introduction

WILLIAM D. BERRY
MICHAEL S. LEWIS-BECK

In scientific research, we generally aim to make inferences about cause and effect. Obviously, an experiment allows the strongest inference about whether or not X caused Y. Take, for example, the following simple experiment in applied medicine. Imagine a large sample of patients is suffering from a newly discovered flu strain, Z–7, and some investigating physicians hypothesize that antibiotic A will bring about a cure, but the others are skeptical of this claim. Hence, following a classical experimental design, they randomly assign one-half of the sufferers to Group A (for treatment with antibiotic A), the other half to Group B (for no treatment). After two days, 90% of Group A is free from all traces of the flu, while only 20% of Group B shows any improvement. Therefore, the investigators conclude, with some confidence, that antibiotic A is highly effective in combatting the Z–7 flu. Seldom, in social science research, is cause and effect inference as powerful as in this medical example. One reason for this is that the bulk of social science investigation is nonexperimental, which robs it of two critical features: (1) random assignment of subjects to treatment, and (2) observation of the variables across time. The lack of the first means that we must worry that an observed relationship between X and Y is not causal, but rather a spurious product of the common influence of a "third" variable, Z. The absence of the second means that we do not know the timing of X, which may even have actually occurred after Y instead of before, thereby violating a necessary requirement of causality.

A widely used source of nonexperimental data, national election surveys conducted at a single time-point, can be used to illustrate these difficulties. Currently, political scientists and economists are busily engaged in assessing the impact of economic conditions on electoral behavior in the United States and Western Europe (for an up-to-date collection of papers, see Eulau and Lewis-Beck, 1985). In a national survey of voters from, say, the United States, assume we find a correlation of .4 between dissatisfaction with national economic performance (X) and disapproval of the president (Y). Before asserting that economic discontent is a cause of presidential disapproval one should, among other things, rule out the following possibilities: (1) this observed relationship is spurious, the product of a third variable such as party identification, and (2) presidential disapproval is not actually producing the perception of poor economic performance; that is, Y is causing X. The first possibility may be reasonably well ruled out by including the appropriate control variables in a multiple regression model. However, the second possibility is not at all easy to rule out within the constraints of a single survey. We must simply assume, on grounds of theory, that the causal arrow flows one way, from X to Y.[1] Further, we are forced into speculation about the timing of such a response. For example, does the formation of a negative opinion about the president come from the voter's evaluation of the economic news of last month? Last quarter? Last year?

Although confrontation of these issues surrounding the time dimension is integral to establishing firmly the presence and nature of a causal relationship, resolution is extremely difficult with cross-sectional data, such as an election survey. This dilemma suggests the real strength of investigations based on time-series data, that is, repeated measures on the same unit of analysis across time. Such data permit us to model explicitly the essential before-and-after-character of any real-world cause and effect process. The undergirding hypothesis of empirical research, "If X changes, *then* Y changes," implies movement in time. This dynamic quality is clearly evident in the "quasi-experimental" design of interrupted time-series (ITS) analysis, discussed in Chapter 9. Here the question is whether a relatively discrete event—suppose a change in law or policy—influences the behavior of a dependent variable, as measured over time. For example, does a lowered speed limit reduce traffic fatalities? Has federal legislation increased safety in U.S. coal mines? Did the Cuban Revolution harm economic growth in that country?

The impact of such interventions can be studied usefully in an ITS analysis. The basic strategy is simple: Compare the course of the dependent variable before the occurrence of the event to the course after, and determine if the differences are statistically significant. In this endeavor, Lewis-Beck relies on a straightforward extension of classical regression, modeling the "interruptions" by means of dummy variables that count time. Typical problems of making valid causal inferences from regression estimates—specification error, measurement error, multicollinearity—are discussed fully in the context of an ITS analysis. Particular attention is given to the problem of autocorrelated error terms, which is pervasive in time-series work. Diagnostic techniques for different autoregressive and moving-average error processes are provided, and a generalized least-squares correction for a first-order autoregressive process is described.

The second chapter in this part on dynamic analysis—Helmut Norpoth on transfer functions—moves time-series estimation beyond these generalized least-squares procedures. Further, it directs the reader's attention away from an ITS design, because the focus is on independent variables that are continuous, rather than discrete, phenomena. How does X (say, national unemployment) relate to Y (say, presidential popularity in a Gallup poll)? Is the relationship instantaneous (for example, an increase in unemployment immediately lowers presidential approval)? Or, does X influence Y at a lag (for instance, impact of last quarter's unemployment registers itself on this quarter's popularity rating)? According to Norpoth, to estimate such a relationship, traditional econometric methods should not be relied upon, because they contain two flaws: (1) they tend to postulate, rather than establish empirically, the timing of the cause and effect relationship between X and Y; and, (2) they can correct only fairly simple autocorrelation problems, such as a first-order autoregressive error process. In contrast, the transfer function approach, applying Box-Jenkins (1976) methods of prewhitening variables and ARIMA modeling, promises to identify the actual dynamics of the relationship and generate desirable nonlinear parameter estimates. To illustrate, he examines the relationship of national unemployment and inflation to presidential popularity in the United States, a subject much studied but little agreed upon. It is interesting to note that he finds inflation exercises its impact on presidential approval from the contemporaneous (t) and previous (t-1) quarters, but the influence of unemployment occurs only during the contemporaneous quarter (t).

Given the strengths of transfer-function analysis, one may ask why it has not been more widely used. An obvious reason is that, with the exception of Chapter 10, past methodological work has left the statistics and computer routines largely inaccessible to the reader. Another, more lasting, reason is the fear that the technique tends to "throw out the baby with the bathwater." That is, once the trends and the autocorrelation have been removed from the time-series variables under study, too little systematic variation may be left to form a valid transfer function. Thus the final models unduly favor the hypothesis of no causal effects. Norpoth suggests that this criticism, although not without merit, has been carried too far. He argues, first, that with large samples, say N = 100, this bias toward the null hypothesis disappears. Further, his own investigation of presidential popularity illustrates, convincingly, that transfer function analysis can yield positive results.

Chapter 11, by John Wanat, also employs data on United States presidential popularity to illustrate the solution to an apparently intractable problem: how to make inferences of individual change from a limited number of aggregate time-series observations. One common frustration with time-series data is a perilously small number of available observations, which makes statistical significance so difficult to achieve. Another is the aggregate nature of the data, which makes inferences to individual behavior very risky. Consider Wanat's example, which is the impact of the Cuban missile crisis on President Kennedy's popularity. Before the crisis, in September 1962, he received an approval of 62%, and after the crisis, in November 1962, his rating rose to 74%. Overall, it looks like the crisis was an intervention that boosted President Kennedy's approval. But who shifted what way? Were "disapprovers" more likely to become "approvers" than those with "no opinion" were? These two Gallup polls appear to tell us nothing about such interesting cross-time shifts of individual opinion. According to Wanat, however, creative use of the percentage marginals from the 3 × 3 table relating the two polls, along with a few modest assumptions, can permit the analyst to approximate a panel data-set, that is, surveys on the same sample of individuals at the two points in time.

To arrive at an estimate of individual shifts of opinion, he explores, with the aid of the computer, all possible solutions, given this 3 × 3 table, the marginal values, and the other constraints imposed. This possibilities approach leads, among other things, to the identification of limits to the cells and some cell groupings. For instance, in none of the 9858 possible solutions, each of which could have accounted for what did happen in 1962, does the value of cell a (those "approving" in both September and November) fall below 36%. Further, in virtually all these solutions, "disapprovers" changing to "approvers" exceeded "approvers" changing to "disapprovers." Thus through exhaustive, careful exploration of the possibilities for different cell values, given a particular set of marginals, apparently uninformative aggregate time-series data can be made to generate hard conclusions about certain changes in individual opinion over time.

In this section, we have reviewed three chapters on dynamic analysis. Although each emphasizes a different technique—interrupted time-series analysis, transfer-function analysis, the enumeration of possibilities—all are united in their focus on change. With each, the variables under investigation are observed to move over time. Of course, this allows surer inferences about changes and their causes. Given such an obvious advantage, in comparison to cross-sectional research, it does not seem unreasonable to call for more frequent incorporation of the time dimension in future social science research.

NOTE

1. Another alternative is to use a cross-sectional nonrecursive causal (or simultaneous equation) model, in which X is viewed as both a cause and an effect of Y. However, to obtain meaningful coefficient estimates for such a model, several strict assumptions—including error terms that are completely uncorrelated with each other—must be met. Carmines discusses nonrecursive models very briefly in Chapter 2, and Berry (1984) offers a more exhaustive treatment.

references

Berry, William D. (1984) Nonrecursive Causal Models. Beverly Hills, CA: Sage.

Box, George E. P. and Gwilym M. Jenkins (1976) Time Series Analysis. San Francisco: Holden-Day.

Eulan, Heinz and Michael Lewis-Beck (1985) Economic Conditions and Electoral Outcomes: United States and Western Europe. New York: Agathen Press.

9

Interrupted Time Series

MICHAEL S. LEWIS-BECK

Interrupted time-series (ITS) analyses are becoming rather widely applied in social science research. The technique attempts to answer a simple question: Does the occurrence of a particular event change a variable's behavior over time? The substantive literature offers several examples that pursue this inquiry. An ITS approach has been employed as follows: (1) to assess the impact of new public policies, in areas such as social security, coal mine safety, and civil rights (Albritton, 1979; Lewis-Beck and Alford, 1980; McCrone and Hardy, 1978); (2) to evaluate the effects of specific laws, such as traffic and gun control measures (Campbell and Ross, 1968; Glass, 1968; Deutsch and Alt, 1977; Zimring, 1975); and, (3) to determine the influence of major political shifts, including reform and revolution (Campbell, 1969; Caporaso and Pelowski, 1971; Lewis-Beck, 1979). With respect to the methodology of ITS analysis, work has tended to emphasize the broad issue of research design or the narrow issue of modeling the autocorrelation process (see, in order, Campbell and Stanley, 1966; Campbell, 1969; Cook and Campbell, 1979; Hibbs, 1977; Box and Tiao, 1975; McDowall et al., 1980). Although this effort benefits from both of these past emphases, the focus here is different from either. Simply put, I view ITS models as an interesting variation on the classic multiple regression model, which can be estimated with ordinary least squares, once the standard assumptions are satisfied. Below, I first consider how much can be learned about the effect of an "interruption" merely by "eyeballing" the time series. Then, I present a straightforward ordinary least-squares method for assessing more precisely the effects of both simple and multiple interruptions. Next, I discuss how to bolster confidence in the causal inferences made from these regression estimates, examining in particular the assumptions of no specification error, no measurement error, no perfect multicollinearity and, finally, no autocorrelation. Throughout, in order to make the presentation concrete, I draw on data examples.

EYEBALLING

An ITS analysis should be used whenever the investigator is interested in the effect of a relatively discrete event on a phenomenon observed over time. Normally, the research question is whether or not the event (X) caused a change in the phenomenon (Y). Occasionally, a glance at the scatterplot provides at least a preliminary answer. However, some plots are easier to decipher than others. Different possibilities will be evaluated, as they are sketched in Figure 9.1, where "X" marks the time the event took place. Further, to make the example less abstract, suppose the research question concerns the impact on traffic fatalities (Y) of a hypothetical 1972 reduction (X) in the Kentucky speed limit for automobiles to 50 mph (the example is inspired, of course, by Glass, 1968; Campbell and Ross, 1968). As can be seen immediately, there exists a class of plots (9.1a to 9.1e) that reveal little, if anything, about a cause-and-effect relationship. The first, Figure 9.1a, merely looks at fatalities the year after the new speed limit was imposed, completely ignoring what happened before. Although it is perhaps of interest as a "case study," this single post-event observation really suggests nothing about the effect of the speeding reduction. The second, Figure 9.1b, which records a pre-event observation as well, points to some influence from the 1972 speeding crackdown. However, this influence cannot be asserted with any confidence, for either observation could be a poor representative of Kentucky driving patterns. In other words, because we are not able to rule out the possibility that one or both of the observations are "outliers," causal inference is exceedingly weak.

In Figure 9.1c, the additional data allow the conclusion that observations made regarding 1971 and 1973 are probably not outliers. Still, it is far from clear that the speeding crackdown had any impact. Is the post-event scatter of points generally lower than the pre-event scatter, or is it the same height? Visually, one cannot be sure, because the data are so "noisy." For all these Figures (9.1a–9.1c), inference is difficult because the observations are so few. With ITS analysis, then, as with time-series analysis generally, the more cases the better. But, with ITS analysis an additional concern emerges, which is that enough observations be available before and after the event. For instance, in Figure 9.1d, there are several observations after 1972, but only one before. Given the almost total lack of prior data, it is quite difficult to assess whether the fatality rate actually changed after the speed limit imposition. The same holds true for Figure 9.1e; with no more than one observation after the event,

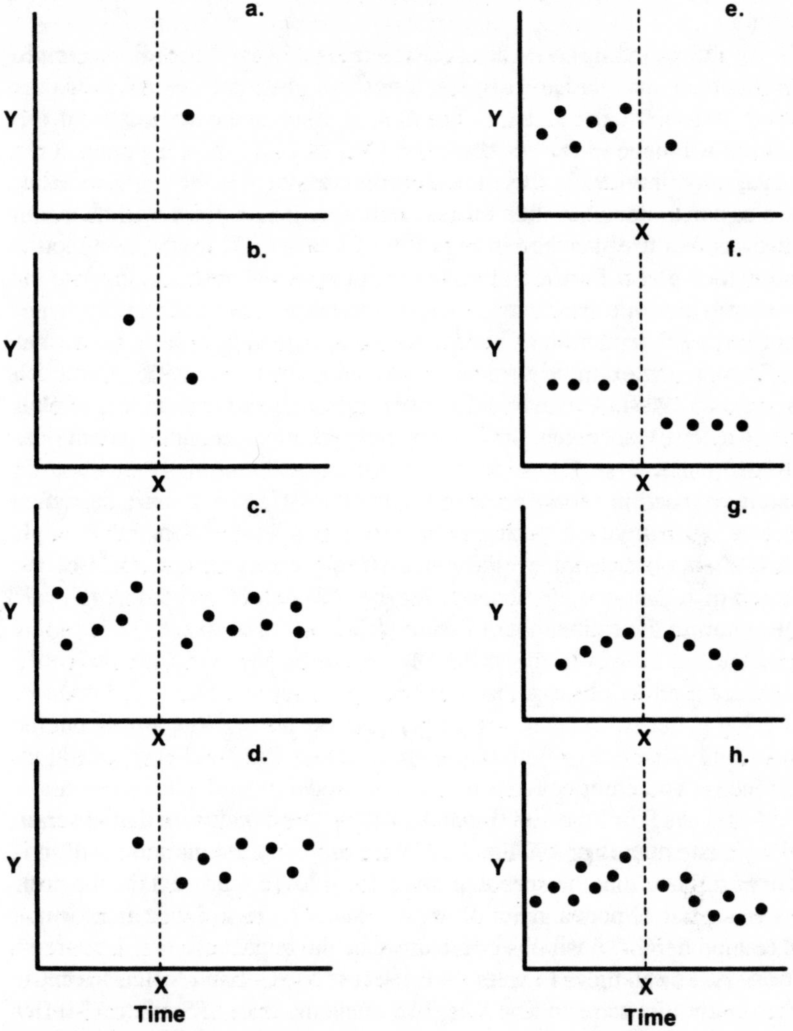

NOTE: X = the 1972 speed limit change; Y = annual traffic fatalities.

Figure 9.1 a-h: Various Interrupted Time Series Plots

change assessment is highly problematic, despite the relatively large number of pre-event observations.

From Figures 9.1a–9.1e, one sees that the number of observations in general, and their placement to the left and right sides of the event in particular, are important for easy visual diagnosis of the impact of an intervention. But, even a scarcity of cases does not automatically prevent accurate eyeballing, provided the pattern of effect is sharp. For example, in Figure 9.1f, there are only eight observations, but they form two distinct plateaus before and after the event, which clearly indicates a downward shift in the level of fatalities subsequent to the speeding crackdown. Again, in Figure 9.1g, there are few observations, but those before form a rising line, and those after form a declining line, suggesting a change in the trend in fatalities as a result of the 1972 law. Of course, the plots in Figures 9.1f and 9.1g are idealized. Time series of observations from the real world never unerringly track straight lines, so we are always eager for more cases in order to better discern what linearity might be present. The scatterplot in Figure 9.1h offers a more realistic picture of such data. Here, the level of fatalities appears to have dropped immediately after the speeding crackdown. Further, the trend in the fatality rate has changed, and is now heading downward. From just eyeballing the scatterplot of Figure 9.1h, it seems that the 1972 speed limit altered the Kentucky traffic fatality rate for the better, both in the short and long run. Exactly how much did it change? Did it really even change at all? Because these questions require answers more precise than eyeballing allows, I turn now to the estimation of ITS models.

ESTIMATION

The basic interrupted time-series model postulates intervention-induced changes in the level (mean) and/or trend (slope) of a time series. The least-squares procedure for estimating an ITS equation is straightforward, involving the use of dummy variables to represent the intervention (see also Draper and Smith, 1966: 134–142). First, I look at the simple ITS model (SITS), which aims to estimate the impact of a single intervention. As an example, I explore the effect of the Cuban revolution on Cuban economic growth. Then, I go on to the multiple ITS model (MITS), which estimates the impact of multiple interventions. That example examines the impact of the various U.S. coal mine safety laws on the mine fatality rate. After presenting these estimation procedures, I turn to the problems of making causal inferences from these ordinary least-squares (OLS) results.

The most uncomplicated SITS model evaluates the change in the level of the time series after the intervention occurs. One such change in level is diagrammed in Figure 9.2a, where the series jumps to a new plateau following the intervention. The data evidence no trend, and Y_t is a perfect function of the intervention, yielding the following regression equation:

$$Y_t = b_0 + b_1 (D_{1t}) \quad [9.1]$$

where Y_t = the value of the dependent variable at time point t; D_{1t} = a dichotomous dummy variable scored 0 for those observations before the event and 1 for those observations after the event, and data are available for N time points denoted 1, 2, . . . N. For the preintervention period, then, equation 9.1 for Y_t simplifies to

$$Y_t = b_0 + b_1 (0) \quad [9.2]$$

$$Y_t = b_0 \quad [9.3]$$

but for the postintervention period,

$$Y_t = b_0 + b_1(1) \quad [9.4]$$

$$Y_t = b_0 + b_1 \quad [9.5]$$

Hence the bivariate regression equation 9.1 estimates the change in the level (the change in the mean value) of the series, which is "$+b_1$". Observe that this change in level is actually a change in the intercept of the prediction equation, from b_0 to $b_0 + b_1$.

The Figure 9.2a diagram is unrealistic in several respects, one of which is its lack of any trend. Time-series data often exhibit a trend, which may obscure the change in level, and which may even change itself. In Figure 9.2b, the trend in the time series changes after an intervention. This postintervention change in trend can be estimated with the following multiple regression equation:

$$Y_t = b_0 + b_1 X_{1t} + b_2 D_{2t} \quad [9.6]$$

where Y_t = N time-series observations on the dependent variable; X_{1t} = a dummy variable counter for time from 1 to N; D_{2t} = a dummy variable counter of time scored 0 for observations before the event and 1, 2, 3 . . . . for observations after the event. For the preintervention period, then, the prediction equation simplifies to

$$Y_t = b_0 + b_1 X_{1t} + (0) \quad [9.7]$$

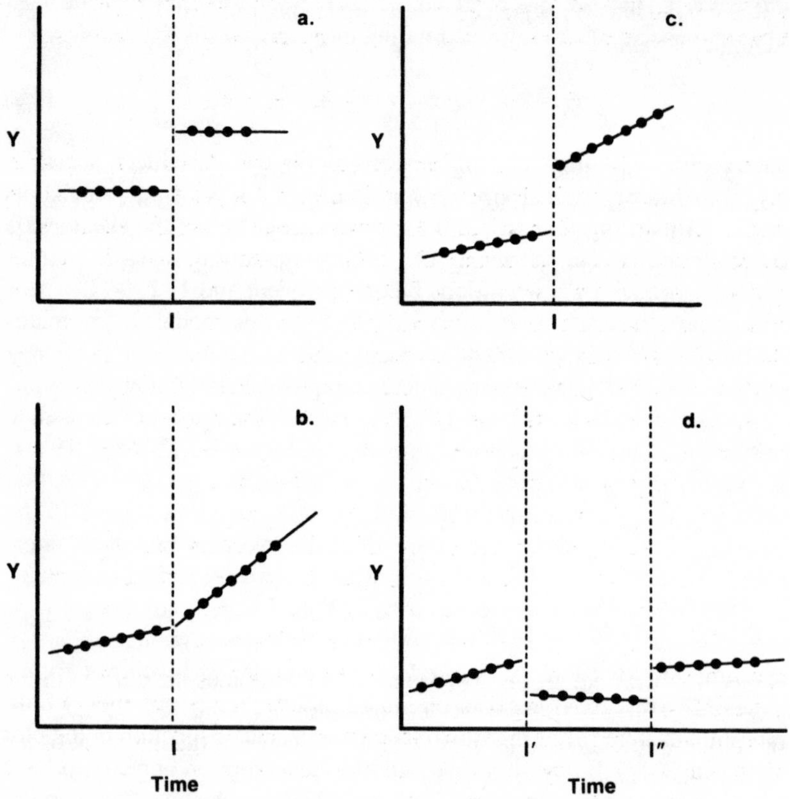

NOTE: Y = the dependent variable; I = the point of intervention.

Figure 9.2 a-d: Some Idealized Interrupted Time Series Plots

$$Y_t = b_0 + b_1 X_{1t} \quad [9.8]$$

Thus the slope (b_1) estimates the trend before the intervention. For the postintervention period, however, the prediction equation does not so simplify, because the values of D_{2t} increase incrementally with time. The trend for the postintervention period, then, is actually $b_1 + b_2$. Therefore, b_2 estimates the change in the trend (slope) of the time series subsequent to the intervention.

The more general SITS model allows for the possibility of estimating simultaneously both an intercept change and a slope change. (An example in which both occur is depicted in Figure 9.2c.) The appropriate multiple regression equation for estimating these changes is the following:

$$Y_t = b_0 + b_1X_{1t} + b_2X_{2t} + b_3X_{3t} \qquad [9.9]$$

where Y_t = N time-series observations on the dependent variable; X_{1t} = a dummy variable counter for time from 1 to N; X_{2t} = a dichotomous dummy variable scored 0 for observations before the event and 1 for observations after (formerly D_{1t}); X_{3t} = a dummy variable counter of time scored 0 for observations before the event and 1, 2, 3 . . . . for observations after the event (formerly D_{2t}). In this model, b_2 estimates the postintervention change in intercept, and b_3 estimates the postintervention change in slope. Perhaps a data example will clarify how this is so.

An earlier investigation used SITS to explore the impact of the Cuban revolution on national economic growth (see Lewis-Beck, 1979, 1981). In the scatterplot of Figure 9.3 are annual observations (1949-1980) on national energy consumption (in millions of metric tons logged to the base e), the proxy variable used for GNP. The vertical line that "interrupts" the series marks the beginning of the Cuban revolution on January 8, 1959, when Castro assumed control. Thus virtually all energy consumption for 1959 and after was under Castro's government, but energy consumption for 1958 and before took place under prerevolutionary regimes. The research question, of course, is whether or not energy consumption changed after the Castro takeover. Visual inspection of the plot hints that it did. In the short run, energy consumption appears to have taken an unusual jump from 1958 to 1959, suggesting an intercept change. In the long run, the trend looks a bit less steep after 1958, implying a slope change. Are these changes apparent rather than real, being in fact no more than products of chance? Further, if they are real changes, exactly how much do they amount to? OLS estimates of the general SITS model provide answers to these queries:

$$G_t = .840 + .076X_{1t} + .110X_{2t} - .034X_{3t} + e_t$$

$$(34.97) \quad (19.60) \quad (4.27) \quad (-8.43) \qquad [9.10]$$

$$\text{R-squared} = .996 \quad N = 32 \quad \text{D-W} = 1.42$$

where G_t = annual Cuban energy consumption (millions of metric tons, natural logs); X_{1t} = a dummy variable counter for time from 1 to 32; X_{2t} = a dichotomous dummy variable scored 0 for observations before 1959 and 1 for observation 1959 and after; X_{3t} = a dummy vari-

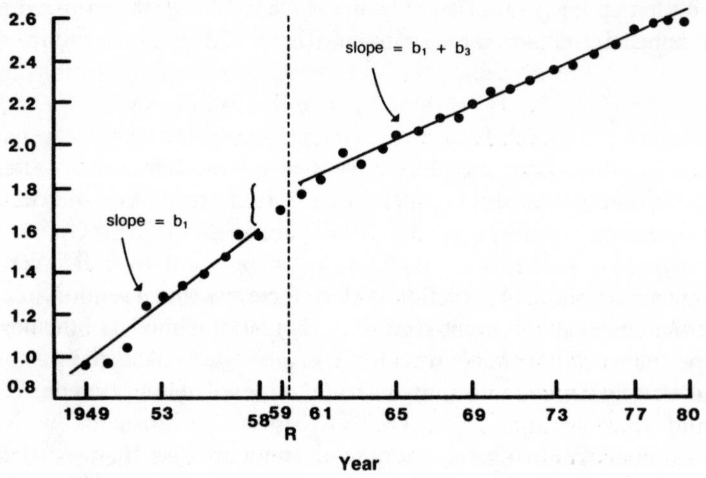

NOTE: R = revolution.

Figure 9.3: Simple Interrupted Time Series Plots of Annual Cuban Energy Consumption (1949-1980)

ables counter for time scored 0 for observations before 1959 and 1 (at 1959), 2 (at 1960), . . . , 22 (at 1980); e_t = the error term; the figures in parentheses = the t-ratios; the R-squared = the coefficient of multiple determination; D–W = the Durbin-Watson statistic; N = the number of annual observations (from 1949-1980, gathered from various issues of the *United Nations Statistical Yearbook*).

According to the t-ratios for b_2 and b_3, respectively, the level and the trend in energy consumption shifted significantly after Castro came to power (for statistical significance at .05, one-tail, $/t/ > 2.05$). Let us consider precisely how the SITS design captures these shifts, initially by examining the trend change. Using equation 9.10, we will predict the energy consumption values first for each of the preintervention years, then for each of the postintervention years. If the predicted values are now plotted, as in Figure 9.3, they are seen to form two straight lines. (These lines would also be produced by the bivariate regression of energy consumption on time, within each period; skeptics should demonstrate this for themselves.) Visually, the slopes of these lines appear different. Indeed, the slope of the preintervention line is .076 (b_1), but the slope of the postintervention line is only .042 ($b_1 - b_3$). As noted, this drop in slope of .034 (b_3) is statistically significant, indicating that the growth of energy consumption has slowed under Castro.

With regard to the positive change in the level, this is suggested by the gap between the two lines occurring from 1958 to 1959. For the years before the revolution, the prediction equation simplifies to $\hat{G}_t = b_0 + b_1 X_{1t}$ (given that X_{2t} and X_{3t} assume zero values). If the revolution had not taken place, then the prediction for 1959 on the basis of this equation for prerevolutionary Cuba would be 1.676 (that is, $\hat{G}_{59} = .840 + .076(11) = 1.676$). But, the revolution did occur, so the preferred prediction for 1959 becomes 1.752 ($\hat{G}_{59} = .840 + .076(11) + .11(1) - .034(1) = 1.676 + .076 = 1.752$). This .076 increase in the prediction is due to the post-intervention intercept rise (b_2) and would be still larger if the depressing impact of the negative slope change (b_3) were not working, $b_2 - b_3 = .110 - .034 = .076$. (It is strictly coincidental that this value is identical to b_1; in general, this would not be so.)

It is possible to refine further the meaning of these changes. Because the dependent variable is logged, a percentage change interpretation of the parameter estimates can be made (Tufte, 1974: 124–126). For example, a one-year change in X_{1t} produces a (b_1 x 100) percentage change in energy consumption. That is, b_1 estimates that energy consumption increased at the rate of 7.6% a year prior to the revolution. Then, after Castro came to power, the rate dropped 3.4 percentage points, according to b_3. Put another way, the estimated annual rate of energy consumption increase under the revolutionary government is 4.2% ($b_1 - b_3$). Therefore, in the long run, the Cuban revolution is associated with a diminished upward trend in energy consumption. But, in the short run, the picture is different. The estimated growth from 1958 to 1959 is 15.2 %, which reflects the substantial intercept shift measured by $b_2(\hat{G}_{59} - \hat{G}_{58} = b_1 + b_2 + b_3 = .076 + .11 - .034 = .152)$. In sum, this SITS analysis suggests that the arrival of the Cuban revolution was followed in the short term by increased economic growth (indicated by a significant intercept change, b_2), and in the long term by decreased economic growth (indicated by the significant slope change, b_3).

SITS analysis focuses on the impact of a single intervention. Obviously, however, a researcher might also be interested in the impact of multiple interventions. Suppose, to resume the traffic fatalities example, that the Kentucky speed limit was again changed, and this time it was raised to 65 mph. There are now two "interruptions" in the time series of fatalities, which is plotted in Figure 9.2d. These apparent slope and intercept changes can be estimated in a multiple interrupted times series (MITS) model, which straightforwardly extends the SITS model, as follows:

$$Y_t = b_0 + b_1 X_{1t} + b_2X_{2t} + b_3X_{3t} + b_4X_{4t} + b_5 X_{5t} + e_t \quad [9.11]$$

where Y_t, X_{1t}, X_{2t}, and X_{3t} are defined as in the SITS model of equation 9.9, thereby capturing the first event; X_{4t} = a dichotomous dummy variable scored 0 for observations before the second event and 1 for observations after; X_{5t} = a dummy counter of time scored 0 for observations before the second event and 1, 2, 3. . . . for after the second event; e_t = the error term. As is readily seen, the model is general in form, for any number of interventions can be incorporated by merely adding the appropriate variables.

Although examples of SITS analysis are not uncommon in the research literature, examples of MITS analysis are almost nonexistent, despite its undoubted applicability to numerous research questions. In earlier work, I utilized MITS analysis to assess the effect of three coal mine safety laws (from 1941, 1952, and 1969) on the fatality rate among miners (for details and follow-up studies, see Lewis-Beck and Alford, 1980; Perry, 1982; Nelson and Neumann, 1982). Here, I update these findings to 1980, and use the results to explicate a MITS analysis. Figure 9.4 is a plot of annual observations on the fatality rate in U.S. coal mines from 1932-1980. The vertical lines mark the introduction of the three different pieces of safety legislation. Eyeballing the scatter, it seems that the 1941 and 1969 laws influenced the fatality trend. Further, it appears that the 1941 law did not influence the level, but the 1969 law may have. The other possibilities are difficult to assess visually. To clarify what is going on, I formulate a full MITS model and estimate it with OLS, yielding

$$\begin{aligned} F_t = \ & \underset{(18.91)}{1.493} - \underset{(-.05)}{.001X_{1t}} - \underset{(-.95)}{.096X_{2t}} - \underset{(-2.66)}{.045X_{3t}} + \underset{(1.72)}{.151X_{4t}} \\ & \underset{(3.76)}{.047X_{5t}} - \underset{(-2.48)}{.228X_{6t}} - \underset{(-4.71)}{.058X_{7t}} + e_t \qquad [9.12] \\ & \text{R-squared} = .916 \quad N = 49 \quad \text{D–W} = 2.28 \end{aligned}$$

where F_t = annual fatalities per million hours worked; X_{1t} = a dummy counter for years, from 1 to 49; X_{2t} = a dichotomous dummy variable scored 0 for observations before 1942 and 1 for 1942 and after; X_{3t} = a dummy counter for years, scored 0 for observations before 1942, and 1, 2, 3 . . . . for 1942 and after; X_{4t} = a dichotomous dummy variable scored 0 for observations before 1953 and 1 for 1953 and

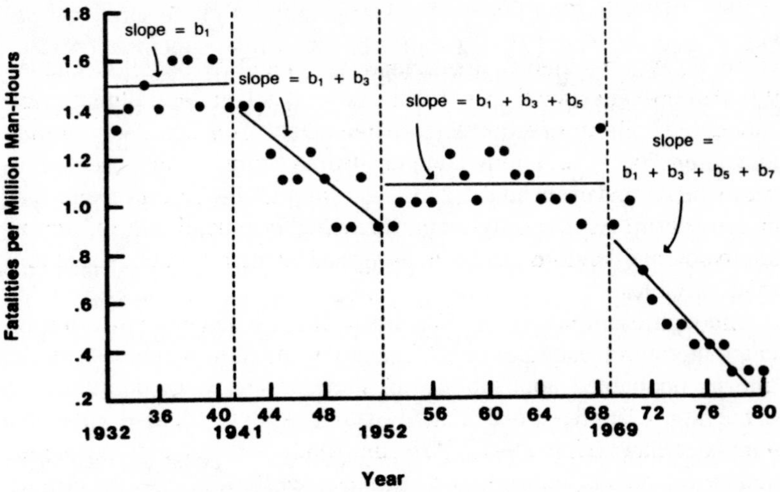

Figure 9.4: Multiple Interrupted Time Series Plots of the Annual Coal Mining Fatality Rate (1932-1980)

after; X_{5t} = a dummy counter for years, scored 0 for observations before 1953 and 1, 2, 3 . . . . for 1953 and after; X_{6t} = a dichotomous dummy variable scored 0 for observations before 1970 and 1 for 1970 and after; X_{7t} = a counter for years scored 0 for observations before 1970 and 1, 2, 3 . . . . for 1970 and after; e_t = the error term; the figures in parentheses = the t-ratios; the R-squared = the coefficient of multiple determination; N = number of annual observations (1932-1980); D–W = the Durbin-Watson statistic; the data are gathered from various publications of the *Bureau of Mines* and its successors.

The parameter estimates $\hat{b}_0$ and $\hat{b}_1$ indicate, respectively, the level and trend of the time series before imposition of the 1941 law. In order to assess whether b_0 and b_1 were changed by this new legislation, it is necessary to study b_2 and b_3. Given that, according to the t-ratios, the estimate for b_2 is not significantly different from zero, the inference is that these regulations had no impact on the level of fatalities (for statistical significance at .05, two-tail, $/t/ > 2.2$). However, the b_3 estimate is significant, which indicates that the 1941 law did change the slope of the time series, substantially lowering the fatality rate. Indeed, the slope before the 1941 legislation is $\hat{b}_1$ (–.001), whereas after the 1941 legislation it is $\hat{b}_1 + \hat{b}_3 = -.046$, showing that the fatality rate changed from a stable to a declining condition.

The 1952 and 1969 interventions are evaluated in the same manner. One observes that the 1952 legislation has an insignificant intercept effect (see $\hat{b}_4$), but a significant positive slope effect (see $\hat{b}_5$). The result is that the 1952 legislation apparently arrested the downward movement in the fatality rate instituted by the 1941 legislation. (The trend line for this post-1952 period is flat, $\hat{b}_1 + \hat{b}_3 + \hat{b}_5 = -.001 - .045 + .047 \cong 0$). Finally, with respect to the 1969 regulations, the estimates for b_6 and b_7 suggest they brought about significant reductions in the fatality rate, in both the short and the long run. The slope of the time series in the post-1969 period equals $b_1 + b_3 + b_5 + b_7$. In general, the slope of the time series within any postintervention period, for example, post-1969, can be estimated by adding to the initial slope estimate (for example, $\hat{b}_1$) all the slope change parameter estimates calculated up to and including that period, e.g., $\hat{b}_3 + \hat{b}_5 + \hat{b}_7$. (In Figure 9.4, observe that if one fits a simple regression line within each time period, each has a slope equal to this combination of MITS coefficients.) Overall, this collection of dummy variables, which have been scored to reflect multiple federal interventions in the area of coal mine safety, does an excellent job of accounting for the changes in the mining fatality rate, as the R-squared = .92 demonstrates.

PROBLEMS OF INFERENCE

From an ITS analysis, one hopes to make causal inferences. Did the intervention produce the change observed? Fortunately, the ITS design, which is quasi-experimental, seems relatively strong in this regard. One can observe the pattern of behavior in Y before the intervention occurs, then after. In appearance, this is similar to an experiment with a control group and a treatment group. Experimental design, of course, allows the surest inferences about causality. However, what is missing here with an ITS analysis is random assignment to groups, which means it remains an essentially nonexperimental approach. Therefore, in order to make causal inferences, it is necessary to meet the assumptions of a nonexperimental multiple regression model. These assumptions include absence of specification error for the model, absence of measurement error in the variables, absence of perfect multicollinearity among the independent variables and—for the error term—a zero mean, homoscedasticity, no autocorrelation, no correlation with independent variables, and normality. (For regression analysis generally, these assumptions are discussed elsewhere; Berry and Feldman, 1985; Lewis-Beck, 1980.) Below, I give particular attention to specification error, measurement error, and perfect multicollinearity. Lastly, I consider the no-autocorrelation assumption, too often the exclusive focus of concern in other treatments of ITS analysis.

THE PROBLEM OF SPECIFICATION ERROR

A regression model is properly specified when each independent variable is linearly related to the dependent variable, no irrelevant independent variables have been included, and no relevant independent variables have been excluded. Let me address how each of these conditions apply in an ITS analysis. With respect to linearity, the best equation in the pre- and postintervention periods must yield a straight line. One observes this most clearly in Figure 9.3 of the Cuban example, where the trends are straight both before and after Castro took control. Overall, the linearity assumption appears quite sound for this SITS model which, it should be recalled, produced an R-squared = .996, an almost perfect linear fit. Obviously, however, a time trend need not always be straight, as it is not in the diagram of Figure 9.5a, in which Y follows an exponential path. If an ordinary SITS model were estimated with these data, it would fit two straight lines (see broken lines) to the curved trends on either side of the intervention. This erroneous specification leads to faulty inference from these ITS estimates, which would indicate a large positive slope shift ($+b_3$).

The solution for this predicament is a transformation that will make the relationship linear, thus allowing the proper use of OLS. The pattern in Figure 9.5a is a fairly common one, depicting the trajectory of an absolute growth figure, such as GNP, over time. Such trends can usually be linearized with a logarithmic transformation of the dependent variable. Indeed, recall this was initially done with the data in the Cuban revolution example, where the energy consumption variable was logged in order to overcome such curvilinearity. In general, as with any regression analysis, if the scatterplot of the raw observations reveals nonlinearity, a transformation should be sought to make the relationship linear. A variety of variable transformations—logarithmic, reciprocal, square root, polynomial—can be used (see Berry and Feldman, 1985, chap. 5). Careful choice here is important, for an improper transformation could increase, rather than decrease, the observed nonlinearity. The preferred transformation depends heavily, of course, upon the shape of the nonlinearity. Look, for example, at the nature of the nonlinearity in the postintervention period in Figure 9.5b. Because of the inverted bowl shape, a second-order polynomial is suggested, which would involve adding a variable,

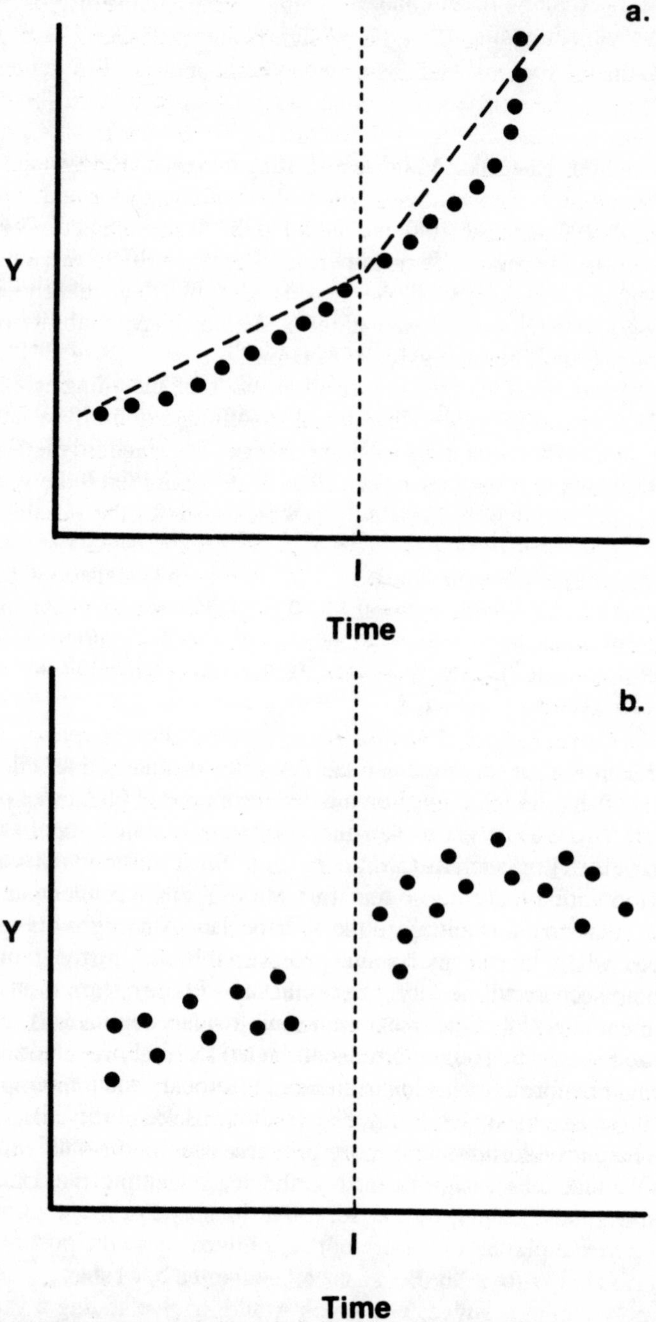

Figure 9.5 a, b: Examples of Nonlinear Interrupted Time Series

X^2_{3t}, the square of the postintervention time counter, to the original SITS equation. If this variable, X^2_{3t}, had a significant coefficient, one might infer that the intervention had changed the shape of trend. But, it may not be clear, from visual inspection alone, which transformation should be chosen. For instance, in Figure 9.5b, the log or reciprocal of X_{3t} might also be candidates because of the decelerating increase visible in the time series. In this case, the rival transformations could be performed, and the changes in the R-squared from one model to the next evaluated. Overall, if no one transformation seems superior to another (or to the untransformed model) in improving the goodness of fit, then the choice of models should be based on other criteria, such as interpretability of the results or preservation of degrees of freedom.

Let us now consider the specification error of including irrelevant variables. For an ITS model, this means including a dummy variable to capture a nonexistent intercept or slope change. The standard method for assessing whether or not such an error has been committed is the application of a significance test. If the parameter estimate for the variable fails to achieve statistical significance, then the conclusion is that the variable should be omitted from the equation. (Of course, this decision would be wrong one time in twenty, assuming a .05 significance level.) Using the rule for the coal mining fatalities equation, it appears that the intercept change variables X_{2t} and X_{4t} should be excluded in a reestimation, which I carry out below.

The last aspect of specification error, the exclusion of relevant variables, raises the question of spuriousness. An estimated ITS equation may indicate that an intervention significantly alters the phenomenon under study. However, it is possible that this impact is only apparent, the product of the common prior influence of a "third variable" (Z_t) on the intervention and on the dependent variable. Suppose, in the coal mine example, that fatalities are more likely to occur in underground mines, measured by Z_{1t}, and in small mines, measured by Z_{2t}; further, suppose that when more small, underground mines are in operation, the federal government more vigorously intervenes with safety regulations. In this situation, the significant coefficients of the MITS safety regulation variables might be spurious, having been brought about by the joint impact of these "third variables," Z_{1t} and Z_{2t}. To test for this possibility, these variables were introduced into the more properly specified MITS equation (which excludes the insignificant X_{2t} and X_{4t}), yielding the following OLS estimates:

$$F_t = .030 - .006X_{1t} - .042X_{3t} + .057X_{5t} - .128X_{6t}$$
$$(.06) \quad (-.59) \quad (-2.89) \quad (5.32) \quad (-1.36)$$

$$-.050X_{7t} + .87Z_{1t} + .010Z_{2t} + e_t \qquad [9.13]$$
$$(-4.00) \qquad (1.38) \qquad (2.08)$$
$$\text{R-squared} = .928 \qquad N = 49 \qquad \text{D-W} = 2.33$$

where F_t, X_{1t}, X_{3t}, X_{5t}, X_{6t}, X_{7t} and the statistics are defined as with equation 9.12; Z_{1t} = annual percentage of miners working underground; Z_{2t} = annual percentage of mines producing less than 50,000 tons (data on Z_{1t} and Z_{2t} are from *Minerals Yearbook*, various issues).

According to these results, the significant, long-run slope changes ($\hat{b}_3$, $\hat{b}_5$, $\hat{b}_7$) captured in the initial MITS model (equation 9.12) are not spurious. But, the introduction of controls, Z_{1t} and Z_{2t}, indicates that the significant short-run intercept change (b_6) of the initial model was spurious. Moreover, the findings of equation 9.13 suggest, quite plausibly, that the fatality rate is responsive to something besides federal regulation, namely, mine size. (However, the other control variable, percentage of miners underground, appears not to affect fatalities.) These pieces of evidence enable further improvements in model specification. Coal mining fatalities seem to be a function of the long-run impact of federal safety legislation in 1941, 1952, and 1969 (X_{3t}, X_{5t}, X_{7t}), plus mine size (Z_{2t}). Estimating such a revised model with OLS yields

$$F_t = .315 - .014X_{1t} - .039X_{3t} + .060X_{5t} - .063X_{7t} + .017Z_{2t} + e_t$$
$$(1.05) \quad (-1.43) \quad (-2.62) \quad (5.98) \quad (-5.76) \quad (4.21)$$
$$\text{R-squared} = .921 \qquad N = 49 \qquad \text{D-W} = 2.10 \qquad [9.14]$$

where the definitions of the variables and the statistics are as with equation 9.13. This final specification is an advance over the initial specification in several important ways: (1) it is more parsimonious, explaining the same amount of variance with fewer independent variables; (2) it is theoretically more plausible, indicating that federal safety legislation yields long-term rather than short-term results; and, (3) it is theoretically more complete, incorporating a substantive variable, that is, coal mine size, into the model along with the dummy variable time counters.

With ITS analysis, there is also a particular kind of specification error involving the omission of a relevant variable, which comes from the occasional seasonality of time-series data. Although relatively rare in annual series, cycles may be exhibited in quarterly or monthly series. The classic example is the December jump in department store sales. A dummy variable would easily incorporate such a twelfth-month rise into an ITS model. Suppose, for instance, that our Kentucky traffic fatalities data were recorded on a monthly, rather than an annual, basis. If we repeatedly observed a leap in fatalities in December, perhaps due to the holiday season, then we might develop a monthly SITS equation that included a December dummy, scored 1 = December and 0 = other months. Then, the slope and intercept changes produced by the speeding crackdown could be assessed free of any distorting influence from the December cycle.

At this point, I would like to consider how to reduce the risk of specification error by drawing on corroborative evidence from the analysis of other, relevant, time series. One type of relevant time series is a related dependent variable that would be expected to respond similarly to the intervention. For example, in my coal mine safety investigation, I reasoned that actual safety enforcement activity (measured by the annual size of the health and safety budget) should mirror the pattern of interruptions in the fatality rate, if in fact the federal regulations were operating as postulated. One observes that this is actually so, by eyeballing the time-series plot of the coal mine health and safety budget (natural logs) in Figure 9.6 (see Lewis-Beck and Alford, 1980). For instance, the trend changes in the pattern of budget growth from period to period appear to reflect the changes in the law. Estimation of the full MITS model, with an R-squared = .99, nicely confirms this general picture. (In addition, the significant short-term budget spurts would seem plausible, immediate consequences of the introduction of new legislation).

$$
\begin{aligned}
B_t = {} & 6.497 - .007X_{1t} + .582X_{2t} + .135X_{3t} - .125X_{4t} \\
& (58.5) \quad (-.4) \quad (4.1) \quad (5.7) \quad (-1.0) \\
& -.067X_{5t} + 1.174X_{6t} + .007X_{7t} + e_t \qquad [9.15] \\
& (-3.9) \quad (7.5) \quad (2.4) \\
& \text{R-squared} = .99 \quad N = 45 \quad \text{D-W} = 1.5
\end{aligned}
$$

where B_t = annual coal mine health and safety budget (thousands of dollars, natural logs) 1932-1976, (gathered from the *Budget of the United States Government*, various issues); the other variables are defined as in equation 9.12.

Another kind of relevant time series useful for checking specification error is a "nonequivalent no-treatment control group time series"; that is, a time series from a population that is as similar as possible to the one under study, except it has not experienced the intervention. Applying this idea to the Kentucky speeding crackdown example, one might put together the time series of traffic fatalities in Tennessee, which had had no

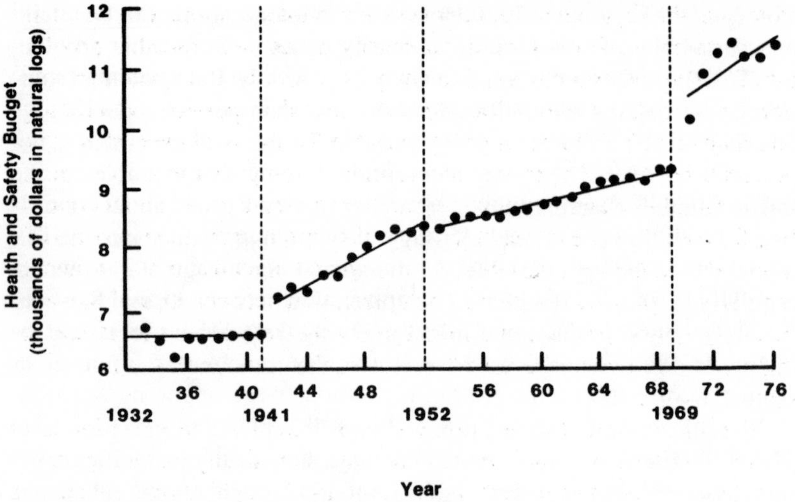

Figure 9.6: MITS Analysis of Federal Coal Mine Health and Safety Budget

crackdown. On the one hand, then, if the Kentucky series manifests a significant slope change and the Tennessee series does not, one gains confidence that the speeding limitation caused the fatality rate reduction. On the other hand, if both states show a significant decline in fatalities after 1972, then the suspicion would be that the Kentucky results were not caused by the new speed limit. Rather, the decline in both states would then appear to be a product of a more general influence affecting both states at the same time, such as (hypothetically) the introduction of a national auto seatbelt requirement in 1972.

PROBLEMS OF MULTICOLLINEARITY

The foregoing example leads to the problem of perfect multicollinearity in an ITS context. The intervention may occur at the same time as another possibly relevant event. Suppose, for example, that the Kentucky traffic safety researchers hypothesize that the 1972 speeding crackdown changed the level of the time series, and therefore they formulate a model with D_t scored 0 before 1972 and 1 for 1972 and after. However, they realize that in the same year the national seatbelt law was introduced; hence they try to control for this rival influence on fatalities by introducing a third variable, E_t, scored 0 before 1972 and 1 for 1972 and after. Of course, D_t and E_t will be perfectly correlated, estimation will be impossible, and the separate influence of these two interventions will be totally unascertainable. Perfect multicollinearity poses an intractable problem for ITS analysis, as for regression analysis generally. But a potential solution lies in making the multicollinearity less than perfect. Specifically, one may be able to locate a proxy variable for the rival event that is not perfectly correlated with the intervention dummy. For example, in the traffic fatalities example, if the researchers are concerned about controlling for the influence of seatbelt usage, they might introduce into the ITS model the continuous variable, S_t, the annual percentage of car owners regularly employing seatbelts. The correlation between D_t and S_t would certainly not be perfect, and might allow the researchers to assess the impact of the speeding crackdown free of the confounding influence of seatbelt usage.

The substitution of such a proxy variable could still leave a high level of multicollinearity, which might generate a statistically insignificant parameter estimate even though the intervention brought about real change in the population (on the multicollinearity problem, see Berry and Feldman, 1985, chap. 4; Lewis-Beck, 1980: 58–63). Generally, in an ITS model, high multicollinearity may be introduced if one attempts to include a rival event that occurred at almost the same time as the intervention of interest. In the Cuban example, is the revolution responsible for the economic growth pattern, or is the U.S. embargo, which began in 1960, responsible? One approach is to simply think of the embargo as part of the revolutionary experiment, which included a shift in trade partners from the United States to the Soviet Union. Then, the embargo is captured, along with the other aspects of the revolution, in the ITS dummies of the original model (see equation 9.10). However, if one wishes to distinguish conceptually between the domestic and the international aspects of revolutionary change, a solution is more difficult. The U.S. embargo took place a year after the revolution began; therefore, a dummy time counter for the embargo would have the same values as X_{3t} in the original model, except for the 1959 observation. This high degree of multicollinearity makes reliable separation of the slope changes impossible. (However, it does not prohibit assessment of the intercept shift, from 1958 to 1959. For that brief period, there was domestic revolution operating without the potentially confounding effects of the U.S. embargo. As the coefficient for X_{2t} in the original model shows, energy consumption jumped significantly in this period, hinting that, at least in the short run, the revolution positively influenced growth.) Broadly speaking, in ITS analysis, when several interventions are being considered that are fairly closely spaced in time, one should be alert to the possibility of multicollinearity problems. Insignificant coefficients may simply be the product of a high degree of linear dependency among the intervention dummy variables.

Another way in which high multicollinearity can arise with ITS analysis is when the number of observations before and after the event are seriously uneven (recall Figures 9.1d–9.1e). For instance, if the researcher has a much longer string of observations before the event, then X_{2t} and X_{3t} in the SITS model (equation 9.9) will tend to be highly correlated because the large number of pre-event values will equal zero. For example, in my study of the Cuban revolution, I also carried out a SITS analysis of annual sugar production from 1929-1974. The SITS results showed that the coefficients for X_{2t} and X_{3t} were statistically insignificant (Lewis-Beck, 1979). However, I worried that this lack of significance was a product of the high correlation between X_{2t} and X_{3t}, which was .85. (This correlation results from the fact that there were 39 observations before the Castro takeover compared to 16 after, which means that X_{2t} and X_{3t} share many identical, zero, values). I explored the drastic solution of dropping first X_{2t}, then X_{3t}, from the model. (Such a solution is drastic because it implies willful commission of specification error. Technically, the preferred solution is the standard econometric recommendation of increasing the sample size, which is usually not possible in practice.) Thus each variable, in turn, is allowed to account for as much sugar production as it can, independent of the control of the other. Still, neither X_{2t} nor X_{3t} managed to exhibit a significant impact. Therefore, I concluded that there was no multicollinearity problem, and that the insignificant results of the original model were valid.

SOME MEASUREMENT ERROR PROBLEMS

Measurement error problems can take a special form with ITS analysis. In order to construct the independent variables, the intervention must be clearly marked in time. When exactly did the event occur? In the case of the Cuban revolution, Batista fled the island on December 31, 1958, and Castro marched victoriously into Havana on January 8, 1959. Therefore, given that the data are annual observations, I regarded 1959 as the year the revolution began. The next question is, "Should the year (quarter, month) of the event be scored on the "before" or "after" side of the intervention dummies?" With annual data, if the event took place in the first half of the year, then that whole year should generally be coded as a postintervention value, because the behavior of the dependent variable would happen mostly after the event. For example, because Castro came to power in January 1959, X_{2t} and X_{3t} in the basic SITS model are scored "1" for the year 1959 (see equation 9.10).

One problem that can arise is uncertainty as to the precise date the event occurred. Although the ITS model requires definite cut-points, we know that social processes are not always so easily pulled apart. For instance, suppose someone argued that the Cuban revolution did not really get underway until 1960. If this is so, then year 1 for the ITS dummies should be 1960, rather than 1959. One strategy for resolving this disagreement is to specify different intervention points, estimate the rival ITS models, and observe which more clearly supports the dominant hypothesis. With the Cuban example, I altered the intervention point to 1960, 1961, 1962, and 1963, respectively. (That is, I reestimated the SITS model, each time making these years the first postintervention observation, with a score of 1 on X_{2t} and X_{3t}.) These estimates confirmed my preference for the original intervention scoring (1959 = 1). In particular, the various estimates for b_2 steadily decline as the intervention point is moved away from 1959, and actually cease to be significant at 1962 = 1. These results clearly support the impression of careful observers of the Cuban scene that 1959 was a revolutionary peak in economic growth.

The last difficulty that crops up is whether or not the intervention effect occurs with a lag. We may expect the effect of the intervention to appear after the passage of some time, rather than immediately. In our hypothetical example of the 1972 Kentucky speeding crackdown, for example, we might think that the law would not significantly affect fatalities until the following year, because it takes people a while to learn of the law and see that it is actually being enforced. If the law is operating with this one-year lag, then the preferred scoring of the SITS dummy variables X_{2t} and X_{3t} would be year 1 = 1973 (instead of 1972).

THE PROBLEM OF AUTOCORRELATION

Finally, I turn to the regression assumption of no autocorrelation. In order to make valid causal inferences from the OLS estimates of an ITS equation, error terms must not be correlated, that is, $E(e_t\, e_{t-j}) = 0$, where $j \neq 0$ (for a general reference on this problem in time series, see Ostrom, 1978). This assumption is routinely violated in the analysis of time-series data (data involving repeated observations on the same unit of analysis over time). Almost always, the autocorrelation is positive. In the presence of positive autocorrelation, the regression residuals ($\hat{e}_t = Y_t - \hat{Y}_t$) will tend to track each other when plotted across time, with positive residuals followed by positive residuals until a "shock" occurs, then negative residuals follow negative residuals. It is not difficult to imagine why such a pattern appears so often with time series. The error term of the regression equation stands for an ensemble of variables that influence Y but are left out of the model. These variables shaping Y at time t-1 would likely be related to the variables shaping Y at time t, which implies autocorrelation. Consider the following simple model, in which the annual United States defense budget (Y_t) is a function of the annual presidential defense budget request (X_t):

$$Y_t = b_0 + b_1X_t + e_t \qquad [9.16]$$

Upon contemplation of what variables are likely in that collection represented by the error term, e_t, a candidate that comes easily to mind is the annual Gross National Product (GNP). Obviously, GNP from the prior year, GNP_{t-1}, is correlated with GNP from the present year, GNP_t; therefore, the correlation between e_t and e_{t-1} is not equal to zero. Such a pattern, in which error from the immediately prior time (e_{t-1}) is correlated with error at the current time (e_t), depicts a first-order autoregressive process, AR(1), by far the most common form.

In the face of this autocorrelation, the OLS parameter estimates, $\hat{b}_0 + \hat{b}_1$, nevertheless remain unbiased. Hence when the primary focus of the ITS analysis is on the magnitude of the parameter changes brought about by an intervention unambiguously known to have altered the level and/or slope of the series, then the autocorrelation problem is less important. However, such certain knowledge about an intervention's effectiveness is usually lacking. For most ITS analysis, the critical question is not, How big was the effect of the intervention?; rather, it is simply, Did the intervention have an effect? When the latter question is paramount, the presence of autocorrelation is problematic for OLS estimation because it invalidates the significance tests, our essential tool for assessing whether the intervention had an effect.

These significance tests are rendered invalid due to the bias that autocorrelation creates in the estimation of the coefficient variances. These estimated variances are typically too small, given that most autocorrelation is positive. The more the true variance is underestimated, the more the t-ratio from the OLS results is inflated, as its formula makes clear:

$$t = \frac{\hat{b}}{\sqrt{\operatorname{var} \hat{b}}} \qquad [9.17]$$

The underestimated denominator gives the t-ratio too large a value. It can too easily surpass the value of 2.00, thus erroneously suggesting significance at the .05 level, with a two-tailed test. Thus, in the presence of positive autocorrelation, OLS tends to make the coefficients appear significant when they are not. We risk, in other words, committing the Type I error of rejecting the null hypothesis when it is correct. Further, this risk is far from trivial, for this inflation of the t-ratio can be substantial. Indeed, according to McDowall and his colleagues (1980: 13), it is commonly inflated 300% to 400%. The implication is that, in the face of autocorrelation, one cannot safely infer significance from OLS t-ratios even when they well exceed the rule-of-thumb value of 2.00.

Clearly, any ITS analysis that aims to assess the statistical significance of an intervention must explicitly deal with the autocorrelation problem. Until the data suggest otherwise, the presumption must be that the error terms of an OLS model are not independent. There are two basic types of dependent error processes, the autoregressive and the moving average. A positive first-order autoregressive process, AR(1), by far the most common, takes the form

$$e_t = p\, e_{t-1} + u_t \qquad [9.18]$$

where e_t = the error term; p = rho, the population correlation between e_t and e_{t-1}. Here, the error at time t is a function of the error at time t-1, plus a random variable, u_t. An AR(1) model yields a particular "autocorrelation function" such as that in Figure 9.7a, which shows the correlation of the error terms at an increasing lag. This theoretical correlogram graphs the correlation of $e_t\, e_{t-1}$ (A_1), $e_t\, e_{t-2}$ (A_2), $e_t\, e_{t-3}$ (A_3) . . . and $e_t\, e_{t-10}$ (A_{10}). As with all positive AR(1) error processes, these correlations follow a steady exponential decline. Very rarely, a first-order autoregressive process is negative,

$$e_t = -p\, e_{t-1} + u_t \qquad [9.19]$$

In this case, the theoretical correlogram looks like Figure 9.7b, where the autocorrelation functions oscillate from positive to negative as they exponentially decline.

The moving-average process is the second basic error pattern. A positive first-order moving-average process, MA(1), takes the form,

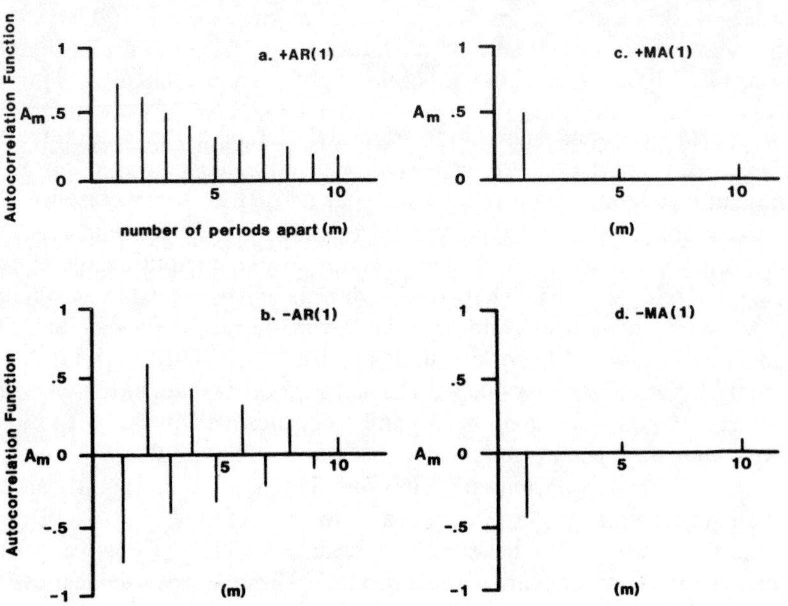

Figure 9.7 a-d: Theoretical Autocorrelation Functions ($A_m = Pe_te_{t-m}$) for Different Error Processes

$$e_t = u_t + p\,u_{t-1} \qquad [9.20]$$

where the error at time t is strictly a function of a random variable at time t, plus a portion of that random variable at time t-1. The autocorrelation function of a moving average process is quite different from an autoregressive process. The theoretical correlograms in Figures 9.7c and 9.7d describe, respectively, a positive and a negative MA(1) pattern. The distinguishing characteristic of an MA(1) error process is a spike at the first lag, followed by correlations of zero at greater lags.

In practice, one may encounter a mixed autoregressive-moving average process. Further, higher-order processes are possible. For example, an AR(2) model takes the form,

$$e_t = p_1e_{t-1} + p_2e_{t-2} + u_t \qquad [9.21]$$

However, mixed processes and higher-order processes are in fact very rare in time series of social science data (McDowall et al., 1980: 28-29, 46). Instead, evidence indicates that positive AR(1) processes dominate these series. For instance, Ames and Reiter (1961) examine 100 annual time series randomly selected from statistical abstracts and report that, on average, the autocorrelation function exhibits exponential decay. Thus because any error process of error dependency is almost always AR(1), the discussion below focuses on its detection and correction. (Other forms of error are generally less tractable; for an introduction to estimation procedures in this case, see Hibbs, 1974.)

The most widely used method of assessing the presence of first-order autocorrelation is the Durbin-Watson statistic, which has the following formula:

$$\text{D–W} = \frac{\sum_{t=2}^{N} (\hat{e}_t - \hat{e}_{t-1})^2}{\sum_{t=1}^{N} \hat{e}_t^2} \qquad [9.22]$$

where $\hat{e}_t$ = OLS residuals. Glancing at this formula, one sees that the more positive the autocorrelation the smaller the numerator, thus diminishing the D-W value. In opposite fashion, the more negative the autocorrelation, the larger the D-W value. More formally, assuming first-order autocorrelation, the following generalizations hold for ρ (rho):

$$\text{if } p = +1 \quad \text{then D–W} \cong 0$$

$$\text{if } p = -1 \quad \text{then D–W} \cong 4$$

$$\text{if } p = 0 \quad \text{then D–W} \cong 2.$$

Hence, in terms of accepting the null hypothesis of no autocorrelation, the closer D-W is to 2.00, the better. To evaluate precisely whether a particular D-W value allows acceptance of the null, one consults a D-W table (see any standard econometrics text). Assuming the table provides a .05, two-tail significance test, we look up the values appropriate to the number of observations, N, and the number of independent variables, K. Two values will be provided, a lower-bound, d_t, and an upper-bound, d_u. With positive autocorrelation, a D-W value less than d_ℓ leads to rejection of the null hypothesis of no autocorrelation, whereas a D-W value exceeding d_u leads to acceptance of the null of no autocorrelation. Unfortunately, if the D-W value falls between d_ℓ and d_u, then there is an uncertainty over whether to accept or reject the null hypothesis. (This uncertainty exists because, in this region, apparent autocorrelation of the error terms may actually be due to autocorrelation of the independent variables; Pindyck and Rubinfeld, 1976: 115.) The major drawback, then, of the D-W test for first-order autocorrelation is the presence of this range of uncertainty, which may prevent a clear decision. Therefore, one might prefer a less ambiguous statistic. Rao and Griliches (1969) conclude, from Monte Carlo experiments, that when an AR(1) error process with $p > .30$ exists, OLS should not be employed. With this rule of thumb, we would simply decide significant first-order autocorrelation was present when the estimate of p surpassed .30. (The estimate of p comes from correlating the residuals for the original OLS equation, $\hat{e}_t$ and $\hat{e}_{t-1}$. Note that, because of the lag, one case would necessarily be lost.)

If the ITS analyst, upon application of an appropriate test, discovers a significant AR(1) process, then the OLS t-ratios can no longer be safely employed in making causal inferences. A straightforward remedy is the method of generalized differences, which involves the transformation of the variables using the autocorrelation coefficient, p, thereby rendering the error terms independent. With this assumption met, it is then correct to apply OLS.

Suppose a very simple ITS model were used positing only a slope change, the results of which are generalizable to more complicated cases,

$$Y_t = b_0 + b_1X_{1t} + b_2X_{2t} + e_t \quad [9.23]$$

where Y_t = N time series observations on the dependent variable; X_{1t} = a dummy time counter from 1 to N; X_{2t} = a dummy variable scored 0 before the event and 1, 2, 3 . . . . for observations after the event; e_t = the error term. Assume, further, that the following first-order autoregressive process is operating,

$$e_t = p\,e_{t-1} + u_t \quad [9.24]$$

Applying generalized differences to these variables yields the following transformed equation:

$$Y_t^* = b_0^* + b_1X_{1t}^* + b_2X_{2t}^* + e_t^* \quad [9.25]$$

where

$$Y_t^* = Y_t - pY_{t-1}$$
$$X_{1t}^* = X_{1t} - pX_{1t-1}$$

$$X_{2t}^* = X_{2t} - pX_{2t-1}$$

$$b_0^* = b_0(1 - p)$$

$$e_t^* = e_t - pe_{t-1} = (pe_{t-1} + u_t) - pe_{t-1} = u_t$$

Because the revised error term, e_t^*, is now equal to the random variable, u_t, the regression assumption of independent error terms is met, and OLS can be appropriately applied to the transformed variables in order to secure efficient parameter estimates (see Hibbs, 1974: 269; Pindyck and Rubinfeld, 1976: 108-110). In practice, of course, we seldom actually know the autocorrelation coefficient, p, and so we must utilize an estimate, $\hat{p}$.

In sum, a generalized difference approach to correcting for first-order autoregression includes estimation of the autocorrelation coefficient, transformation of the variables with that estimated autocorrelation coefficient, and application of OLS to the transformed variables. Below, I describe the steps of such a procedure. For simplicity, I develop the SITS model shown above.

$$Y_t = b_0 + b_1X_{1t} + b_2X_{2t} + e_t \qquad [9.26]$$

Step 1. Estimate the ITS equation with OLS.

Step 2. Calculate the residuals, $\hat{e}_{1t}, \hat{e}_{2t} \ldots . \hat{e}_{nt}$.

Step 3. Obtain the first-order autocorrelation estimate, $\hat{p}$, by correlating $\hat{e}_t$ with $\hat{e}_{t-1}$.

Step 4. Construct the transformed variables, $Y_t^* = Y_t - \hat{p}Y_{t-1}$, $X_{1t}^* = X_{1t} - \hat{p}X_{1t-1}$, $X_{2t}^* = X_{2t} - \hat{p}X_{2t-1}$. (Note that this lagging necessarily involves the loss of one observation from the beginning of the time period.)

Step 5. Get efficient parameter estimates by applying OLS to the following transformed equation:

$$Y_t^* = b_0^* + b_1X_{1t}^* + b_2X_{2t}^* + e_t^* \qquad [9.27]$$

The parameter estimates from this transformed equation have the desirable properties of consistency and efficiency. Further, the resulting t-ratios provide a more valid assessment of the slope change postulated in this model. (Strictly speaking, these t-ratios are approximations in finite samples; see Kelejian and Oates, 1974: 200.) This is a "two-stage" technique, so called because it estimates the parameters only twice (at Step 1 and at Step 5). It is possible to employ an iterative technique, such as the

Cochrane-Orcutt procedure, involving a repetition of the above described steps until the parameter estimates stabilize, which in my experience typically occurs after a few rounds. However, the two-stage procedure described above generates estimators with properties identical to those from Cochrane-Orcutt, at least for large samples. Furthermore, this two-stage procedure has the advantage of being easily computed without a special computer program. (On these matters, see Kmenta, 1971: 287-289; Kelejian and Oates, 1974: 200; Pindyck and Rubinfeld, 1976: 111-112; Ostrom, 1978: 39-40.)

Let us now apply this general discussion of autocorrelation to the specific ITS data examples at hand, the one from the Cuban revolution and the other from U.S. coal mine safety. With regard to the latter, an initial assessment of the presence of first-order autocorrelation comes from a glance at the D-W statistic. In the final specification for the coal mining fatalities equation (that is, equation 14), the D–W = 2.10 which, by its closeness to the rule-of-thumb value of 2.00, indicates that first-order autocorrelation is quite unlikely. More precisely, given a two-tailed, .05 significance test, with 49 observations and 5 independent variables, the D–W value must fall between 1.69 (d_u) and 2.31 ($4\text{-}d_u$) so that we can accept the null hypothesis. Because this D–W value of 2.10 clearly lies within this range, we accept the null hypothesis, concluding that no significant first-order autocorrelation is operating.

Turning to the SITS equation on Cuban energy consumption (equation 9.10), the picture is more cloudy. Here, the D–W statistic is 1.42, which lies in an uncertainty region. (With a two-tailed, .05 significance test, 32 observations, and 3 independent variables, $d_l = 1.16$ and $d_u = 1.55$). Thus on the basis of this test alone, it is not clear whether or not significant autocorrelation exists. This is a case in which the Rao and Griliches rule of thumb for diagnosing a first-order autocorrelation problem, that is, $p < .30$, is useful. Calculating the correlation, $\hat{p}$, between the OLS residuals, $\hat{e}_t$ and $\hat{e}_{t-1}$, yields $\hat{p} = .25$. By this criterion, then, OLS still appears preferred. Therefore, I resolve my uncertainty in favor of the null hypothesis of no first-order autocorrelation.

Despite these assurances, the possibility remains that some other error dependency process is working, besides AR(1). Because different error processes generate different correlograms, it is helpful to calculate the autocorrelation functions for these examples. In composing an empirical correlogram, a decision must be made regarding the length of the last lag, for effective sample size quickly dwindles, increasing the imprecision of the estimates. As a rule of thumb, it has been recommended that these autocorrelations be calculated to lag N/4 (see Hibbs, 1974, p. 280). For the coal mine example, this means computing about 12 empirical

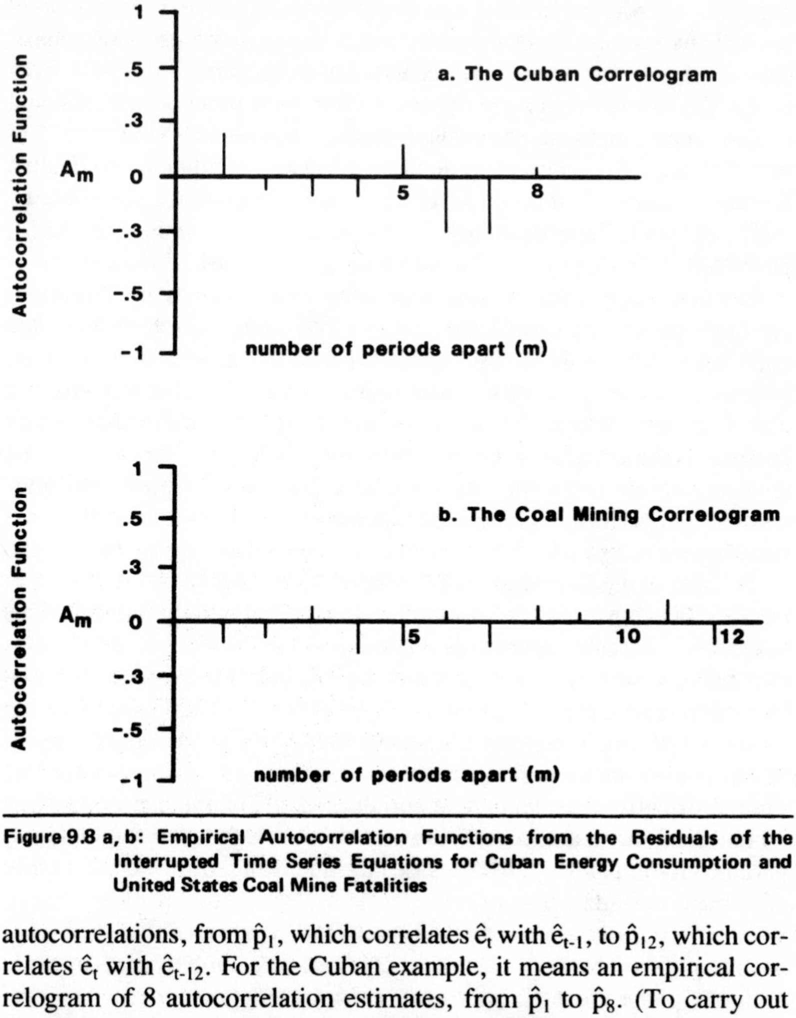

Figure 9.8 a, b: Empirical Autocorrelation Functions from the Residuals of the Interrupted Time Series Equations for Cuban Energy Consumption and United States Coal Mine Fatalities

autocorrelations, from $\hat{p}_1$, which correlates $\hat{e}_t$ with $\hat{e}_{t-1}$, to $\hat{p}_{12}$, which correlates $\hat{e}_t$ with $\hat{e}_{t-12}$. For the Cuban example, it means an empirical correlogram of 8 autocorrelation estimates, from $\hat{p}_1$ to $\hat{p}_8$. (To carry out these calculations, a special Box-Jenkins or ARIMA computer program is helpful, but not essential.) In Figures 9.8a–9.8b these empirical correlograms are shown.

In order to diagnose the particular error process, these empirical autocorrelations can be compared to theoretical ones, always bearing in mind that perfect correspondence cannot be expected. For example, by chance alone, one or two autocorrelation estimates might have some size, even though there was no autocorrelation in the population. Let us look first at the coal mine fatalities correlogram, which is more extended. First, the hypothesis of no significant first-order autocorrelation, earlier supported by the D-W statistic, is again confirmed. Clearly, no positive AR(1) process is at work, for there is exponential damping off of coefficients from $\hat{\rho}_1$. (Also, no positive second-order autoregressive process, which would exhibit steady, but not exponential, decay, is present.) With regard to negative autoregression, its systematic pattern of oscillation and decline is totally absent. Further, no MA(1) process is in evidence, as would be indicated by a spike at $\hat{\rho}_1$, followed by near zero coefficients. [An MA(2) process, which is also absent, would spike at $\hat{\rho}_2$ as well]. In sum, the autocorrelation function for the coal mine fatalities equation manifests no error dependency. Instead, it shows a random pattern. Note how all the coefficients are small, and scattered haphazardly around the zero line. Indeed, all 12 of the coefficients are far from statistical significance at .05. The implications of this "white noise" process are heartening. In particular, the OLS assumption of no autocorrelation is met. Therefore, the original OLS parameter estimates of equation 9.14 appear efficient, and the t-ratios valid. The causal inferences made from them have not been overturned by any discovery of an autocorrelation problem.

Turning to the Cuban case, the picture is somewhat less clear, in part because the empirical correlogram is shorter, going only to lag 8. This autocorrelation function reveals no obvious pattern of error dependency. Five negative and three positive autocorrelation estimates are distributed aimlessly around the zero horizon. Especially noteworthy is the fact that these coefficients are generally small. In fact, even the largest, $\hat{\rho}_7 = -.30$, is quite far from statistical significance at .05, given an effective sample size of 25 at that point. Again, the overall picture does not signal a violation of the no autocorrelation assumption. Hence the original OLS parameter estimates and t-ratios of the SITS model for Cuban energy consumption stand.

SUMMARY AND CONCLUSIONS

When the researcher wants to assess the effect of a relatively discrete event on a phenomenon observed across time, interrupted time-series analysis is applicable. Informally, the scatterplot is eyeballed to detect patterns of intervention. Formally, dummy variable time counters capturing the intervention are constructed and included in an ITS model. Then, the estimates record changes in the level (intercept) and trend (slope) of the time series that are associated with the intervention. The preferred estimation technique is OLS, provided the usual regression assumptions are met. ITS analysts must pay particular attention to the assumptions of no specification error, no measurement error, no perfect multicollinearity, and no autocorrelation. Fortunately, however, violations of these assumptions are generally remediable, after which OLS can be applied. Briefly, here are some of the remedies already considered. Nonlinearity can usually be eliminated through variable transformation. Spuriousness can be controlled for by including other relevant variables. Improper measurement of the intervention point can be avoided by theoretical and empirical consideration of various lags. Perfect multicollinearity can be overcome by locating a proxy measure for the offending variable. First-order autocorrelation can be removed by generalized differencing, after which OLS is appropriate.Furthermore, by correcting one violation, another may also be corrected. For instance, accurate measurement of the intervention point avoids the specification error of including an irrelevant variable. Or, a remedy for nonlinearity may cure an autocorrelation problem. (Because the ITS variables are ordered by time, the D-W statistic can indicate nonlinearity, as well as autocorrelation; see Kmenta, 1971: 471.) Certainly, it is not possible to salvage the regression assumptions in every instance. Nevertheless, in general, OLS estimators for ITS models, at least after appropriate adjustments or transformation, clearly yield sound causal inferences. Of course, this prescription for using OLS, or a generalized version of it, may err. For instance, rarely, the problem may involve a mixed autoregressive-moving average error process, in which case a nonlinear estimation procedure may be preferred. However, such techniques are beyond the scope of this brief chapter.

references

Albritton, Robert B. (1979) "Measuring public policy: impacts of the Supplemental Social Security program." American Journal of Political Science 23: 559-578.

Ames, E. and S. Reiter (1961) "Distributions of correlation coefficients in economic time series." Journal of the American Statistical Association 56: 637-656.

Berry, William D. (1984) Nonrecursive Causal Models. Beverly Hills, CA: Sage.

———and Stanley Feldman (1985) Problems in Multiple Regression. Beverly Hills, CA: Sage.

Box, George E.P. and Gwilym M. Jenkins (1976) Time Series Analysis. San Francisco: Holden-Day.

Box, George E. P. and G. C. Tiao (1975) "Intervention analysis with applications to economic and environmental problems." Journal of the American Statistical Association 70: 70-92.

Campbell, D. T. (1969) "Reforms as experiments." American Psychologist 24: 409-429.

———and H. L. Ross (1968) "The Connecticut crackdown on speeding: time series data in quasi-experimental analysis. "Law and Society Review 3: 33-53.

Campbell, D. T. and J. C. Stanley (1966) Experimental and Quasi-Experimental Designs for Research. Skokie, IL: Rand McNally.

Caporaso, J. A. and A. L. Pelowski (1971) "Economic and political integration in Europe: a time series quasi-experimental analysis." American Political Science Review 65: 418-433.

Cook, T. D. and D. T. Campbell (1979) Quasi-Experimentation: Design and Analysis Issues for Field Settings. Chicago: Rand McNally.

Deutsch, S. J. and F. B. Alt (1977) "The effect of Massachusetts' gun control law on gun-related crimes in the city of Boston." Evaluation Quarterly 1: 543-568.

Draper, N. R. and H. Smith (1966) Applied Regression Analysis. New York: John Wiley.

Eulau, Heinz and Michael S. Lewis-Beck (1985) Economic Conditions and Electoral Outcomes: The United States and Western Europe. New York: Agathon.

Glass, G. V (1968) "Analysis of data on the Connecticut speeding crackdown as a time series quasi-experiment." Law and Society Review 3: 55-76.

Hibbs, D. A., Jr. (1974) "Problems of statistical estimations and causal inference in time series regression models," in H. L. Costner (ed.) Sociological Methodology 1973-74. San Francisco: Jossey-Bass.

——— (1977) "On analyzing the effects of policy interventions: Box-Jenkins vs. structural equation models," in D. R. Heise (ed.) Sociological Methodology 1977. San Francisco: Jossey-Bass.

Kelejian, H. H. and W. E. Oates (1974) Introduction to Econometrics: Principles and Applications. New York: Harper & Row.

Kmenta, J. (1971) Elements of Econometrics. New York: Macmillan.

Lewis-Beck, M. S. (1979) "Some economic effects of revolution: models, measurement, and the Cuban evidence." American Journal of Sociology 84: 1127-1149.

——— (1980) Applied Regression: An Introduction. Beverly Hills, CA: Sage.

———(1981) "Can we assess the effects of revolution: a third look at the Cuban evidence." American Journal of Sociology 86: 1130-1133.

———and J. R. Alford (1980) "Can government regulate safety? The coal mine example." American Political Science Review 74: 745-756.

McCrone, Donald. J. and Richard J. Hardy (1978) "Civil rights policies and the achievement of racial income equality." American Journal of Political Science 22: 1-17.

McDowall, D., R. McCleary, E. E. Meidinger, and R. A. Hay, Jr. (1980) Interrupted Time Series Analysis. Beverly Hills, CA: Sage.

Nelson, J. P. and G. R. Neumann (1982) "Safety regulation and firm size: effects of the coal mine Health and Safety Act of 1969." Journal of Law and Economics 25: 183-199.

Ostrom, Charles W., Jr. (1978) Time Series Analysis: Regression Techniques. Beverly Hills, CA: Sage.

Perry, C. (1982) "Government regulation of coal mine safety: Effects of spending under strong and weak law." American Politics Quarterly 10: 303-314.

Pindyck, R. S. and D. L. Rubinfeld (1976) Econometric Models and Economic Forecasts. New York: McGraw-Hill.

Rao, P. and Griliches, Z. (1969) "Small-sample properties of several two-stage regression methods in the context of auto-correlated errors." Journal of the American Statistical Association 64: 253-272.

Tufte, E. R. (1974) Data Analysis for Politics and Policy. Englewood Cliffs, NJ: Prentice-Hall.

Zimring, F. E. (1975) "Firearms and federal law: The Gun Control Act of 1968." Journal of Legal Studies 4: 133-198.

10

Transfer Function Analysis

HELMUT NORPOTH

Like the federal government, the science of government lives by borrowing. Whereas the government borrows money to pay for many of its bills, political science borrows models to conduct much of its research. And, like the budget deficit in the public sector, resulting from a spendthrift government, there is something of an understanding deficit in the political science community. To many students of politics, the names of the borrowed concepts are unfamiliar and their meanings mystifying. The notations of the borrowed concepts deviate from familiar patterns; there are Greek characters to become familiar with in unfamiliar assignments. All that proves rather annoying if it turns out at the end that the new method is just old wine with a new label.

Transfer Function analysis is a recent addition to the methodological borrowing done by political scientists. The attempt to adopt this concept for the analysis of political data reveals all the troubles engendered by such borrowing. As introduced by Box and Jenkins (1976), transfer function analysis is largely geared to students of engineering and operations research.[1]

> Suppose X measures the level of an *input* to a system . . . the concentration of some constituent in the feed of a chemical process. Suppose that the level of X influences the level of a system *output* Y . . . the yield of product from the chemical process. It will usually be the case that, because of the inertia of the system, a change in X from one level to another will have no immediate effect on the output but, instead, will produce a delayed response with Y eventually coming to equilibrium at a new level. . . . A model which describes this dynamic response is called a *transfer function model* [Box and Jenkins, 1976: 335].

It is easy to think of inputs and outputs closer to home for most political scientists. One could take the rate of unemployment prevailing in the country as input to a system of voter evaluation of government, and the output of that system would be government popularity. Assume that unemployment has risen this month: By how much and over how many months is government popularity going to change as the result of higher unemployment? That, of course, is a classic research problem that has not exactly been ignored even before something like transfer function analysis was known, or known to exist. Why bother with transfer function analysis and the slew of foreign sounding terms (ARIMA, prewhitening, impulse response, white noise, and so forth) coming along with it? Why not simply apply ordinary least-squares regression? Or generalized least squares, correcting for autocorrelation among residuals?

The general reason is twofold: (1) The familiar methods are of little help in establishing the *dynamic* nature of the process being studied. That is to say, they do not indicate over what time span the effect of X on Y occurs and how this effect is distributed. (2) They are severely limited in what kinds of models they can specify for autocorrelated behavior in time series. Transfer function analysis is geared to both of these concerns: identifying dynamic models—how one variable affects another over time—and laying bare the nature of dependence within a variable over time. Hence this method offers considerable payoff to anyone interested in examining how one or more series affect another series. What follows in this chapter is a demonstration of transfer function analysis.

BASIC TRANSFER FUNCTION MODELS

Say we are interested in determining the effect of unemployment and other macroeconomic conditions on overall government popularity. Monthly measures of the unemployment rate are available, as are monthly measures of presidential approval ratings through the Gallup poll. Each of these series could be aggregated quarterly, semi-annually or annually, depending on the whims of the researcher. Figure 10.1 presents quarterly readings of presidential approval ratings from 1961 to 1980. Figure 10.2 shows the rate of unemployment for the same period.[2]

Let us designate the unemployment level at a given time t as X_t and the level of government popularity at that same time as Y_t. A change in the level of X_t will be denoted as

$$\nabla X_t = X_t - X_{t-1}$$

and a change in the level of Y as

$$\nabla Y_t = Y_t - Y_{t-1}$$

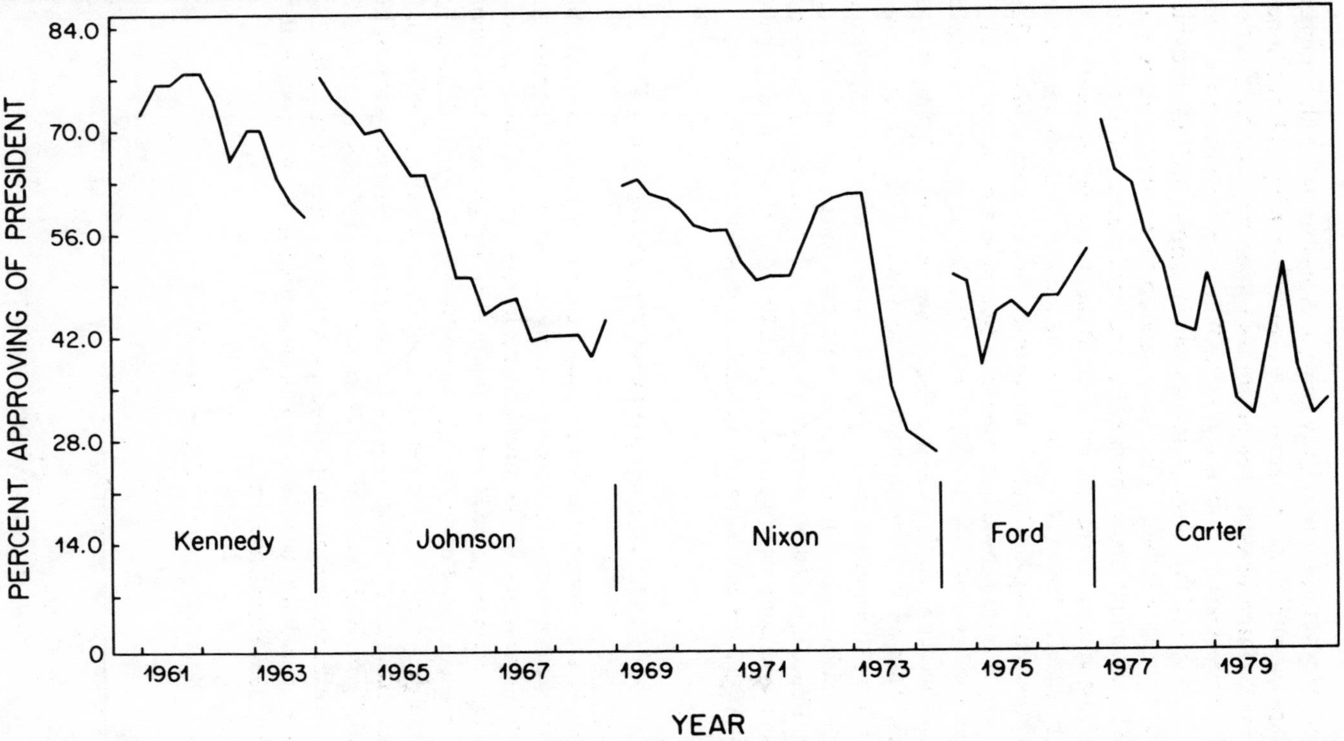

Figure 10.1: Quarterly Readings of Presidential Approval Ratings, 1961-1980

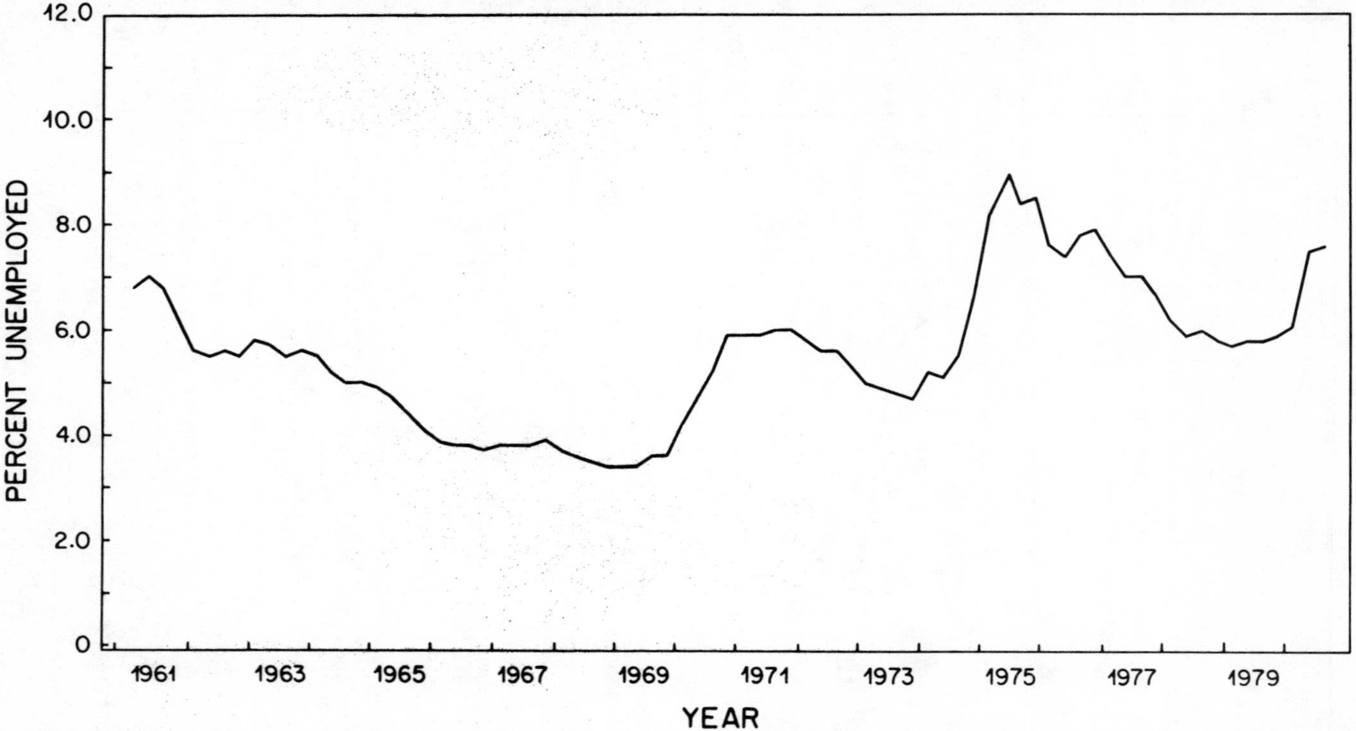

Figure 10.2: Unemployment Rates, 1961-1980

For time series that are in a state of equilibrium, that is, they fluctuate around a fixed mean level, we can safely deal with X_t and Y_t. For series not in equilibrium, however, it is better to deal with ∇X_t and ∇Y_t, the changes from one time to another. (More on this below.)

Whichever way this matter is settled, the same transfer function models apply. The simplest such model—a rather undynamic one—specifies the relationship as,

$$Y_t = \omega_0 X_t + N_t \qquad [10.1]$$

where ω_0 denotes a parameter that indicates what proportion of X_t is transferred to Y_t. There is no delay. The transfer occurs contemporaneously, according to this model. Strictly speaking, nothing ever does in real life, but when X_t and Y_t are measured monthly and the transfer from X_t to Y_t has a delay of only a day or so, such a delay cannot be detected. From a monthly perspective, then, the transfer is contemporaneous. N_t represents "noise," also referred to as error, the behavior of which will be discussed below.

Once the delay is long enough to be detectable, a more dynamic model can be stipulated:

$$Y_t = \omega_0 X_{t-b} + N_t \qquad [10.2]$$

where the output Y_t is proportional to the input X_t, according to parameter ω_0, but is now displaced by b time intervals.

In the event that present and past values of X_t influence the current value of Y_t, the transfer function model might read

$$Y_t = \omega_0 X_t + \omega_1 X_{t-1} + N_t \qquad [10.3]$$

or if there is a constant delay b,

$$Y_t = \omega_0 X_{t-b} + \omega_1 X_{t-b-1} + N_t \qquad [10.4]$$

With regard to our illustrative example, model 10.3 implies that this month's unemployment affects not only this month's government popularity but also next month's popularity. Of course, it would be easy to include further effects in models 10.3 or 10.4 if that proved necessary.

A long chain of such weights, however, is not a very attractive feature of parsimonious modeling. In the event that the weights of model 10.5

$$Y_t = \omega_0 X + \omega_1 X_{t-1} + \omega_2 X_{t-2} + \ldots + \omega_m X_{t-m} + N_t \qquad [10.5]$$

obey the following geometric rule:

$$\omega_1 = \delta\omega_o$$
$$\omega_2 = \delta^2\omega_o$$
$$\omega_3 = \delta^3\omega_o$$
$$\cdot$$
$$\cdot$$
$$\omega_m = \delta^m\omega_o$$

Model 10.5 can be rewritten as

$$Y_t = \delta Y_{t-1} + \omega_o X_t + N_t \qquad 0<\delta<1 \qquad [10.6]$$

or if the effect of X_t is delayed by b time intervals as

$$Y_t = \delta Y_{t-1} + \omega_o X_{t-b} + N_t \qquad [10.7]$$

Models 10.6 and 10.7 represent a distributed lag structure that is geometric in nature (Koyck, 1954; Pindyck and Rubinfeld, 1976: 211-218). The effect of X on Y is distributed over time and follows the rule described above. Ultimately, a change in the level of X that is not reversed results in an asymptotic change in Y equal to

$$\frac{\omega o}{1 - \delta}$$

For example, assuming $\omega_o = -.6$ and $\delta = .8$ a 1% rise in unemployment (X) would lead to an asymptotic drop in government popularity (Y) equal to 3%.

$$\frac{-.6}{1 - .8} = -3.0$$

With model 10.6 the distributed-lag process would commence at the same time that the change in X occurred, whereas with model 10.7 b time intervals would elapse before any effect of a change in X would begin to be felt in Y.

The geometric lag structure has inspired several recent studies of the popularity function (Rivers, 1980; Kernell, 1980; Hibbs et al., 1982). Exceedingly high estimates are reported for the geometric lag parameter, and the models appear to fit the time-series data rather well. It is not clear, however, whether the geometric lag structure is the only one to do so, and how it was identified. Moreover, when time series are not stationary they exhibit such strong autocorrelations as to inflate the lag estimate. The δ-parameter, after all, is tied to the correlation between Y_t and Y_{t-1}.

What is needed, then, is a search procedure for lag structures that is not misled by such correlation. A transformation of time series known as "prewhitening" removes the troublesome autocorrelation stemming from nonstationarity, autoregressive or moving-average processes (ARIMA; see Box and Jenkins, 1976). This transformation sets the stage for taking an unobstructed look at the correlation between the input and output variables of interest, so-called "cross-correlations." The aim is to obtain reliable clues regarding the following:

(1) The delay with which the effect of X on Y occurs (after how many b time intervals)
(2) The number of past X-values that affect Y (how many ω's, and which ones in particular), and
(3) The need for a δ-parameter (or several ones) attached to past values of Y.

Information on these three points may not always lead to just one plausible transfer function model. But at the very least it helps us narrow the range of such models, and perhaps only one model emerges as a likely candidate to account for the effect of X on Y.

The cross-correlation function between the input and output series furnishes the clues for the identification of transfer function models. It is introduced in the next section, after which we turn to the transformation called "prewhitening."

CROSS-CORRELATIONS BETWEEN TIME SERIES

A cross-correlation between two time series X_t and Y_t, where none trails or leads the other, is simply the familiar correlation between X and Y.

$$\rho_{xy} = \text{cov}(X_t, Y_t)/\sigma_x \sigma_y$$

But when Y leads X, or what is the same, X trails Y, by, say, one time unit, we are correlating X_t with Y_{t-1}, which is represented as

$$\rho_{xy}^{(+1)} = \text{cov}(X_t, Y_{t+1})/\sigma_x \sigma_y$$
$$= \text{cov}(X_{t-1}, Y_t)/\sigma_x \sigma_y$$

This case should not be confused with the situation in which X leads Y (same as Y trailing X) by one time unit, which is

$$\rho_{xy}^{(-1)} = \text{cov}\,(X_{t+1}, Y_t)/\sigma_x\sigma_x$$
$$= \text{cov}\,(X_t, Y_{t-1})/\sigma_x\sigma_y$$

By chance, $\rho_{xy}^{(+1)}$ may turn out to be equal to $p_{xy}^{(-1)}$ but not by any necessity. A positive value in parenthesis after ρ_{xy} indicates that X is being lagged whereas a negative value indicates that Y is being lagged.

In order to obtain reliable clues regarding the transfer function model for X and Y we have to examine cross-correlations up to a reasonable lag (K) in either direction. One rule of thumb is to go as far as one-quarter of the length of series,

$$K \leqslant N/4$$

For a series 240 months long, that could mean 60 separate correlations either way, extending up to 60 months. Other concerns, such as the continuity of each series must be weighed and it may not be advisable in certain situations to lag up to one-quarter of the length of the series. An example is provided below.

In any event, we are much less interested in cross-correlations with negative lags than in those with positive lags. If we are correct in assuming that X is the input and Y the output, all correlations between lagged Y's and X, $\rho_{xy}^{(-K)}$, ought to be zero anyway, unless there is feedback of Y on X. Whereas today's inflation rate (X_t) may bear on tomorrow's presidential approval rating (Y_{t+1}), we do not expect yesterday's presidential approval rating (Y_{t-1}) to influence today's inflation rate (X_t). Our search for tell-tale signs of a particular transfer function model focuses on $\rho_{xy}^{(+K)}$ coefficients. Figure 10.3 depicts a number of theoretical cross-correlation functions (CCF), the first four of which correspond to the transfer function models outlined above. CCF(A) reveals but one spike at K = O; all other cross-correlations are zero. That means that whatever effect X has on Y occurs contemporaneously. Model (1) is suggested. Any causal inference in this case must rest on considerations unrelated to transfer function analysis. CCF(B), where a lone spike occurs at K = 3, suggests model (2) what with a delay (b) of 3 time intervals. In this case the cross-correlation finding supports the assumption of the causal arrow running from X to Y. CCF(C) points to model (4), again with a delay parameter equal to 3 time intervals. And CCF(D) suggests a geometric lag structure of the sort described by model 10.7.

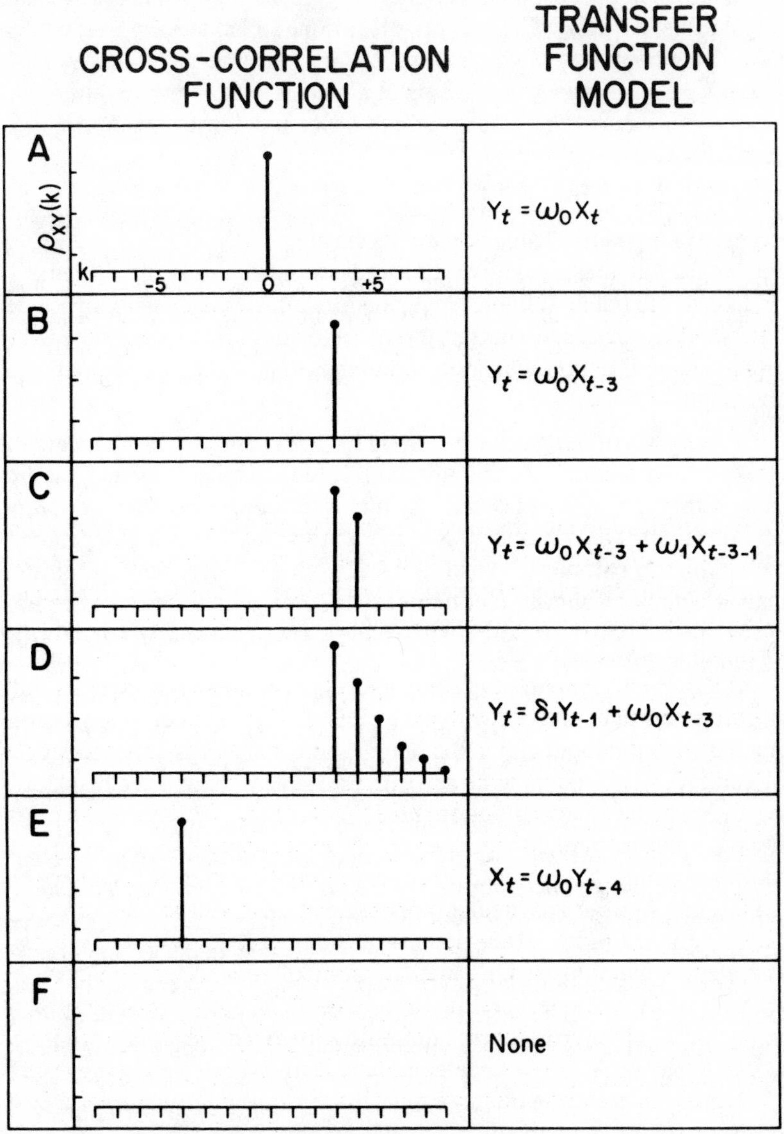

Figure 10.3: Theoretical Cross-Correlation Functions

In addition to these four patterns, Figure 10.3 depicts two that are bound to be unsettling. CCF(E) reveals but one spike, at K = –4, which is on the wrong side of the tracks. We are told that with a delay of 4 time intervals, a change in Y leads to a change of X, not the other way around. This contradicts our assumption of the causal arrow running from X to Y.

If one encounters a "wrong" cross-correlation, there are several options one can entertain in order to try to resolve this problem. First of all, one should double check the computer printout, making sure that one is right about which variable is being lagged; then check for data errors and computing errors. If that does not help, examine the over-time behavior of each series separately for possible clues of spurious correlations. And if all that fails, you are probably wrong about X being the input and Y the output.

No less discouraging is the pattern in CCF(F). This one is not meant as a joke, or as an exercise in finding the invisible; no mistake of the graphic artist, either. The point of this empty plot is to suggest the absence of *any* relationship between X and Y. X and Y in this case are two independent series, and no parameter ω or δ links X with Y or vice versa. For any analyst who is convinced that there exists some relationship between X and Y, and the only question is with what, if any, delay and in what form, the empty CCF-plot is disheartening.

The example of CCF(F) is included in Figure 10.3 not for completeness' sake, as something that the reader should know about for the rare instance when it might occur. On the contrary, it is a pattern that, I bet, any user of this type of analysis has encountered more often than he or she cares to remember. It may have convinced some of them that this type of analysis is not a worthwhile exercise of one's time or scholarly resources.

Of course, no estimated cross-correlation function will turn out to be so flat that all values are exactly zero; some mechanical error would have to be responsible for that. What is meant here is that an inspection of estimated cross-correlations fails to turn up a single one exceeding the 95% confidence limits. It is statistically significant cross-correlations that provide us with clues to transfer function models governing the relationship between the time series of interest.

It cannot be stressed enough, however, that unless those series are stationary, cross-correlations estimated with observed time series are more likely to mislead than to enlighten the analyst. For a series to be stationary, it must be free of trends, drifts, or other features suggesting that over time the expected value or the variance of the series change. Such changes, for the most part, inflate the (absolute) value of cross-correlations, the sign of which may even be reversed. As an example,

```
            -1.0  -.8  -.6  -.4  -.2   .0   .2   .4   .6   .8  1.0
LAG   CORR.  +----+----+----+----+----+----+----+----+----+----+
                                         I
-12    .305                         +    IXXXXXX+X
-11    .337                         +    IXXXXXX+X
-10    .391                         +    IXXXXXX+XXX
 -9    .454                         +    IXXXXXX+XXXX
 -8    .491                         +    IXXXXXX+XXXXX
 -7    .530                         +    IXXXXXX+XXXXXX
 -6    .587                         +    IXXXXXX+XXXXXXXX
 -5    .634                         +    IXXXXXX+XXXXXXXXX
 -4    .688                          +   IXXXXX+XXXXXXXXXXX
 -3    .747                          +   IXXXXX+XXXXXXXXXXXXX
 -2    .805                          +   IXXXXX+XXXXXXXXXXXXXX
 -1    .860                          +   IXXXXX+XXXXXXXXXXXXXXX
  0    .905                          +   IXXXXX+XXXXXXXXXXXXXXXXX
  1    .873                          +   IXXXXX+XXXXXXXXXXXXXXXX
  2    .842                          +   IXXXXX+XXXXXXXXXXXXXXX
  3    .815                          +   IXXXXX+XXXXXXXXXXXXXX
  4    .790                          +   IXXXXX+XXXXXXXXXXXXXX
  5    .747                         +    IXXXXXX+XXXXXXXXXXXX
  6    .726                         +    IXXXXXX+XXXXXXXXXXX
  7    .686                         +    IXXXXXX+XXXXXXXXXX
  8    .652                         +    IXXXXXX+XXXXXXXXX
  9    .615                         +    IXXXXXX+XXXXXXXX
 10    .588                         +    IXXXXXX+XXXXXXXX
 11    .558                         +    IXXXXXX+XXXXXXX
 12    .528                         +    IXXXXXX+XXXXXX
```

Figure 10.4: Cross-Correlations Between Unemployment and Lyndon Johnson's Popularity Measured Monthly

consider the plot in Figure 10.4 of cross-correlations between unemployment and Lyndon Johnson's popularity, measured monthly.

All correlations between Johnson's approval ratings and unemployment lagged up to 12 months exceed the 95% confidence limits, and not by a small margin. The problem is that the sign of all those correlations is "wrong." It is positive, suggesting that the higher the unemployment rate, the higher LBJ's approval rating, even after 12 months have elapsed (see cross-correlations with positive lags). Without a lag, unemployment and approval ratings for LBJ correlate with each other at a staggering +.9.

Likewise, with LBJ's approval ratings lagged (see values with negative lags), cross-correlations are positive and significant. At least, this permits us to discount the troubling cross-correlations between approval ratings and lagged unemployment. No inference as to the dynamic relationship between unemployment and presidential popularity ratings can be drawn from Figure 10.4, nor should one ever be tempted to do so from CCFs that rely on raw and unexamined time series.

The reason for this caution can be quickly inferred from the charts of unemployment and popularity. Although presenting quarterly readings, Figures 10.1 and 10.2 make the point rather well. They show that LBJ's popularity fell steadily throughout his tenure, from roughly 77 percentage points approving to 44, while unemployment dropped from 5.5% to 3.4%. It is the parallelism of these two downward *trends* that is highlighted by the CCF in Figure 10.4, not any relationship between unemployment and presidential popularity as such.

In the Johnson case the trends were parallel and produced cross-correlations with the "wrong" sign. What if the trends had run into opposite directions, popularity down and unemployment up? In that event, the cross-correlations might have proved equally impressive, and what is more, they would have had the "correct" sign. Nevertheless they should be dismissed with the same incredulity as those with the "wrong" sign. CCFs of trendy series are poor guides for transfer function modeling.

Trends, however, are not the only source of mischief. In fact, they are usually so conspicuous that corrective action can be quickly taken. More pernicious because they are less easy to spot are drifts and stochastic processes that generate autocorrelations within series that at first glance appear to fluctuate randomly. For someone interested in coming to grips with the dynamic relationship between variables all these internal features of time series pose pitfalls and obstacles. Hence Box and Jenkins (1976: 379) argue that

> considerable simplification in the identification process [of the transfer function] would occur if the input of the system were white noise. . . . When the original input follows some other stochastic process, simplification is possible by "prewhitening."

PREWHITENING

In the vernacular of time-series analysis, "white noise" essentially denotes a time series the observations of which are not correlated with each other over any lag. Hardly any real-life series of observations fits this description. But it can be made to fit through a procedure, evoking laundry imagery, called "prewhitening." This transformation not only wrings out nonstationarity but also removes autoregressive and moving-average components to the extent that they are present.

Any stationary series can be treated as the realization of an ARMA (autoregressive, moving-average) process. For example,

$$X_t = \phi X_{t-1} - \theta a_{t-1} + a_t \qquad [10.8]$$

would represent a first-order autoregressive, moving-average process, ARMA (1,1). X_t denotes the observation of the series at t, X_{t-1} at the immediately previous time point; a_t the random disturbance at time t, a_{t-1} at the immediately previous time point. ϕ and θ represent linear coefficients linking, respectively, past observations of the series and past random disturbances to present observations of the series. More to the point, a_t is assumed to be white noise. Hence by rewriting model 10.8,

$$X_t - (\phi X_{t-1} - \theta a_{t-1}) = a_t \qquad [10.9]$$

we are prewhitening the series X_t. All one needs to know is (1) whether or not the ARMA(1,1) model is correct and (2) what the values are for ϕ and θ. The rest is simple.

If the series of interest happens to be nonstationary, then this transformation would have to be applied not to X_t but to the properly differenced series, say

$$\nabla X_t = X_t - X_{t-1}$$

In that event,

$$\nabla X_t - (\phi \nabla X_{t-1} - \theta a_{t-1}) = a_t \qquad [10.10]$$

would furnish the required white-noise series. And the process underlying the series X_t would be referred to as an autoregressive, integrated, moving-average process, what with each component being of order one: ARIMA (1,1,1).

Returning to our series of interest, shown in Figures 10.1 and 10.2, we can say that both are candidates for prewhitening. Unemployment drifts, first downward until 1968, then upward in leaps and bounds. There is no indication that it fluctuates around a stable mean, returning to that mean quickly after departing from it. For long stretches it hovers below the overall mean, then above it. The unemployment series, in other words, appears to be nonstationary. The identification of autoregressive,

```
          -1.0 -.8  -.6  -.4  -.2   .0   .2   .4   .6   .8  1.0
LAG   CORR. +----+----+----+----+----+----+----+----+----+----+
                                     I
  1    .449                     +    IXXXX+XXXXXX
  2    .148                    +     IXXXX +
  3    .048                   +      IX     +
  4   -.034                   +     XI      +
  5   -.072                   +    XXI      +
  6   -.075                   +    XXI      +
  7    .007                   +      I      +
  8   -.218                   + XXXXXI      +
  9   -.230                   +XXXXXXI      +
 10   -.107                   +   XXXI      +
 11   -.106                   +   XXXI      +
 12   -.211                   + XXXXXI      +
 13   -.107                   +   XXXI      +
 14    .025                   +      IX     +
 15    .068                   +      IXX    +
 16    .066                   +      IXX    +
 17    .028                   +      IX     +
 18    .160                   +      IXXXX  +
 19    .054                  +       IX      +
 20    .195                  +       IXXXXX  +
```

Figure 10.5: Autocorrelation Function Estimated for ∇X_t

moving-average components henceforth focuses on the first differences of the unemployment series, X_t.

Figure 10.5 depicts the autocorrelation function estimated for ∇X_t, with lags up to 20 quarters. The pattern shown is one of rapid decay, which leads us to suspect a first-order autoregressive process at work on unemployment. For this model the following estimate, with parameter standard errors in parentheses, is obtained by way of an estimation procedure outlined below:

$$\hat{\nabla X_t} \doteq .45\, \nabla X_{t-1} \qquad [10.11]$$
$$(.10)$$
$$Q = 25 \qquad DF = 19 \qquad p > .10$$

The model easily passes the "white noise" diagnostics.[3] That is to say, the residuals produced by model 10.11 are not significantly correlated with each other at the .05 level up to 20 lags. They can be safely treated as white noise, and the series

$$\alpha_t = \nabla X_t - .45\nabla X_{t-1} \qquad [10.12]$$

supplies us with a prewhitened unemployment series.

Now let us turn our attention to the series supposedly influenced by unemployment. As one can glean from Figure 10.1, the presidential popularity series also violates stationarity assumptions. The curve for almost every president points downward. These "local trends" of the overall popularity series are invariably reversed by spectacular leaps once a new president takes office. There can be no question that the mean of the popularity series from 1961 to 1980 changes over time. Differencing is required to render the popularity series stationary. It is the differenced popularity series that is then subjected to the same transformation as the unemployment series. This yields a "prefiltered" popularity series denoted by Box and Jenkins as β:

$$\beta_t = \nabla Y_t - .45\ Y_{t-1} \qquad [10.13]$$

This step removes from the popularity series the autoregressive component detected in the unemployment series and eliminates any possibility that that component might be responsible for correlations between unemployment and popularity.[4]

The cross-correlations between the (prewhitened) unemployment series and the (prefiltered) presidential popularity series provide interpretable, though perhaps not altogether satisfactory clues for identifying a suitable transfer function.[5] In Figure 10.6 just one cross-correlation estimate exceeds the 95% confidence limit. It does have the correct sign, namely negative, but it happens at lag 0. There are no signs of any delayed effects, just a contemporaneous one. A rise (drop) in the unemployment rate appears to be matched by a drop (rise) of some magnitude in presidential approval ratings during the same quarter. No delay is involved, at least none exceeding a time span equal to a quarter of a year, though there may be shorter lags. However meager, the finding of a negatively signed CCF-estimate at lag 0 is preferable to the semblance of a dynamic effect with the wrong sign.

Based on the clues provided by Figure 10.6 we tentatively identify a transfer function model for unemployment and popularity as

$$\nabla Y_t = \omega_0\ X_t + \nabla N_t \qquad [10.14]$$

```
          -1.0 -.8  -.6  -.4  -.2   .0   .2   .4   .6   .8  1.0
LAG   CORR. +----+----+----+----+----+----+----+----+----+----+

 -8    .025                    +     IX    +
 -7   -.082                    +   XXI     +
 -6   -.101                    +  XXXI     +
 -5   -.084                    +   XXI     +
 -4    .016                    +     I     +
 -3   -.178                    + XXXXI     +
 -2    .189                    +     IXXXXX+
 -1    .045                    +     IX    +
  0   -.243                   X+XXXXXI    +
  1    .122                    +     IXXX  +
  2    .098                    +     IXX   +
  3    .027                    +     IX    +
  4   -.098                    +   XXI     +
  5    .182                    +     IXXXXX+
  6    .077                    +     IXX   +
  7    .014                    +     I     +
  8    .068                    +     IXX   +
```

Figure 10.6: Cross-Correlation Estimates

If this were all we were interested in we would now begin to focus on the disturbance term (∇N_t), identify its autoregressive, moving-average components, and then estimate the whole transfer function model. But in order to come to grips with macroeconomic effects on presidential popularity we must also take account of at least one other condition—inflation. As postulated by the Phillips curve, unemployment and inflation sit at opposite ends of a macroeconomic seesaw.

In fact, as Cameron (1984) points out, inflation was the more salient macroeconomic problem throughout most of the 1961-1980 period. Quarterly readings for a measure of inflation are charted in Figure 10.7. The inflation measure shown there represents quarter-to-quarter changes of the logged consumer-price index; taking the (natural) logarithm of the CPI numbers is necessary because of the accelerating pace of the CPI in the 1970s.

As can quickly be gleaned from Figure 10.7, our measure of inflation drifts upward in leaps and bounds. Its behavior over time is not that of a stationary series. After being differenced once,

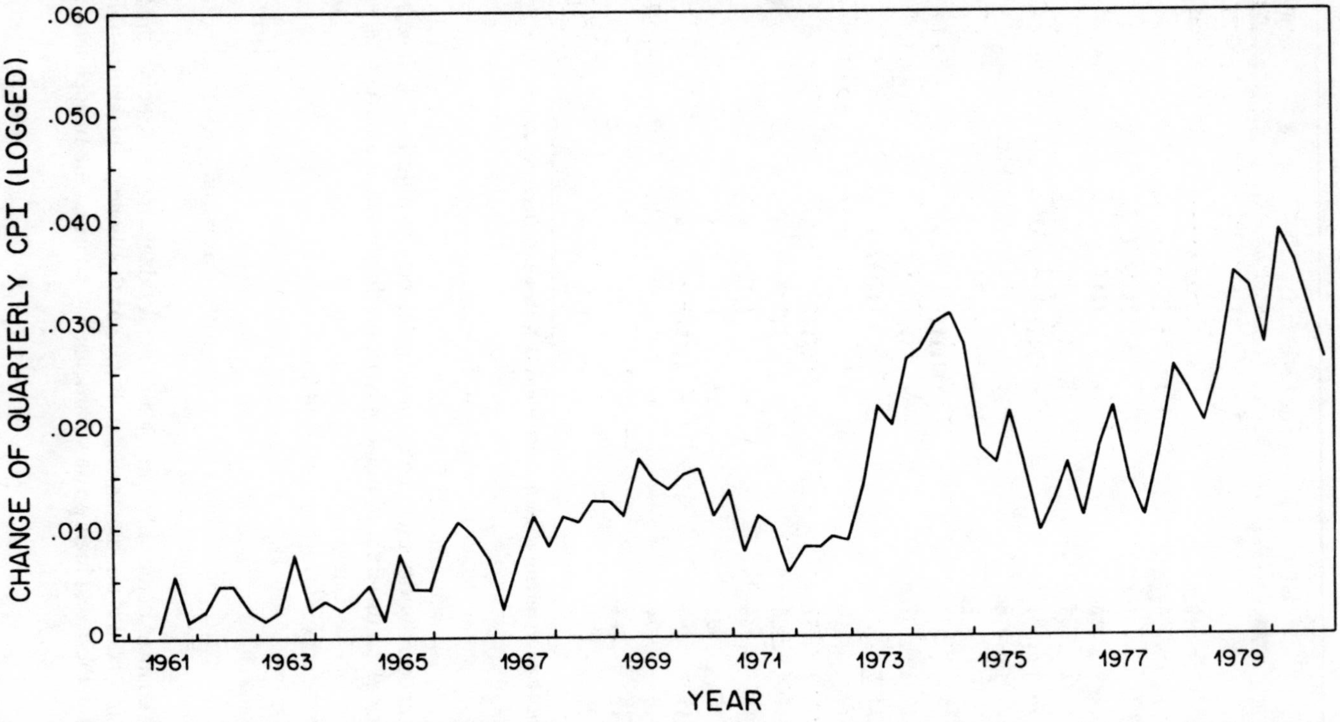

Figure 10.7: Quarterly Readings for a Measure of Inflation, 1961-1980

```
          -1.0  -.8  -.6  -.4  -.2  .0   .2   .4   .6   .8  1.0
LAG   CORR. +----+----+----+----+----+----+----+----+----+----+
                                     I
  1   -.162                     +XXXXI    +
  2   -.374                 XXX+XXXXXI     +
  3    .254                    +     IXXXXXX
  4    .163                   +      IXXXX  +
  5   -.134                   +   XXXI      +
  6   -.190                   + XXXXXI      +
  7    .098                   +      IXX    +
  8    .051                   +      IX     +
  9   -.257                   +XXXXXXI      +
 10   -.107                   +   XXXI      +
 11    .182                   +      IXXXXX +
 12    .018                   +      I      +
 13   -.147                   +  XXXXI      +
 14   -.128                  +    XXXI       +
 15    .136                  +       IXXX    +
 16    .083                  +       IXX     +
 17   -.190                  +  XXXXXI       +
 18    .124                  +       IXXX    +
 19    .069                  +       IXX     +
 20   -.054                  +      XI       +
```

Figure 10.8: Function of Autocorrelations of Inflation Differenced Once

$$\nabla Z_t = Z_t - Z_{t-1}$$

its autocorrelations produce a function depicted in Figure 10.8. The behavior of the differenced inflation series is diagnosed as autoregressive:

$$\nabla \hat{Z}_t = -.48\, \nabla Z_{t-2}$$

$$(.11) \qquad [10.15]$$

$$Q = 31 \quad DF = 19 \quad p = .05$$

With chances being only 5 in 100 that the residuals are white noise, the fit of this model is not breathtaking. But given that none of the autocorrelations of these residuals prove significant, we consider the fit adequate. In

```
          -1.0 -.8  -.6  -.4  -.2   .0   .2   .4   .6   .8  1.0
LAG   CORR. +----+----+----+----+----+----+----+----+----+----+
 -8    .084                    +     IXX   +
 -7    .052                    +     IX    +
 -6    .138                    +     IXXX  +
 -5    .189                    +     IXXXXX+
 -4    .064                    +     IXX   +
 -3    .023                    +     IX    +
 -2   -.240                    XXXXXXI     +
 -1    .057                    +     IX    +
  0   -.120                     + XXXI    +
  1   -.311                  XX+XXXXXI     +
  2   -.039                    +    XI     +
  3   -.140                    +  XXXI     +
  4   -.173                    + XXXXI     +
  5   -.175                    + XXXXI     +
  6    .099                    +     IXX   +
  7    .034                    +     IX    +
  8    .029                    +     IX    +
```

Figure 10.9: Cross-Correlations

any event, all that is required at this point is a reasonable success in filtering out nonstationarity and autocorrelation, so that the cross-correlations between input and output series are not totally misleading.

As with the unemployment series shown above, we prewhiten the inflation series and prefilter the popularity series, this time according to model 10.15 estimates, and obtain estimated cross-correlations between the resulting series. As can be seen in Figure 10.9, one estimate clearly exceeds the 95% confidence limits. This happens at lag 1, and the estimate has the correct sign, namely a negative one. That is to say, an effect of inflation on presidential popularity with a one-quarter delay is suggested. The estimated CCF hints at no further effects. There is a faint hint, however, at an effect without a delay (lag 0). Because the CCF for unemployment and popularity also hinted at a lag-0 effect, and given the trade-off between unemployment and inflation, it may be worthwhile, at least tentatively, to specify a lag-0 effect for inflation, in addition to a lag-l effect.

TRANSFER FUNCTION ESTIMATES

The estimated cross-correlations between unemployment and popularity, and between inflation and popularity, all properly prewhitened, lead us to specify, tentatively, the following transfer function model:

$$\nabla Y_t = \theta_o + \omega_{xo} \nabla X_t + \omega_{zo} \nabla Z_t + \omega_{z1} \nabla Z_{t-1} + \nabla N_t \quad [10.16]$$

Note that a constant (θ_0) has also been entered into the model specification. The reason for this step is that the overall mean of the differenced popularity series (∇Y_t) is nonzero, a sign of the downward trend in the undifferenced popularity series (Y_t). The disturbance term (∇N_t), which like all the other variables is treated in differenced form, will receive our attention after preliminary estimates for the model parameters have been obtained. They are given in model 10.17 with standard errors in parentheses.[6]

$$\hat{Y}_t = \underset{(.49)}{-1.33} - \underset{(1.28)}{1.64} \nabla X_t - \underset{(109.3)}{168.7} \nabla Z_t - \underset{(106.8)}{400.9} \nabla Z_{t-1} \quad [10.17]$$

The residuals of equation 10.17

$$\nabla N_t = \nabla Y_t - \nabla \hat{Y}_t$$

can now be probed for traces of stochastic processes of the autoregressive or moving-average sort.

The autocorrelations of those residuals (∇N_t) have been charted in Figure 10.10. They hint at a low order and fairly weak moving-average process, MA(1). With this specification of the disturbance included in model 10.16, the estimates are now as follows,

$$\hat{Y}_t = \underset{(.61)}{-1.33} \underset{(1.36)}{-1.88} \nabla X_t \underset{(103.9)}{-183.5} \nabla Z_t \underset{(105.3)}{-402.9} \nabla Z_{t-1} + \underset{(.11)}{.29} a_{t-1} \quad [10.18]$$

where a_{t-1} represents the lagged value of a_t. Whether or not a_t behaves like white noise is judged through an examination of the autocorrelations of the residuals produced by equation 10.18.

As can be easily seen from Figure 10.11, none of the first 20 autocorrelations even as much as reach the 95% confidence limits. The hypothesis that a time series with an ACF of this sort is white noise cannot be

```
          -1.0  -.8  -.6  -.4  -.2   .0   .2   .4   .6   .8  1.0
LAG   CORR. +----+----+----+----+----+----+----+----+----+----+
                                     I
  1    .209                     +    IXXXXX
  2   -.160                    + XXXXI     +
  3   -.207                    +XXXXXI     +
  4   -.141                    + XXXXI     +
  5    .093                    +     IXX   +
  6   -.019                    +     I     +
  7   -.130                    +  XXXI     +
  8   -.105                    +  XXXI     +
  9    .023                    +     IX    +
 10   -.044                    +    XI     +
 11    .061                    +     IXX   +
 12    .034                    +     IX    +
 13    .035                    +     IX    +
 14   -.013                    +     I     +
 15   -.056                    +    XI     +
 16    .032                    +     IX    +
 17    .158                    +     IXXXX +
 18    .078                   +      IXX    +
 19   -.092                   +    XXI      +
 20   -.159                   +  XXXXI      +
```

Figure 10.10: Autocorrelations of Residuals

rejected at the .05 level. As a matter of fact, the Q-diagnostic based on those 20 estimates comes to 13, which, with nineteen degrees of freedom corresponds to a probability of roughly .75. The parameter estimates suggest that the effect of inflation on presidential popularity is more substantial after a lag of one quarter than within the same quarter; the t-ratio for contemporary inflation (−1.77) is just above the requirement for one-tailed .05 significance. As for contemporary unemployment, its estimate makes only the .10 grade of significance. But because the sign is correct and the series is relatively short, we do not want to be overly picky about the .05 level of significance here.

It is important to recall that the series of interest have been treated in differenced form; in the raw they are simply not stationary. Strictly speaking, we should be referring to "quarterly changes in inflation" and "quarterly changes in unemployment" having such and such an effect on

```
          -1.0  -.8  -.6  -.4  -.2   .0   .2   .4   .6   .8  1.0
LAG   CORR. +----+----+----+----+----+----+----+----+----+----+
                                     I
  1   -.025                     +   XI    +
  2   -.111                     + XXXI    +
  3   -.136                    +  XXXI     +
  4   -.143                    + XXXXI     +
  5    .132                    +     IXXX  +
  6   -.025                    +    XI     +
  7   -.094                    +   XXI     +
  8   -.094                    +   XXI     +
  9    .073                    +     IXX   +
 10   -.084                    +   XXI     +
 11    .083                    +     IXX   +
 12    .000                    +     I     +
 13    .033                    +     IX    +
 14   -.005                    +     I     +
 15   -.059                    +    XI     +
 16    .002                    +     I     +
 17    .141                    +     IXXXX +
 18    .057                    +     IX    +
 19   -.063                    +   XXI     +
 20   -.140                    + XXXXI     +
```

Figure 10.11: Autocorrelations of Residuals

"quarterly changes in popularity" rather than inflation and unemployment having an effect on popularity. It is at the level of quarterly changes that the transfer function analysis done here has been able to demonstrate effects. Sometimes in the course of the discussion this qualification may get lost as it is so cumbersome to spell out each time. No doubt the estimates presented here, obtained as they are from the differenced series, prove less overpowering than some, though by no means all, estimates obtained from raw series lacking in stationarity. But there can be no question that the findings reported in this chapter have passed a more demanding test. They are not suspect because of trends, drifts, or stochastic processes that drive the observed time series.

Given the transformations that have been applied to the observed series, it is not easy to see how much difference inflation and unemployment make for presidential popularity. This is especially true for inflation, where the parameter estimates may boggle the mind. So let us

TABLE 10.1
Inflation, Unemployment, and Change of Presidential Popularity

	Change in Percentage Approving of President	
President	*Inflation Induced*	*Unemployment Induced*
Kennedy	+.5	+1.7
Johnson	–6.0	+4.1
Nixon	–9.1	–3.2
Ford	+8.7	–5.3
Carter	–5.8	+.8

NOTE: The entries were obtained by taking the mean quarterly change of each economic series for a given president and multiplying it by the respective parameter provided in equation 10.18. The entries in the inflation column combine inflation and inflation lagged.

translate them into effects on the popularity of specific presidents. For each of the five presidents included in the 1961-1980 period we have calculated the amount by which his approval rating fell or rose as the result of the movement of the two macroeconomic indicators throughout his term of office.

According to the estimates provided in Table 10.1, Kennedy appears to have gained a negligible one-half percentage point as the result of a drop in inflation, which was low to begin with. His successor, on the other hand, suffered a considerable loss of 6 points due to inflation, which worsened during LBJ's term. Nixon fared even worse, what with an estimated popularity loss due to inflation of 9 points. His successor, however, seems to have been able to capitalize on a declining inflation, ending up with a gain estimated here in the order of 8.7 points. When inflation rose sharply again during Carter's presidency, it appears to have cost the incumbent approximately 6 points in popularity. All these gain-loss figures include both the contemporary and the lagged inflation effects.

Nevertheless they represent only one side of the macroeconomic coin. It is quite possible that these losses or gains were offset by the effects of unemployment, however marginal in significance, on popularity. Johnson, for example, as can be seen in Table 10.1, was helped by the decline in unemployment during his tenure, estimated here to have boosted his popularity by 4 points. This is still short of the 6 points he is seen losing because of rising inflation, but it leaves him with only a net loss of 2 points attributable to macroeconomic performance. In any event, the finding that the drop in unemployment during LBJ's term of office helped rather than hurt his popular standing, as was implied by the perplexing cross-correlations of raw series (see Figure 10.3, above), demonstrates the usefulness of transfer function analysis over analysis that ignores the time-series nature of time series.

Like LBJ, the next Democrat in the White House was also able to trim his inflation losses through improvements on unemployment, though to a lesser degree. Carter, we estimate, gained approximately one popularity point from a decline in unemployment throughout most of his term. In contrast, his predecessor had some of his inflation-induced gains canceled by a worsening of unemployment. Ford nevertheless came out with a net gain of 3 points. Nixon, on the other hand, was unfortunate enough to lose on both counts. Unemployment subtracted 3 more points from his popularity, which was also severely cut by inflation.

There is no point, however, in getting carried away with those gain-loss estimates. They are not meant as a verdict on the economic performance of the five presidents, but rather as an illustration of what the transfer function estimates may be able to tell us. Before taking those estimates too seriously, we must specify the model from which they are derived more fully. "Honeymoon effects," "rally 'round the flag" effects, the occurrence of wars, and Watergate, among others, beg for specification (Mueller, 1973; Kernell, 1978). How these variables may be incorporated in a transfer function model is shown elsewhere (Norpoth, 1984).

ESTIMATION PROCEDURE

It will come as no surprise to anyone that the model estimates reported in this chapter were not obtained by hand. They were produced by an algorithm embodied in the BMDP2T routine of the Biomedical Computer Programs.[7] This author has found BMDP2T (Box-Jenkins Time Series Analysis) a convenient program for analyzing not only the ARIMA-properties of single series, but also the relationships among several time series, with cross-correlations, prewhitening, and transfer function identification, noise model estimation and all. The program language is straightforward and the output intelligible for someone reasonably familiar with ARIMA modeling.

To illustrate the estimation of such models, consider a single series assumed to be stationary and generated by a first-order moving-average process,

$$X_t = a_t - \theta a_{t-1}$$

The parameters of this model cannot be directly estimated by ordinary least squares. After all, a_{t-1} is an unobserved random variable. The quantity the sum of squares of which is to be minimized is,

$$a_t = X_t + \theta a_{t-1}$$

which can be expanded to yield,

$$\begin{aligned} a_t &= X_t + \theta (X_{t-1} + \theta a_{t-2}) \\ &= X_t + \theta (X_{t-1} + \theta(X_{t-2} + \theta a_{t-3}) \end{aligned}$$

$$= \sum_{K=0}^{\infty} \theta^k X_{t-k}$$

The sum of squares for errors of this type leads to nonlinear normal equations for which the ordinary least squares algorithm provides no solution. A nonlinear method is required instead (Box and Jenkins, 1976, chap. 7; Marquardt, 1963; McCleary and Hay, 1980, chap. 6; Pindyck and Rubinfeld, 1976, chap. 7.5).

Iteration provides the key for the nonlinear estimation strategy. We begin by making some initial guesses about the parameters to be estimated, only one in the example shown above (θ). Such a guess need not be a shot in the dark. The autocorrelation function of the observed time series, or the cross-correlation function in case of bivariate parameters, furnishes a tool for making reasonably informed guesses. These guesses are entered into a *Taylor series expansion* of the nonlinear model (Bishir and Drewes, 1970, chap. 16), to which ordinary least squares can be applied. In this way, we obtain a new estimate for the parameter of interest (θ), which deviates from the old one by a certain amount (d),

$$\hat{\theta}_{new} = \hat{\theta}_{old} + d$$

Using $\hat{\theta}_{new}$ now as our best guess for θ, we relinearize the model, and reestimate it with ordinary least squares. This sequence of steps is repeated until a certain degree of precision has been reached. This may happen when from one iteration to the next the θ-estimate changes by less than a certain predetermined degree,

$$\frac{\hat{\theta}\text{ new} - \hat{\theta}\text{ old}}{\hat{\theta}\text{ old}}$$

or, alternatively, when the residual sum of squares, $S(\hat{\theta})$, changes by less than a certain degree,

$$\frac{S(\hat{\theta}_{new}) - S(\hat{\theta}_{old})}{S(\hat{\theta}_{old})}$$

whichever comes first. It is up to the analyst to set these precision criteria. Of course, he or she may elect to go along with preassigned ones; the BMDP2T defaults are quite conservative, .0001 for change in parameter estimates and .00001 for change in the residual sum of square. Once either of these precision criteria is reached, the algorithm stops iterating and produces the solution on which it has converged. It should be noted, however, that the algorithm may also stop because the maximum number of iterations set by the analyst has been reached (the BMDP2T default is 10). In that event the algorithm has not converged on a solution. The analyst should now either increase the maximum number of iterations or reexamine the model; perhaps the parameters of the tentatively specified model are so highly correlated with each other as to prevent convergence.

It goes without saying that setting reasonable starting values for the parameters to be estimated speeds up convergence, although in my experience convergence has not been unduly delayed when BMDP2T default values (.1) were used. But because by the time one is ready to get estimates for transfer function models so much labor has been invested in locating preliminary parameter estimates of an appropriate model, it would be foolish to ignore all that work and simply go with program defaults for starters.

When it comes to the mechanics of estimating the parameters of a time-series model, yet another decision must be made by the analyst. That is so because in many instances the initial value of a time series is undefined. Again, consider the MA(1) model:

$$x_t = a_t - \theta a_{t-1}$$

or

$$a_t = X_t + \theta a_{t-1}$$

TABLE 10.2
Transfer Function Estimation by Conditional Least-Squares and Backcasting

		Constant (Θ_0)	*Inflation* (ω_{Z0}	ω_{Z1})	*Unemployment* (ω_{X0})	*MA (1)* (Θ)	*Residual SS*
Starting values		–1.5	–132	–343	–3	–.21	
		(a) Conditional Least Squares Only					
Iteration	(1)	–1.32	–182	–398	–1.91	–.273	1336
	(2)	–1.31	–184	–403	–1.87	–.283	1336
	(3)	–1.31	–184	–402	–1.87	–.285	1336
		(b) Backcasting Only					
Iteration	(1)	–1.33	–182	–399	–1.91	–.273	1336
	(2)	–1.31	–183	–403	–1.87	–.284	1335
	(3)	–1.31	–184	–403	–1.88	–.285	1335
		(c) Backcasting After Conditional Least Squares					
Iteration	(1)	–1.31	–184	–403	–1.88	–.286	1335

NOTE: The iteration results are entered with the precision provided by the BMDP2T printout.

To obtain the value for a_1,

$$a_1 = X_1 + \theta a_o$$

we need a_o, something that is not available. We do know X_1 and can make guesses about θ, but what do we do about a_o? One suggestion is to set a_o equal to zero, the expectation of a_t. Then a value for a_1 can be calculated for a given guess of θ, then a_2, and so forth. With the series of a_t values in hand, the iterative algorithm can proceed to estimate the model parameters in the fashion outlined above.

This "conditional" approach ($a_o = 0$) is one way of calculating a_t's. The alternative involves "backcasting." Here, one begins at the end of the series, and moving backward through the series ends up with a "backcast" value for a_o. That value for a_o can then be used to calculate a_1, a_2, and so forth by going forward until the end of the series is reached. Box and Jenkins (1976: 209-220), who present detailed examples for both approaches, favor backcasting over conditional least-squares. BMDP2T allows the analyst to use either one alone or both in succession, with backcasting following conditional least-squares.

For the transfer function model estimated in this chapter both approaches work reasonably well and with just a few iterations. Both conditional least-squares and backcasting converge on practically the same solution after only three iterations. The one additional iteration performed by backcasting, with initial parameter estimates provided by the final iteration of conditional least-squares, leaves those estimates virtually unchanged.

DISCUSSION

Transfer function analysis, admittedly, is not the vogue in political analysis; of course, if it were, a chapter such as this would not be needed. One simple reason for the less than frequent use of the type of analysis outlined above is that time series are not the most common data staple in social and political analysis. Another is that user-friendly computer algorithms have not been available until very recently. Whoever wanted to apply transfer function analysis either had to build his or her own routines or work from routines requiring a great deal of preparation. A third reason, I suspect, is that many attempts to put this type of analysis to work have come up empty-handed. After running one's time series of interest through the prewhitening filter many users may have wondered whether or not there was any transfer function model to be identified and estimated. In several applications of ARIMA modeling the conventional wisdom has not seemed to be faring too well (Pierce, 1977; Norpoth and Yantek, 1983a, 1983b). But reports that life is white noise and that one thing does not lead to another neither excite not convince many people. Those claims may also prove premature and call for special care in applying this methodology.

Even when applied with seeming success, Box-Jenkins models are often presented with reservations. Hibbs (1977), in one of the earlier introductions of Box-Jenkins models provided for political and social scientists, concluded on a downbeat note:

> Box-Jenkins methods are essentially models of "ignorance" that are not based on theory and in a sense are void of explanatory power [Hibbs, 1977: 172].

Strong words, especially after an elegant presentation of the method coupled with an empirical demonstration of the effect of party in government on unemployment in Britain.

Others have warned that Box-Jenkins methods are prone to throwing out the baby with the bathwater (Feige and Pearce, 1979: 531). Special blame is put on differencing and prewhitening. These filters are said to remove much of the substantive relationship between the series of interest. As a result, there is a heightened risk that the null hypothesis of no effect is *not* rejected when it should be rejected. Nelson and Schwert (1982) argue that compared with other methods such as the Direct Granger Approach (Freeman, 1983) cross-correlations between prewhitened time-series lack statistical power. Hence the lack of success of many attempts to enlist ARIMA models for the task of identifying dynamic models should not be surprising or reason for disappointment; it is simply due to a defect of the instrument.

These objections are examined here one by one. First, the notion that Box-Jenkins methods are "models of ignorance." Is it true that these methods are "essentially sophisticated noise models that make no attempt to represent the behavioral structure" (Hibbs, 1977: 173)? Is it true that they fail to tell us anything about causal relationships? The answer may indeed be "yes" for instances in which only a single explanatory variable is considered, especially in the form of a single intervention such as the adoption of a new policy, a change of government, or an international event. The omission of relevant variables would raise serious doubts regarding the estimate for the lone variable, if that is even the right term here for a single intervention. No doubt, a transfer function model of presidential popularity containing only unemployment as an explanatory series would be suspect, and rightfully so, the continuous nature of that variable notwithstanding. The problem is simply one of omitted variables and even the most sophisticated ARIMA noise model could not hope to make up for that.

As demonstrated above, transfer function analysis is *not* confined to situations involving just one explanatory variable. It permits as much imagination in model specification as do other approaches. What is more, it promises to furnish clues for model identification. Cross-correlations help us detect effects that the explanatory series may be exerting on the dependent series.

This brings us to the second bone of contention, the "lack of power" objection. How much can we trust cross-correlation estimates derived from prewhitened series? A skeptical attitude is voiced by Nelson and Schwert (1982) and Geweke et al (1979). Nelson and Schwert's (1982) Monte Carlo study, for example, noted a considerable failure rate for cross-correlations to flag causal effects. Before generalizing too far, however, one should realize that although the point was well taken for series of 50 observations there was no problem with series of 100 and 200 observations (Nelson and Schwert, 1982: 15). Box and Jenkins (1976: 387) themselves make the point that "cross-correlation estimates will be buried in noise . . . unless n is large." There is, of course, no absolute rule as to what is "large." Nelson and Schwert's analysis suggests that 50 is not, whereas 100 is. But whether or not a series is large enough may also depend on other factors, especially the relative size of residual error. The less the residual noise, the louder the cross-correlations speak.

> The identification procedure [for transfer function models] requires that the variation in the input X shall be reasonably large compared with the variation due to the noise [Box and Jenkins, 1976: 387].

With short series, the presence of only a little noise may still lead to success in identifying the transfer function model. On the other hand, a longer series afflicted with a case of deafening noise may not, its welcome length notwithstanding.

The example used in this chapter relied on series 80 observations long, neither large nor small. These are 80 quarterly observations that were derived from 240 monthly observations. Why turn a decidedly "large" series into one that falls into the grey zone between large and small, and no longer allows one to estimate short-term lag structures occurring within a three-month span? The reason is "noise." From one month to the next, presidential approval ratings typically do not change a great deal. Shifts of one or two points are of a size that is indistinguishable from the margin of sampling error. Being based on surveys of samples of the public the approval ratings reported for any given month may deviate from the "true" level by amounts that can easily surpass the shift in reported readings from one month to the next. Hence differencing such a series of monthly observations produces a largely random series, which is made up of sampling error differences. Quarterly aggregates of such monthly observations, on the other hand, filter out much of this noise, though not all of it, and enable us to identify models with series of 80 observations that would go unrecognized in series of 240. No dumb rule of thumb, however, should be derived from this example. There is no substitute for good judgment of how sample size and residual noise should be balanced.

Transfer function analysis may be tough regarding what it demands of time-series data, but not to the degree that null findings are a foregone conclusion. In return it rewards us with estimates that are not confounded by all the built-in artifacts that invariably come with time-series observations.

NOTES

1. Box and Jenkins (1976) provide the most thorough treatment of transfer function and ARIMA modeling. Although the coverage is quite mathematical, examples and illustrations are plentiful, though not especially intriguing for social scientists. For a more ap-

plied approach with social science examples, see McCleary and Hay (1980). A condensed version, which concentrates on analyzing interrupted time series and presents a handy overview of univariate ARIMA modeling, is available in the Sage series on quantitative applications, McDowall et al. (1980). Pindyck and Rubinfeld (1976), and Nelson (1973) also cover univariate modeling but have little to say about transfer function models. Yantek (1985) provides a readable exposition of transfer function methodology for political scientists.

2. The monthly data from which the quarterly unemployment data were derived come from the *Monthly Labor Review* (U.S. Department of Labor). The consumer price index, on which the measure of inflation used below is based, was taken from *Business Statistics* (U.S. Department of Commerce). For 1979 and 1980, the data come from the *Survey of Current Business* (U.S. Department of Commerce). The popularity series is based on the percentage "approve" of monthly Gallup surveys ("Do you approve or disapprove of the way . . . is handling his job as president?"). See *The Gallup Opinion Index*, Report No. 182, October-November 1980. The monthly figures, sometimes based on more than one survey a month, were averaged by quarters. For the fourth quarter of 1963 and the third quarter of 1974, when the presidency changed hands in the middle of a term, only values of the new president were used each time. Popularity values were interpolated for the third quarters of election years 1964, 1972, and 1976.

3. The Q-diagnostic, which has a chi-square distribution, is computed by summing the squared autocorrelations of residuals up to a certain lag, say 20, and then multiplying that sum by the length of the series (Box and Jenkins, 1976: 290-294). In this case,

$$Q = 80 \quad \{(.03)^2 + (-.05)^2 + \ldots + (.16)^2\} = 25$$

with degrees of freedom equal to the number of autocorrelations (20) minus the number of model parameters (one in this case):

$$DF = 20 - 1 = 19$$

Using a chi-square tabulation, we determine whether or not chances are fewer than 5 in 100 of getting such a Q-estimate, given the number of degrees of freedom. If so, the hypothesis of white noise residuals is rejected at the .05 level; if not, we consider it safe to treat the residuals as white noise.

4. As an alternative, one could prewhiten the output series according to its own dynamic, and not the dynamic of the input series. See Haugh (1976) and Pierce (1977). This procedure, which results in two white noise series, might be preferable if one cannot safely assume which of the two series is the causal one.

5. It should be noted that for the transition quarters, when the presidency changed hands, the (differenced) popularity series was set equal to zero. This step removes any inauguration or "honeymoon" effect, which is not of interest here. This adjustment, however, does not settle all issues raised by an analysis of the popularity of five different presidents in the 1961-1980 period. In computing cross-correlations between popularity and lagged values of unemployment or inflation, one connects some of the unemployment (or inflation) prevailing under one president with the popularity of the next one—the more so, the longer the lag. To be sure, this poses a less severe problem for presidents of the same party, such as Kennedy and Johnson, or Nixon and Ford, but neither Nixon in 1969 nor Carter in 1977 should be thought of as being influenced in their public standing by eco-

nomic conditions prevailing under their respective predecessors belonging to the opposite party. There is no quick and easy way to handle this problem and still examine the whole series. The best that one can do by way of subseries analysis is to estimate separate CCFs for the Kennedy-Johnson years, the Nixon-Ford years, and the Carter years. This was done and it disclosed no more extended effects than did the CCF for the whole series, neither for unemployment nor for inflation. In any event, it seemed prudent to lag the economic series no further than 8 lags, as was done in Figures 10.6 and 10.9.

6. Note that the parameter estimates for inflation are so much bigger than the estimate for unemployment only because the CPI used for constructing the inflation measure was log-transformed.

7. The analysis results reported in this chapter were performed with the 1981 BMDP2T version. Since then the 1983 version has become available, to which students interested in this methodology might want to turn. BMDP2T is part of the Biomedical Computer Program package (BMDP), University of California, Los Angeles.

references

Bishir, J. W. and D. W. Drewes (1970) Mathematics in the Behavioral and Social Sciences. New York: Harcourt.

Box, George E.P. and Gwilym M. Jenkins (1976) Time Series Analysis. San Francisco: Holden-Day.

Cameron, David R. (1984) "Elections and the economy." Presented at the annual meeting of the American Political Science Association, Washington, DC.

Feige, Edgar L. and Douglas K. Pearce (1979) "The causal relationship between money and income: some caveats for time series analysis." Review of Economics and Statistics 76: 363-373.

Freeman, John R. (1983) "Granger causality and the time series analysis of political relationships." American Journal of Political Science 27 (May): 325-355.

Geweke, J., R. Meese and W. Dent (1979) "Comparing alternative tests of causality in temporal systems: analytic results and experimental evidence." Social Systems Research Institute Workshop Paper 7928, University of Wisconsin, Madison.

Haugh, Larry D. (1976) "Checking the independence of two covariance-stationary time series: a univariate residual cross correlation approach." Journal of the American Statistical Association 71: 375-385.

Hibbs, Douglas A., Jr. (1977) "On analyzing the effects of policy interventions: Box-Jenkins and Box-Tiao vs. structural equation models," pp 137-179 in David Heise (ed.) Sociological Methodology 1977. San Francisco: Jossey-Bass.

Hibbs, Douglas A., Jr., with R. Douglas Rivers and Nicholas Vasilatos (1982) "On the demand for economic outcomes: macroeconomic performance and mass political support in the United States, Great Britain, and Germany." Journal of Politics 43: 426-462.

Kernell, Samuel (1978) "Explaining presidential popularity." The American Political Science Review 72 (June): 506-522.

———(1980) "Strategy and ideology: the politics of unemployment and inflation in modern capitalist democracies." Presented at the annual meeting of the American Political Science Association, Washington, DC.

Koyck, L. M. (1954) Distributed Lags and Investment Analysis. Amsterdam: North-Holland.

Marquardt, D. W. (1963) "An algorithm for least-squares estimation of nonlinear parameters." Journal of the Society for Industrial and Applied Mathematics 2: 431-441.

McCleary, Richard and Richard A. Hay, Jr. (1980) Applied Time Series Analysis. London: Sage.

McDowall, David, Richard McCleary, Errol E. Meidinger, and Richard A. Hay, Jr. (1980) Interrupted Time Series Analysis. London: Sage.

Mueller, John C. (1973) War, Presidents, and Public Opinion. New York: John Wiley.

Nelson, Charles R. (1973) Applied Time Series Analysis for Managerial Forecasting. San Francisco: Holden-Day.

Nelson, Charles R. and G. Schwert (1982) "Tests for predictive relationships between time series variables: a Monte Carlo investigation." Journal of the American Statistical Association 77: 11-17.

Norpoth, Helmut and Thom Yantek (1983) "Macroeconomic conditions and fluctuations of presidential popularity: the question of lagged effects." American Journal of Political Science 27 (November): 785-807.

———(1983b) Von Adenauer bis Schmidt: Wirtschaftslage und Kanzlerpopularitat, pp. 198-221 in Max Kaase and Hans-Dieter Klingemann (eds.) Wahlen und Politisches System. Opladen: Westdeutscher Verlag.

Norpoth, Helmut (1984) "Economics, politics, and the cycle of presidential popularity." Political Behavior 6 (No. 3): 253-273.

Pierce, David A. (1977) "Relationships—and the lack thereof—between economic time series, with special reference to money and interest rates." Journal of the American Statistical Association 72 (March): 11-26.

Pindyck, Robert S. and Donald L. Rubinfeld (1976) Econometric Models and Economic Forecasts. New York: McGraw-Hill.

Rivers, Douglas (1980) "Distributed-lag models in political research." Presented at the 1980 annual meeting of the Midwest Political Science Association, Chicago, IL.

Yantek, Thom (forthcoming) "Box-Jenkins transfer function analysis." Political Methodology.

11

The Use of Limits and Possibility in Social Science Research

JOHN WANAT

Political research encompasses many endeavors, of which prediction, explanation, and description are some of the major ones. The more glamorous and sophisticated research usually focuses on prediction and explanation. But all that depends on having decent data describing the phenomena being investigated. Description is the basis for any further political research. But, comparatively speaking, descriptive research is not emphasized in most treatises on social science research. With the possible exception of the attention paid to gathering data by means of surveys, data of reasonably good quality describing political phenomena are assumed. Yet I would hazard the guess that most dollars of funded research are spent to answer the question: "What happens or happened when . . . ?" Policymakers are notoriously not interested in sophisticated measures and models, but in description.

In spite of the need for good data on which to base policy or to explain and predict, the tools available for collecting good quality data are at times somewhat primitive and are frequently expensive. Sophisticated survey skills exist but implementing them takes a lot of money. Interview skills and personal observation cannot always be employed. And archival data are frequently not in a usable form for secondary analysis, despite their pervasiveness and relative cheapness.

This essay tries to show how certain kinds of archival data can be milked to yield information not readily apparent. A technique will be used to approximate panel data. By doing this, the descriptive task of accounting for shifts among the categories will be furthered. Three examples should clarify this endeavor.

(1) The Gallup organization and many other polling firms ask essentially the same question time after time. The classic question of whether or not the president is doing a good job is asked at least every few weeks. But although changes in the aggregate approval scores occur after various presidential actions, the cross-sectional nature of the samples precludes

inferences about whether or not the shifts in approval came as a result of changes to or from disapprovers or to or from those holding no opinion. If such inferences could be made, enormous survey archives could conceivably generate new insight into the questions of what caused people to change opinions and how those changes came about.

(2) Scholars have mountains of electoral data in aggregated form. For most major races far back in time we can report how many people voted for major party contenders in successive elections. That is a low level "what" question. But the real interest comes in explaining electoral changes. When a critical election occurs and party hegemony shifts, scholars want to know whether that occurred because, for example, one-time Republicans voted Democratic or because new voters predominantly voted Democratic. Once again repeated cross-sectional data are, with present common analytic tools, not amenable to approximating panel data that would answer the more interesting descriptive questions of how a critical election takes place.

(3) At times agencies collect data that will not be released to the public for fear of violating privacy rights of certain citizens. To illustrate, consider the practice of many juvenile courts of not identifying young offenders. To avoid stigmatizing a youth for illegal actions committed while presumably too young or at least too immature to know better, courts publish only aggregate data on how many juvenile arrests and/or convictions took place in a given time period. These repeated statistics do not really allow researchers to estimate recidivism because individual level data either are not released or are prohibitively expensive to procure. But imaginative uses of the available aggregate data could allow the researcher to answer some of the cross-level and cross-time descriptive questions.

The three illustrations mentioned above all exemplify attempts to use sparse, aggregate, categorical data collected at two times on largely the same population to infer changes in subpopulations. If effect, we would like to approximate panel data by using repeated cross-sectional data. If this could be done, better description (and later explanation and prediction) would be secured. This essay will advance a technique that promises some movement in that direction. But first one illustration will be formalized to specify the kind of problem undertaken here.

PROBLEM FORMALIZATION

Consider the first illustration mentioned earlier. To advance explanation and prediction of how presidential popularity shifts, the descriptive question of how many shifted what way must be answered. One important shift in popularity occurred when presidential popularity surged after the

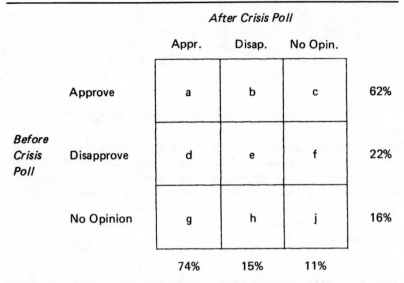

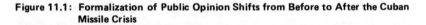

		After Crisis Poll			
		Appr.	Disap.	No Opin.	
Before Crisis Poll	Approve	a	b	c	62%
	Disapprove	d	e	f	22%
	No Opinion	g	h	j	16%
		74%	15%	11%	

NOTE: The pre-event poll was taken from 20-25 September, 1962 and the post-event poll was taken from 16-21 November, 1962. Data come from the Gallup poll.

Figure 11.1: Formalization of Public Opinion Shifts from Before to After the Cuban Missile Crisis

Cuban missile crisis. Gallup polls conducted just before and after the essential event show aggregate data representing public opinion from the nation as a whole. Because the two polls were so close together, augmentation and diminution of the population is not a problem. The raw percentages expressing the approval, disapproval, and no-opinion holding portions of the population can be considered the marginals of the 3×3 table that shows the behavior of those three opinion holding groups over time.

The descriptive problem is to identify the values of cells a,b,c, . . . j, given the marginals. Knowing those cell values would allow the analyst to test hypotheses about how and why the shifts in opinion took place, as well as permitting predictions about opinion changes under conditions similar to the Cuban missile crisis. But given only the marginals there are an infinite number of solutions to our descriptive problem. That is clear if we consider the 3×3 table to exemplify the following relations among rows, columns, and the respective marginals. In general,

$$a + b + c = 62 \quad [11.1]$$

$$d + e + f = 22 \quad [11.2]$$

$$g + h + j = 16 \quad [11.3]$$

$$a + d + g = 74 \quad [11.4]$$

$$b + e + h = 15 \quad [11.5]$$

$$c + f + j = 11 \quad [11.6]$$

Equations 11.1 through 11.6 involve nine variables. But high school algebra says that a system of six linear equations involving nine unknowns is indeterminant. That is, there are numerous solutions. If the cells can take on real number values, there are an infinite number of solutions. But because the poll data represent a large, but finite number of people (the adult population in the United States), the number of solutions, if only nonnegative integer cell entries are allowed, will be finite but very large. Our problem can be made a bit more tractable if cell values in solutions to 11.1 through 11.6 must sum to 100. In other words, by considering each cell count to represent 1% of the total population, the Gallup marginals for pre- and post-event reduce the number of solutions to our problem to a finite, but usually very large number.

In historical fact, some fixed number of pre-event approvers stayed approvers and some fixed number of disapprovers became approvers, and so on. The problem is to find out exactly how many fell into any one cell in the crosstabulation. Knowing that there were a fixed but large number of possible solutions does not engender great solace in the heart of the researcher who wants to know what actually happened. But the large number of solutions or scenarios each solution represents can be reduced somewhat by recognizing additional relationships.

People tend to be inertial. For example, most observers would say that, in the aggregate, persons voting Republican in one election are more likely to vote Republican in the next than not. Particularly if the activity or opinion is being measured over a relatively short time period, the likelihood of change is small because the shift in the aggregate normally is small. If the shift in the aggregate is large the likelihood of change is larger. In terms of our problem, although any person could change his or her evaluation of JFK over the few weeks surrounding the missile crisis, in the aggregate those approving of JFK before the crisis were more likely to continue in that opinion than to shift. The following models express these constraints more succinctly:

$$a \geqslant b \quad [11.7]$$

$$a \geqslant c \quad [11.8]$$

Imposition of inequality constraints 11.7 and 11.8 on the set of nonnegative integer solutions to equations 11.1 through 11.6 reduces the number of possible scenarios that conform to the known aggregate data. How much the added constraints restrict the solution set cannot, unfortunately, be known by any neat analytical technique. The only way to know how many possible scenarios could have occurred is to count them.

THE POSSIBILITY APPROACH

Most approaches to problems reflect the tools that are or were available to the researchers. For instance our problem can be conceived as an estimation problem. Given the 3×3 table and the marginals, what is the "best" estimate for the cell entries? When forced to make such an estimate for the purposes of prediction or for use as a null hypothesis in testing, the notion of "maximum likelihood" is considered the "best" estimate. Why? Likelihood is an easily agreed upon criterion, but to maximize likelihood requires knowledge of or willingness to assume what is likely. Because of the lack of computers and the consequent reliance on the law of large numbers, statisticians traditionally assume that cell values would be distributed according to multinominal or normal distributions. The analytic neatness of such assumptions affords the researcher some ease in maximizing the likelihood of various cell outcomes.

In brief, by assuming that cell values were distributed in accordance with the analytically well understood distributions, researchers were able to use the tools at hand. But later analysts with other tools at their disposal must ask if other assumptions might be more appropriately made. Can we assume, for example, that the normal distribution is ever pervasive?

Most approaches to the kind of problem at hand have sought one specific solution, a "best" solution. That approach is optimistic at best, most likely foolhardy or arrogant, and probably in error most of the time. The philosophy underlying traditional approaches is somewhat deductive: Assume the nature of the distribution is known, then seek to deduce from that a most likely outcome. In a sense this is working from the inside out.

This chapter is more timid in its approach. Rather than working out the logical consequences of heroic assumptions and empirical boundary conditions, its approach is to work from the outside in by seeing how the boundary conditions limit the possible solutions. No attempt is made to pick out one solution as what "really" happened. Given that the change in public opinion occurred over twenty years ago, no one can know what actually took place. But examining the constraints and working out how those constraints restrict what could have happened can yield important information. By knowing what could not have happened, we may gain some knowledge of what did happen. In some situations the constraints are sufficiently powerful to identify not a specific solution but a set of solutions sharing certain characteristics, characteristics that represent important information.

The technical mechanism behind this possibility approach is enumeration. Simply put, the analyst examines all possible solutions to the set of equations and inequalities characterizing the problem. Because of computers, the assumed nature of the distributions underlying each cell is irrelevant. The brute force of the computer is the tool that allows this approach. We simply have the computer search out all possible solutions and identify characteristics that are common to the restricted or constrained set of solutions.

To further elaborate the enumeration of possibilities approach, return to the problem of trying to understand the dynamics of opinion change from before to after the Cuban missile crisis. First, limits to the cells and certain cell groupings will be identified. Second, the frequency of certain relationships among cells and cell groupings will be investigated. And third, structural relations among cells will be treated.

ANALYSIS OF LIMITS

Consider Table 11.1, which displays the frequency distribution of cell values for each cell for the set of all possible solutions to conditions 11.1 through 11.8. A computer program written for use with any 3×3 table and available from the author searched through all possible values of cells a, c, e, and j from 0 through 62, 11, 15 and 11, respectively. By knowing the marginals and fixing cells a and c, cell b is easily computed. Knowing cells b and e along with the marginals permits calculation of cell h. For any given combination of cells a, c, e, and j, the program generates the remaining cell values. Out of the more than 145 thousand combinations of values of a, c, e, and j within the ranges just specified, the program identified 9858 solutions and scenarios. A tally was kept of, for instance, how many times cell b was 0, was 1, was 2, was 3, and so forth. More than that, the program also kept track of how many scenarios had, for instance, cell b exceeding cell h.

Table 11.1 defines what we may call the possibility distribution for each cell. Note that the word probability was not used. We have no way of

TABLE 11.1
Frequency Distributions of Possible Cell Values for the Cuban Missile Crisis Problem

Cell Value	Cells a	b	c	d	e	f	g	h	j
0	0	1008	1392	35	1028	1412	286	1228	1616
1	0	995	1321	56	1005	1331	364	1160	1486
2	0	968	1236	84	972	1240	442	1088	1346
3	0	929	1139	120	930	1140	520	1013	1196
4	0	880	1032	165	880	1032	598	936	1040
5	0	823	917	220	823	917	676	858	882
6	0	760	796	286	760	796	737	770	726
7	0	692	670	364	692	670	780	675	575
8	0	620	540	442	620	536	804	576	432
9	0	545	407	520	545	398	808	476	300
10	0	468	272	598	468	260	791	378	182
11	0	390	136	676	390	126	752	285	81
12	0	312	0	737	308	0	690	200	0
13	0	234	0	770	225	0	600	126	0
14	0	156	0	777	144	0	484	66	0
15	0	78	0	760	68	0	344	23	0
16	0	0	0	721	0	0	182	0	0
17	0	0	0	662	0	0	0	0	0
18	0	0	0	585	0	0	0	0	0
19	0	0	0	492	0	0	0	0	0
20	0	0	0	385	0	0	0	0	0
21	0	0	0	266	0	0	0	0	0
22	0	0	0	137	0	0	0	0	0
36	1	0	0	0	0	0	0	0	0
37	4	0	0	0	0	0	0	0	0
38	10	0	0	0	0	0	0	0	0
39	20	0	0	0	0	0	0	0	0
40	35	0	0	0	0	0	0	0	0
41	56	0	0	0	0	0	0	0	0
42	84	0	0	0	0	0	0	0	0
43	120	0	0	0	0	0	0	0	0
44	165	0	0	0	0	0	0	0	0
45	220	0	0	0	0	0	0	0	0
46	286	0	0	0	0	0	0	0	0
47	364	0	0	0	0	0	0	0	0
48	442	0	0	0	0	0	0	0	0
49	520	0	0	0	0	0	0	0	0
50	598	0	0	0	0	0	0	0	0
51	676	0	0	0	0	0	0	0	0
52	737	0	0	0	0	0	0	0	0
53	770	0	0	0	0	0	0	0	0
54	777	0	0	0	0	0	0	0	0
55	760	0	0	0	0	0	0	0	0
56	721	0	0	0	0	0	0	0	0
57	662	0	0	0	0	0	0	0	0
58	585	0	0	0	0	0	0	0	0
59	488	0	0	0	0	0	0	0	0
60	376	0	0	0	0	0	0	0	0
61	254	0	0	0	0	0	0	0	0
62	127	0	0	0	0	0	0	0	0

knowing whether each of the 9858 solutions representing real-world states was as likely as any other. If they were we could talk about probability. To illustrate this distinction, if two dice were thrown there would be 36 possible combinations: (1,1), (1,2), (1,3) . . . (6,4), (6,5), and (6,6), where the first number in each pair represents the number on the first die and the second stands for the number on the second die. If we are using unbiased dice, each of the 36 combinations is equally likely. The sum of the dots on the two dice vary and a sum of 7 occurs in more combinations than a sum of 11. This allows us to say that a 7 is more probable than an 11. More precisely, in 5 of the equally likely 36 scenarios the dots on the dice sum to 7, which allows assigning the number 5/36 as the probability of throwing a 7.

The data in Table 11.1 is analogous to counting how many of the 36 possibilities had various sums of dots on the dice. The only difference is that with the dice we know that each of the 36 combinations is equally likely. In the case of opinion change there is no way of knowing whether or not each solution is as likely as any other with anything like the certainty of equipossibility in the dice example. Because we are investigating events far in the past, we are condemned to ignorance. To be safe, therefore, it is best to speak of posssibility density functions being exemplified or defined by Table 11.1 rather than speaking of probability density functions. But if we are willing to make that assumption, estimates with desirable properties are forthcoming (Wanat, 1982b).

But must that ignorance prove incapacitating? We can make some inferences about the opinion change without assuming anything. For example, the frequencies of possible solutions in Table 1 indicate maxima and minima for each cell. The theoretically possible extremes to cells b through j may be logically deducible from the nonnegativity constraint and the smallest of the row and column marginals for each cell. But certainly in the case of cell a the inequality constraints 11.7 and 11.8 and the complexity of interdependence among the cells prevent straightforward identification of at least the minimum value. Yet enumeration of the solutions says that in none of the 9858 solutions, each corresponding to a scenario in the real world of 1962, did the value of cell a drop below 36. In other words, at least 58% (36/62) of those approving the president before the crisis did so immediately afterward. The enumeration of all possibilities has provided a floor value, one not obvious.

The enumeration strategy outlined above is not restricted to values of single cells. When the computer program is identifying solutions, cells are grouped together and their extreme values are tallied. For instance, cells a + e + j represent people who did not change their opinion. The tally of 9858 solutions implies that at most 88% of the populace and at least 36% of the populace did not change opinion. So we now know that at least 12% did change opinion. In similar fashion, by examining the range of values of those leaving the disapproval state in all possible solutions (cells d + f), extreme values are such that at least 27% and at most 85% of precrisis disapprovers changed opinion. Other combinations of cells can be examined to identify limits on behavior of those represented in the 3×3 crosstabulation. These limits may prove useful at times.

ANALYSIS OF DEGREES OF POSSIBILITY

The possibility approach so far is only somewhat different from that of Davis and Duncan (1953) who derived extreme values for cells from marginals. Their approach, however, was generally restricted to 2×2 tables. Further it was not applied to groups of cells, and it was not able to incorporate inequality relations as our enumeration approach does. Although the means used to ascertain limits differed, the general goal of seeking limits is the same in both approaches. But enumeration with the notion of possibility can move far beyond the limits of values for cells and cell groups.

Frequently, social scientists seek unrealistically exact answers to questions. In our illustration the ideal answer would give specific numerical values for each cell. But at times important questions can be answered with inexact responses, responses that express relations. For example, if we want to understand the dynamics of opinion shift after decisive presidential action in foreign affairs, the relative size of cell b (approvers turned disapprovers) and cell d (disapprovers turned approvers) merits attention. The enumeration of all 9858 solutions allowed the comparison of those two cells in every solution and indicated that in 97.7% of all solutions cell d exceeded or equaled cell b. In other words, in only 2.3% of all possibilities did the number of approvers turned disapprovers outnumber their opposites.

For some analysts the information that disapprovers become approvers exceeds approvers turned disapprovers in 97.7% of all possible scenarios is compelling. Hypothesis testing typically uses 95% as an appropriate level of certainty and our finding in a sense exceeds that. We should note, however, that we are talking about possibilities and not necessarily talking about probabilities. We perhaps cannot assume that all possible outcomes or solutions are as likely as all others. But lacking any evidence to say that such an assumption is unreasonable many will grasp it to their bosom, especially if decisions must be made and no other information is available. Once again the difference between probability and possibility arises.

ANALYSIS OF STRUCTURAL RELATIONS

If the analyst is unhappy with the ambiguities associated with possibilities gained through enumeration, he or she may take solace in the fact that on occasion the percentage of scenarios in which one cell or group of cells exceeds anothers is 100%. Although that occasionally does happen (for example, Wanat and Burke, 1982), some certain though imprecise information can be gathered from any 3 × 3 crosstabulation. Although we may not be able to specify what values certain cells will take, the relations among certain cell groups can be specifically known. In our example consider the "defecting approvers" (cells b + c) and the "new approvers" (cells d + g). We may never know just how many fell into each group; that is, just what numbers occurred in reality. But no matter what the possibilities, we can establish the specific numerical relation between those two groups.

To derive that relationship recall that cell a occurs in equations 11.1 and 11.4. If we recast both of those equations to isolate a, we get

$$62 - b - c = a$$

$$74 - d - g = a$$

or, by equating them,

$$74 - d - g = 62 - b - c$$

or,

$$12 + (b + c) = d + g \qquad [11.9]$$

Verbally this says new approvers, whatever their number, outnumber defecting approvers by 12.

$$12 + (\text{defecting approvers}) = \text{new approvers}$$

By focusing on cell e, the people who steadfastly disapprove of the president, the logic used above says that 7 + (b + h) = d + f. Verbally this states that defecting disapprovers, whatever their number, outnumber new disapprovers by 7. Similarly it is easy to show that 5 + (c + f) = h + g, or no-opinion holders who now take an opinion outnumber by 5 opinion holders who have ceased to hold opinion.

Thus creative use of the marginals permits specific relations among certain, but not all, subpopulations. This approach can be extended to take advantage of the inequality relations to which enumeration may point. To illustrate, our enumeration suggested that cell d exceeds cell b in over 97% of all possible cases. By algebraically manipulating relations 11.1 through 11.6 we can express the relations between cell d and cell b in such a way that other relations among other cells must obtain with the same certainty that holds between d and b.

By expressing d and b in terms of their marginals it is easy to show that

$$d = 74 - a - g = 26 - e - f$$

and

$$b = 62 - a - c = 15 - h - e$$

Subtracting yields,

$$d - b = 12 + c - g = 11 + h - f \qquad [11.10]$$

Hence if $d > b$, then $12 + c - g > 0$ or $12 + c > g$. Verbally interpreted, if d exceeds b, then $g - c$ is less than 12. At the same time if $d > b$, then $f - h$ is less than 11. Because we know that disapprovers turned approvers outnumber their counterparts in 97% of the possible cases, the relations between f and h and between c and g laid out just above must also hold in 97% of the possible scenarios.

The relation between d and b allows going beyond the inequality relations into the realm of possibility in another way. Again, although the researcher will never know for certain what happened in 1962, we can say that if d exceeded b by, say, 4 percentage points, then $12 + c - g = 4$, which says that cell g exceeded cell c by 8 percentage points. It would also imply that f exceeded h by 7 percentage points. Relation 11.10 thus allows the researcher to express exact but conditional relations among pairs of cells.

The clever researcher may express relations among various cells and cell groups to show the structure of relations among other cell groupings. No matter what the relations among cells actually was, investigation of the possibilities and the limits on the possibilities can generate insight into the dynamics of opinion change and other changes expressed in terms of crosstabulations.

CONCLUDING COMMENTS

This essay was intended to demonstrate the value of working with possibilities. In the context of a 3×3 table representing repeated cross-sectional aggregate data, I have suggested that important information may be elicited without demanding certainty. By looking at the limits of possible cell values, by looking at the frequency with which given cells exceed others, and by looking at contingent structural relations among cells, this essay has shown that important and nonobvious information may be secured. The emphasis on precise estimates that are purchased with the expensive currency of assumptions was shown to be a poor bargain in comparison with the value of ranges of estimates and relations purchased with few if any assumptions.

I do not argue that this possibility approach will always provide new and valuable information. Depending on the marginals, this approach may not give usably restrictive cell values or relations, but some information generally can be derived even where many relations are inconclusive (Wanat, 1982a, 1983). The relative cheapness of enumeration and the ease of establishing structural relations as exemplified in relations 11.10 argue for exploring the possibilities immanent in a crosstabulation before imposing assumptions.

references

Davis, B. and O. D. Duncan (1953) "An alternative to ecological correlation." American Sociological Review 18: 665-666.

Wanat, J. and K. Burke (1982) "Estimating the degree of mobilization and conversion in the 1890s." American Political Science Review 76 (June): 360-370.

Wanat, J. (1982a) "The dynamics of presidential popularity shifts." American Politics Quarterly 10 (April): 181-196.

Wanat, J. (1982b) "Most possible estimates and maximum likelihood estimates." Sociological Methods and Research 10 (May): 453-462.

Wanat, J. (1983) "Estimation with sparse nominal data: the case of differential compliance with the 55 mph limit." Transportation Research 17A (March): 115-120.

about the contributors

JOHN H. ALDRICH is Professor of Political Science at the University of Minnesota. He has taught courses in statistics and formal modeling at the University of Minnesota and at Michigan State University. His major area of research is the development and testing of models of parties and electoral choice. He has published numerous articles in scholarly journals, and he is also the author of *Before the Convention* (University of Chicago Press, 1980) and coauthor of *Change and Continuity in the 1980 Elections* (Congressional Quarterly Press, rev. ed., 1983, with Paul Abramson and David Rohde).

WILLIAM D. BERRY is Associate Professor of Political Science at the University of Kentucky. He earned his Ph.D. at the University of Minnesota. He is author of *Nonrecursive Causal Models* and coauthor of *Multiple Regression in Practice*. He has also published numerous articles in scholarly journals, including papers on several methodological problems in the social sciences. His substantive areas of interest are public policy, political economy, and intergovernmental relations.

STEVEN R. BROWN is Professor of Political Science at Kent State University. He received a Ph.D. from the University of Missouri—Columbia and teaches in the areas of political psychology and research methodology. He is the author of *Political Subjectivity* and editor of *Operant Subjectivity: The Q Methodology Newsletter*, and his papers have appeared in *American Political Science Review, Journal of Educational Measurement, Political Methodology, Political Psychology, Handbook of Political Communication*, and *Political Behavior Annual*.

EDWARD G. CARMINES is Professor of Political Science at Indiana University, Bloomington. His methodological interests focus on statistical analysis, measurement models, and scaling techniques. He is the coauthor of *Statistical Analysis of Social Data* (Rand-McNally, 1978), *Measurement in the Social Sciences* (Cambridge University Press, 1980), *Reliability and Validity Assessment* (Sage, 1979) and *Unidimen-*

sional Scaling (Sage, 1981) as well as a number of articles and chapters focusing on these topics. His most recent work concerns the application of time series methods and covariance structure models.

HERBERT M. KRITZER is Professor of Political Science at the University of Wisconsin-Madison. He has published a number of articles on the analysis of contingency tables in *Sociological Methods and Research, Political Methodology*, and the *American Journal of Political Science*. His substantive research is on civil justice, and in recent years he has authored or coauthored articles in *American Bar Foundation Research Journal, UCLA Law Review, Law and Society Review, Journal of Politics, Judicature, Justice System Journal, American Behavioral Scientist, Policy Studies Journal* and *Law and Contemporary Problems*. He is currently working on an analysis of the negotiation process in ordinary civil litigation.

MICHAEL S. LEWIS-BECK is Professor of Political Science at the University of Iowa. He is the author of several methodological papers, and *Applied Regression: An Introduction*. Professor Lewis-Beck received his Ph.D. from the University of Michigan in 1973, and has taught methods courses at Michigan, Iowa, the Inter-University Consortium for Political and Social Research (University of Michigan), the European Consortium for Political Research (University of Essex, England), and the Catholic University (Lima, Peru). His substantive areas of interest include political economy and public policy.

FORREST D. NELSON is Associate Professor of Economics at the University of Iowa. He has taught in statistics and econometrics at the University of Iowa and at California Institute of Technology. His major area of research is methods of analysis for economic models with quantitative and limited dependent variables. Professor Nelson has published numerous articles on theoretical and applied econometrics in scholarly journals, including *Econometria* and *Journal of Econometrics*. Nelson and John Aldrich have coauthored *Linear Probability, Logit, and Probit Models* (Sage, 1984).

HELMUTH NORPOTH is Professor of Political Science at the State University of New York at Stony Brook. He received his M.A. and Ph.D. from the University of Michigan. From 1978 on, he has taught every summer a course on time series analysis in the ECPR Summer School at Essex, England. Prior to that, he also taught courses on dynamic analysis in the ICPSR Summer Program at the University of Michigan. He is coauthor (with Gudmund Iversen) of the Sage monograph *Analysis of Variance*. He has published articles on the dynamics of party identification in the *American Political Science Review* and the *British Journal of Political Science*. His analyses of Presidential popularity series have appeared in the *American Journal of Political Science* and *Political Behavior*. In 1984, he served as a consultant to the *New York Times* for its election campaign polling done jointly with CBS News.

GEORGE RABINOWITZ is Associate Professor of Political Science at the University of North Carolina. Professor Rabinowitz did his undergraduate work at Hobart College where he obtained a B.S. degree in Chemistry and Mathematics. He did his graduate work at the University of Michigan where he received an M.A. in mathematics and a Ph.D. in Political Science. He has contributed articles on measurement and scaling to *Psychometrika*, the *American Political Science Review*, the *American Journal of Political Science*, and the *Journal of Politics*. His substantive interests are U.S. electoral politics and political psychology.

JOHN WANAT is Professor of Political Science at the University of Illinois at Chicago. He received his Ph.D. at the University of Illinois at Urbana-Champaign. Professor Wanat's major areas of interest are budgeting and bureaucratic politics. He has published numerous articles in journals such as *Sociological Methods and Research*, *Political Methodology* and *American Political Science Review*, and is on the editorial board of several scholarly journals.